'Le Guin is a writer of phenomenal power' *Observer*

'She is unique. She is legend' *The Times*

'An important writer, period' *Washington Post*

'Le Guin writes with painstaking intelligence' *Time*

Also by Ursula K. Le Guin

NOVELS
Rocannon's World (1966)
Planet of Exile (1966)
City of Illusions (1967)
A Wizard of Earthsea (1968)
The Left Hand of Darkness (1969)
The Tombs of Atuan (1971)
The Lathe of Heaven (1971)
The Farthest Shore (1972)
The Dispossessed (1974)
The Word for World is Forest (1976)
The Eye of the Heron (1978)
Malafrena (1979)
The Beginning Place (aka Threshold) (1980)
Always Coming Home (1985)
Tehanu (1990)
The Telling (2000)
The Other Wind (2001)
Gifts (2004)
Voices (2006)
Powers (2007)
Lavinia (2008)

SHORT STORY COLLECTONS
The Wind's Twelve Quarters (1975)
Orsinian Tales (1976)
The Compass Rose (1982)
Buffalo Gals and Other Animal Presences (1987)
Searoad: Chronicles of Klatsand (1991)
A Fisherman of the Inland Sea (1994)
Four Ways to Forgiveness (1995)
Unlocking the Air and Other Stories (1996)
Tales from Earthsea (2001)
The Birthday of the World and Other Stories (2002)
Changing Planes (2003)
The Unreal and the Real Volume 1: Where on Earth (2012)
The Unreal and the Real Volume 2: Outer Space, Inner Lands (2012)

NON-FICTION
The Language of the Night (1979)
Way of the Water's Going (1989)
Dancing at the End of the World (1989)
Lao Tzu: Tao Te Ching (1997)
Steering the Craft (1998)
The Wave in the Mind (2004)
Cheek by Jowl (2009)
Words are my Matter (2012)

Dreams Must Explain Themselves

and Other Essays

1972-2004

Ursula K. Le Guin

GOLLANCZ

LONDON

First published in Great Britain in 2018 by Gollancz
an imprint of the Orion Publishing Group Ltd
Carmelite House, 50 Victoria Embankment
London EC4Y 0DZ

An Hachette UK Company

The authorised representative in the EEA is Hachette Ireland,
8 Castlecourt Centre, Dublin 15, D15 XTP3, Ireland (email: info@hbgi.ie)

11 13 15 17 19 20 18 16 14 12

A CIP catalogue record for this book is
available from the British Library.

ISBN 978 1 473 20594 9

Typeset by Input Data Services Ltd, Somerset

Printed and bound in Great Britain by Clays Ltd, Elcograf S.p.A.

www.ursulakleguin.com
www.orionbooks.co.uk
www.gollancz.co.uk

Contents

Preface

These essays, talks, introductions, reviews, and meditations, published from 1972 to 2004, mostly in America, were reprinted in the collections *The Language of the Night, Dancing at the Edge of the World, The Wave in the Mind,* and *Cheek by Jowl.* From these four books my British publisher and I selected forty-nine pieces for British readers – plus a fiftieth, a balance or update to the opening piece. Both were brief talks given at the National Book Award ceremony, one in 1972, one in 2014.

The earlier pieces were written when critics and academics generally refused to consider fantasy or science fiction as literature at all, and when the protest against social injustice to women was in its fiery youth. The defensive or aggressive tone of some of these talks and writings mellows somewhat over the years in response to material changes in literary criticism and in society at large. But in 2004 the ivory barricades defending realistic fiction were still being hotly defended against the uprising of the genre ghettos. As for the mighty fortress walls guarding masculine prerogative, some had fallen, but already an increasingly politicized fundamentalism was industriously rebuilding them. If the general tone of the pieces becomes more equable and meditative, it probably reflects less a sense of victory over prejudice and injustice than the greater willingness to settle for very relative gains that comes with age; I was in my thirties in 1972, my seventies in 2004.

But the years after 2004, not represented in this collection, were years of steady drift towards reactionary extremism. The two speeches that begin and end the book address much the same issues, but the difference is striking: the literary-critical debate of 1972 appears, forty-two years later, as an element of the struggle of imaginative art to exist at all in the increasingly hostile economic and moral environment of corporation capitalism.

That said, I'm not sure what else to say about the book. It's a carrier

I

bag full of ideas and responses, thoughts and rethinkings. Some themes and subjects keep coming up over the years: the place of imaginative fiction in literature, discussions of the relationship between writer and reader, between the writer and the written, and between the artist and society, along with considerations of problems of defining fantasy and its uses. Forewords to some of my own books and reviews of books by other authors touch on these and other topics. There are a couple of talks addressed to women graduating from college, and a couple made to groups active in women's rights and the politics of gender. There are also thoughts about where writers get their ideas and how they invent worlds, studies of utopia and of animals in fiction, an analysis of Tolkien's prose style, three efforts to come to terms with Doris Lessing's view of the universe, and an argument with Tolstoy. I can only hope that readers wandering in this garden of forking paths will find themselves in a rose plot or a bed of mandrake-root or a small grove of mallorns or sequoias where they feel at home.

Ursula K. Le Guin
(January 2017)

National Book Award Acceptance Speech

1972

I am very pleased, very proud, and very startled to accept the National Book Award in children's literature for my novel *The Farthest Shore*.

Nothing could give me greater joy than to share that honor, as it should be shared, with the people whose work and patience and constant trust were essential to the writing and publication of the book: the people at Atheneum Press, especially my editor, Jean Karl, and illustrator, Gail Garraty; and my literary agent, Virginia Kidd; and – last of all and first of all – my husband and our children.

And I also rejoice in the privilege of sharing this honor, if I may, with my fellow writers, not only in the field of children's books, but in that even less respectable field, science fiction. For I am not only a fantasist but a science fiction writer, and odd though it may seem, I am proud to be both.

We who hobnob with hobbits and tell tall tales about little green men are quite used to being dismissed as mere entertainers, or sternly disapproved of as escapists. But I think that perhaps the categories are changing, like the times. Sophisticated readers are accepting the fact that an improbable and unmanageable world is going to produce an improbable and hypothetical art. At this point, realism is perhaps the least adequate means of understanding or portraying the incredible realities of our existence. A scientist who creates a monster in the laboratory; a librarian in the library of Babel; a wizard unable to cast a spell; a space ship having trouble in getting to Alpha Centauri: all these may be precise and profound metaphors of the human condition. Fantasists, whether they use the ancient archetypes of myth and legend or the younger ones of science and technology, may be talking as seriously as any sociologist – and a good deal more directly – about human life as it is lived, and as it might be lived, and as it ought to be lived. For after all, as great scientists have said and as all children know, it is above all by the imagination that we achieve perception, and compassion, and hope.

3

Dreams Must Explain Themselves

●

1973

Andy Porter called from New York earlier this year to try and tell me what he hoped I'd write for *Algol*. The conversation was pleasant, though disarranged by a bad connection, several explosive intrusions by a person at this end who wanted some cookies and attention, and a slight degree of misunderstanding. Andy kept saying things like, "Tell the readers about yourself," and I kept saying things like, "How? Why?"

Some people can talk on the telephone. They must really believe in the thing. For me the telephone is for making appointments with the doctor and canceling appointments with the dentist. It is not a medium of human communication. I can't stand there in the hall with the child and the cat both circling around my legs frisking and purring and demanding cookies and catfood, and explain to a disembodied voice in my ear that the Jungian spectrum of introvert/extrovert can usefully be applied not only to human beings but also to authors. That is, that there are some authors who want and need to tell about themselves, you know, like Norman Mailer, and there are others who want and need privacy. Privacy! What an elitist, Victorian concept. These days it sounds almost as quaint as modesty. But I can't say all that on the telephone, it just won't come out. Nor can I say (although I made a feeble effort to, about the time the connection failed entirely, probably because the cat, in despair, had settled for chewing on the telephone cord) that the problem of communication is a complex one, and that some of us introverts have solved it in a curious, not wholly satisfactory, but interesting way: we communicate (with all but a very few persons) in writing, but indirectly in writing. As if we were deaf and dumb. And not just in writing, but indirectly in writing. We write stories about imaginary people in imaginary situations. Then we publish them (because they are, in their strange way, acts of communi-cation – addressed to others). And then people read them and call up and say But who are you? tell us about yourself! And we say, But I have.

It's all there, in the book. All that matters. – But you made all that up! – Out of what?

Where Andy and I temporarily misunderstood each other was at this point. Wanting me to write about the Earthsea trilogy, the background of it, he said (excuse me, Andy, for misquoting) something like, "People would be interested in knowing things like how you planned the Earthsea world, and how you developed the languages, and how you keep lists of places and characters and so on." To which I returned some kind of garble-garble, of which I recall only one sentence, "But I didn't plan anything, I found it."

Andy (not unnaturally): "Where?"

Me: "In my subconscious."

Now as I think about it, perhaps this is worth talking about a little. Andy and I surprised each other because we had different unexamined notions of how writing is done; and they were so different that their collision produced a slight shock. Both of them are completely valid; they're just different methodologies. As mine is the one not talked about in writers' manuals, however, perhaps it needs some explanation.

All my life I have written, and all my life I have (without conscious decision) avoided reading how-to-write things. The *Shorter Oxford Dictionary* and Follett's and Fowler's manuals of usage are my entire arsenal of tools.* However, in reading and teaching and talking with other writers one does arrive at a certain consciousness of technique. The most different technique from my own, the one that starts from the point farthest removed, is just this one of preliminary plans and lists and descriptions. The technique of keeping a notebook and describing all the characters in it before the story is begun: how much William weighs and where he went to school and how his hair is cut and what his dominant traits are.

I do have notebooks, in which I worry at plot ideas as if they were old bones, growling and snarling and frequently burying them and digging them up again. Also, during the writing of a piece, I often make notes concerning a character, particularly if it's a novel. My memory is very poor, and if there's something I just noticed about the character, but this is

---

* Note (1989). I use Fowler and Follett rarely now, finding them authoritarian. Strunk and White's *Elements of Style*, corrected and supplemented by Miller and Swift's *Words and Women*, are my road atlas to English, and have never led me astray. A secondhand copy of the small-print Oxford English Dictionary in two volumes has been an infinite source of learning and pleasure, but the Shorter Oxford is still good for a quick fix.

not the right point to put it into the book, then I make a note for future reference. Something like:

W. d not appr H's ing. – Repr!!

Then I lose the note.

But I don't write out descriptions beforehand, and would indeed feel ridiculous, even ashamed, to do so. If the character isn't so clear to me that I know all *that* about him, what am I doing writing about him? What right have I to describe what William did when Helen bit his knee, if I don't even know what he looks like, and his past, and his psyche, inside and out, as well as I know myself? Because after all he is myself. Part of myself.

If William is a character worthy of being written about, then he exists. He exists, inside my head to be sure, but in his own right, with his own vitality. All I have to do is look at him. I don't plan him, compose him of bits and pieces, inventory him. I find him.

There he is, and Helen is biting his knee, and he says with a little cough, "I really don't think this is relevant, Helen." What else, being William, could he say?

This attitude toward action, creation, is evidently a basic one, the same root from which the interest in the *I Ching* and Taoist philosophy evident in most of my books arises. The Taoist world is orderly, not chaotic, but its order is not one imposed by man or by a personal or humane deity. The true laws – ethical and aesthetic, as surely as scientific – are not imposed from above by any authority, but exist in things and are to be found – discovered.

To return circuitously to Earthsea: this anti-ideological, pragmatic technique applies to places, as well as people. I did not deliberately invent Earthsea. I did not think "Hey wow – islands are archetypes and archipelagoes are superarchetypes and let's build us an archipelago!" I am not an engineer, but an explorer. I discovered Earthsea.

Plans are likely to be made, if well made, inclusively; discoveries are made bit by bit. Planning negates time. Discovery is a temporal process. It may take years and years. People are still exploring Antarctica.

The history of the discovery of Earthsea is something like this:

In 1964 I wrote a story called "The Word of Unbinding" about a wizard. Cele Goldsmith Lalli bought it for *Fantastic*. (Cele Lalli gave me and a lot of other people their start in SF; she was one of the most sensitive and audacious editors the field has ever had.) I don't recall now whether the fact is made much of in the story, but it was perfectly clear in my mind

6

that it took place on an island, one among many islands. I did not give much attention to the setting, as it was (as William would say) not relevant, and developed only such rules of magic as were germane to the very small point the very minor story made.

Soon after, I wrote a story, "The Rule of Names," in which both the islands and the rules of magic were considerably more developed (Cele published it too). This story was lighthearted (the other one was glum), and I had fun playing around a bit with the scenery, and with the old island ladies drinking rushwash tea, and so on. It was set on an island called Sattins, which I knew to be one of an outlying group east of the main archipelago. The main character, a dragon known first as Mr. Underhill and then, when his nature is revealed, by his true name Yevaud, came from a westerly isle called Pendor.

I did not much bother with all the islands that I knew lay between Sattins and Pendor, and north and south of them. They weren't involved. I had the distinct feeling, however, that the island of "Word of Unbinding" lay up north of Pendor. I am not now sure which island it actually is, that one I first landed on. Later voyages of discovery have so complicated the map that the first landfall, like that of the Norsemen in the New World, is hard to pin down for certain. Sattins, however, is on the map, high in the East Reach between Yore and Vemish.

Along in 1965 or 1966 I wrote a longish story about a prince who travels down through the archipelago from its central island, Havnor, in search of the Ultimate. He goes southwest out into the open sea, beyond all islands, and finds there a people who live on rafts all their lives long. He ties his boat to a raft and settles down with them, content with this as the Ultimate, until he realizes that out past the farthest journey of the drifting raft-colony there are sea-people, living in the sea itself. He joins them. I think the implication was that (not being a merman) he'll wear out eventually, and sink, and find the ultimate Ultimate. This story wasn't submitted for publication as it never worked itself out at all well; but I felt strongly that the basic image – the raft-colony – was a lulu, and would find itself its home somewhere eventually. It did, in the third of the Earthsea books, *The Farthest Shore*.

I explored Earthsea no further until 1967, when the publisher of Parnassus Press, Herman Schein, asked me if I'd like to try writing a book for him. He wanted something for older kids; till then Parnassus had been mainly a young-juvenile publisher, putting out the handsomest and best-made picture books in America. He gave me complete freedom as to subject and approach. Nobody until then had ever asked me to write anything. I had just done so, relentlessly. To be asked to do it was a great boon. The exhilaration carried me over my apprehensions about writing "for young people," something I had never seriously tried. For some weeks or months I let my imagination go groping around in search of what was wanted, in the dark. It stumbled over the Islands, and the magic employed there. Serious consideration of magic, and of writing for kids, combined to make me wonder about wizards. Wizards are usually elderly or ageless Gandalfs, quite rightly and archetypically. But what were they before they had white beards? How did they learn what is obviously an erudite and dangerous art? Are there colleges for young wizards? And so on.

The story of the book is essentially a voyage, a pattern in the form of a long spiral. I began to see the places where the young wizard would go. Eventually I drew a map. Now that I knew where everything was, now was the time for cartography. Of course a great deal of it only appeared above water, as it were, in drawing the map.

Three small islands are named for my children, their baby-names; one gets a little jovial and irresponsible, given the freedom to create a world out of nothing at all. (Power corrupts.) None of the other names "means" anything that I know of, though their sound is more or less meaningful to me.

People often ask how I think of names in fantasies, and again I have to answer that I find them, that I hear them. This is an important subject in this context. From that first story on, *naming* has been the essence of the art-magic as practiced in Earthsea. For me, as for the wizards, to know the name of an island or a character is to know the island or the person. Usually the name comes of itself, but sometimes one must be very careful: as I was with the protagonist, whose true name is Ged. I worked (in collaboration with a wizard named Ogion) for a long time trying to "listen for" his name, and making certain it really was his name. This all sounds very mystical and indeed there are aspects of it *I* do not understand, but it is a pragmatic business too, since if the name had been wrong the character would have been wrong – misbegotten, misunderstood.

A man who read the ms. for Parnassus thought "Ged" was meant to suggest "God." That shook me badly. I considered changing the name in case there were other such ingenious minds waiting to pounce. But I couldn't do so. The fellow's name was Ged and no two ways about it.

It isn't pronounced Jed, by the way. That sounds like a mountain moonshiner to me. I thought the analogy with "get" would make it clear, but a lot of people have asked. One place I do exert deliberate control in name-inventing is in the area of pronounce-ability. I try to spell them so they don't look too formidable (unless, like Kurremkarmerruk, they're meant to look formidable), and they can be pronounced either with the English or the Italian vowels. I don't care which.

Much the same holds for the bits of invented languages in the text of the trilogy.

There are words, like rushwash tea, for which I can offer no explanation. They simply drink rushwash tea there; that's what it's called, like lapsang soochong or Lipton's here. Rushwash is a Hardic word, of course. If you press me, I will explain that it comes from the rushwash bush, which grows both wild and cultivated everywhere south of Enlad, and bears a small round leaf which when dried and steeped yields a pleasant brownish tea. I did not know this before I wrote the foregoing sentence. Or did I know it, and simply never thought about it? What's in a name? A lot, that's what.

There are more formal examples of foreign languages in the trilogy; in *The Farthest Shore* there are several whole sentences in the Language of the Making, as dragons will not speak anything else. These arrived, spelling (formidable) and all, and I wrote them down without question. No use trying to make a lexicon of Hardic or of the True Speech; there's not enough in the books. It's not like Tolkien, who in one sense wrote *The Lord of the Rings* to give his invented languages somebody to speak them. That is lovely, that is the Creator Spirit working absolutely unhindered – making the word flesh. But Tolkien is a linguist, as well as a great creator.

(In other books I have taken the invented languages further. I knew enough Karhidish, when I was writing *The Left Hand of Darkness*, to write a couple of short poems in it. I couldn't do so now. I made no methodical lexicon or grammar, only a word list for my own reference.)

I said that to know the true name is to know the thing, for me, and for the wizards. This implies a good deal about the "meaning" of the trilogy, and about me. The trilogy is, in one aspect, about the artist. The artist as magician. The Trickster. Prospero. That is the only truly allegorical aspect it has of which I am conscious. If there are other allegories in it please don't tell me; I hate allegories. A is "really" B, and a hawk is "really" a handsaw – bah. Humbug. Any creation, primary or secondary, with any vitality to it, can "really" be a dozen mutually exclusive things at once, before breakfast.

Wizardry is artistry. The trilogy is then, in this sense, about art, the creative experience, the creative process. There is always this circularity in fantasy. The snake devours its tail. Dreams must explain themselves.

What I wanted to send Andy Porter was a long passionate article about the status of "children's books." He wanted something more personal. But as an SF writer I resent being low paid in comparison to dreck-writers; and if SF writers think they're low paid, they should look at writers for children. I am not complaining personally. Atheneum, who now publish my children's books, have treated me well, and with great personal civility; the same goes for Gollancz in England; and both firms have given me splendid (woman) editors. What is wrong is the whole scale – all the publishers' budgets for their children's books. There is seldom big quick money in kiddylit, but a successful kids' book has an unusually long life. It sells to schools, to libraries, and to gift-giving adults, and it goes on selling, and making money, for years and years and years. This is not reflected in the advances or the royalties. It is a very badly paid field, in general.

But the economic discrimination is only an element, as usual, of the real problem: a reflection of a prejudice. The real trouble isn't the money, it's the adult chauvinist piggery.

"You're a juvenile writer, aren't you?"

Yeth, Mummy.

"I love your books – the real ones, I mean, I haven't read the ones for children, of course!"

Of courthe not, Daddy.

"It must be relaxing to write *simple* things for a change."

Sure it's simple, writing for kids. Just as simple as bringing them up.

All you do is take all the sex out, and use little short words, and little dumb ideas, and don't be too scary, and be sure there's a happy ending. Right? Nothing to it. Write down. Right on.

If you do all that, you might even write *Jonathan Livingston Seagull* and make twenty billion dollars and have every adult in America reading your book.

But you won't have every kid in America reading your book. They will look at it, and they will see straight through it, with their clear, cold, beady little eyes, and they will put it down, and they will go away. Kids will devour vast amounts of garbage (and it is good for them) but they are not like adults: they have not yet learned to eat plastic.

The British seem not to believe publishers' categorizations of "juvenile," "teenage," "young adult," etc. so devoutly as we do. It's interesting that, for instance, Andre Norton is often reviewed with complete respect by English papers, including *The Times Literary Supplement*. No pats, no sniggers, no put-downs. They seem to be aware that fantasy is the great age-equalizer; if it's good when you're twelve, it's quite likely to be just as good, or better, when you're thirty-six.

Most of my letters about the Earthsea books from American readers are from people between sixteen and twenty-five. The English who write me tend to be, as well as I can guess, over thirty, and more predominantly male. (Several of them are Anglican clergymen. As a congenital non-Christian I find this a little startling; but the letters are terrific.) One might interpret this age difference to mean that the English are more childish than the Americans, but I see it the other way. The English readers are grownup enough not to be defensive about being grownup.

The most childish thing about *A Wizard of Earthsea*, I expect, is its subject: coming of age.

Coming of age is a process that took me many years; I finished it, so far as I ever will, at about age thirty-one; and so I feel rather deeply about it. So do most adolescents. It's their main occupation, in fact.

The subject of *The Tombs of Atuan* is, if I had to put it in one word, sex. There's a lot of symbolism in the book, most of which I did not, of course, analyze consciously while writing; the symbols can all be read as sexual. More exactly, you could call it a feminine coming of age. Birth, rebirth, destruction, freedom are the themes.

The Farthest Shore is about death. That's why it is a less well built, less sound and complete book than the others. They were about things I had already lived through and survived. *The Farthest Shore* is about the thing you do not live through and survive. It seemed an absolutely suitable subject to me for young readers, since in a way one can say that the hour when a child realizes, not that death exists – children are intensely aware of death – but that he/she, personally, is mortal, will die, is the hour when childhood ends, and the new life begins. Coming of age again, but in a larger context.

In any case I had little choice about the subject. Ged, who was always very strong-minded, always saying things that surprised me and doing things he wasn't supposed to do, took over completely in this book. He was determined to show me how his life must end, and why. I tried to keep up with him, but he was always ahead. I rewrote the book more times than I want to remember, trying to keep him under some kind of control. I thought it was all done when it was printed here, but the English edition differs in three long passages from the earlier American one: my editor at Gollancz said, "Ged is talking too much," and she was quite right, and I shut him up three times, much to the improvement of the whole. If you insist upon discovering instead of planning, this kind of trouble is inevitable. It is a most uneconomical way to write. The book is still the most imperfect of the three, but it is the one I like best. It is the end of the trilogy, but it is the dream I have not stopped dreaming.[1]

---

1 (1989) Nor have I yet stopped dreaming it.
It was a pleasant surprise to me to discover that Ged was in fact quite mistaken about how his life must end, and that the person who would guide me through the last book of Earthsea was Tenar. That last book – *Tehanu* – though I longed to call it Better Late Than Never – is to be published soon.

A Citizen of Mondath

1973

One evening when I was about twelve I was looking through the living room bookshelves for something to read, and pulled out a little Modern Library book, in the old limp leather binding; it had a queer title, *A Dreamer's Tales*. I opened it, standing beside the battered green armchair by the lamp; the moment is perfectly vivid to me now. I read:

> Toldees, Mondath, Arizim, these are the Inner Lands, the lands whose sentinels upon their borders do not behold the sea. Beyond them to the east there lies a desert, for ever untroubled by man: all yellow it is, and spotted with shadows of stones, and Death is in it, like a leopard lying in the sun. To the south they are bounded by magic, to the west by a mountain.

I don't entirely understand why Dunsany came to me as a revelation, why that moment was so decisive. I read a lot, and a lot of my reading was myth, legend, fairy tale; first-rate versions, too, such as Padraic Colum, Asbjornsson, etc. I had also heard my father tell Indian legends aloud, just as he had heard them from informants, only translated into a rather slow, impressive English; and they were impressive and mysterious stories. What I hadn't realized, I guess, is that people were still making up myths. One made up stories oneself, of course; but here was a grownup doing it, for grownups, without a single apology to common sense, without an explanation, just dropping us straight into the Inner Lands. Whatever the reason, the moment was decisive. I had discovered my native country.

The book belonged to my father, a scientist, and was a favorite of his; in fact he had a large appetite for fantasy. I have wondered if there isn't some real connection between a certain kind of scientific-mindedness (the explorative, synthesizing kind) and fantasy-mindedness. Perhaps "science fiction" really isn't such a bad name for our genre after all. Those who dislike fantasy are very often equally bored or repelled by science. They don't like either hobbits or quasars; they don't feel at home with them; they don't want complexities, remoteness. If there is any such connection, I'll bet that it is basically an aesthetic one.

I wonder what would have happened if I had been born in 1939 instead of 1929, and had first read Tolkien in my teens, instead of in my twenties. That achievement might have overwhelmed me. I am glad I had some sense of my own direction before I read Tolkien. Dunsany's influence was wholly benign, and I never tried much to imitate him, in my prolific and derivative adolescent scribblings. I must have known already that this sort of thing is inimitable. He was not a model to me but a liberator, a guide.

However, I was headed toward the Inner Lands before I ever heard of them. I still have my first completed short story, written at age nine. It is about a man persecuted by evil elves. People think he is mad, but the evil elves finally slither in through the keyhole and get him. At ten or eleven I wrote my first science fiction story. It involved time travel and the origin of life on Earth, and was very breezy in style. I submitted it to *Amazing Stories*. There's another vivid memory, my brother Karl on the stairs, looking up at me on the landing and saying very reluctantly, "I'm afraid this is your story come back." I don't remember being very downcast, rather flattered by a real rejection slip. I never submitted anything else to anybody till I was twenty-one, but I think that was less cowardice than wisdom.

We kids read science fiction, in the early forties: *Thrilling Wonder*, and *Astounding* in that giant format it had for a while, and so on. I liked "Lewis Padgett" best, and looked for his stories, but we looked for the trashiest magazines, mostly, because we *liked* trash. I recall one story that began, "In the beginning was the Bird." We really dug that bird. And the closing line from another (or the same?) – "Back to the saurian ooze from whence it sprung!" Karl made that into a useful chant: The saurian ooze from which it sprung/Unwept, unhonor'd, and unsung. I wonder how many hack writers who think they are writing down to "naive kids" and "teenagers" realize the *kind* of pleasure they sometimes give their readers. If they did, they would sink back into the saurian ooze from whence they sprung.

I never read only science fiction, as some kids do. I read everything I could get my hands on, which was limitless; there was a house full of books, and a good public library. I got off science fiction some time in the late forties. It seemed to be all about hardware and soldiers. Besides, I was busy with Tolstoy and things. I did not read any science fiction at all for about fifteen years, just about that period which people now call The Golden Age of Science Fiction. I almost totally missed Heinlein, et al. If I glanced at a magazine, it still seemed to be all about starship captains in black with lean rugged faces and a lot of fancy artillery. Possibly I would never have gone back to reading science fiction, and thence to writing it, if it hadn't been for a friend of ours in Portland in 1960 and 1961 who had a small collection and lent me whatever I glommed on to. One of the things he lent me was a copy of *Fantasy and Science Fiction* containing a story called "Alpha Ralpha Boulevard," by Cordwainer Smith.

I don't really remember what I thought when I read it; but what I think now I ought to have thought when I read it is, *My God! It can be done!*

After that I read a good deal of science fiction, looking for "that kind" of writing; and found some, here and there. Presently it seemed that since there was so little of it, why not do some myself?

No, that is not true. It is much more complicated, and boring.

To put it briefly, I had been writing all my life, and it was becoming a case of publish or perish. You cannot keep filling up the attic with mss. Art, like sex, cannot be carried on indefinitely solo; after all, they have the same enemy, sterility. I had had a number of poems published, and one short story, in little magazines; but this wasn't enough, considering that I had written five novels in the last ten years. I had either to take off or give up.

One of the novels was set in contemporary San Francisco, but the others were set in an invented though nonfantastic Central European country, as were the best short stories I had done. They were not science fiction, they were not fantasy, yet they were not realistic. Alfred Knopf said (in 1951) that he would have published the first of them, ten years earlier, but he'd lose too much money on it now. Viking and other publishers merely remarked that "this material seems remote." It was remote. It was meant to be. Searching for a technique of distancing, I had come on this one. Unfortunately it was not a technique used by anybody else at the moment, it was not fashionable, it did not fit into any of the categories. You must either fit a category or "have a name," to publish a book in America. As the only way I was ever going to achieve Namehood was *by* writing, I was reduced to fitting a category. Therefore my first efforts to write science fiction were motivated by a pretty distinct wish to get published: nothing higher or lower. The stories reflect this extrinsic motivation. They are kind of amiable but not very good, not serious, essentially slick. They were published by Cele Goldsmith Lalli, the kindly and outrageous editor of *Amazing* and *Fantastic*, in the early sixties.

The shift from the kind of writing I had done before to categorizable "fantasy" and "science fiction" was not a big one, but I had a good deal to learn all the same. Also I was pretty ignorant of science, and was just beginning to educate myself (a hopeless job, but one which I continue to enjoy immensely). At first I knew too little science to use it as the framework, as part of the essential theme of a story, and so wrote fairy tales decked out in space suits. If anything gives these merit, it would be my long apprenticeship in poetry and in the psychologically realistic kind of novel.

The first science fiction story I wrote that begins to break from the trivial became the source, and prologue, of the little novel *Rocannon's World*. I was beginning to get the feel of the medium. In the next books I kept on pushing at my own limitations and at the limits of science fiction. That is what the practice of an art is, you keep looking for the outside edge. When you find it you make a whole, solid, real and beautiful thing; anything less is incomplete. These books were certainly incomplete, especially *City of Illusions*, which I should not have published as it stands. It has some good bits, but is only half thought out. I was getting vain and hasty.

That is a real danger, when you write science fiction. There is so little real criticism, that despite the very delightful and heartening feedback from and connection with the fans, the writer is almost her only critic. Second-rate stuff will be bought just as fast, maybe faster sometimes, by the publishers, and the fans will buy it because it is science fiction. Only the writer's conscience remains to insist that she try *not* to be second-rate. Nobody else seems much to care.

Of course this is basically true of the practice of all writing, and all art; but it is exaggerated in science fiction. And equally, of course, it is not true in the long run of science fiction or any other form. But it is an awfully long run. One can trust in the verdict of posterity, but it's not a handy tool to apply in specific instances. What almost all of us need is some genuine, serious, literate criticism: some standards. I don't mean pedantry and fancy academic theorizing. I mean just the kind of standards which any musician, for instance, has to meet. Whether she plays rock on the electric piccolo or Bach on the cello, she is listened to by informed, profoundly interested people, and if she's second-rate she will be told so; ditto if she's good. In science fiction, sometimes it seems that so long as it's science fiction at all, the fans will love it – briefly; therefore the publishers will put it in print – briefly; therefore the writer is likely to settle for doing much less than her best. The mediocre and the excellent are praised alike by aficionados, and ignored alike by outsiders. In such a situation it is simply amazing that writers like Philip K. Dick continue in excellence. It is not at all amazing, though very sad, that writers like Roger Zelazny may be forced into a long period of floundering and groping, after initial sureness. After all, writing is not only an originative act, it is a responsive one. The lack of genuine response, and therefore the lack of the sense of responsibility, is painfully clear in those writers who simply go on and on imitating themselves – or others.

I think the standards are rising, however. In fact, I know they are, when I think back to the saurian ooze from whence we sprung.

Along in 1967–8 I finally got my pure fantasy vein separated off from my science fiction vein, by writing *A Wizard of Earthsea* and then *Left Hand of Darkness*, and the separation marked a very large advance in both skill and content. Since then I have gone on writing, as it were, with both the left and the right hands; and it has been a matter of keeping on pushing out toward the limits – my own, and those of the medium. Very much the largest push was made in my last (not yet published) novel, *The Dispossessed*. I hope rending sounds and cries of dismay are not heard when it comes out. Meanwhile, people keep predicting that I will bolt science fiction and fling myself madly into the Mainstream. I don't know why. The limits, and the great spaces of fantasy and science fiction, are precisely what my imagination needs. Outer Space, and the Inner Lands, are still, and always will be, my country.

From Elfland to Poughkeepsie

1973

Elfland is what Lord Dunsany called the place. It is also known as Middle Earth, and Prydain, and the Forest of Broceliande, and Once Upon a Time; and by many other names.

Let us consider Elfland as a great national park, a vast and beautiful place where a person goes alone on foot, to get in touch with reality in a special, private, profound fashion. But what happens when it is considered merely as a place to "get away to"?

Well, you know what has happened to Yosemite. Everybody comes, not with an ax and a box of matches, but in a trailer with a motorbike on the back and a motorboat on top and a butane stove, five aluminum folding chairs, and a transistor radio on the inside. They arrive totally encapsulated in a secondhand reality. And then they move on to Yellowstone, and it's just the same there, all trailers and transistors. They go from park to park, but they never really go anywhere; except when one of them who thinks that even the wildlife isn't real gets chewed up by a genuine, firsthand bear.

The same sort of thing seems to be happening in Elfland, lately. A great many people want to go there, without knowing what it is they're really looking for, driven by a vague hunger for something real. With the intention or under the pretense of obliging them, certain writers of fantasy are building six-lane highways and trailer parks with drive-in movies, so that the tourists can feel at home just as if they were back in Poughkeepsie.*

But the point about Elfland is that you are not at home there. It's not Poughkeepsie. It's different.

What is fantasy? On one level, of course, it is a game: a pure pretense

---

* Note for the British edition (1989). I don't know where "Poughkeepsie" is, in England. Reading, perhaps, or Surbiton?

with no ulterior motive whatever. It is one child saying to another child, "Let's be dragons," and then they're dragons for an hour or two. It is escapism of the most admirable kind – the game played for the game's sake.

On another level, it is still a game, but a game played for very high stakes. Seen thus, as art, not spontaneous play, its affinity is not with daydream, but with dream. It is a different approach to reality, an alternative technique for apprehending and coping with existence. It is not anti-rational, but para-rational; not realistic, but surrealistic, superrealistic, a heightening of reality. In Freud's terminology, it employs primary, not secondary process thinking. It employs archetypes, which, as Jung warned us, are dangerous things. Dragons are more dangerous, and a good deal commoner, than bears. Fantasy is nearer to poetry, to mysticism, and to insanity than naturalistic fiction is. It is a real wilderness, and those who go there should not feel too safe. And their guides, the writers of fantasy, should take their responsibilities seriously.

After all these metaphors and generalities, let us get down to some examples; let us read a little fantasy.

This is much easier to do than it used to be, thanks very largely to one man, Lin Carter of Ballantine Books, whose Adult Fantasy Series of new publications and reprints of old ones has saved us all from a lifetime of pawing through the shelves of used bookstores somewhere behind several dusty cartons between "Occult" and "Children's" in hopes of finding, perhaps, the battered and half-mythical odd volume of Dunsany. In gratitude to Mr. Carter for the many splendid books, both new and old, in his series, I will read anything his firm sends me; and last year when they sent me a new one, I settled down with a pleasant sense of confidence to read it. Here is a little excerpt from what I read. The persons talking are a duke of the blood royal of a mythical Celtic kingdom, and a warrior-magician – great Lords of Elfland, both of them.

"Whether or not they succeed in the end will depend largely on Kelson's personal ability to manipulate the voting."

"Can he?" Morgan asked, as the two clattered down a half-flight of stairs and into the garden.

"I don't know, Alaric," Nigel replied. "He's good – damned good – but I just don't know. Besides, you saw the key council lords. With Ralson dead and Bran Coris practically making open accusations – well, it doesn't look good."

"I could have told you that at Cardosa."[1]

At this point I was interrupted (perhaps by a person from Porlock, I don't remember), and the next time I sat down I happened to pick up a different kind of novel, a real Now novel, naturalistic, politically conscious, relevant, set in Washington, D.C. Here is a sample of a conversation from it, between a senator and a lobbyist for pollution control.

"Whether or not they succeed in the end will depend largely on Kelson's personal ability to manipulate the voting."

"Can he?" Morgan asked, as the two clattered down a half-flight of stairs and into the White House garden.

"I don't know, Alaric," Nigel replied. "He's good – damned good – but I just don't know. Besides, you saw the key committee chairmen. With Ralson dead and Brian Corliss practically making open accusations – well, it doesn't look good."

"I could have told you that at Poughkeepsie."

Now, I submit that something has gone wrong. The book from which I first quoted is not fantasy, for all its equipment of heroes and wizards. If it was fantasy, I couldn't have pulled that dirty trick on it by changing four words. You can't clip Pegasus' wings that easily – not if he has wings.

Before I go further I want to apologize to the author of the passage for making a horrible example of her. There are infinitely worse examples I could have used; I chose this one because in this book something good has gone wrong – something real has been falsified. There would be no use at all in talking about what is generally passed off as "heroic fantasy," all the endless Barbarians, with names like Barp and Klod, and the Tarnsmen and the Klansmen and all the rest of them – there would be nothing whatever to say. (Not in terms of art, that is; in terms of ethics, racism, sexism, and politics there would be a great deal to say.)[*]

What is it, then, that I believe has gone wrong in the book and the passage quoted from it? I think it is the *style*. Presently I'll try to explain why I think so. It will be convenient, however, to have other examples at hand. The first passage was dialogue, and style in a novel is often particularly

---

1 Katherine Kurtz, *Deryni Rising* (New York: Ballantine Books, August 1970), p. 41

[*] Note (1989). I don't find it as easy as I did in 1973 to separate "art" from "ethics, racism, sexism, and politics" – a dangerous, usually illusory, separation.

visible in dialogue; so here are some bits of conversations from other parts of Elfland. The books from which they were taken were all written in this century, and all the speakers are wizards, warriors, or Lords of Elfland, as in the first selection. The books were chosen carefully, of course, but the passages were picked at random; I just looked for a page where two or three suitably noble types were chatting.

Now spake Spitfire saying, "Read forth to us, I pray thee, the book of Gro; for my soul is afire to set forth on this faring."

"'Tis writ somewhat crabbedly," said Brandoch Daha, "and most damnably long. I spent half last night a-searching on't, and 'tis most apparent no other way lieth to these mountains save by the Moruna, and across the Moruna is (if Gro say true) but one way . . ."

"If he say true?" said Spitfire. "He is a turncoat and a renegado. Wherefore not therefore a liar?"[2]

"Detestable to me, truly, is loathsome hunger; abominable an insufficiency of food upon a journey. Mournful, I declare to you, is such a fate as this, to one of my lineage and nurture!"

"Well, well," said Dienw'r Anffodion, with the bitter hunger awaking in him again, "common with me is knowledge of famine. Take you the whole of the food, if you will."

"Yes," said Goreu. "That will be better."[3]

"Who can tell?" said Aragorn. "But we will put it to the test one day."

"May the day not be too delayed," said Boromir. "For though I do not ask for aid, we need it. It would comfort us to know that others fought also with all the means that they have."

"Then be comforted," said Elrond.[4]

Now all those speakers speak English differently; but they all have the genuine Elfland accent. You could not pull the trick on them that I pulled on Morgan and Nigel – not unless you changed half the words in every

2 E.R. Eddison, *The Worm Ouroboros* (New York: Ballantine Books, April 1967), p. 137.

3 Kenneth Morris, *Book of the Three Dragons*, Junior Literary Guild, copyright 1930 (New York: Longmans, Green and Company), p. 8. (This excerpt also contained in *Dragons, Elves and Heroes*, ed. Lin Carter [New York: Ballantine Books, October 1969], p. 59.)

4 J. R. R. Tolkien, *The Fellowship of the Ring* (New York: Ballantine Books, October 1965), p. 351.

sentence. You could not possibly mistake them for anyone on Capitol Hill.

In the first selection they are a little crazy, and in the second one they are not only crazy but Welsh – and yet they speak with power, with a wild dignity. All of them are heroic, eloquent, passionate. It may be the passion that is most important. Nothing is really going on in those first two passages: in one case they're reading a book, in the other they're dividing a cold leg of rabbit. But with what importance they invest these trivial acts, what emotion, what vitality!

In the third passage, the speakers are quieter, and use a less extraordinary English, or rather an English extraordinary for its simple timelessness. Such language is rare on Capitol Hill, but it has occurred there. It has sobriety, wit and force. It is the language of men* of character.

Speech expresses character. It does so whether the speaker or the author knows it or not. (Presidential speech writers know it very well.) When I hear a man say, "I could have told you that at Cardosa," or at Poughkeepsie, or wherever, I think I know something about that man. He is the kind who says, "I told you so."

Nobody who says, "I told you so" has ever been, or will ever be, a hero.

The Lords of Elfland are true lords, the only true lords, the kind that do not exist on this earth: their lordship is the outward sign or symbol of real inward greatness. And greatness of soul shows when a man* speaks. At least, it does in books. In life we expect lapses. In naturalistic fiction, too, we expect lapses, and laugh at an "overheroic" hero. But in fantasy, which, instead of imitating the perceived confusion and complexity of existence, tries to hint at an order and clarity underlying existence – in fantasy, we need not compromise. Every word spoken is meaningful, though the meaning may be subtle. For example, in the second passage, the fellow called Goreu is moaning and complaining and shamelessly conning poor Dienw'r out of the only thing he has to eat. And yet you feel that anybody who can talk like that isn't a mean-spirited man. He would never say, "I told you so." In fact, he's not a man at all, he is Gwydion son of Don in disguise, and he has a good reason for his tricks, a magnanimous reason. On the other hand, in the third quotation, the very slight whine in Boromir's tone is significant also. Boromir is a noble-hearted person, but there is a tragic flaw in his character and the flaw is envy.

---

* Note (1989). All the heroes in the fantasies I quoted from, even the one written by a woman, are men.

I picked for comparison three master stylists: E.R. Eddison, Kenneth Morris, and J.R.R. Tolkien; which may seem unfair to any other authors mentioned. But I do not think it is unfair. In art, the best is the standard. When you hear a new violinist, you do not compare her to the kid next door; you compare her to Stern and Heifetz. If she falls short, you will not blame her for it, but you will know what she falls short of. And if she is a real violinist, she knows it too. In art, "good enough" is not good enough.

Another reason for picking those three is that they exemplify styles which are likely to be imitated by beginning writers of fantasy. There is a great deal of quite open influencing and imitating going on among the writers of fantasy. I incline to think that this is a very healthy situation. It is one in which most vigorous arts find themselves. Take for example music in the eighteenth century, when Handel and Haydn and Mozart and the rest of them were borrowing tunes and tricks and techniques from one another and building up the great edifice of music like a lot of masons at work on one cathedral; well, we may yet have a great edifice of fantasy. But you can't imitate what somebody does until you've learned how they do it.

The most imitated, and the most inimitable, writer of fantasy is probably Lord Dunsany. I did not include a passage of conversation from Dunsany, because I could not find a suitable one. Genuine give-and-take conversations are quite rare in his intensely mannered, intensely poetic narratives, and when they occur they tend to be very brief, as they do in the Bible. The King James Bible is indubitably one of the profoundest formative influences on Dunsany's prose; another, I suspect, is Irish daily speech. Those two influences alone, not to mention his own gifts of a delicate ear for speech rhythms and a brilliantly exact imagination, remove him from the reach of any would-be imitator or emulator who is not an Irish peer brought up from the cradle on the grand sonorities of Genesis and Ecclesiastes. Dunsany mined a narrow vein, but it was all pure ore, and all his own. I have never seen any imitation Dunsany that consisted of anything beyond a lot of elaborate made-up names, some vague descriptions of gorgeous cities and unmentionable dooms, and a great many sentences beginning with "And."

Dunsany is indeed the First Terrible Fate that Awaiteth Unwary Beginners in Fantasy. But if they avoid him, there are others – many others. One of these is archaicizing, the archaic manner, which Dunsany and other master fantasists use so effortlessly. It is a trap into which almost all very young fantasy writers walk. I know; I did myself. They know instinctively that what is wanted in fantasy is a *distancing from the ordinary*. They see it done beautifully in old books, such as Malory's *Morte d'Arthur*, and in new books the style of which is grounded on the old books, and they think, "Aha! I will do it too." But alas, it is one of those things, like bicycling and computer programming, that you have got to know how to do before you do it.

"Aha!" says our novice. "You have to use verbs with thee and thou." So she does. But she doesn't know how. There are very few Americans now alive who know how to use a verb in the second person singular. The general assumption is that you add *-est* and you're there. I remember Debbie Reynolds telling Eddie Fisher – do you remember Debbie Reynolds and Eddie Fisher? – "Whithersoever thou goest there also I goest." Fake feeling; fake grammar.

Then our novice tries to use the subjunctive. All the was's turn into were's, and leap out at the reader snarling. And the Quakers have got us all fouled up about which really is the nominative form of Thou. Is it Thee, or isn't it? And then there's the She-To-Whom Trap. "I shall give it to she to whom my love is given!" – "Him whom this sword smites shall surely die!" – Give it to she? Him shall die? It sounds like Tonto talking to the Lone Ranger. This is distancing with a vengeance. But we aren't through yet, no, we haven't had the fancy words. Eldritch. Tenebrous. Smaragds and chalcedony. Mayhap. It can't be maybe, it can't be perhaps; it has to be mayhap, unless it's perchance. And then comes the final test, the infallible touchstone of the seventh-rate: Ichor. You know ichor. It oozes out of severed tentacles, and beslimes tessellated pavements, and bespatters bejeweled courtiers, and bores the bejesus out of everybody.

The archaic manner is indeed a perfect distancer, but you have to do it perfectly. It's a high wire: one slip spoils all. The man who did it perfectly was, of course, Eddison. He really did write Elizabethan prose in the 1930s. His style is totally artificial, but it is never faked. If you love language for its own sake he is irresistible. Many, with reason, find him somewhat crabbed and most damnably long; but he is the real thing, and just to reaffirm that strange, remote reality, I am placing a longer quotation from him here. This is from *The Worm Ouroboros*. A dead king is being carried, in secrecy, at night, down to the beach.

> The lords of Witchland took their weapons and the men-at-arms bare the goods, and the King went in the midst on his bier of spear-shafts.

So went they picking their way in the moonless night round the palace and down the winding path that led to the bed of the combe, and so by the stream westward toward the sea. Here they deemed it safe to light a torch to show them the way. Desolate and bleak showed the sides of the combe in the windblown flare; and the flare was thrown back from the jewels of the royal crown of Witchland, and from the armored buskins on the King's feet showing stark with toes pointing upward from below his bear-skin mantle, and from the armor and the weapons of them that bare him and walked beside him, and from the black cold surface of the little river hurrying for ever over its bed of boulders to the sea. The path was rugged and stony, and they fared slowly, lest they should stumble and drop the King.[5]

That prose, in spite of or because of its archaisms, is good prose: exact, clear, powerful. Visually it is precise and vivid; musically – that is, in the sound of the words, the movement of the syntax, and the rhythm of the sentences – it is subtle and very strong. Nothing in it is faked or blurred; it is all seen, heard, felt. That style was his true style, his own voice; that was how Eddison, an artist, spoke.

The second of our three "conversation pieces" is from *Book of the Three Dragons*, by Kenneth Morris. This book one must still seek on the dusty shelves behind the cartons, probably in the section marked "Children's" – at least that's where I found it – for Mr. Carter has not yet reprinted more than a fragment of it, and if it ever had a day of fame it was before our time. I use it here partly in hopes of arousing interest in the book, for I think many people would enjoy it. It is a singularly fine example of the recreation of a work magnificent in its own right (the *Mabinogion*) – a literary event rather rare except in fantasy, where its frequency is perhaps proof, if one were needed, of the ever-renewed vitality of myth. But Morris is also useful to my purpose because he has a strong sense of humor; and humor in fantasy is both a lure and a pitfall to imitators. Dunsany is often ironic, but he does not mix simple humor with the heroic tone. Eddison sometimes did, but I think Morris and James Branch Cabell were the masters of the comic-heroic. One does not smile wryly, reading them; one laughs. They achieve their comedy essentially by their style – by an eloquence, a fertility and felicity of invention that is simply overwhelming. They are

---

5 Eddison, *The Worm Ouroboros*, pp. 56–7.

outrageous, and they know exactly what they're doing.

Fritz Leiber and Roger Zelazny have both written in the comic-heroic vein, but their technique is different: they alternate the two styles. When humor is intended the characters talk colloquial American English, or even slang, and at earnest moments they revert to old formal usages. Readers indifferent to language do not mind this, but for others the strain is too great. I am one of these latter. I am jerked back and forth between Elfland and Poughkeepsie; the characters lose coherence in my mind, and I lose confidence in them. It is strange, because both Leiber and Zelazny are skillful and highly imaginative writers, and it is perfectly clear that Leiber, profoundly acquainted with Shakespeare and practiced in a very broad range of techniques, could maintain any tone with eloquence and grace. Sometimes I wonder if these two writers underestimate their own talents, if they lack confidence in themselves. Or it may be that, since fantasy is seldom taken seriously at this particular era in this country, they are afraid to take it seriously. They don't want to be caught believing in their own creations, getting all worked up about imaginary things; and so their humor becomes self-mocking, self-destructive. Their gods and heroes keep turning aside to look out of the book at you and whisper, "See, we're really just plain folks."

Now Cabell never does that. He mocks everything: not only his own fantasy, but our reality. He doesn't believe in his dreamworld, but he doesn't believe in us, either. His tone is perfectly consistent: elegant, arrogant, ironic. Sometimes I enjoy it and sometimes it makes me want to scream, but it is admirable. Cabell knew what he wanted to do and he did it, and the marketplace be damned.

Evangeline Walton, whose books, like Kenneth Morris's, are reworkings of the *Mabinogion*, has achieved her own beautifully idiosyncratic blend of humor and heroism; there is no doubt that the Celtic mythos lends itself to such a purpose. And while we are on the subject of humor, Jack Vance must be mentioned, though his humor is so quiet you can miss it if you blink. Indeed the whole tone of his writing is so modest that sometimes I wonder whether, like Leiber and Zelazny, he fails to realize how very good a writer he is. If so, it is probably a result of the patronizing attitude American culture affects toward works of pure imagination. Vance, however, never compromises with the patronizing and ignorant. He never lets his creation down in order to make a joke and he never shows a tin ear for tone. The conversation of his characters is aloof and restrained, very like his own narrative prose; an unusual kind of English, but clear, graceful, and precisely suited to Vance's extraordinary imagination. It is an achieved style. And it contains no archaisms at all.

After all, archaisms are not essential. You don't have to know how to use the subjunctive in order to be a wizard. You don't have to talk like Henry the Fifth to be a hero.*

Caution, however, is needed. Great caution. Consider: Did Henry the Fifth of England really talk like Shakespeare's Henry? Did the real Achilles use hexameters? Would the real Beowulf please stand up and alliterate? We are not discussing history, but heroic fantasy. We are discussing a modern descendant of the epic.

Most epics are in straightforward language, whether prose or verse. They retain the directness of their oral forebears. Homer's metaphors may be extended, but they are neither static nor ornate. The *Song of Roland* has four thousand lines, containing one simile and no metaphors. The *Mabinogion* and the Norse sagas are as plainspoken as they could well be. Clarity and simplicity are permanent virtues in a narrative. Nothing highfalutin is needed. A plain language is the noblest of all.

It is also the most difficult.

Tolkien writes a plain, clear English. Its outstanding virtue is its flexibility, its variety. It ranges easily from the commonplace to the stately, and can slide into metrical poetry, as in the Tom Bombadil episode, without the careless reader's even noticing. Tolkien's vocabulary is not striking; he has no ichor; everything is direct, concrete and simple.

Now the kind of writing I am attacking, the Poughkeepsie style of fantasy, is also written in a plain and apparently direct prose. Does that makes it equal to Tolkien's? Alas, no. It is a fake plainness. It is not really simple, but flat. It is not really clear, but inexact. Its directness is specious. Its sensory cues – extremely important in imaginative writing – are vague and generalized; the rocks, the wind, the trees are not there, are not felt; the scenery is cardboard, or plastic. The tone as a whole is profoundly inappropriate to the subject.

To what then is it appropriate? To journalism. It is journalistic prose. In journalism, the suppression of the author's personality and sensibility is deliberate. The goal is an impression of objectivity. The whole thing is meant

---

* Note (1989). I'm more certain than ever of the second statement, but I think the preceding one is wrong. Wizards operate in the subjunctive mode.

to be written fast and read faster. This technique is right, for a newspaper. It is wrong for a novel, and dead wrong for a fantasy. A language intended to express the immediate and the trivial is applied to the remote and the elemental. The result, of course, is a mess.

Why do we seem to be achieving just that result so often, these days? Well, undoubtedly avarice is one of the reasons. Fantasy is selling well, so let's all grind out a fantasy. The Old Baloney Factory. And sheer ineptness enters in. But in many cases neither greed nor lack of skill seems to be involved, and in such cases I suspect a failure to take the job seriously: a refusal to admit what you're in for when you set off with only an ax and a box of matches into Elfland.

A fantasy is a journey. It is a journey into the subconscious mind, just as psychoanalysis is. Like psychoanalysis, it can be dangerous; and *it will change you.*

The general assumption is that, if there are dragons or hippogriffs in a book, or if it takes place in a vaguely Celtic or Near Eastern medieval setting, or if magic is done in it, then it's a fantasy. This is a mistake.

A writer who doesn't know the West may deploy acres of sagebrush and rimrock without achieving a real Western. A writer may fumble about with space ships and strains of mutant bacteria and never be anywhere near real science fiction. A writer may even write a five-hundred-page novel about Sigmund Freud which has absolutely nothing to do with Sigmund Freud; it has been done; it was done just a couple of years ago. And in the same way, a writer may use all the trappings of fantasy without ever actually imagining anything.

My argument is that this failure, this fakery, is visible instantly in the style.

Many readers, many critics and most editors speak of style as if it were an ingredient of a book, like the sugar in a cake, or something added on to the book, like the frosting on the cake. The style, of course, *is* the book. If you remove the cake, all you have left is a recipe. If you remove the style, all you have left is a synopsis of the plot.

This is partly true of history; largely true of fiction; and absolutely true of fantasy.

In saying that the style is the book, I speak from the reader's point of view. From the writer's point of view, the style is the writer. Style isn't just how you use English when you write. It isn't a mannerism or an affectation (though it may be mannered or affected). It isn't something you can do without, though that is what people assume when they announce that they intend to write something "like it is." You can't do without it. There is no "is" without it. Style is how you as a writer see and speak. It is how you see: your vision, your understanding of the world, your voice.

This is not to say that style cannot be learned and perfected, or that it cannot be borrowed and imitated. We learn to see and speak, as children, primarily by imitation. The artist is merely the one who goes on learning after growing up. A good learner will finally learn the hardest thing: how to see one's own world, how to speak one's own words.

Still, why is style of such fundamental significance in fantasy? Just because a writer gets the tone of a conversation a bit wrong, or describes things vaguely, or uses an anachronistic vocabulary or shoddy syntax, or begins going a bit heavy on the ichor before dinner – does that disqualify the book as a fantasy? Just because the style is weak and inappropriate – is that so important?

I think it is, because in fantasy there is nothing but the writer's vision of the world. There is no borrowed reality of history, or current events, or just plain folks at home in Peyton Place. There is no comfortable matrix of the commonplace to substitute for the imagination, to provide ready-made emotional response, and to disguise flaws and failures of creation. There is only a construct built in a void, with every joint and seam and nail exposed. To create what Tolkien calls "a secondary universe" is to make a new world. A world where no voice has ever spoken before; where the act of speech is the act of creation. The only voice that speaks there is the creator's voice. And every word counts.

This is an awful responsibility to undertake, when all the poor writer wants to do is play dragons, to entertain us all for a while. Nobody should be blamed for falling short of it. But all the same, if one undertakes a responsibility one should be aware of it. Elfland is not Poughkeepsie; the voice of the transistor is not heard in that land.

And lastly I believe that the reader has a responsibility; if we love the stuff we read, we have a duty toward it. That duty is to refuse to be fooled; to refuse to permit commercial exploitation of the holy ground of Myth; to reject shoddy work, and to save our praise for the real thing. Because when fantasy is the real thing, nothing, after all, is realer.

Why Are Americans Afraid of Dragons?

1974

This was to be a talk about fantasy. But I have not been feeling very fanciful lately, and could not decide what to say; so I have been going about picking people's brains for ideas. "What about fantasy? Tell me something about fantasy." And one friend of mine said, "All right, I'll tell you something fantastic. Ten years ago, I went to the children's room of the library of such-and-such a city, and asked for *The Hobbit*; and the librarian told me, 'Oh, we keep that only in the adult collection; we don't feel that escapism is good for children.'"

My friend and I had a good laugh and shudder over that, and we agreed that things have changed a great deal in these past ten years. That kind of moralistic censorship of works of fantasy is very uncommon now, in the children's libraries. But the fact that the children's libraries have become oases in the desert doesn't mean that there isn't still a desert. The point of view from which that librarian spoke still exists. She was merely reflecting, in perfect good faith, something that goes very deep in the American character: a moral disapproval of fantasy, a disapproval so intense, and often so aggressive, that I cannot help but see it as arising, fundamentally, from fear.

So: Why are Americans afraid of dragons?

Before I try to answer my question, let me say that it isn't only Americans who are afraid of dragons. I suspect that almost all very highly technological peoples are more or less antifantasy. There are several national literatures which, like ours, have had no tradition of adult fantasy for the past several hundred years: the French, for instance. But then you have the Germans, who have a good deal; and the English, who have it, and love it, and do it better than anyone else. So this fear of dragons is not merely a Western, or a technological, phenomenon. But I do not want to get into these vast historical questions; I will speak of modern Americans, the only people I know well enough to talk about.

In wondering why Americans are afraid of dragons, I began to realize that a great many Americans are not only antifantasy, but altogether anti-fiction. We tend, as a people, to look upon all works of the imagination either as suspect or as contemptible.

"My wife reads novels. I haven't got the time."

"I used to read that science fiction stuff when I was a teenager, but of course I don't now."

"Fairy stories are for kids. I live in the real world."

Who speaks so? Who is it that dismisses *War and Peace*, *The Time Machine* and *A Midsummer Night's Dream* with this perfect self-assurance? It is, I fear, the man in the street – the hard-working, over-thirty American male – the men who run this country.

Such a rejection of the entire art of fiction is related to several American characteristics: our Puritanism, our work ethic, our profit-mindedness, and even our sexual mores.

To read *War and Peace* or *The Lord of the Rings* plainly is not "work" – you do it for pleasure. And if it cannot be justified as "educational" or as "self-improvement," then, in the Puritan value system, it can only be self-indulgence or escapism. For pleasure is not a value, to the Puritan; on the contrary, it is a sin.

Equally, in the businessman's value system, if an act does not bring in an immediate, tangible profit, it has no justification at all. Thus the only person who has an excuse to read Tolstoy or Tolkien is the English teacher, who gets paid for it. But our businessman might allow himself to read a best-seller now and then: not because it is a good book, but because it is a best-seller – it is a success, it has made money. To the strangely mystical mind of the money-changer, this justifies its existence; and by reading it he may participate, a little, in the power and mana of its success. If this is not magic, by the way, I don't know what it is.

The last element, the sexual one, is more complex. I hope I will not be understood as being sexist if I say that, within our culture, I believe that this antifiction attitude is basically a male one. The American boy and man is very commonly forced to define his maleness by rejecting certain traits, certain human gifts and potentialities, which our culture defines as "womanish" or "childish." And one of these traits or potentialities is, in cold sober fact, the absolutely essential human faculty of imagination.

Having got this far, I went quickly to the dictionary.

The *Shorter Oxford Dictionary* says: "Imagination. 1. The action of imagining, or forming a mental concept of what is not actually present to the senses; 2. The mental consideration of actions or events not yet in existence."

Very well; I certainly can let "absolutely essential human faculty" stand. But I must narrow the definition to fit our present subject. By "imagination," then, I personally mean the free play of the mind, both intellectual and sensory. By "play" I mean recreation, re-creation, the recombination of what is known into what is new. By "free" I mean that the action is done without an immediate object of profit – spontaneously. That does not mean, however, that there may not be a purpose behind the free play of the mind, a goal; and the goal may be a very serious object indeed. Children's imaginative play is clearly a practicing at the acts and emotions of adulthood; a child who did not play would not become mature. As for the free play of an adult mind, its result may be *War and Peace*, or the theory of relativity.

To be free, after all, is not to be undisciplined. I should say that the discipline of the imagination may in fact be the essential method or technique of both art and science. It is our Puritanism, insisting that discipline means repression or punishment, which confuses the subject. To discipline something, in the proper sense of the word, does not mean to repress it, but to train it – to encourage it to grow, and act, and be fruitful, whether it is a peach tree or a human mind.

I think that a great many American men have been taught just the opposite. They have learned to repress their imagination, to reject it as something childish or effeminate, unprofitable, and probably sinful.

They have learned to fear it. But they have never learned to discipline it at all.

Now, I doubt that the imagination can be suppressed. If you truly eradicated it in a child, that child would grow up to be an eggplant. Like all our evil propensities, the imagination will out. But if it is rejected and despised, it will grow into wild and weedy shapes; it will be deformed. At its best, it will be mere ego-centered daydreaming; at its worst, it will be wishful thinking, which is a very dangerous occupation when it is taken seriously. Where literature is concerned, in the old, truly Puritan days, the only permitted reading was the Bible. Nowadays, with our secular Puritanism, the man who refuses to read novels because it's unmanly to do so, or because they aren't true, will most likely end up watching bloody detective thrillers on the television, or reading hack Westerns or sports stories, or going in for pornography, from *Playboy* on down. It is his starved imagination, craving nourishment, that forces him to do so. But he can rationalize such entertainment by saying that it is realistic – after all, sex exists, and there are criminals, and there are baseball players, and there used to be cowboys – and also by saying that it is virile, by which he means that it doesn't interest most women.

That all these genres are sterile, hopelessly sterile, is a reassurance to him, rather than a defect. If they were genuinely realistic, which is to say genuinely imagined and imaginative, he would be afraid of them. Fake realism is the escapist literature of our time. And probably the ultimate escapist reading is that masterpiece of total unreality, the daily stock market report.

Now what about our man's wife? She probably wasn't required to squelch her private imagination in order to play her expected role in life, but she hasn't been trained to discipline it either. She is allowed to read novels, and even fantasies. But, lacking training and encouragement, her fancy is likely to glom on to very sickly fodder, such things as soap operas, and "true romances," and nursy novels, and historico-sentimental novels, and all the rest of the baloney ground out to replace genuine imaginative works by the artistic sweatshops of a society that is profoundly distrustful of the uses of the imagination.

What, then, are the uses of imagination?

You see, I think we have a terrible thing here: a hardworking, upright, responsible citizen, a full-grown, educated person, who is afraid of dragons, and afraid of hobbits, and scared to death of fairies. It's funny, but it's also terrible. Something has gone very wrong. I don't know what to do about it but to try and give an honest answer to that person's question, even though he often asks it in an aggressive and contemptuous tone of voice. "What's the good of it all?" he says. "Dragons and hobbits and little green men – what's the *use* of it?"

The truest answer, unfortunately, he won't even listen to. He won't hear it. The truest answer is, "The use of it is to give you pleasure and delight."

"I haven't got the time," he snaps, swallowing a Maalox pill for his ulcer and rushing off to the golf course.

So we try the next-to-truest answer. It probably won't go down much better, but it must be said: "The use of imaginative fiction is to deepen your understanding of your world, and your fellow men, and your own feelings, and your destiny."

To which I fear he will retort, "Look, I got a raise last year, and I'm giving my family the best of everything, we've got two cars and a color TV. I understand enough of the world!"

And he is right, unanswerably right, if that is what he wants, and all he wants.

The kind of thing you learn from reading about the problems of a hobbit who is trying to drop a magic ring into an imaginary volcano has very little to do with your social status, or material success, or income. Indeed, if there is any relationship, it is a negative one. There is an inverse correlation between fantasy and money. That is a law, known to economists as Le Guin's Law. If you want a striking example of Le Guin's Law, just give a lift to one of those people along the roads who own nothing but a backpack, a guitar, a fine head of hair, a smile and a thumb. Time and again, you will find that these waifs have read *The Lord of the Rings* – some of them can practically recite it. But now take Aristotle Onassis or J. Paul Getty: could you believe that those men ever had anything to do, at any age, under any circumstances, with a hobbit?

But, to carry my example a little further, and out of the realm of economics, did you ever notice how very gloomy Mr. Onassis and Mr. Getty and all those billionaires look in their photographs? They have this strange, pinched look, as if they were hungry. As if they were hungry for something, as if they had lost something and were trying to think where it could be, or perhaps what it could be, what it was they've lost.

Could it be their childhood?

So I arrive at my personal defense of the uses of the imagination, especially in fiction, and most especially in fairy tale, legend, fantasy, science fiction and the rest of the lunatic fringe. I believe that maturity is not an outgrowing, but a growing up: that an adult is not a dead child, but a child who survived. I believe that all the best faculties of a mature human being exist in the child, and that if these faculties are encouraged in youth they will act well and wisely in the adult, but if they are repressed and denied in the child they will stunt and cripple the adult personality. And finally, I believe that one of the most deeply human, and humane, of these faculties is the power of imagination: so that it is our pleasant duty, as librarians, or teachers, or parents, or writers, or simply as grownups, to encourage that faculty of imagination in our children, to encourage it to grow freely, to flourish like the green bay tree, by giving it the best, absolutely the best and purest, nourishment that it can absorb. And never, under any circumstances, to squelch it, or sneer at it, or imply that it is childish, or unmanly, or untrue.

For fantasy is true, of course. It isn't factual, but it is true. Children know that. Adults know it too, and that is precisely why many of them are afraid of fantasy. They know that its truth challenges, even threatens, all that is false, all that is phony, unnecessary, and trivial in the life they have let themselves be forced into living. They are afraid of dragons, because they are afraid of freedom.

So I believe that we should trust our children. Normal children do not confuse reality and fantasy — they confuse them much less often than we adults do (as a certain great fantasist pointed out in a story called "The Emperor's New Clothes"). Children know perfectly well that unicorns aren't real, but they also know that books about unicorns, if they are good books, are true books. All too often, that's more than Mummy and Daddy know; for, in denying their childhood, the adults have denied half their knowledge, and are left with the sad, sterile little fact: "Unicorns aren't real." And that fact is one that never got anybody anywhere (except in the story "The Unicorn in the Garden," by another great fantasist, in which it is shown that a devotion to the unreality of unicorns may get you straight into the loony bin). It is by such statements as, "Once upon a time there was a dragon," or "In a hole in the ground there lived a hobbit" — it is by such beautiful non-facts that we fantastic human beings may arrive, in our peculiar fashion, at the truth.

Is Gender Necessary? Redux

●

1976/1988

In the mid-1960s the women's movement was just beginning to move again, after a fifty-year halt. There was a groundswell gathering. I felt it, but I didn't know it was a groundswell; I just thought it was something wrong with me. I considered myself a feminist: I didn't see how you could be a thinking woman and not be a feminist; but I had never taken a step beyond the ground gained for us by Emmeline Pankhurst and Virginia Woolf.[1]

Along about 1967, I began to feel a certain unease, a need to step on a little farther, perhaps, on my own. I began to want to define and under-stand the meaning of sexuality and the meaning of gender, in my life and in our society. Much had gathered in the unconscious – both personal and collective – which must either be brought up into consciousness or else turn destructive. It was that same need, I think, that had led de Beauvoir to write *The Second Sex*, and Friedan to write *The Feminine Mystique*, and that was, at the same time, leading Kate Millett and others to write their books, and to create the new feminism. But I was not a theoretician, a political thinker or activist, or a sociologist. I was and am a fiction writer. The way I did my thinking was to write a novel. That novel, *The Left Hand of Darkness*, is the record of my consciousness, the process of my thinking.

Perhaps, now that we have all[2] moved on to a plane of heightened consciousness about these matters, it might be of some interest to look back on the book, to see what it did, what it tried to do, and what it might have done, insofar as it is a "feminist"[3] book. (Let me repeat the

---

1 Feminism has enlarged its ground and strengthened its theory and practice immensely, and enduringly, in these past twenty years; but has anyone actually taken a step "beyond" Virginia Woolf? The image, implying an ideal of "progress," is not one I would use now.
2 Well, quite a lot of us, anyhow.
3 Strike the quotation marks from the word "feminist," please.

last qualification, once. The fact is that the real subject of the book is not feminism or sex or gender or anything of the sort; as far as I can see, it is a book about betrayal and fidelity. That is why one of its two dominant sets of symbols is an extended metaphor of winter, of ice, snow, cold: the winter journey. The rest of this discussion will concern only half, the lesser half, of the book.)[4]

It takes place on a planet called Gethen, whose human inhabitants differ from us in their sexual physiology. Instead of our continuous sexuality, the Gethenians have an oestrous period, called *kemmer*. When they are not in kemmer, they are sexually inactive and impotent; they are also androgynous. An observer in the book describes the cycle:

In the first phase of kemmer [the individual] remains completely androgynous. Gender, and potency, are not attained in isolation . . . Yet the sexual impulse is tremendously strong in this phase, controlling the entire personality . . . When the individual finds a partner in kemmer, hormonal secretion is further stimulated (most importantly by touch – secretion? scent?) until in one partner either a male or female hormonal dominance is established. The genitals engorge or shrink accordingly, foreplay intensifies, and the partner, triggered by the change, takes on the other sexual role (apparently without exception) . . . Normal individuals have no predisposition to either sexual role in kemmer; they do not know whether they will be the male or the female, and have no choice in the matter . . . The culminant phase of kemmer lasts from two to five days, during which sexual drive and capacity are at maximum. It ends fairly abruptly, and if conception has not taken place, the individual returns to the latent phase and the cycle begins anew. If the individual was in the female role and was impregnated, hormonal activity of course continues, and for the gestation and lactation periods this individual remains female . . . With the cessation of lactation the female becomes once more a perfect androgyne. No physiological habit is established, and the mother of several children may be the father of several more.

★

---

4 This parenthesis is overstated; I was feeling defensive, and resentful that critics of the book insisted upon talking only about its "gender problems," as if it were an essay not a novel. "The fact is that the real subject of the book is . . ." This is bluster. I had opened a can of worms and was trying hard to shut it. "The fact is" however, that there are other aspects to the book, which are involved with its sex/gender aspects quite inextricably.

Why did I invent these peculiar people? Not just so that the book could contain, halfway through it, the sentence "The king was pregnant" – though I admit that I am fond of that sentence. Not, certainly not, to propose Gethen as a model for humanity. I am not in favor of genetic alteration of the human organism – not at our present level of understanding. I was not recommending the Gethenian sexual setup: I was using it. It was a heuristic device, a thought-experiment. Physicists often do thought-experiments. Einstein shoots a light ray through a moving elevator; Schrödinger puts a cat in a box. There is no elevator, no cat, no box. The experiment is performed, the question is asked, in the mind. Einstein's elevator, Schrödinger's cat, my Gethenians, are simply a way of thinking. They are questions, not answers; process, not stasis. One of the essential functions of science fiction, I think, is precisely this kind of question-asking: reversals of a habitual way of thinking, metaphors for what our language has no words for as yet, experiments in imagination.

The subject of my experiment, then, was something like this: Because of our lifelong social conditioning, it is hard for us to see clearly what, besides purely physiological form and function, truly differentiates men and women. Are there real differences in temperament, capacity, talent, psychic process, etc.? If so, what are they? Only comparative ethnology offers, so far, any solid evidence on the matter, and the evidence is incomplete and often contradictory. The only going social experiments that are truly relevant are the kibbutzim and the Chinese communes, and they too are inconclusive – and hard to get unbiased information about. How to find out? Well, one can always put a cat in a box. One can send an imaginary, but conventional, indeed rather stuffy, young man from Earth into an imaginary culture which is totally free of sex roles because there is no, absolutely no, physiological sex distinction. I eliminated gender, to find out what was left. Whatever was left would be, presumably, simply human. It would define the area that is shared by men and women alike.

I still think that this was a rather neat idea. But as an experiment, it was messy. All results were uncertain; a repetition of the experiment by someone else, or by myself seven years later, would probably[5] give quite different results. Scientifically, this is most disreputable. That's all right; I am not a scientist. I play the game where the rules keep changing.

---

5 Strike the word "probably" and replace it with "certainly."

Among these dubious and uncertain results, achieved as I thought, and wrote, and wrote, and thought, about my imaginary people, three appear rather interesting to me.

First: the absence of war. In the thirteen thousand years of recorded history on Gethen, there has not been a war. The people seem to be as quarrelsome, competitive and aggressive as we are; they have fights, murders, assassinations, feuds, forays and so on. But there have been no great invasions by peoples on the move, like the Mongols in Asia or the Whites in the New World: partly because Gethenian populations seem to remain stable in size, they do not move in large masses, or rapidly. Their migrations have been slow, no one generation going very far. They have no nomadic peoples, and no societies that live by expansion and aggression against other societies. Nor have they formed large, hierarchically governed nation-states, the mobilizable entity that is the essential factor in modern war. The basic unit all over the planet is a group of two hundred to eight hundred people, called a hearth, a structure founded less on economic convenience than on sexual necessity (there must be others in kemmer at the same time), and therefore more tribal than urban in nature, though overlaid and interwoven with a later urban pattern. The hearth tends to be communal, independent, and somewhat introverted. Rivalries between hearths, as between individuals, are channeled into a socially approved form of aggression called *shif-grethor*, a conflict without physical violence, involving one-upmanship, the saving and losing of face – conflict ritualized, stylized, controlled. When shifgrethor breaks down there may be physical violence, but it does not become mass violence, remaining limited, personal. The active group remains small. The dispersive trend is as strong as the cohesive. Historically, when hearths gathered into a nation for economic reasons, the cellular pattern still dominated the centralized one. There might be a king and a parliament, but authority was not enforced so much by might as by the use of shifgrethor and intrigue, and was accepted as custom, without appeal to patriarchal ideals of divine right, patriotic duty, etc. Ritual and parade were far more effective agents of order than armies or police. Class structure was flexible and open; the value of the social hierarchy was less economic than aesthetic, and there was no great gap between rich and poor. There was no slavery or servitude. Nobody owned anybody. There were no chattels. Economic organization was rather communistic or syndicalistic than capitalistic, and was seldom highly centralized.

During the time span of the novel, however, all this is changing. One of the two large nations of the planet is becoming a genuine nation-state, complete with patriotism and bureaucracy. It has achieved state capitalism and the centralization of power, authoritarian government, and a secret police; and it is on the verge of achieving the world's first war.

Why did I present the first picture, and show it in the process of changing to a different one? I am not sure. I think it is because I was trying to show a balance – and the delicacy of a balance. To me the "female principle" is, or at least historically has been, basically anarchic. It values order without constraint, rule by custom not by force. It has been the male who enforces order, who constructs power structures, who makes, enforces and breaks laws. On Gethen, these two principles are in balance: the decentralizing against the centralizing, the flexible against the rigid, the circular against the linear. But balance is a precarious state, and at the moment of the novel the balance, which had leaned toward the "feminine," is tipping the other way.[6]

Second: the absence of exploitation. The Gethenians do not rape their world. They have developed a high technology, heavy industry, automobiles, radios, explosives, etc., but they have done so very slowly, absorbing their technology rather than letting it overwhelm them. They have no myth of Progress at all. Their calendar calls the current year always the Year One, and they count backward and forward from that.

In this, it seems that what I was after again was a balance: the driving linearity of the "male," the pushing forward to the limit, the logicality that admits no boundary – and the circularity of the "female," the valuing of patience, ripeness, practicality, livableness. A model for this balance, of course, exists on Earth: Chinese civilization over the past six millennia. (I

---

6 At the very inception of the whole book, I was interested in writing a novel about people in a society that had never had a war. That came first. The androgyny came second. (Cause and effect? Effect and cause?)

I would now write this paragraph this way: . . . The "female principle" has historically been anarchic; that is, anarchy has historically been identified as female. The domain allotted to women – "the family," for example – is the area of order without coercion, rule by custom not by force. Men have reserved the structures of social power to themselves (and those few women whom they admit to it on male terms, such as queens, prime ministers); men make the wars and peaces, men make, enforce and break the laws. On Gethen, the two polarities we perceive through our cultural conditioning as male and female are neither, and are in balance: consensus with authority, decentralizing with centralizing, flexible with rigid, circular with linear, hierarchy with network. But it is not a motionless balance, there being no such thing in life, and at the moment of the novel, it is wobbling perilously.

did not know when I wrote the book that the parallel extends even to the calendar; the Chinese historically never had a linear dating system such as the one that starts with the birth of Christ.)[7]

Third: the absence of sexuality as a continuous social factor. For four-fifths of the month, a Gethenian's sexuality plays no part of all in his social life (unless he's pregnant); for the other one-fifth, it dominates him absolutely. In kemmer, one must have a partner, it is imperative. (Have you ever lived in a small apartment with a tabby-cat in heat?) Gethenian society fully accepts this imperative. When a Gethenian has to make love, he does make love, and everybody expects him to, and approves of it.[8]

But still, human beings are human beings, not cats. Despite our continuous sexuality and our intense self-domestication|(domesticated animals tend to be promiscuous, wild animals pair-bonding, familial, or tribal in their mating), we are very seldom truly promiscuous. We do have rape, to be sure – no other animal has equaled us there. We have mass rape, when an army (male, of course) invades; we have prostitution, promiscuity controlled by economics; and sometimes ritual abreactive promiscuity controlled by religion; but in general we seem to avoid genuine license. At most we award it as a prize to the Alpha Male, in certain situations; it is scarcely ever permitted to the female without social penalty. It would seem, perhaps, that the mature human being, male or female, is not satisfied by sexual gratification without psychic involvement, and in fact may be *afraid of it*, to judge by the tremendous variety of social, legal and religious controls and sanctions exerted over it in all human societies. Sex is a great mana, and therefore the immature society, or psyche, sets great taboos about it. The mature culture, or psyche, can integrate these taboos or laws into an internal ethical code, which, while allowing great freedom, does

---

7 A better model might be some of the pre-Conquest cultures of the Americas, though not those hierarchical and imperialistic ones approvingly termed, by our hierarchical and imperialistic standards, "high." The trouble with the Chinese model is that their civilization instituted and practiced male domination as thoroughly as the other "high" civilizations. I was thinking of a Taoist ideal, not of such practices as bride-selling and foot-binding, which we are trained to consider unimportant, nor of the deep misogyny of Chinese culture, which we are trained to consider normal.

8 I would now write this paragraph this way: ... For four-fifths of the month, sexuality plays no part at all in a Gethenian's social behavior; for the other one-fifth, it controls behavior absolutely. In kemmer, one must have a partner, it is imperative. (Have you ever lived in a small apartment with a tabby-cat in heat?) Gethenian society fully accepts this imperative. When Gethenians have to make love, they do make love, and everybody else expects it and approves of it.

not permit the treatment of another person as an object. But, however irrational or rational, there is always a code.

Because the Gethenians cannot have sexual intercourse unless both partners are willing, because they cannot rape or be raped, I figured that they would have less fear and guilt about sex than we tend to have; but still it is a problem for them, in some ways more than for us, because of the extreme, explosive, imperative quality of the oestrous phase. Their society would have to control it, though it might move more easily than we from the taboo stage to the ethical stage. So the basic arrangement, I found, in every Gethenian community, is that of the kemmerhouse, which is open to anyone, in kemmer, native or stranger, so that he can find a partner.[9] Then there are various customary (not legal) institutions, such as the kemmering group, a group who choose to come together during kemmer as a regular thing; this is like the primate tribe, or group marriage. Or there is the possibility of vowing kemmering, which is marriage, pair-bonding for life, a personal commitment without legal sanction. Such commitments have intense moral and psychic significance, but they are not controlled by Church or State. Finally, there are two forbidden acts, which might be taboo or illegal or simply considered contemptible, depending on which of the regions of Gethen you are in: first, you don't pair off with a relative of a different generation (one who might be your own parent or child); second, you may mate, but not vow kemmering, with your own sibling. These are the old incest prohibitions. They are so general among us – and with good cause, I think, not so much genetic as psychological – that they seemed likely to be equally valid on Gethen.

These three "results," then, of my experiment, I feel were fairly clearly and successfully worked out, though there is nothing definitive about them.

In other areas where I might have pressed for at least such plausible results, I see now a failure to think things through, or to express them clearly. For example, I think I took the easy way in using such familiar governmental structures as a feudal monarchy and a modern-style bureaucracy for the two Gethenian countries that are the scene of the novel. I doubt that Gethenian governments, rising out of the cellular hearth, would resemble any of our own so closely. They might be better, they might be worse, but they would certainly be different.

---

9 Read: . . . so that they can find sexual partners.

I regret even more certain timidities or ineptnesses I showed in following up the psychic implications of Gethenian physiology. Just for example, I wish I had known Jung's work when I wrote the book: so that I could have decided whether a Gethenian had *no* animus or anima, or *both*, or an animum.[10] ... But the central failure in this area comes up in the frequent criticism I receive, that the Gethenians seem like *men*, instead of menwomen.

This rises in part from the choice of pronoun. I call Gethenians "he" because I utterly refuse to mangle English by inventing a pronoun for "he/she."[11]

"He" is the generic pronoun, damn it, in English. (I envy the Japanese, who, I am told, do have a he/she pronoun.) But I do not consider this really very important.[12]

The pronouns wouldn't matter at all if I had been cleverer at *showing* the "female" component of the Gethenian characters in *action*.[13]

Unfortunately, the plot and structure that arose as I worked the book out cast the Gethenian protagonist, Estraven, almost exclusively into roles that we are culturally conditioned to perceive as "male" – a prime minister (it takes more than even Golda Meir and Indira Gandhi to break a

---

10 For another example (and Jung wouldn't have helped with this, more likely hindered) I quite unnecessarily locked the Gethenians into heterosexuality. It is a naively pragmatic view of sex that insists that sexual partners must be of opposite sex! In any kemmerhouse homosexual practice would, of course, be possible and acceptable and welcomed – but I never thought to explore this option; and the omission, alas, implies that sexuality is heterosexuality. I regret this very much.

11 This "utter refusal" of 1968 restated in 1976 collapsed, utterly, within a couple of years more. I still dislike invented pronouns, but now dislike them less than the so-called generic pronoun he/him/his, which does in fact exclude women from discourse; and which was an invention of male grammarians, for until the sixteenth century the English generic singular pronoun was they/them/their, as it still is in English and American colloquial speech. It should be restored to the written language, and let the pedants and pundits squeak and gibber in the streets.

In a screenplay of The Left Hand of Darkness written in 1985, I referred to Gethenians not pregnant or in kemmer by the invented pronouns a/un/a's, modeled on a British dialect. These would drive the reader mad in print, I suppose; but I have read parts of the book aloud using them, and the audience was perfectly happy, except that they pointed out that the subject pronoun, "a" pronounced "uh" [a], sounds too much like "I" said with a Southern accent.

12 I now consider it very important.

13 If I had realized how the pronouns I used shaped, directed, controlled my own thinking, I might have been "cleverer."

stereotype), a political schemer, a fugitive, a prison-breaker, a sledge-hauler
... I think I did this because I was privately delighted at watching, not a
man, but a manwoman, do all these things, and do them with considerable
skill and flair. But, for the reader, I left out too much. One does not see
Estraven as a mother, with his children,[14] in any role that we automatically
perceive as "female": and therefore, we tend to see him as a man.[15] This
is a real flaw in the book, and I can only be very grateful to those readers,
men and women, whose willingness to participate in the experiment led
them to fill in that omission with the work of their own imagination, and
to see Estraven as I saw him,[16] as man and woman, familiar and different,
alien and utterly human.

It seems to be men, more often than women, who thus complete
my work for me: I think because men are often more willing to identify as they read with poor, confused, defensive Genly, the Earthman,
and therefore to participate in his painful and gradual discovery
of love.[17]

Finally, the question arises, Is the book a Utopia? It seems to me that
it is quite clearly not; it poses no *practicable* alternative to contemporary
society, since it is based on an imaginary, radical change in human anatomy.
All it tries to do is open up an alternative viewpoint, to widen the imagination, without making any very definite suggestions as to what might be
seen from that new viewpoint. The most it says is, I think, something like
this: If we were socially ambisexual, if men and women were completely
and genuinely equal in their social roles, equal legally and economically,
equal in freedom, in responsibility, and in self-esteem, then society would
be a very different thing. What our problems might be, God knows; I only
know we would have them. But it seems likely that our central problem
would not be the one it is now: the problem of exploitation – exploitation of the woman, of the weak, of the earth. Our curse is alienation,
the separation of yang from yin.[18] Instead of a search for balance and

---

14 Strike "his."

15 Place "him" in quotation marks, please.

16 Read: ... as I did.

17 I now see it thus: Men were inclined to be satisfied with the book, which allowed them a safe
trip into androgyny and back, from a conventionally male viewpoint. But many women wanted
it to go further, to dare more, to explore androgyny from a woman's point of view as well as a
man's. In fact, it does so, in that it was written by a woman. But this is admitted directly only in
the chapter "The Question of Sex," the only voice of a woman in the book. I think women were
justified in asking more courage of me and a more rigorous thinking-through of implications.

18 – and the moralization of yang as good, of yin as bad.

integration, there is a struggle for dominance. Divisions are insisted upon, interdependence is denied. The dualism of value that destroys us, the dualism of superior/inferior, ruler/ruled, owner/owned, user/used, might give way to what seems to me, from here, a much healthier, sounder, more promising modality of integration and integrity.

Introduction to
The Left Hand of Darkness

✦

1976

Science fiction is often described, and even defined, as extrapolative. The science fiction writer is supposed to take a trend or phenomenon of the here and now, purify and intensify it for dramatic effect, and extend it into the future. "If this goes on, this is what will happen." A prediction is made. Method and results much resemble those of a scientist who feeds large doses of a purified and concentrated food additive to mice, in order to predict what may happen to people who eat it in small quantities for a long time. The outcome seems almost inevitably to be cancer. So does the outcome of extrapolation. Strictly extrapolative works of science fiction generally arrive about where the Club of Rome arrives: somewhere between the gradual extinction of human liberty and the total extinction of terrestrial life.

This may explain why many people who do not read science fiction describe it as "escapist," but when questioned further, admit they do not read it because "it's so depressing."

Almost anything carried to its logical extreme becomes depressing, if not carcinogenic.

Fortunately, though extrapolation is an element in science fiction, it isn't the name of the game by any means. It is far too rationalist and simplistic to satisfy the imaginative mind, whether the writer's or the reader's. Variables are the spice of life.

This book is not extrapolative. If you like you can read it, and a lot of other science fiction, as a thought-experiment. Let's say (says Mary Shelley) that a young doctor creates a human being in his laboratory; let's say (says Philip K. Dick) that the Allies lost the Second World War; let's say this or that is such and so, and see what happens . . . In a story so conceived, the moral complexity proper to the modern novel need not be sacrificed, nor is there any built-in dead end; thought and intuition can move freely within bounds set only by the terms of the experiment, which may be very large indeed.

The purpose of a thought-experiment, as the term was used by Schrödinger and other physicists, is not to predict the future – indeed Schrödinger's most famous thought-experiment goes to show that the "future," on the quantum level, *cannot* be predicted – but to describe reality, the present world.

Science fiction is not predictive; it is descriptive.

Predictions are uttered by prophets (free of charge); by clairvoyants (who usually charge a fee, and are therefore more honored in their day than prophets); and by futurologists (salaried). Prediction is the business of prophets, clairvoyants and futurologists. It is not the business of novelists. A novelist's business is lying.

The weather bureau will tell you what next Tuesday will be like, and the Rand Corporation will tell you what the twenty-first century will be like. I don't recommend that you turn to the writers of fiction for such information. It's none of their business. All they're trying to do is tell you what they're like, and what you're like – what's going on – what the weather is now, today, this moment, the rain, the sunlight, look! Open your eyes; listen, listen. That is what the novelists say. But they don't tell you what you will see and hear. All they can tell you is what they have seen and heard, in their time in this world, a third of it spent in sleep and dreaming, another third of it spent in telling lies.

"The truth against the world!" – Yes. Certainly. Fiction writers, at least in their braver moments, do desire the truth; to know it, speak it, serve it. But they go about it in a peculiar and devious way, which consists in inventing persons, places and events which never did and never will exist or occur, and telling about these fictions in detail and at length and with a great deal of emotion, and then when they are done writing down this pack of lies, they say, There! That's the truth!

They may use all kinds of facts to support their tissue of lies. They may describe the Marshalsea Prison, which was a real place, or the battle of Borodino, which really was fought, or the process of cloning, which really takes place in laboratories, or the deterioration of a personality, which is described in real textbooks of psychology; and so on. This weight of verifiable place-event-phenomenon-behavior makes readers forget that they are reading a pure invention, a history that never took place anywhere but in that unrealizable region, the author's mind. In fact, while we read a novel, we are insane – bonkers. We believe in the existence of people who aren't there, we hear their voices, we watch the battle of Borodino

47

with them, we may even become Napoleon. Sanity returns (in most cases) when the book is closed.

Is it any wonder that no truly respectable society has ever trusted its artists?

But our society, being troubled and bewildered, seeking guidance, sometimes puts an entirely mistaken trust in its artists, using them as prophets and futurologists.

I do not say that artists cannot be seers, inspired: that the *awen* cannot come upon them, and the god speak through them. Who would be an artist if they did not believe that that happens? If they did not *know* it happens, because they have felt the god within them use their tongue, their hands? Maybe only once, once in their lives. But once is enough.

Nor would I say that the artist alone is so burdened and so privileged. The scientist is another who prepares, who makes ready, working day and night, sleeping and awake, for inspiration. As Pythagoras knew, the god may speak in the forms of geometry as well as in the shapes of dreams; in the harmony of pure thought as well as in the harmony of sounds; in numbers as well as in words.

But it is words that make the trouble and confusion. We are asked now to consider words as useful in only one way: as signs. Our philosophers, some of them, would have us agree that a word (sentence, statement) has value only in so far as it has one single meaning, points to one fact which is comprehensible to the rational intellect, logically sound, and – ideally – quantifiable.

Apollo, the god of light, of reason, of proportion, harmony, number – Apollo blinds those who press too close in worship. Don't look straight at the sun. Go into a dark bar for a bit and have a beer with Dionysus, every now and then.

I talk about the gods, I an atheist. But I am an artist too, and therefore a liar. Distrust everything I say. I am telling the truth.

The only truth I can understand or express is, logically defined, a lie. Psychologically defined, a symbol. Aesthetically defined, a metaphor.

Oh, it's lovely to be invited to participate in Futurological Congresses where Systems Science displays its grand apocalyptic graphs, to be asked to tell the newspapers what America will be like in 2001, and all that, but it's a terrible mistake. I write science fiction, and science fiction isn't about the future. I don't know any more about the future than you do, and very likely less.

This book is not about the future. Yes, it begins by announcing that it's set in the "Ekumenical Year 1490–97," but surely you don't *believe* that?

Yes, indeed the people in it are androgynous, but that doesn't mean that I'm predicting that in a millennium or so we will all be androgynous, or announcing that I think we damned well ought to be androgynous. I'm merely observing, in the peculiar, devious and thought-experimental manner proper to science fiction, that if you look at us at certain odd times of day in certain weathers, we already are. I am not predicting, or prescribing. I am describing. I am describing certain aspects of psychological reality in the novelist's way, which is by inventing elaborately circumstantial lies.

In reading a novel, any novel, we have to know perfectly well that the whole thing is nonsense, and then, while reading, believe every word of it. Finally, when we're done with it, we may find – if it's a good novel – that we're a bit different from what we were before we read it, that we have been changed a little, as if by having met a new face, crossed a street we never crossed before. But it's very hard to *say* just what we learned, how we were changed.

The artist deals with what cannot be said in words.

The artist whose medium is fiction does this *in words*. The novelist says in words what cannot be said in words.

Words can be used thus paradoxically because they have, along with a semiotic usage, a symbolic or metaphoric usage. (They also have a sound – a fact the linguistic positivists take no interest in. A sentence or paragraph is like a chord or harmonic sequence in music: its meaning may be more clearly understood by the attentive ear, even though it is read in silence, than by the attentive intellect.)

All fiction is metaphor. Science fiction is metaphor. What sets it apart from older forms of fiction seems to be its use of new metaphors, drawn from certain great dominants of our contemporary life – science, all the sciences, and technology, and the relativistic and the historical outlook, among them. Space travel is one of these metaphors; so is an alternative society, an alternative biology; the future is another. The future, in fiction, is a metaphor.

A metaphor for what?

If I could have said it nonmetaphorically, I would not have written all these words, this novel; and Genly Ai would never have sat down at my desk and used up my ink and typewriter ribbon in informing me, and you, rather solemnly, that the truth is a matter of the imagination.

The Space Crone

·

1976

The menopause is probably the least glamorous topic imaginable; and this is interesting, because it is one of the very few topics to which cling some shreds and remnants of taboo. A serious mention of menopause is usually met with uneasy silence; a sneering reference to it is usually met with relieved sniggers. Both the silence and the sniggering are pretty sure indications of taboo.

Most people would consider the old phrase "change of life" a euphemism for the medical term "menopause," but I, who am now going through the change, begin to wonder if it isn't the other way round. "Change of life" is too blunt a phrase, too factual. "Menopause," with its chime-suggestion of a mere pause after which things go on as before, is reassuringly trivial.

But the change is not trivial, and I wonder how many women are brave enough to carry it out wholeheartedly. They give up their reproductive capacity with more or less of a struggle, and when it's gone they think that's all there is to it. Well, at least I don't get the Curse any more, they say, and the only reason I felt so depressed sometimes was hormones. Now I'm myself again. But this is to evade the real challenge, and to lose, not only the capacity to ovulate, but the opportunity to become a Crone.

In the old days women who survived long enough to attain the menopause more often accepted the challenge. They had, after all, had practice. They had already changed their life radically once before, when they ceased to be virgins and became mature women/wives/matrons/mothers/mistresses/whores/etc. This change involved not only the physiological alterations of puberty – the shift from barren childhood to fruitful maturity – but a socially recognized alteration of being: a change of condition from the sacred to the profane.

With the secularization of virginity now complete, so that the once awesome term "virgin" is now a sneer or at best a slightly dated word for a person who hasn't copulated yet, the opportunity of gaining or regaining the dangerous/sacred condition of being at the Second Change has ceased to be apparent.

Virginity is now a mere preamble or waiting room to be got out of as soon as possible; it is without significance. Old age is similarly a waiting room, where you go after life's over and wait for cancer or a stroke. The years before and after the menstrual years are vestigial: the only meaningful condition left to women is that of fruitfulness. Curiously, this restriction of significance coincided with the development of chemicals and instruments that make fertility itself a meaningless or at least secondary characteristic of female maturity. The significance of maturity now is not the capacity to conceive but the mere ability to have sex. As this ability is shared by pubescents and by postclimacterics, the blurring of distinctions and elimination of opportunities is almost complete. There are no rites of passage because there is no significant change. The Triple Goddess has only one face: Marilyn Monroe's, maybe. The entire life of a woman from ten or twelve through seventy or eighty has become secular, uniform, changeless. As there is no longer any virtue in virginity, so there is no longer any meaning in menopause. It requires fanatical determination now to become a Crone.

Women have thus, by imitating the life condition of men, surrendered a very strong position of their own. Men are afraid of virgins, but they have a cure for their own fear and the virgin's virginity: fucking. Men are afraid of crones, so afraid of them that their cure for virginity fails them; they know it won't work. Faced with the fulfilled Crone, all but the bravest men wilt and retreat, crestfallen and cockadroop.

Menopause Manor is not merely a defensive stronghold, however. It is a house or household, fully furnished with the necessities of life. In abandoning it, women have narrowed their domain and impoverished their souls. There are things the Old Woman can do, say, and think that the Woman cannot do, say, or think. The Woman has to give up more than her menstrual periods before she can do, say, or think them. She has got to change her life.

The nature of that change is now clearer than it used to be. Old age is not virginity but a third and new condition; the virgin must be celibate, but the crone need not. There was a confusion there, which the separation of female sexuality from reproductive capacity, via modern contraceptives, has cleared up. Loss of fertility does not mean loss of desire and fulfillment.

But it does entail a change, a change involving matters even more important – if I may venture a heresy – than sex.

The woman who is willing to make that change must become pregnant with herself, at last. She must bear herself, her third self, her old age, with travail and alone. Not many will help her with that birth. Certainly no male obstetrician will time her contractions, inject her with sedatives, stand ready with forceps, and neatly stitch up the torn membranes. It's hard even to find an old-fashioned midwife, these days. That pregnancy is long, that labor is hard. Only one is harder, and that's the final one, the one that men also must suffer and perform.

It may well be easier to die if you have already given birth to others or yourself, at least once before. This would be an argument for going through all the discomfort and embarrassment of becoming a Crone. Anyhow it seems a pity to have a built-in rite of passage and to dodge it, evade it, and pretend nothing has changed. That is to dodge and evade one's womanhood, to pretend one's like a man. Men, once initiated, never get the second chance. They never change again. That's their loss, not ours. Why borrow poverty?

Certainly the effort to remain unchanged, young, when the body gives so impressive a signal of change as the menopause, is gallant; but it is a stupid, self-sacrificial gallantry, better befitting a boy of twenty than a woman of forty-five or fifty. Let the athletes die young and laurel-crowned. Let the soldiers earn the Purple Hearts. Let women die old, white-crowned, with human hearts.

If a space ship came by from the friendly natives of the fourth planet of Altair, and the polite captain of the space ship said, "We have room for one passenger; will you spare us a single human being, so that we may converse at leisure during the long trip back to Altair and learn from an exemplary person the nature of the race?" – I suppose what most people would want to do is provide them with a fine, bright, brave young man, highly educated and in peak physical condition. A Russian cosmonaut would be ideal (American astronauts are mostly too old). There would surely be hundreds, thousands of volunteers, just such young men, all worthy. But I would not pick any of them. Nor would I pick any of the young women who would volunteer, some out of magnanimity and intellectual courage, others out of a profound conviction that Altair couldn't possibly be any worse for a woman than Earth is.

What I would do is go down to the local Woolworth's, or the local village marketplace, and pick an old woman, over sixty, from behind the costume jewelry counter or the betel-nut booth. Her hair would not be red or blonde or lustrous dark, her skin would not be dewy fresh, she would not have the secret of eternal youth. She might, however, show you a small snapshot of her grandson, who is working in Nairobi. She is a bit vague about where Nairobi is, but extremely proud of the grandson. She has worked hard at small, unimportant jobs all her life, jobs like cooking, cleaning, bringing up kids, selling little objects of adornment or pleasure to other people. She was a virgin once, a long time ago, and then a sexually potent fertile female, and then went through menopause. She has given birth several times and faced death several times – the same times. She is facing the final birth/death a little more nearly and clearly every day now. Sometimes her feet hurt something terrible. She never was educated to anything like her capacity, and that is a shameful waste and a crime against humanity, but so common a crime should not and cannot be hidden from Altair. And anyhow she's not dumb. She has a stock of sense, wit, patience, and experiential shrewdness, which the Altaireans might, or might not, perceive as wisdom. If they are wiser than we, then of course we don't know how they'd perceive it. But if they are wiser than we, they may know how to perceive that inmost mind and heart which we, working on mere guess and hope, proclaim to be humane. In any case, since they are curious and kindly, let's give them the best we have to give.

The trouble is, she will be very reluctant to volunteer. "What would an old woman like me do on Altair?" she'll say. "You ought to send one of those scientist men, they can talk to those funny-looking green people. Maybe Dr. Kissinger should go. What about sending the Shaman?" It will be very hard to explain to her that we want her to go because only a person who has experienced, accepted, and acted the entire human condition – the essential quality of which is Change – can fairly represent humanity. "Me?" she'll say, just a trifle slyly. "But I never did anything."

But it won't wash. She knows, though she won't admit it, that Dr. Kissinger has not gone and will never go where she has gone, that the scientists and the shamans have not done what she has done. Into the space ship, Granny.

Introduction to
The Word for World is Forest

●

1977

On What the Road to Hell Is Paved With

There is nothing in all Freud's writing that I like better than his assertion that artists' work is motivated by the desire "to achieve honor, power, riches, fame, and the love of women." It is such a comforting, such a complete statement; it explains everything about the artist. There have even been artists who agreed with it; Ernest Hemingway, for instance; at least, he said he wrote for money, and since he was an honored, powerful, rich, famous artist beloved by women, he ought to know.

There is another statement about the artist's desire that is, to me, less obscure; the first two stanzas of it read,

Riches I hold in light esteem
And Love I laugh to scorn
And lust of Fame was but a dream
That vanished with the morn –
And if I pray, the only prayer
That moves my lips for me
Is – "Leave the heart that now I bear
And give me liberty."

Emily Brontë wrote those lines when she was twenty-two. She was a young and inexperienced woman, not honored, not rich, not powerful, not famous, and you see that she was positively rude about love ("of women" or otherwise). I believe, however, that she was rather better qualified than Freud to talk about what motivates the artist. He had a theory. But she had authority.

It may well be useless, if not pernicious, to seek a single motive for a pursuit so complex, long-pursued, and various as art; I imagine that Brontë

54

got as close to it as anyone needs to get, with her word "liberty."

The pursuit of art, then, by artist or audience, is the pursuit of liberty. If you accept that, you see at once why truly serious people reject and mistrust the arts, labeling them as "escapism." The captured soldier tunneling out of prison, the runaway slave, and Solzhenitsyn in exile are escapists. Aren't they? The definition also helps explain why all healthy children can sing, dance, paint and play with words; why art is an increasingly important element in psychotherapy; why Winston Churchill painted, why mothers sing cradle songs, and what is wrong with Plato's *Republic*. It really is a much more useful statement than Freud's, though nowhere near as funny.

I am not sure what Freud meant by "power," in this context. Perhaps significantly, Brontë does not mention power. Shelley does, indirectly: "Poets are the unacknowledged legislators of the world." This is perhaps not too far from what Freud had in mind, for I doubt he was thinking of artists' immediate and joyous power over their material – the shaping hand, the dancer's leap, the novelist's power of life and death over characters; it is more probable that he meant the power of the idea to influence other people.

The desire for power, in the sense of power over others, is what pulls most people off the path of the pursuit of liberty. The reason Brontë does not mention it is probably that it was never even a temptation to her, as it was to her sister Charlotte. Emily did not give a damn about other people's morals. But many artists, particularly artists of the word, whose ideas must actually be spoken in their work, succumb to the temptation. They begin to see that they can do good to other people. They forget about liberty, then, and instead of legislating in divine arrogance, like God or Shelley, they begin to preach.

In this tale, *The Word for World is Forest*, which began as a pure pursuit of freedom and the dream, I succumbed, in part, to the lure of the pulpit. It is a very strong lure to a science fiction writer, who deals more directly than most novelists with ideas, whose metaphors are shaped by or embody ideas, and who therefore is always in danger of inextricably confusing ideas with opinions.

I wrote *The Little Green Men* (its first editor, Harlan Ellison, retitled it, with my rather morose permission) in the winter of 1968, during a year's stay in London. All through the sixties, in my home city in the States, I had been helping organize and participating in nonviolent demonstrations, first against atomic bomb testing, then against the pursuance of the war in Vietnam. I don't know how many times I walked down Alder Street in the rain, feeling useless, foolish and obstinate, along with ten or twenty or a hundred other foolish and obstinate souls. There was always somebody taking pictures of us – not the press – odd-looking people with cheap cameras: John Birchers? FBI? CIA? Crackpots? No telling. I used to grin at them, or stick out my tongue. One of my fiercer friends brought a camera once and took pictures of the picture-takers. Anyhow, there was a peace movement, and I was in it, and so had a channel of action and expression for my ethical and political opinions totally separate from my writing.

In England that year, a guest and a foreigner, I had no such outlet. And 1968 was a bitter year for those who opposed the war. The lies and hypocrisies redoubled; so did the killing. Moreover, it was becoming clear that the ethic which approved the defoliation of forests and grainlands and the murder of non-combatants in the name of "peace" was only a corollary of the ethic which permits the despoliation of natural resources for private profit or the GNP, and the murder of the creatures of the Earth in the name of "man." The victory of the ethic of exploitation, in all societies, seemed as inevitable as it was disastrous.

It was from such pressures, internalized, that this story resulted: forced out, in a sense, against my conscious resistance. I have said elsewhere that I never wrote a story more easily, fluently, surely – and with less pleasure.

I knew, because of the compulsive quality of the composition, that it was likely to become a preachment, and I struggled against this. Say not the struggle naught availeth. Neither Lyubov nor Selver is mere Virtue Triumphant; moral and psychological complexity was salvaged, at least, in those characters. But Davidson is, though not uncomplex, pure; he is purely evil – and I don't, consciously, believe purely evil people exist. But my unconscious has other opinions. It looked into itself and produced, from itself, Captain Davidson. I do not disclaim him.

American involvement in Vietnam is now past; the immediately intolerable pressures have shifted to other areas; and so the moralizing aspects of the story are now plainly visible. These I regret, but I do not disclaim them either. The work must stand or fall on whatever elements it preserved of the yearning that underlies all specific outrage and protest, whatever tentative outreaching it made, amidst anger and despair, toward justice, or wit, or grace, or liberty.

Synchronicity Can Happen at Almost Any Time

A few years ago, a few years after the first publication in America of *The Word for World is Forest*, I had the great pleasure of meeting Dr. Charles Tart, a psychologist well known for his researches into and his book on *Altered States of Consciousness*. He asked me if I had modeled the Athsheans of the story upon the Senoi people of Malaysia. The who? said I, so he told me about them. The Senoi, are, or were, a people whose culture includes and is indeed substantially based upon a deliberate training in and use of the dream. Dr. Tart's book includes a brief article on them by Kilton Stewart.[1]

Breakfast in the Senoi is like a dream clinic, with the father and older brothers listening to and analyzing the dreams of all the children . . .

When the Senoi child reports a falling dream, the adult answers with enthusiasm, "That is a wonderful dream, one of the best dreams a man can have. Where did you fall to, and what did you discover?"

The Senoi dream is meaningful, active and creative. Adults deliberately go into their dreams to solve problems of interpersonal and intercultural conflict. They come out of their dreams with a new song, tool, dance, idea. The waking and the dreaming states are equally valid, each acting upon the other in complementary fashion.

The article implies, by omission rather than by direct statement, that the men are the "great dreamers" among the Senoi; whether this means that the women are socially inferior or that their role (as among the Athsheans) is equal and compensatory is not clear. Nor is there any mention of the Senoi conception of divinity, the numinous, etc.; it is merely stated that they do not practice magic, though they are perfectly willing to let neighboring peoples think they do, as this discourages invasion.

They have built a system of inter-personal relations which, in the field of psychology, is perhaps on a level with our attainments in such areas as television and nuclear physics.

---

[1] "Dream Theory in Malaya," by Kilton Stewart, in *Altered States of Consciousness*, ed. Charles T. Tart (Wiley & Sons, 1969; Anchor-Doubleday, 1972). The quotations are on pp. 164 and 163 of the Anchor second edition.

It appears that the Senoi have not had a war, or a murder, for several hundred years.

There they are, twelve thousand of them, farming, hunting, fishing, and dreaming, in the rain forests of the mountains of Malaysia. Or there they were, in 1935 – perhaps. Kilton Stewart's report on them has had no professional sequels that I know of.* Were they ever there, and if so, are they still there? In the waking time, I mean, in what we so fantastically call "the real world." In the dream time, of course, they are there, and here. I thought I was inventing my own lot of imaginary aliens, and I was only describing the Senoi. It is not only the Captain Davidsons who can be found in the unconscious, if one looks. The quiet people who do not kill each other are there, too. It seems that a great deal is there, the things we most fear (and therefore deny), the things we most need (and therefore deny). I wonder, couldn't we start listening to our dreams, and our children's dreams?

"Where did you fall to, and what did you discover?"

---

* Note (1989). It has since been pretty conclusively shown that his work was closer to fiction than to field work – if not totally invented, almost unsubstantiated.

Close Encounters, Star Wars, and the Tertium Quid

1978

A dark screen. The title, *Close Encounters of the Third Kind*, appears in silence. The sound begins very, very softly; rises slowly; explodes into a roaring fortissimo – and stays there during the rest of the movie.

The light is often at top brightness too, but it is almost impossible to make the light from a projector painful; and anyhow, we have eyelids. But no earlids. The light is used with variety and a great deal of beauty. The sound is used with brutality.

Very seldom can one understand a complete sentence. Words are mumbled and slurred off, Method-style, shouted or screamed into dust storms, wind storms, helicopter backwash, yelled simultaneously in French and English, redoubled and self-effaced by loudspeaker echo. A few lines come through clear, and they are effective:

"*I* didn't *want* to see it."

"Yes, I saw you going up in the air, did you see me running after you?"

And my favorite, whispered: "*Mince alors* . . ."

Just enough comes through to convince the middle-aged moviegoer in the fourth row extreme left (does Pauline Kael ever have to sit in the fourth row extreme left?) that she isn't going deaf and that the unintelligibility is deliberate. Perhaps it is used to disguise the banality of most of the dialogue. Certainly there were moments in *Star Wars* when one prayed in vain for unintelligibility . . . Possibly the high proportion of noise to meaning *has* a meaning. But I am afraid that it serves merely to augment the hysterical tension established in the opening scene and never relaxed thereafter.

Why, after all, does there have to be a dust storm in the Sonora Desert just then? Why does everyone rush about screaming in three languages? The discovery of mysteriously just-abandoned World War II planes might very well take place quietly, eerily; and deserts aren't noisy, crowded places, as a rule. But no. The wind and all the performers have to howl in unison.

When humans and aliens finally communicate, it is by musical tones. In that one scene the noise gimmickry all comes together; it is at last a genuine climax. If it rose to true music, it would be a great moment.

But even then it would not justify the rest of the soundtrack, which uses noise to whip up emotion, the same trick that's so easy to do with electronically amplified instruments: decibellicosity. Exposed to aggression by loud noise, the body must continually resist its own fight/flight reaction, thus building up an adrenaline high, thus feeling surges of unfocused emotion, increased pulse rate, etc. – thrills and chills. No harm. Same kick as a rollercoaster. But a rollercoaster doesn't pretend to have a message.

On the other hand . . . *Star Wars*, which rather ostentatiously pretends not to have any message, may be even tricksier.

The end of *Star Wars* kept bothering me after I saw it the first time. I kept thinking, such a funny silly beautiful movie, why did George Lucas stick on that wooden ending, a high-school graduation, with prizes for good citizenship? But when I saw it again I realized it wasn't high school but West Point: a place crawling with boots and salutes. Aren't there any civilians in this Empire, anyhow? Finally a friend who knows films explained to me that the scene is a nostalgic evocation or imitation of Leni Riefenstahl's famous film of the 1936 Olympics, with the German winners receiving a grateful ovation from the Thousand-Year Reich. Having dragged Dorothy and Toto and that lot around the cosmos a bit, Lucas cast about for another surefire golden oldie and came up with Adolf Hitler.

Anyhow, what the hell is nostalgia doing in a science-fiction film? With the whole universe and all the future to play in, Lucas took his marvelous toys and crawled under the fringed cloth on the parlor table, back into a nice safe hideyhole, along with Flash Gordon and the Cowardly Lion and Huck Skywalker and the Flying Aces and the Hitler Jugend. If there's a message there, I don't think I want to hear it.

There are gorgeous moments in *Star Wars*, especially on the desert planet (before everybody gets into uniform): the little desert people, the caravan, the behemoth, the town, R2D2 lost, and so on. Through the impasto of self-indulgence and the comic-book compulsion to move-move-move, there breaks a childlike, radical, precise gesture of the imagination: and you glimpse what a science-fiction movie might be like, when they get around to making one.*

---

* They did get around to making two, so far (1988) – *Time Bandits* and *Brother from Another Planet*.

Close Encounters has science-fictional elements – the space ship is even more splendid than the ones in *Star Wars* – but it seems to me essentially an occultist movie. It's much more amiable than the endless nasties about little girls possessed by devils; it's definitely on the side of the angels. But the arrival of benevolent aliens in saucers is a theme science fiction hasn't dealt with, except facetiously, for at least a generation. Fiction writers got out long ago, leaving the field to believers, faddists, amateur photographers, psychologists, and the Air Force. Saucerism has a lot to do with religion, as Jung pointed out, but nothing at all to do with either science or science fiction.

Indeed, the movie seemed almost entirely irrational. Perhaps, being middle-aged and seeing it from a highly oblique angle, I missed some explanations. I ought to see it again before saying this; but my impression is that the plot abounds in giant loopholes, as the universe abounds in black holes. How does the U.S. government know *when* to expect the aliens? Why do they have a troop of – well, exchange students, I guess – all dressed up in red pantsuits (one woman, or was it two, in the whole troop) ready to go aboard the saucer? How do they know they'll be wanted? What the dickens is François Truffaut doing there? And if he's there, amidst all the security officers and dead sheep, why aren't there any Mexicans or Chinese or Russians or Canadians or Peruvians or Samoans or Swahili or Thai? Why does the United States get to hog the cosmic show? Why does – Oh, well. Shoot. Why do you spoil it, asking questions? everybody snarls at me.

Well, because both movies come on as science fiction, or as "sci fi," anyhow; and I was brought up to believe that science fiction, whatever its shortcomings in the way of character, catharsis, and grammar, was supposed to try to be intellectually coherent: to have an idea and to follow it through. Neither of these movies would know an idea if they fell over it (which, of course, given their subject matter, they frequently do). *Star Wars* is all action and *Close Encounters* is all emotion, and both are basically mindless.

The emotional bias interests me somewhat more – it's a greater artistic risk to take. In *Close Encounters* sometimes the emotions do move. Children are genuinely important throughout it, and so there is a deep resonance for a moment when the aliens first appear, childlike, gracile, almost fetal forms bathed in pure light. But then Spielberg blows it with a disastrous close-up. His hand is so heavy! Nobody is allowed to do anything, even load a camera, quietly or easily; all movements are frenetic, violent, as if the characters were being pursued by giant sharks. Yet the actors are so good they establish personality and believable response against all the odds. You begin to feel with them, to go along with them . . . and then another load of hysteria gets dumped on and the volume gets turned up another notch.

The end, for instance. I think we're supposed to be sort of misty-eyed; but what about? I want to be clear about what I'm misty about. Is it because they didn't blow us up? Because we didn't blow them up? Because the hero's doing what he wanted and going off in a really gorgeous supersaucer? But what happened to the other guys (and gal) in red pantsuits? They don't seem to be going into the saucer with him. And why does the heroine express her emotion by suddenly ignoring her beautiful kid and shooting a full twenty-four-shot roll of snapshots, color slides no doubt, of the hero's exodus? There she is, smiling through her tears, pressing the shutter again – and again – and again – and again – Is that an adequate dramatic expression of human emotion at a peak experience? Is it even appropriate? I find it pitiful: and, since this is a movie, grotesquely self-conscious. It happened, because it's on film . . .

Well, it's real pretty. And some day they'll make a science-fiction movie. Meanwhile, I think I'll go back and see *Dersu Uzala* for the third time. Because that is a movie about a world and a time none of us will ever see; about aliens; about fear, and love; and because it lets us see that the universe really is endless, and terrible, and beautiful.

Shikasta
by Doris Lessing

●

1979

Doris Lessing takes risks but does not play games. One does not turn
to her books for humor or wit or playfulness, nor will one find in them
any game-playing in the sense of one-upping, faking, posturing. In her
introductory remarks to *Shikasta* she states with characteristic straightfor-
wardness what she sees as the modern novelist's debt to science fiction.
Not even taking refuge in the respectability of "speculative fiction," she
presents her book as science fiction, and I shall review it as such, gratefully;
for science fiction has wasted far too much time apologizing to the pre-
tentious and explaining itself to the willfully ignorant.

Doris Lessing, *Canopus in Argos – Archives. Re: Colonised Planet 5. Shikasta,*
Personal, Psychological, Historical Documents Relating to Visit by Johor (George
Sherban) Emissary (Grade 9). 87th of the Period of the Last Days (New York:
Alfred A. Knopf, 1979; London: Jonathan Cape Ltd, 1979).

If I had read *Shikasta* without knowing who wrote it, I do not think I
would have guessed it to be the work of an established author writing with
some awkwardness in a new mode. I am afraid I would have said: A first
novel, typically earnest and overambitious, badly constructed, badly edited,
showing immense promise; when this writer has learned the art, we'll have
a first-ranker . . . Novel-making is novel-making, whether imagination or
observation dominates, and given Lessing's experience with the fiction of
ideas and with near-future settings, the unshapeliness of *Shikasta* is surprising; the rambling title is only too descriptive. To be sure, the subject is
no less than a history of human life on earth, past, present, and future, not
the sort of thing novelists who play safe, winners of fictional parlor games,
are likely to attempt. Lessing mentions Olaf Stapledon in her introduction,
and in scope the book – especially as the first of a series – indeed vies with

Last and First Men; but the almost obsessive organization, the unity of Stapledon's thought, is wanting. The majesty of the vision is fitful. Sometimes it is majestic, sometimes it is little more than a pulp Galactic Empire with the Goodies fighting the Baddies. Then again it goes off into allegory, like C. S. Lewis, for a while; and there are moments – the bad moments, for me – when it all seems to have been inspired by the Velikovsky–Von Däniken school of, as it were, thought.

The aesthetic incoherence is not due to the plurality of viewpoints, but it may be connected to Lessing's use of the alien viewpoint: most of the events are recounted by an extraterrestrial witness. This is of course one of the basic devices of science fiction (and of prescientific ironic tales), but familiar as the technique is, it requires very great care. Only intense and continual imaginative effort by the author can keep the "alien" voice from sounding human, all too human – thus subverting the estrangement that is the goal of the technique, and so disastrously shrinking, instead of expanding, the universe. This is what has happened in those dreary backwaters of science fiction where the heroes fight the dirty (Commies) (Capitalists) from Aldebaran. Lessing commits no such political imbecilities; the trouble lies more with ethics, I think. The morality voiced by her aliens seems less universal than sectarian, and at times Canopus in Argos sounds strangely like a pulpit in Geneva.

The villains of the piece, from a planet called Shammat, part of the Empire of Puttiora, remain offstage. Though Shammat is the author of evil on earth, all the agents of evil we meet in the book are human beings. But the agents of good we meet are not human; they come from Canopus. One is left in doubt whether mankind has any moral being at all; perhaps we are all puppets of either Shammat or Canopus. In any case, the logic of the book is inescapable: humanity is incapable of doing good on its own, without direct and continual prompting by Benevolences from Outer Space. (The behavior of these guardian angels I personally find, on the evidence given, paternalistic, imperialist, authoritarian, and male supremacist. The latter trait is particularly galling; they claim to be bisexual, but if you notice, they always impregnate human women and never permit themselves to be impregnated by human men.) The picture, then, is, or resembles, one currently very popular indeed, that of the chariots of the gods, or *dei ex machina;* and the message is: In us there is no truth or power. All great events on earth result from decisions made elsewhere; all our inventions were given us by extraterrestrials; all our religions feebly reflect the glory of an unhuman Founder. We have done, and can do, unaided and by ourselves, nothing. Except, perhaps – this is not clear – evil.

To find this projective ethic stated by a considerable writer, no hack or crank, is disquieting to me. Though *Shikasta* is not a Christian book, I think it is a Calvinist one: it affirms the radical irresponsibility of mankind. Salvation not by works but by grace alone, not by the soul's effort but by intercession/intervention – for a few, the chosen, the elect: the rest consigned to damnation by judgment/holocaust/apocalypse. The theme has recently been common in pseudoscience and of course is a cornerstone of fundamentalism. Its roots I suppose are in the Near East. It turns up in the West in hard centuries, whenever people seek the counsels of despair. It has no claim to universality, however, since it remains unsympathetic and essentially unintelligible to the great majority of people. It is not a position sympathetic to most artists, either, since it leaves no room in the world for tragedy, or for charity.

There is much self-hatred in *Shikasta* – hatred of the feminine, the middle-class, the national, the White, the Western, the human – which all comes to a head in the strange episode of the Trial, late in the story, and there perhaps self-destructs. But there is no catharsis; the ethic of guilt forbids it. A brief utopian coda rings false to my ear – the usual Luddite prigs sharing everything with nary a cross word. And all through these final sections the protagonist, Johor, in his last incarnation as George, stalks about bearing the White Man's Burden until you want to kick him. We never meet the Shammatians, we never meet the Sirians, and the Canopans are twits. But the humans . . . There is the story of Rachel; the story of Lynda; the story of "Individual 6" – the exact, brilliant, compassionate, passionate portrayal of human minds driven out of "sanity," forced on beyond. In such passages, Lessing is incomparable. Does she need to write science fiction to achieve them? Would there not be more place for them in a conventional novel?

She seems to have little real interest in the alien as such, little pleasure in it. Invention is an essential ingredient of science fiction, and she lacks or scants it, letting theory and opinion override the humble details that make up creation (primary or secondary). Canopus and the Canopans remain dead words, a world without a landscape, characters without character. No games, no play. The Canopans are angels, messengers of God, but Lessing's concept of the divine excludes that Trickster who creates and destroys. No Coyote, no Loki, no Hermes. Life is real, life is earnest, and Shiva is not allowed to dance in this universe. Like Solzhenitsyn, like the late Victorians, Lessing denies the value of pure invention, permitting only the "meaningful". The work will be not a mystery but a morality. And so it is. And yet –

Every now and then she stops moralizing and looks around at the world she has got herself into; and at such times there is no doubt at all why she is there, or that she belongs there. She does not write conventional fiction because she does not have a conventional mind. She is not a realist at all. Nor is she a fantasist. The old distinctions are useless and must be discarded. Before the critics can do that, we novelists must get on past them ourselves, clear past. It is not easy; no wonder Lessing moves awkwardly. But she moves forward. I would not wish to dwell upon things like SOWF, or substance-of-we-feeling – is the phrase or its acronym worse? – but maybe we had to go through SOWF to get to Zone 6. Zone 6 – which is Hades, and the landscape of the Tibetan *Book of the Dead*, and certain remote territories of the unconscious mind, and the Borderland, and more – is magnificent in conception and in imagery.

Intellectual fiction, the novel of ideas, all too often slides down into the novel of opinions. Science fiction gone self-indulgent rants and preaches, with no more right to, despite its vast subject matter, than any other kind of art. Lessing's opinions, her diatribes against "science" and "politics" and so forth, are very nearly the ruin of the novel. But beneath and beyond the opinions, not fully under her control, perhaps even disobeying her conscious intent, is the creative spirit that can describe a terrorist's childhood with the authority of a Dostoyevsky, or imagine the crowded souls crying at the gates of life – and the lurching, lumbering, struggling book is redeemed, is worth reading, is immortal diamond.

It was a Dark and Stormy Night: Or,
Why Are We Huddling about the Campfire?

1979/1980

This talk was the last paper read at a three-day symposium on narrative held at
the University of Chicago in 1979. Some of the obscurer bits of it are incorporations
of and jokes about things read or said by other participants in the conference, the
proceedings of which may be found in Critical Inquiry *(vol. 7, no. 1, Autumn*
1980). I had bought my first and only pair of two-inch-heeled shoes, black French
ones, to wear there, but I never dared put them on; there were so many Big Guns
shooting at one another that it seemed unwise to try to increase my stature.

It was a dark and stormy night
and Brigham Young and Brigham Old
sat around the campfire.
Tell us a story, old man!
And this is the story he told:

It was a dark and stormy night
and Brigham Young and Brigham Old
sat around the campfire.
Tell us a story, old man!
And this is the story he told:

It was a dark and stormy night
and Brigham Young and Pierre Menard, author of the *Quixote*,
sat around the campfire,
which is not quite the way my Great-Aunt Betsy told it
when we said Tell us another story!
Tell us, *au juste*, what happened!
And this is the story she told:

It was a dark and stormy night, in the otherwise unnoteworthy year 711

E.C. (Eskimo Calendar), and the great-aunt sat crouched at her typewriter, holding his hands out to it from time to time as if for warmth and swinging on a swing. He was a handsome boy of about eighteen, one of those men who suddenly excite your desire when you meet them in the street, and who leave you with a vague feeling of uneasiness and excited senses. On a plate beside the typewriter lay a slice of tomato. It was a flawless slice. It was a perfect slice of a perfect tomato. It is perfectly boring. I hold out my hands to the typewriter again, while swinging and showing my delicate limbs, and observe that the rows of keys are marked with all the letters of the English alphabet, and all the letters of the French alphabet minus accent marks, and all the letters of the Polish alphabet except the dark L. By striking these keys with the ends of my fingers or, conceivably, a small blunt instrument, the aging woman can create a flaw in the tomato. She did so at once. It was then a seriously, indeed a disgustingly flawed tomato, but it continued to be perfectly boring until eaten. She expires instantly in awful agony, of snakebite, flinging the window wide to get air. It is a dark and stormy night and the rain falling in on the typewriter keys writes a story in German about a great-aunt who went to a symposium on narrative and got eaten in the forest by a metabear. She writes the story while reading it with close attention, not sure what to expect, but collaborating hard, as if that was anything new; and this is the story I wrote:

It was a dark and stormy night
and Brigham al-Rashid sat around the campfire with his wife
who was telling him a story in order to keep her head on her
    shoulders,
and this is the story she told:

The *histoire* is the what
and the *discours* is the how
but what I want to know, Brigham,
is *le pourquoi*.
Why are we sitting here around the campfire?

Tell me a story, great-aunt,
so that I can sleep.
Tell me a story, Scheherazade,
so that you can live.

Tell me a story, my soul, animula, vagula, blandula,
little Being-Towards-Death,
for the word's the beginning of being
if not the middle or the end.

"A beginning is that which is not itself necessarily after anything else, and
which has naturally something else after it; an end, that which is naturally
after something else, either as its necessary or usual consequent, and with
nothing else after it; and a middle, that which is by nature after one thing
and has also another after it."[1]
   But sequence grows difficult in the ignorance of what comes after the
necessary or at least the usual consequent of living, that is, dying,
   and also when the soul is confused by not unreasonable doubts of what
comes after the next thing that happens, whatever that may be.
   It gets dark and stormy when you look away from the campfire.

Tell me what you see in the fire, Lizzie, Lizzie Hexam,
down in the hollow by the flare!
I see storm and darkness, brother.
I see death and running water, brother.
I see loving-kindness, brother.
Is it all right to see that, teacher?
What would Alain Robbe-Grillet say?

Never mind what he says, Lizzie.
Frogs have a lot of trouble with the novel,
even though kissed right at the beginning by the Princesse de Clèves;
maybe they do not want to look down and see Victor Hugo glimmer-
   ing *au fond du puits*.

Brigham, this is stupid stuff!
Tell us a story, old man,
or old woman as the case may be,
or old Tiresias, chirping like a cricket,
tell us a story with a proper end to it

---

1 Aristotle, *On the Art of Poetry*, trans. Ingram Bywater (Oxford: Oxford University Press, 1920).

69

instead of beginning again and again like this
and thereby achieving a muddle
which is not by nature after anything in particular
nor does it have anything consequent to it
but it just hangs there
placidly eating its tail.

In the Far West, where Brigham Young ended up and I started from, they tell stories about hoop snakes. When a hoop snake wants to get some-where – whether because the hoop snake is after something, or because something is after the hoop snake – it takes its tail (which may or may not have rattles on it) into its mouth, thus forming itself into a hoop, and rolls. Jehovah enjoined snakes to crawl on their belly in the dust, but Jehovah was an Easterner. Rolling along, bowling along, is a lot quicker and more satisfying than crawling. But, for the hoop snakes with rattles, there is a drawback. They are venomous snakes, and when they bite their own tail they die, in awful agony, of snakebite. All progress has these hitches. I don't know what the moral is. It may be in the end safest to lie perfectly still without even crawling. Indeed it's certain that we shall all do so in the end, which has nothing else after it. But then no tracks are left in the dust, no lines drawn; the dark and stormy nights are all one with the sweet bright days, this moment of June – and you might as well never have lived at all. And the moral of *that* is, you have to form a circle to escape from the circle. Draw in a little closer around the campfire. If we could truly form a circle, joining the beginning and the end, we would, as another Greek remarked, not die. But never fear. We can't manage it no matter how we try. But still, very few things come nearer the real Hoop Trick than a good story.

There was a man who practiced at the Hoop Trick named Aneirin.

But let us have the footnotes first.

"We have to bear in mind that the *Gododdin* [and its associated lays] are not narrative poems ... Nowhere is there any attempt to give an ac-count of what it was really all about."[2] I disagree with this comment and agree with the next one, which points out that the work goes rolling and bowling all about what it is all about. "While some of these [early Welsh poems] will 'progress' in expected fashion from a beginning through a

---

2 K. H. Jackson, *The Gododdin: The Oldest Scottish Poem* (Edinburgh: Edinburgh University Press, 1969).

middle to an end, the normal structure is 'radial,' circling about, repeating
and elaborating the central theme. It is all 'middle.'"[3]

This is the Gododdin; Aneirin sang it.   [I]

Men went to Catraeth, keen their war-band   [VIII]
Pale mead their portion, it was poison.
Three hundred under orders to fight.
And after celebration, silence.

Men went to Catraeth at dawn: [X]
All their fears had been put to flight.
Three hundred clashed with ten thousand.

Men went to Catraeth at dawn: [XI]
Their high spirits lessened their lifespans.
They drank mead, gold and sweet, ensnaring;   [XVIII]
For a year the minstrels were merry.

Three spears stain with blood
Fifty, five hundred.
Three hounds, three hundred:
Three stallions of war
From golden Eidin,
Three mailclad war-bands,
Three gold-collared kings.

Men went to Catraeth, they were renowned,   [XXI]
Wine and mead from gold cups was their drink,
A year in noble ceremonial,
Three hundred and sixty-three gold-torqued men.
Of all those who charged, after too much drink,
But three won free through courage in strife:
Aeron's two warhounds and tough Cynan,
And myself, soaked in blood, for my song's sake.

---

3 Joseph P. Clancy, introduction to *The Earliest Welsh Poetry* (London: Macmillan, 1970).

My legs at full length   [XLVIII]
In a house of earth.
A chain of iron
About both ankles,
Caused by mead, by horn,
By Catraeth's raiders.
I, not I, Aneirin,
Taliesin knows it,
Master of wordcraft,
Sang to Gododdin
Before the day dawned.

None walk the earth, no mother has borne   [XLIX]
One so fair and strong, dark as iron.
From a war-band his bright blade saved me,
From a fell cell of earth he bore me,
From a place of death, from a harsh land,
Cenan fab Llywarch, bold, undaunted.

Many I lost of my true comrades.   [LXI]
Of three hundred champions who charged to Catraeth,
It is tragic, but one man came back.

On Tuesday they donned their dark armour,   [LXIX]
On Wednesday, bitter their meeting,
On Thursday, terms were agreed on,
On Friday, dead men without number,
On Saturday, fearless, they worked as one,
On Sunday, crimson blades were their lot,
On Monday, men were seen waist-deep in blood.
After defeat, the Gododdin say,
Before Madawg's tent on his return
There came but one man in a hundred.

Three hundred, gold-torqued,   [XCI]
Warlike, well-trained,
Three hundred, haughty,
In harmony, armed.

Three hundred fierce steeds
Bore them to battle.
Three hounds, three hundred:
Tragic, no return.[4]

"I, not I, Aneirin" – "won free" – "for my song's sake." What is Aneirin
telling us? Whether or not we allow that a story so muddled or all middle
can be a narrative, or must be lyric or elegiac, but do classic Greek definitions fit Welsh Dark Ages traditions? – so, as Barbara Myerhoff pleaded, in
all courtesy let us not argue about it at this point, only perhaps admitting
that the spiral is probably the shortest way of getting through spacetime
and is certainly an effective way to recount the *loss* of a battle – in any case,
what is Aneirin trying to tell us? For all we know or shall ever know of the
Battle of Catraeth is what he tells us; and there is no doubt that he very
much wanted us to know about it, to remember it. He says that he won
free for his song's sake. He says that he survived, alone, or with Cynan and
two others, or with Cenan – he seems to have survived in several different
ways, also, which is very Welsh of him – he says that he survived in order
to tell us about his friends who did not survive. But I am not sure whether
he means by this that he must tell the story because he alone survived; or
that he survived because he had the story to tell.

And now for quite another war. I am going to speak in many voices for
a while. Novelists have this habit of ventriloquy.[5]

"The SS guards took pleasure in telling us that we had no chance of
coming out alive, a point they emphasized with particular relish by insisting that after the war the rest of the world would not believe what had
happened; there would be ... no clear evidence" (a survivor of Dachau).

"Those caught were shot, but that did not keep Ringelblum and his
friends from organizing a clandestine group whose job was to gather
information for deposit in a secret archive (much of which survived).
Here ... survival and bearing witness become reciprocal acts" (Des
Pres).

"[In Treblinka] the dead were being unearthed and burned [by work
squads], and soon the work squads too would go up in smoke. If that
had come to pass, Treblinka would never have existed. The aim of the

---

4 Clancy's translation of the text of the *Goddodin*, in ibid.
5 The following citations appear in Terence Des Pres, *The Survivor: An Anatomy of Life in the Death
Camps* (New York: Oxford University Press, 1976).

revolt was to ensure the memory of that place, and we know the story of Treblinka because forty survived" (Des Pres).

"I found it most difficult to stay alive, but I had to live, to give the world the story" (Glatstein, from Treblinka).

"Even in this place one can survive, and therefore one must want to survive, to tell the story, to bear witness" (Primo Levi, from Auschwitz).

"It is a man's way of leaving a trace, of telling people how he lived and died ... If nothing else is left, one must scream. Silence is the real crime against humanity" (Nadyezhda Mandelshtam).

"Conscience ... is a social achievement ... on its historical level, it is the collective effort to come to terms with evil, to distill a moral knowledge equal to the problems at hand ... Existence at its boundary is intrinsically significant ... the struggle to live – merely surviving – is rooted in, and a manifestation of, the form-conferring potency of life itself" (Des Pres).

"We may at least speculate that ... survival depends upon life [considered] as a set of activities evolved through time in successful response to crises, the sole purpose of which is to keep going" (Des Pres).

"Living things act as they do because they are so organized as to take actions that prevent their dissolution into the surroundings" (J. Z. Young).

"It seems as if Western culture were making a prodigious effort of historiographic *anamnesis* ... We may say ... this *anamnesis* continues the religious evaluation of memory and forgetfulness. To be sure, neither myths nor religious practices are any longer involved. But there is this common element: the importance of precise and total recollection ... The prose narrative, especially the novel, has taken the place of the recitation of myths ... The tale takes up and continues 'initiation' on the level of the imaginary ... Believing that he is merely amusing himself or escaping, the man of the modern societies still benefits from the imaginary initiation supplied by tales ... Today we are beginning to realize that what is called 'initiation' coexists with the human condition, that every existence is made up of an unbroken series of 'ordeals,' 'deaths,' and 'resurrections.' ... Whatever the gravity of the present crisis of the novel, it is nonetheless true that the need to find one's way into 'foreign' universes and to follow the complications of a 'story' seems to be consubstantial with the human condition."[6]

"For Heaven only knows why one loves it so, how one sees it so, making

6 Mircea Eliade, *Myth and Reality*, trans. Willard R. Trask (New York: Harper & Row, 1963).

it up, building it round one, tumbling it, creating it every moment afresh
... In people's eyes, in the swing, tramp, and trudge; in the bellow and the
uproar; the carriages, motor cars, omnibuses, vans, sandwich men shuffling
and swinging; brass bands; barrel organs; in the triumph and the jingle and
the strange high singing of some aeroplane overhead was what she loved;
life; London; this moment of June."[7]

Why are we huddling about the campfire? Why do we tell tales, or tales
about tales – why do we bear witness, true or false? We may ask Aneirin
or Primo Levi, we may ask Scheherazade or Virginia Woolf. Is it because
we are so organized as to take actions that prevent our dissolution into the
surroundings? I know a very short story that might illustrate this hypothesis. You will find it carved into a stone about three feet up from the floor
of the north transept of Carlisle Cathedral in the north of England, not
all that far from Catterick, which may have been Catraeth. It was carved
in runes, one line of runes, laboriously carved into the stone. A translation
into English is posted up nearby in typescript under glass. Here is the
whole story:

Tolfink carved these runes in this stone.

Well, this is pretty close to Barbara Herrnstein Smith's earliest form of
historiography – notch-cutting. As a story, it does not really meet the requirement of Minimal Connexity. It doesn't have much beginning or end.
The material was obdurate, and life is short. Yet I would say Tolfink was a
reliable narrator. Tolfink bore witness at least to the existence of Tolfink, a
human being unwilling to dissolve entirely into his surroundings.

It is time to end, an appropriate time for a ghost story. It was a dark and
stormy night, and the man and the woman sat around the campfire in their
tent out on the plains. They had killed the woman's husband and run away
together. They had been going north across the plains for three days now.
The man said, "We must be safe. There is no way the people of the tribe
can track us." The woman said, "What's that noise?" They listened, and
they both heard a scratching noise on the outside of the tent, low down,
near the ground. "It's the wind blowing," the man said. The woman said,
"It doesn't sound like the wind." They listened and heard the sound again,

7 Virginia Woolf, *Mrs. Dalloway* (London: Hogarth Press).

a scraping, louder, and higher up on the wall of the tent. The woman said, "Go and see what it is. It must be some animal." The man didn't want to go out. She said, "Are you afraid?" Now the scraping sound had got very loud, up almost over their heads. The man jumped up and went outside to look. There was enough light from the fire inside the tent that he could see what it was. It was a skull. It was rolling up the outside of the tent so that it could get in at the smokehole at the top. It was the skull of the man they had killed, the husband, but it had grown very big. It had been rolling after them over the plains all along and growing bigger as it rolled. The man shouted to the woman, and she came out of the tent, and they caught each other by the hand and ran. They ran into the darkness, and the skull rolled down the tent and rolled after them. It came faster and faster. They ran until they fell down in the darkness, and the skull caught up with them there. That was the end of them.

There may be some truth in that story, that tale, that discourse, that narrative, but there is no reliability in the telling of it. It was told you forty years later by the ten-year-old who heard it, along with her great-aunt, by the campfire, on a dark and starry night in California; and though it is, I believe, a Plains Indian story, she heard it told in English by an anthropologist of German antecedents. But by remembering it he had made the story his; and insofar as I have remembered it, it is mine; and now, if you like it, it's yours. In the tale, in the telling, we are all one blood. Take the tale in your teeth, then, and bite till the blood runs, hoping it's not poison; and we will all come to the end together, and even to the beginning: living, as we do, in the middle.

The Marriages Between Zones Three, Four, and Five
by Doris Lessing

1980

With a sigh that she refused to deepen into a groan, she again saw him as her fellow prisoner, and marveling that this taut, grief-marked man could be the gross and fleshy Ben Ata of their first days, she enclosed him, as he did her, and their lovemaking was all a consoling and a reassurance. When his hand felt for their child, now responding quite vigorously to their lovemaking, as if wishing to share in it – as if it were the promise of a festival – it was with respect and a promise not to an extension of himself, or of her, but a salute to the possibilities of them both; a considered and informed salute, at that, for Al-Ith, feeling the delicately contained strength of those enquiring fingers, knew that the potentialities he acknowledged were for the unknown and the unexpected, as well as for familiar delight. For this union of incompatibles could not be anything less than a challenge.

A challenge it is, and a reward. The second of the *Canopus in Argos* series of novels is a finer-grained and stronger book than *Shikasta*, the first. *The Marriages* may be read for the pure pleasure of reading it, a tale unencumbered by metaphysical machinery. The Canopans and Sirians, the superhuman powers of good and evil of *Shikasta*, stay offstage this time. The manipulations of the Sirians are only hinted at; the powers of good, here known as the Providers, emit directives by Voice (like Joan of Arc's Voices) and, entertainingly, by beating an invisible drum. The Providers – I kept thinking of Scott's Antarctic crew, who referred to Providence, upon which they depended quite consciously if not always successfully, as "Provvy" – the Providers command Al-Ith, ruler of Zone Three, and Ben Ata, ruler of Zone Four, to marry. Both obey the order not happily but unquestioningly. Theirs not to reason why. (Why not?) Once they meet, however, the two human beings begin to behave very humanly indeed, and what might have been a fable enacted by wooden puppets twitching on the strings of allegory becomes a lively and lovable novel. A novel in the folktale mode, bordering on the mythic.

Doris Lessing, *The Marriages Between Zones Three, Four, and Five* (New York: Alfred A. Knopf, 1980; London: Jonathan Cape Ltd, 1980).

The theme is one of the major themes of both myth and novel: marriage. Lessing's treatment of it is complex and flexible, passionate and compassionate, with a rising vein of humor uncommon in her work, both welcome and appropriate. Marriage in all modes. Marriage sensual, moral, mental, political. Marriage of two people, an archetypally sensitive lady and an archetypally tough soldier. Marriage of female and male; of masculine and feminine; of intuitional and sensational; of duty and pleasure. Marriage of their two countries, which reflect all these opposites and more, including the oppositions wealth/poverty, peace/war. And then suddenly a marriage with Zone Five is ordered, a second marriage, a tertium quid, startling and inevitable.

It may be worth noting that this series of oppositions does not overlap very far with the old Chinese system of opposites, the yin and yang. At female/male and perhaps at intuitional/sensational they coincide; otherwise Lessing simply omits the dark, wet, cold, passive, etc., the whole yin side of the Tai Chi figure. Her dialectic of marriage takes place almost wholly in terms of yang. Its process therefore is Hegelian, struggle and resolution, without the option of a maintained balance (the marriage cannot last). This is illustrative of the extreme Westernness of Lessing's ethic and metaphysic. The *Canopus* books propose a cosmic viewpoint: but it turns out to be so purely European an explanation of human destiny that anyone even slightly familiar with other religious or philosophical systems must find it inadequate, if not presumptuous. In her introduction to *Shikasta*, referring to "the sacred literatures of all races and nations," Lessing said, "It is possible we make a mistake when we dismiss them as quaint fossils from a dead past." Possible, indeed. Who but a bigot or an ignoramus would do so? Lessing is neither, but the parochialism is disturbing.

The landscapes and societies of Zones Three, Four, and Five (and, most tantalizingly, Two) are sketched, not detailed. One cannot live in these lands, as one can in Middle Earth. These are the countries of parable, intellectual nations which one can only visit in a closed car; but the scenery

78

is vastly interesting, and one may wish one could at least stop and get out. The quick-paced plot is kept distanced by several devices: by use of the folktale ambience of faraway lands once upon a time; by frequent reference, in a kind of stop-frame effect, to paintings of the events recounted; and by having the tale told by an elderly male Chronicler of Zone Three.

At first the protagonists also appear at a distance, a bit larger than life, all of a piece, heroic. Perhaps the Ben Hur lurking in the name Ben Ata is even deliberate (though I wish the Alice trying to lisp her way out of Al-Ith were not so audible). As the two enter upon their difficult marriage, however, and are driven through all the changes of fear, patience, lust, rage, liking, masochism, ecstasy, jealousy, rebellion, dependence, friendship, and the rest, they become smaller, more distinct, more complicated. They get older. Their heroism is no longer easy, it has become painful, it has become real. By having the courage to use these great stock characters, the Queen and the King, and to take them seriously as people, Lessing has presented a personal drama of general significance, skillfully and without falsification. Her portrait of a marriage is perfectly clear-sighted and admirably inconclusive. Moralist that she is, she makes no judgment here. Character is destiny: her characters make themselves a human destiny, far more impressive than any conceivable pseudo-divine Five-Year Plan for the good of Zones Three to Five. They might even have risen to tragedy, had the author not opened heaven's trapdoor to them to prevent that chance.

Though accurate, that last sentence is probably unfair. After all, *The Marriages* aspires to myth, not to tragedy. Zone Two is certainly an unconventional and attractive heaven, or stage on the way to heaven; one may be content to leave Al-Ith to it at last. Perhaps it is only mean-mindedness that makes me distrust Zone One, fearing that it will turn out to be not simply better but Perfectly Good, and therefore longing to find something wrong with it: just as we discovered, gradually, guided gently by our author, what was wrong with the utopian Zone Three, that now quite familiar country where nobody is possessive or destructive or macho or has bad taste in furniture.

The Manichaean-Calvinistic hierarchy, the closed system implied by the structure and the more vatic bits of *Shikasta*, seems here to give way to an open source of relative values – a way, a human way. Or does Lessing not agree with the Chronicler who tells her tale so well? I think she does.

*

We chroniclers do well to be afraid when we approach those parts of our histories (our natures) that deal with evil, the depraved, the benighted. Describing, we become . . .

I tell you that goodness – what we in our ordinary daylight selves call goodness: the ordinary, the decent – these are nothing without the hidden powers that pour forth continually from their shadow sides . . .

In those high places there is a dark side, and who knows but that it may be very dark . . .

But the tale is not a fearful one. It is kindly, careful, cheerful. Its teller, knowing the darkness, faces the light.

Some Thoughts on Narrative

1980

This paper incorporates parts of the Nina Mae Kellogg Lecture given at Portland State University in the spring of 1980.

Recently, at a three-day-long symposium on narrative, I learned that it's unsafe to say anything much about narrative, because if a poststructuralist doesn't get you a deconstructionist will. This is a pity, because the subject is an interesting one to those outside the armed camps of literary theory. As one who spends a good deal of her time telling stories, I should like to know, in the first place, why I tell stories, and in the second place, why you listen to them; and vice versa.

Through long practice I know how to tell a story, but I'm not sure I know what a story is; and I have not found much patience with the question among those better qualified to answer it. To literary theorists it is evidently too primitive, to linguists it is not primitive enough; and among psychologists I know of only one, Simon Lesser, who has tried seriously to explain narration as a psychic process. There is, however, always Aristotle.

Aristotle says that the essential element of drama and epic is "the arrangement of the incidents." And he goes on to make the famous and endearing remark that this narrative or plotly element consists of a beginning, a middle, and an end:

> A beginning is that which is not itself necessarily after anything else, and which has naturally something else after it; an end, that which is naturally after something else, either as its necessary or usual consequent, and with nothing else after it; and a middle, that which is by nature after one thing and has also another after it.

According to Aristotle, then, narrative connects events, "arranges incidents," in a directional temporal order analogous to a directional spatial order.

Causality is implied but not exactly stated (in the word "consequent," which could mean "result" or merely "what follows"); the principal linkage as I understand it is temporal (E. M. Forster's story sequence, "and then ... and then ... and then ..."). So narrative is language used to connect events in time. The connection, whether conceived as a closed pattern, beginning-middle-end, or an open one, past-present-future, whether seen as lineal or spiral or recursive, involves a movement "through" time for which spatial metaphor is adequate. Narrative makes a journey. It goes from A to Z, from then to then-prime.

This might be why narrative does not normally use the present tense except for special effect or out of affectation. It locates itself in the past (whether the real or an imagined, fictional past) in order to allow itself forward movement. The present not only competes against the story with a vastly superior weight of reality, but limits it to the pace of watch hand or heartbeat. Only by locating itself in the "other country" of the past is the narrative free to move towards its future, the present.

The present tense, which some writers of narrative fiction currently employ because it is supposed to make the telling "more actual," actually distances the story (and some very sophisticated writers of narrative fiction use it for that purpose). The present tense takes the story out of time. Anthropological reports concerning people who died decades ago, whose societies no longer exist, are written in the present tense; this paper is written in the present tense. Physics is normally written in the present tense, in part because it *generalizes*, as I am doing now, but also because it deals so much with nondirectional time.

Time for a physicist is quite likely to be reversible. It doesn't matter whether you read an equation forwards or backwards – unlike a sentence. On the subatomic level directionality is altogether lost. You cannot write the history of a photon; narration is irrelevant; all you can say of it is that it might be, or, otherwise stated, if you can say where it is you can't say when and if you can say when it is you can't say where.

Even of an entity relatively so immense and biologically so complex as a gene, the little packet of instructions that tells us what to be, there is no story to be told; because the gene, barring accident, is immortal. All you can say of it is that it is, and it is, and it is. No beginning, no end. All middle.

The past and future tenses become useful to science when it gets involved in irreversible events, when beginning, middle, and end will run only in that order. What happened two seconds after the Big Bang?

What happened when Male Beta took Male Alpha's banana? What will happen if I add this hydrochloric acid? These are events that made, or will make, a difference. The existence of a future — a time different from now, a then-prime — depends on the irreversibility of time; in human terms, upon mortality. In Eternity there is nothing novel, and there are no novels.

So when the storyteller by the hearth starts out, "Once upon a time, a long way from here, lived a king who had three sons," that story will be telling us that things change; that events have consequences; that choices are to be made; that the king does not live forever.

Narrative is a stratagem of mortality. It is a means, a way of living. It does not seek immortality; it does not seek to triumph over or escape from time (as lyric poetry does). It asserts, affirms, participates in directional time, time experienced, time as meaningful. If the human mind had a temporal spectrum, the nirvana of the physicist or the mystic would be way over in the ultraviolet, and at the opposite end, in the infrared, would be *Wuthering Heights*.

To put it another way: Narrative is a central function of language. Not, in origin, an artifact of culture, an art, but a fundamental operation of the normal mind functioning in society. To learn to speak is to learn to tell a story.

I would guess that preverbal narration takes place almost continuously on the unconscious level, but pre- or nonverbal mental operations are very hard to talk about. Dreams might help.

It has been found that during REM (rapid eye movement) sleep, the recurrent phase of sleep during which we dream abundantly, the movement of the eyes is intermittent. If you wake the dreamer while the eyes are flickering, the dreams reported are disconnected, jumbled, snatches and flashes of imagery; but, awakened during a quiet-eye period, the dreamer reports a "proper dream," a *story*. Researchers call the image-jumble "primary visual experience" and the other "secondary cognitive elaboration."

Concerning this, Liam Hudson wrote (in the *Times Literary Supplement* of January 25, 1980):

> While asleep, then, we experience arbitrary images, and we also tell ourselves stories. The likelihood is that we weave the second around the first, embedding images that we perceive as bizarre in a fabric that seems to us more reasonable. If I confront myself, while asleep, with

the image of a crocodile on the roof of a German *Schloss*, and then, while still fast asleep, create for myself some plausible account of how this implausible event has occurred, I am engaged in the manoeuvre of rationalisation – of rendering sensible-seeming something that is not sensible in the least. In the course of this manoeuvre, the character of the original image is falsified . . .

The thinking we do without thinking about it consists in the translation of our experience to narrative, irrespective of whether our experience fits the narrative form or not . . . Asleep and awake it is just the same: we are telling ourselves stories all the time, . . . tidier stories than the evidence warrants.

Mr. Hudson's summary of the material is elegant, and his interpretation of it is, I take it, Freudian. Dreamwork is *rationalization*, therefore it is *falsification*: a cover-up. The mind is an endless Watergate. Some primitive "reality" or "truth" is forever being distorted, lied about, tidied up.

But what if we have no means of access to this truth or reality except through the process of "lying," except through the narrative? Where are we supposed to be standing in order to judge what "the evidence warrants"?

Take Mr. Hudson's crocodile on the roof of a German castle (it is certainly more interesting than what I dreamed last night). We can all make that image into a story. Some of us will protest, No no I can't, I can't tell stories, etc., having been terrorized by our civilization into believing that we are, or have to be, "rational." But all of us can make that image into some kind of story, and if it came into our head while we were asleep, no doubt we would do so without a qualm, without giving it a second thought. As I have methodically practiced irrational behavior for many years, I can turn it into a story almost as easily waking as asleep. What has happened is that Prince Metternich was keeping a crocodile to frighten his aunt with, and the crocodile has escaped through a skylight onto the curious, steep, leaden roofs of the castle, and is clambering, in the present tense because it is a dream and outside time, towards a machicolated nook in which lies, in a stork's nest, but the stork is in Africa, an egg, a wonderful, magical Easter egg of sugar containing a tiny window through which you look and you see – But the dreamer is awakened here. And if there is any "message" to the dream, the dreamer is not aware of it; the dream with its "message" has gone from the unconscious to the unconscious, like most dreams, without any processing describable as "rationalization," and without ever being verbalized (unless and until the dreamer, in some kind of therapy, has learned laboriously to retrieve and hold and verbalize dreams). In this case all the dreamer – we need a name for this character, let us call her Edith Driemer – all Edith remembers, fleetingly, is something about a roof, a crocodile, Germany, Easter, and while thinking dimly about her great-aunt Esther in Munich, she is presented with further "primary visual (or sensory) experiences" running in this temporal sequence: A loud ringing in the left ear. Blinding light. The smell of an exotic herb. A toilet. A pair of used shoes. A disembodied voice screaming in Parsee. A kiss. A sea of shining clouds. Terror. Twilight in the branches of a tree outside the window of a strange room in an unknown city . . .

Are these the "primary experiences" experienced while her eyes move rapidly, furnishing material for the next dream? They could well be; but by following Aristotle's directions and making purely temporal connections between them, we can make of them a quite realistic narration of the day Edith woke up and turned off the alarm clock, got up and got dressed, had breakfast listening to the radio news, kissed Mr. Driemer goodbye, and took a plane to Cincinnati in order to attend a meeting of market analysts.

I submit that though this network of "secondary elaboration" may be more rationally controlled than that of the pretended dream, the primary material on which it must work can be considered inherently as bizarre, as absurd, as the crocodile on the roof, and that the factual account of Edith Driemer's day is no more and no less than the dream-story a "manoeuvre," "rendering sensible-seeming something that is not sensible in the least."

Dream narrative differs from conscious narrative in using sensory symbol more than language. In dream the sense of the directionality of time is often replaced by spatial metaphor, or may be lowered, or reversed, or vanish. The connections dream makes between events are most often unsatisfactory to the rational intellect and the aesthetic mind. Dreams tend to flout Aristotle's rules of plausibility and muddle up his instructions concerning plot. Yet they are undeniably narrative: they connect events, fit things together in an order or a pattern that makes, to some portion of our mind, sense.

Looked at as a "primary visual (sensory) experience," in isolation, without connection to any context or event, each of our experiences is equally plausible or implausible, authentic or inauthentic, meaningful or absurd. But living creatures go to considerable pains to escape equality, to evade entropy, chaos, and old night. They arrange things. They make sense, literally. Molecule by molecule. In the cell. The cells arrange themselves. The body is an arrangement in spacetime, a patterning, a process; the mind is a process of the body, an organ, doing what organs do: organize. Order, pattern, connect. Do we have any better way to organize such wildly disparate experiences as a half-remembered crocodile, a dead great-aunt, the smell of coffee, a scream from Iran, a bumpy landing, and a hotel room in Cincinnati, than the narrative? – an immensely flexible technology, or life strategy, which if used with skill and resourcefulness presents each of us with that most fascinating of all serials, The Story of My Life.

I have read of a kind of dream that is symptomatic of one form of schizophrenia. The dream presents an object, a chair perhaps, or a coat, or a stump. Nothing happens, and there is nothing else in the dream.

Seen thus in spatial and temporal isolation, the primary experience or image can be the image of despair itself (like Sartre's tree root). Beckett's work yearns toward this condition. In the other direction, Rilke's celebration of "Things" – a chair, a coat, a stump – offers connection: a piece of furniture is part of the pattern of the room, of the life, a bed is a table in a swoon (in one of his French poems), forests are in the stump, the pitcher is also the river, and the hand, and the cup, and the thirst.

Whether the technique is narrative or not, the primary experience has to be connected with and fitted into the rest of experience to be useful, probably even to be available, to the mind. This may hold even for mystical perception. All mystics say that what they have experienced in vision cannot be fitted into ordinary time and space, but they try – they have to try. The vision is ineffable, but the story begins, "In the middle of the road of our life . . ."

It may be that an inability to fit events together in an order that at least seems to make sense, to make the narrative connection, is a radical incompetence at being human. So seen, stupidity could be defined as a failure to make enough connections, and insanity as severe repeated error in making connections – in telling The Story of My Life.

But nobody does it right all the time, or even most of the time. Even without identifying narration with falsification, one must admit that a vast amount of our life narration is fictional – how much, we cannot tell.

But if narration is a life stratagem, a survival skill, how can I get away, asleep and awake, with mistaking and distorting and omitting data, through wishful thinking, ignorance, laziness, and haste? If the ghostwriter in my

SOME THOUGHTS ON NARRATIVE

head writing The Story of My Life is forgetful, careless, mendacious, a hack who doesn't care what happens so long as it makes some kind of story, why don't I get punished? Radical errors in interpreting and reacting to the environment aren't let off lightly, in either the species or the individual.

Is the truthfulness of the story, then, the all-important value; or is the quality of the fiction important too? Is it possible that we all keep going in very much the same way as Queen Dido or Don Quixote keeps going – by virtue of being almost entirely fictional characters?

Anyone who knows J. T. Fraser's work, such as his book *Of Time, Passion, and Knowledge*, and that of George Steiner, will have perceived my debt to them in trying to think about the uses of narrative. I am not always able to follow Mr. Steiner; but when he discusses the importance of the future tense, suggesting that statements about what does not exist and may never exist are central to the use of language, I follow him cheering and waving pompoms. When he makes his well-known statement "Language is the main instrument of man's refusal to accept the world as it is," I continue to follow, though with lowered pompoms. The proposition as stated worries me. Man's refusal to accept the world as it is? Do women also refuse? What about science, which tries so hard to see the world as it is? What about art, which not only accepts the dreadful world as it is but praises it for being so? "Isn't life a terrible thing, thank God!" says the lady with the backyard full of washing and babies in *Under Milk Wood*, and the sweet song says, "Nobody knows the trouble I seen, Glory, Hallelujah!" I agree with them. All grand refusals, especially when made by Man, are deeply suspect.

So, caviling all the way, I follow Mr. Steiner. If the use of language were to describe accurately what exists, what, in fact, would we want it for?

Surely the primary, survival-effective uses of language involve stating alternatives and hypotheses. We don't, we never did, go about making statements of fact to other people, or in our internal discourse with ourselves. We talk about what may be, or what we'd like to do, or what you ought to do, or what might have happened: warnings, suppositions, propositions, invitations, ambiguities, analogies, hints, lists, anxieties, hearsay, old wives' tales, leaps and cross-links and spiderwebs between here and there, between then and now, between now and sometime, a continual weaving and restructuring of the remembered and the perceived and the imagined, including a great deal of wishful thinking and a variable quantity of deliberate or non-deliberate fictionalizing, to reassure ourselves or for the pleasure of it, and also some deliberate or semi-deliberate falsification in order to mislead a rival or persuade a friend or escape despair; and no sooner have we made one of these patterns of words than we may, like Shelley's cloud, laugh, and arise, and unbuild it again.

In recent centuries we speakers of this lovely language have reduced the English verb almost entirely to the indicative mood. But beneath that specious and arrogant assumption of certainty all the ancient, cloudy, moody powers and options of the subjunctive remain in force. The indicative points its bony finger at primary experiences, at the Things; but it is the subjunctive that joins them, with the bonds of analogy, possibility, probability, contingency, contiguity, memory, desire, fear, and hope: the narrative connection. As J. T. Fraser puts it, moral choice, which is to say human freedom, is made possible "by language, which permits us to give accounts of possible and impossible worlds in the past, in the future, or in a faraway land."

Fiction in particular, narration in general, may be seen not as a disguise or falsification of what is given but as an active encounter with the environment by means of posing options and alternatives, and an enlargement of present reality by connecting it to the unverifiable past and the unpredictable future. A totally factual narrative, were there such a thing, would be passive: a mirror reflecting all without distortion. Stendhal sentimentalized about the novel as such a mirror, but fiction does not reflect, nor is the narrator's eye that of a camera. The historian manipulates, arranges, and connects, and the storyteller does all that as well as intervening and inventing. Fiction connects possibilities, using the aesthetic sense of time's directionality defined by Aristotle as plot; and by doing so it is useful to us. If we cannot see our acts and being under the aspect of fiction, as "making sense," we cannot act as if we were free.

To describe narrative as "rationalization" of the given or of events is a blind alley. In the telling of a story, reason is only a support system. It can provide causal connections; it can extrapolate; it can judge what is likely, plausible, possible. All this is crucial to the invention of a good story, a sane fantasy, a sound piece of fiction. But reason by itself cannot get from the crocodile to Cincinnati. It cannot see that Elizabeth is, in fact, going to marry Darcy, and why. It may not even ever quite understand who it was, exactly, that Oedipus did marry. We cannot ask reason to take us across the gulfs of the absurd. Only the imagination can get us out of the bind of the eternal present, inventing or hypothesizing or pretending or discovering a way that reason can then follow into the infinity of options, a clue through the labyrinths of choice, a golden string, the story, leading us to the freedom that is properly human, the freedom open to those whose minds can accept unreality.

Italian Folktales
by Italo Calvino

1980

Prowling among dictionaries, I discovered that the word "fairy" is *fata* in Italian and that it derives, like the word "fate," from the Latin verb *fari*, "to speak." Fate is "that which is spoken." The Fates that once presided over human life dwindled away in fairies, fairy godmothers, inhabitants of fairytales.

The English word "fable" and the Italian *fiaba* or *favola*, a story, "a narrative or statement not founded on fact," as the *Shorter Oxford* puts it, descend from the Latin *fabula*, which derives from that same verb, *fari*, "to speak." To speak is to tell tales.

The predestined spindle has pricked her thumb; here lies the Sleeping Beauty in the silent castle. The prince arrives. He kisses her. Nothing happens.

So the prince comes back again next day, and the next day too, and his love is

> so intense that the sleeping maiden gave birth to twins, a boy and a girl, and you never saw two more beautiful children in your life. They came into the world hungry, but who was to nurse them if their mamma lay there like a dead woman? They cried and cried, but their mother didn't hear them. With their tiny mouths they began seeking something to suck on, and that way the boy child happened to find his mother's hand and began sucking on the thumb. With all that sucking, the spindle tip lodged under the nail came out, and the sleeper awakened. "Oh, me, how I've slept!" she said, rubbing her eyes.

The two children are named Sun and Moon, and Sleeping Beauty's mother-in-law tries to have them served up stewed for the prince's supper, but he hears the silver bells sewn on his wife's seven skirts ringing, and saves everybody – except the mother-in-law – and they live happily ever after, in Calabria.

90

Italo Calvino, *Italian Folktales*, translated by George Martin (New York: Harcourt Brace Jovanovich, 1980; London: Penguin Books, 1980).

To find the moral, the message, the meaning of a folktale, to describe its "uses," even so circuitously as Bruno Bettelheim has done, is a risky business; it is like stating the meaning of a fish, the uses of a cat. The thing you are talking about is alive. It changes and is never quite what you thought it was, or ought to be.

One of the innumerable delights of *Italian Folktales* is its mixture of the deeply familiar with the totally unexpected.

Most of the basic "story-types," of which Calvino says there are about fifty represented here, are more or less familiar to members of the English folk literary tradition. The themes that recur in all Western folktales run through these; we meet the youngest son of the king, the wicked stepmother, the stupid giant, the helpful animals, the magic boots, the house of the winds, the well that leads to another world: people and places we all recognize, archetypal forms of our perception of life, according to Jung, embodiments of ideas as basic to our subjective existence as the ideas of extension, right/left, reversal, are to our existence in space. But the recombinations of these themes are mostly not familiar. This is much more than Cinderella served up with *salsa di pomodora*. The tales are endlessly surprising. And their mood is quite different from the elegance of the French *contes*, the iconic splendors of Russian *skazki*, the forest darknesses of German *Märchen*. Often they resemble the British tales of the Joseph Jacobs collections in their dry and zany humor, but they have more sunlight in them. Some are wonderfully beautiful. "The natural cruelties of the folktale give way to the rules of harmony," as Calvino says in his introduction.

> Although the notion of cruelty persists along with an injustice bordering on inhumanity as part of the constant stuff of stories, although the woods forever echo with the weeping of maidens or of forsaken brides with severed hands, gory ferocity is never gratuitous; the narrative does not dwell on the torment of the victim, not even under pretense of pity, but moves swiftly to a healing solution.

Italo Calvino's part in this book is not that of the eminent author condescending to honor a collection of popular tales with an introduction

– anything but. Essentially the book is to Italian literature what the Grimms' collection is to German literature. It is both the first and the standard. And its particular glory is that it was done, not by a scholar-specialist, but by a great writer of fiction. The author of *The Baron in the Trees* and *Invisible Cities* used all his skills to bring together the labors of collectors and scholars from all the regions of Italy, to translate the tales out of dialects into standard Italian, and to retell them:

> I selected from mountains of narratives . . . the most unusual, beautiful, and original texts . . . I enriched the text selected from other versions and whenever possible did so without altering its character or unity, and at the same time filled it out and made it more plastic. I touched up as delicately as possible those portions that were either missing or too sketchy.

With absolute sureness of touch Calvino selected, combined, rewove, reshaped, so that each tale and the entire collection would show at its best, clear and strong, without obscurity or repetition. As a teller of tales he had, of course, both the privilege and the responsibility to do so. He assumed his privilege without question and fulfilled his responsibility magnificently. One of the best storytellers alive telling us some of the best stories in the world – what luck!

Fiabe italiane was first published in Italy in 1956. My children grew up with a selected edition of them, *Italian Fables* (Orion Press, 1959). The book was presented for children, without notes, in a fine translation by Louis Brigante, just colloquial enough to be a joy to read aloud, and with line drawings by Michael Train that reflected the wit and spirit of the stories. Perhaps a reading-aloud familiarity with the cadences of this earlier translation has prejudiced my ear; anyhow I find George Martin's version heavier, often pedestrian, sometimes downright ugly. I don't hear the speaking voice of the storyteller in it, or feel the flow and assurance of words that were listened to by the writer as he wrote them. Nor does the occasional antique woodcut in the present edition add much to the stories. But the design of the book is handsome and generous, entirely appropriate to the work, which includes for the first time in English all the tales, as well as Calvino's complete introduction, and his notes (edited by himself for this edition) on each story. The notes illuminate his unobtrusive scholarship and explain his refashionings of the material, and the introduction contains some of the finest things said on folklore since Tolkien – such throwaway lines as:

> No doubt the moral function of the tale, in the popular conception, is to be sought not in the subject matter but in the very nature of the folktale, in the mere fact of telling and listening.

Come and listen, then. Come hear how a girl named Misfortune found her Fate on the seashore of Sicily:

> At the oven, Misfortune found the old woman, who was so foul, blear-eyed, and smelly that the girl was almost nauseated. "Dear Fate of mine, will you do me the honor of accepting – " she began, offering her the bread.
>
> "Away with you! Begone! Who asked you for bread?" And she turned her back on the girl.

But Misfortune persists in showing goodwill towards this nasty hag, and so we find how Fate may turn to Fairy by the magic of Fable.

> The Fate, who was growing tamer, came forward grumbling to take the bread. Then Misfortune reached out and grabbed her and proceeded to wash her with soap and water. Next she did her hair and dressed her up from head to foot in her new finery. The Fate at first writhed like a snake, but seeing herself all spick-and-span she became a different person entirely. "Listen to me, Misfortune," she said. "For your kindness to me, I'm making you a present of this little box," and she handed her a box as tiny as those which contain wax matches.

And what do you think Misfortune found in the little box?

World-Making

1981

I was invited to participate in a symposium called Lost Worlds and Future Worlds, at Stanford University in 1981. The text of my short contribution follows; a slightly garbled version of it was printed in Women Writers of the West Coast, *by Marilyn Yalom (Capra Press, 1983).*

We're supposed to be talking about world-making. The idea of making makes me think of making new. Making a new world: a different world: Middle Earth, say, or the planets of science fiction. That's the work of the fantastic imagination. Or there's making the world new: making the world different: a utopia or dystopia, the work of the political imagination.

But what about making the world, this world, the old one? That seems to be the province of the religious imagination, or of the will to survive (they may be the same thing). The old world is made new at the birth of every baby, and every New Year's Day, and every morning, and the Buddhist says at every instant.

That, in every practical sense, we make the world we inhabit is pretty well beyond question, but I leave it to the philosophers to decide whether we make it all from scratch – mmmm! tastes like a scratch world! but it's Bishop Berkeley's Cosmo-Mix! – or whether we patch it together by a more or less judicious selection of what strikes us as useful or entertaining in the inexhaustible chaos of the real.

In either case, what artists do is make a particularly skillful selection of fragments of cosmos, unusually useful and entertaining bits chosen and arranged to give an illusion of coherence and duration amidst the uncontrollable streaming of events. An artist makes the world her world. An artist makes her world the world. For a little while. For as long as it takes to look at or listen to or watch or read the work of art. Like a crystal, the work of art seems to contain the whole, and to imply eternity. And yet all it is is an explorer's sketch-map. A chart of shorelines on a foggy coast.

94

To make something is to invent it, to discover it, to uncover it, like Michelangelo cutting away the marble that hid the statue. Perhaps we think less often of the proposition reversed, thus: To discover something is to make it. As Julius Caesar said, "The existence of Britain was uncertain, until I went there." We can safely assume that the ancient Britons were perfectly certain of the existence of Britain, down to such details as where to go for the best woad. But, as Einstein said, it all depends on how you look at it, and as far as Rome, not Britain, is concerned, Caesar invented (*invenire*, "to come into, to come upon") Britain. He made it be, for the rest of the world.

Alexander the Great sat down and cried, somewhere in the middle of India, I think, because there were no more new worlds to conquer. What a silly man he was. There he sits sniveling, halfway to China! A conqueror. Conquistadores, always running into new worlds, and quickly running out of them. Conquest is not finding, and it is not making. Our culture, which conquered what is called the New World, and which sees the world of nature as an adversary to be conquered: look at us now. Running out of everything.

The name of our meeting is Lost Worlds and Future Worlds. Whether our ancestors came seeking gold, or freedom, or as slaves, we are the conquerors, we who live here now, in possession, in the New World. We are the inhabitants of a Lost World. It is utterly lost. Even the names are lost. The people who lived here, in this place, on these hills, for tens of thousands of years, are remembered (when they are remembered at all) in the language of the conquistadores: the "Costanos," the "Santa Claras," the "San Franciscos," names taken from foreign demigods. Sixty-three years ago, in the *Handbook of the Indians of California*, my father wrote:

> The Costanoan group is extinct so far as all practical purposes are concerned. A few scattered individuals survive ... The larger part of a century has passed since the missions were abolished, and nearly a century and a half since they commenced to be founded. These periods have sufficed to efface even traditional recollections of the forefathers' habits, except for occasional fragments.

Here is one such fragment, a song; they sang it here, under the live oaks, but there weren't any wild oats here then, only the Californian bunch-grasses. The people sang:

I dream of you,
I dream of you jumping,
Rabbit, jackrabbit, and quail.

And one line is left of a dancing song:

Dancing on the brink of the world.

With such fragments I might have shored my ruin, but I didn't know how. Only knowing that we must have a past to make a future with, I took what I could from the European-based culture of my own forefathers and mothers. I learned, like most of us, to use whatever I could, to filch an idea from China and steal a god from India, and so patch together a world as best I could. But still there is a mystery. This place where I was born and grew up and love beyond all other, my world, my California, still needs to be made. To make a new world you start with an old one, certainly. To find a world, maybe you have to have lost one. Maybe you have to be lost. The dance of renewal, the dance that made the world, was always danced here at the edge of things, on the brink, on the foggy coast.

The Princess

●

1982

I was asked to give a keynote address to open a workshop conference of the Portland branch of the National Abortion Rights Action League, in January of 1982.

You are going to be working hard today on very serious and urgent work, matters literally of life and death, so I thought it might be a good idea to fool around a little first. I am going to tell you a fairy tale.

Once upon a time, long, long ago, in the Dark Ages, there was a princess. She was wealthy, well fed, well educated, and well beloved. She went to a college for training female royalty, and there, at the associated college for training male royalty, she met a prince. He, too, was wealthy, well fed, well educated, and well beloved. And they fell in love with each other and had a really royal time.

Although the princess was on the Honors List and the prince was a graduate student, they were remarkably ignorant about some things. The princess's parents, though modest and even inhibited, had been responsible and informative: she knew all about how babies are made. She had read books about it. But it had not occurred to her parents or the people who wrote the books that she might need to know how to *keep from making babies.* This was long ago, remember, in the Dark Ages, before sex was obligatory, before the Pill. All she knew was that there was something called a rubber, and boys always sniggered when the Trojan War was mentioned in high school. The prince, of course, knew everything. He'd been around. He'd had sex since he was fifteen, he said. He knew you had to wear a condom the first time each night. But the second or third time each night, you didn't. It was safe. He knew that.

Perhaps you can imagine what happens next in this story? Like all fairy tales, it follows a familiar path; there is a certain inevitable quality to the events.

"We have to get married!" the princess said to the prince.

"I'm going home to my mother," the prince said to the princess. And he did. He went home to his family palace in Brooklyn Heights, and hid in the throne room.

The princess went to her family palace on Riverside Drive and cried a lot. She cried the Hudson River full of tears. But, though she had never been punished for anything in her life, she could not bring herself to tell her parents why she was crying. She made up a pretext to go to her mother's gynecologist and get a pregnancy test. They used rabbits; if the test was positive, the rabbit died; remember, this is the Dark Ages. The rabbit died. The princess didn't tell her parents, but went and dug the prince out and said, "We *really* have to get married."

"You're not a member of my religion, and anyhow, it's your baby," said the prince, and went back to Brooklyn Heights. And she went back home and cried so hard that her parents finally saw what had to be the matter. And they said, "O.K., it's O.K., honey, and if he won't marry you, you don't have to have the baby."

Now, you may recall that in the Dark Ages abortion was not legal. It was a crime, and not a minor one.

The princess's parents were not criminal types. They were the kind of people who obey the speed limit, and pay taxes and parking-ticket fines, and return borrowed books. I mean they were honest. They were neither square nor unsophisticated, they were not "religious," but they were intensely moral people, with a love of kindness and decency, and a strong respect for the law. And yet now, without hesitation, they resolved to break the law, to conspire to commit a felony. And they did so in the reasoned and deeply felt conviction that it was right, that indeed it was their *responsibility*, to do so.

The princess herself questioned the decision, not on legal grounds, of course, but ethically. She cried some more and said, "I'm being cowardly. I'm being dishonest. I'm evading the consequence of my own action."

Her father said, "That's right. You are. That cowardice, dishonesty, evasion, is a lesser sin than the crass irresponsibility of sacrificing your training, your talent, and the children you will want to have, in order to have one nobody wants to have."

He was a Victorian, you see, and a bit of a Puritan. He hated waste and wastefulness.

So the princess and her parents tried to find out how to get an abortion – and they got a little panicky, because they didn't know anybody who knew. The gynecologist got huffy when asked for a reference. "I don't handle A.B.'s," he said. After all, his license to a lucrative practice was at stake; he could have gone to jail; you can't blame him. It was an old family friend, a child psychologist, who finally found the right contact, the criminal connection. She made an appointment for "an examination."

They were really slick, that outfit. Dr. So-and-So. Nice office on the Lower East Side, polite smiling receptionist, *Esquire* and *National Geographic* on the waiting-room tables. Their reputation was "the highest-class abortionists in New York City," and it was probably deserved. They charged more for an abortion than most working families made in a year. This was no dirty backroom business. It was clean. It was class. They never said the word "abortion," not even that cute euphemism "A.B." The doctor offered to restore the hymen. "It's easy," he said. "No extra charge." The princess did not wish to be rebuilt like a Buick and said, "No. Get on with it." And they did. Did a fine job, I'm sure. As the princess left that office she passed a girl coming in, a college girl with red eyes and fear in her face, and she wanted to stop and say, "It's O.K., it's not so bad, don't be afraid," but she was afraid to. And she went back uptown in a taxi with her mother, both of them crying, partly out of grief, partly out of relief. "The endless sorrow . . ."

The princess went back to college to finish her degree. From time to time she would see the prince lurking and scuttling around behind the ivy on the buildings. I'm sure he has lived happily ever after. As for the princess, she got her B.A. a few months after she got her A.B., and then went on to graduate school, and then got married, and was a writer, and got pregnant by choice four times. One pregnancy ended in spontaneous abortion, miscarriage, in the third month; three pregnancies ended in live normal birth. She had three desired and beloved children, none of whom would have been born if her first pregnancy had gone to term.

If any birth is better than no birth, and more births are better than fewer births, as the "Right-to-Life" people insist, then they should approve of my abortion, which resulted in three babies instead of one. A curious but logical method of achieving their goal! But the preservation of life seems to be rather a slogan than a genuine goal of the anti-abortion forces; what they want is control. Control over behavior: power over women. Women in the anti-choice movement want to share in male power over women, and do so by denying their own womanhood, their own rights and responsibilities.

If there is a moral to my tale, it's something like this. In spite of everything the little princess had been taught by the male-supremacist elements of her society, by high-school scandals about why Sallie dropped out of school in March, by novels extolling motherhood as woman's sole function, by the gynecologist's furtiveness, by the existence of a law declaring abortion to be a crime, by the sleek extortionism of the abortionist – despite all those messages repeating ABORTION IS WRONG! – when the terror was past, she pondered it all, and she thought, "I have done the right thing."

What was wrong was not knowing how to prevent getting pregnant. What was wrong was my ignorance. To legislate that ignorance, that's the crime. I'm ashamed, she thought, for letting bigots keep me ignorant, and for acting willfully in my ignorance, and for falling in love with a weak, selfish man. I am deeply ashamed. But I'm not guilty. Where does guilt come in? I did what I had to do so that I could do the work I was put here to do. I will do that work. That's what it's all about. It's about taking responsibility.

So I thought at the time, not very clearly. That I can think more clearly about it now, and talk about it, to you and to others, is entirely due to the moral courage and strength of women and men who have been working these thirty years for the rights and dignity and freedom of women, including the right to abortion. They set me free, and I am here to thank them, and to promise solidarity.

Why did I tell you this tale, which is only too familiar? Well, I called myself a princess in it, partly for the joke, and partly because my parents were indeed royal, where it counts, in the soul; but also to keep reminding myself and you that *I was privileged.* I had "the best abortion in New York City." What was it like, in the Dark Ages when abortion was a crime, for the girl whose dad couldn't borrow the cash, as my dad could? What was it like for the girl who couldn't even tell her dad, because he'd go crazy with shame and rage? Who couldn't tell her *mother*? Who had to go alone to that filthy room and put herself body and soul into the hands of a professional criminal? – because that's what every doctor who did an abortion was, whether he was an extortionist or an idealist. You know what it was like for her. You know and I know; that's why we're here. We are not going back to the Dark Ages. We are not going to let anybody in this country have that kind of power over any girl or woman. There are great powers, outside the government and in it, trying to legislate the return of darkness. We are not great powers. But we are the light. Nobody can put us out. May all of you shine very bright and steady, today and always.

Facing It

●

1982

In December of 1982, the Portland Fellowship of Reconciliation held a symposium called Facing It. I was invited to join one of the panels and give a short talk about science fiction and how it faces the issue of nuclear war.

Modern science fiction begins with H. G. Wells, and as far as I know, it is also with Wells that the apocalypse, the end of the world, becomes a subject of fiction. The stories he called his "scientific romances" run the apocalyptic gamut, from a cometary Judgment Day followed by a very boring earthly paradise, to one of the most terribly beautiful nightmares of all fiction, the beach at the end of the world at the end of *The Time Machine*.

That great vision is the end as seen by science: entropy, the cold, dark chaos that is the target of Time's arrow. Usually, since Wells, the speculative storyteller has chosen a livelier finale. The sun goes nova, or aliens invade, or we perish from overpopulation or pollution or plague, or we mutate into higher forms, or whatever. Round about 1945 a specific kind of apocalypse, not surprisingly, became common in science fiction: the After-the-Bomb, or Post-Holocaust, story.

In the typical After-the-Bomb story, the characters are survivors of what is typically referred to as the Five-Minute War. Some of the options offered these survivors are:

1. Not to survive at all. The characters all kill each other off in the shelters and the ruins. Or, more tidily, as in *On the Beach*, they commit suicide.

2. To survive by killing and dominating other survivors who happen not to be Social Darwinists.

3. To survive by digging in and hanging on and battling mutant monsters with strange powers in the ruins of Chicago.

4. To survive by *being* mutants – often living a pleasant, rural life, far from the ruins of Chicago; kind of like Grandma Moses with telepathy.

5. To survive by leaving the Earth and getting away just in time in a space ship. These characters may sit by a canal on Mars and watch the rest of us go incandescent, or dwell for generations in their space ship, or colonize other planets; they certainly have the best options.

Many, many stories using these or similar scenarios were written and published between the late forties and the present. I wrote some myself, in the early sixties. Most of them were trivial, inadequate to their terrible subject. Some, like Walter Miller's *A Canticle for Leibowitz*, remain rich and durable works of imagination. The radioactive wasteland of glowing slagheaps populated by feral mutants is now a commonplace, perhaps a genuine archetype, available to beginners, hacks, film-makers, and the Collective Unconscious. Recently the Post-Holocaust story seems to be enjoying a revival, I should like to say thanks to President Reagan, but more honestly perhaps as a symptom of the world mood of which the Reagan presidency, and our presence here tonight, are also symptoms.

The Post-Holocaust story must be in part rehearsal, or acting out, variously motivated. One motivation is unmistakably desire. Rage, frustration, and infantile egoism play out the death wish: *Let's press that button and see what happens!* Another motivation is fear, the obsessive anxiety that keeps the mind upon the worst that could happen, dwelling on it, in the not entirely superstitious hope that *if I talk enough about it maybe it won't happen.* Rationally controlled, this fear motivates the cautionary tale: *Look what would happen if – ! so don't!* And the stories where people flee the Earth altogether would seem to be pure wish fulfillment, escapism.

Very few After-the-Bomb tales seem to have come out of South America, I wish I had time to speculate why; but a great many have come from America and England. (One might propose Samuel Beckett as the prophet of the post-apocalypse; his writings are drawn towards, yearn towards, the condition of utter silence.) European science-fiction writers have done their share, but across the Iron Curtain writers seem not to write about World War III. It may be the government demanding optimism, censoring speculation. Or perhaps those Russian and Polish science-fiction writers who are not timid yes-men, and often use their art to say quite subversive and unacceptable things, feel it ethically wrong to write about nuclear holocaust, because by doing so they would trivialize and familiarize the ultimate act of evil.

And this is a real issue, I think: the question of "the unspeakable." If one believes that words are acts, as I do, then one must hold writers responsible for what their words do.

The pornography of violence of course far exceeds, in volume and general acceptance, sexual pornography, in this Puritan land of ours. Exploiting the apocalypse, selling the holocaust, is a pornography; the power fantasies of the survivalists, which seem to originate in certain works of science fiction such as Robert Heinlein's *Farnham's Freehold*, are pornographic. But for the ultimate selling job on ultimate violence one must read those works of fiction issued by our government as manuals of civil defense, in which, as a friend of mine puts it, you learn that there's nothing to be afraid of if you've stockpiled lots of dried fruit.

The question is that of false reassurance. Is the writer "facing it" or, by pretending to face it, evading, lying? In many cases it's not easy to decide. Those stories in which Life Goes On, even though two-headed and glowing faintly in the dark, may be seen as false reassurance or may find justification in the necessity of hope. However ill-founded, however misguided, hope is the basic stratagem of mortality. We need it, and an art that fails to offer it fails us.

Still, I see much current fantasy and science fiction in full retreat from real human needs. Where a Tolkien prophetically faced the central fact of our time, our capacity to destroy ourselves, the present spate of so-called heroic fantasy, in which Good defeats Evil by killing it with a sword or staff or something phallic, seems to have nothing in mind beyond instant gratification, the avoidance of discomfort, in a fake-medieval past where technology is replaced by magic and wishful thinking works. But the science-fiction books about endless wars in space, where technology *is* magic and the killing proceeds without moral or psychological justification of any kind, probably are written from the same unadmitted despair. The future has become uninhabitable. Such hopelessness can arise, I think, only from an inability to face the present, to live in the present, to live as a responsible being among other beings in this sacred world here and now, which is all we have, and all we need, to found our hope upon.

A Non-Euclidean View of California
as a Cold Place to Be

●

1982/1983

Robert C. Elliott died in 1981 in the very noon of his scholarship, just after completing his book *The Literary Persona*. He was the truest of teachers, the kindest of friends. This paper was prepared to be read as the first in a series of lectures at his college of the University of California, San Diego, honoring his memory.

We use the French word *lecture*, "reading," to mean reading and speaking aloud, a performance; the French call such a performance not a *lecture* but a *conférence*. The distinction is interesting. Reading is a silent collaboration of reader and writer, apart; lecturing, a noisy collaboration of lecturer and audience, together. The peculiar patchwork form of this paper is my attempt to make it a "conference," a performable work, a piece for voices. The time and place, a warm April night in La Jolla in 1982, are past, and the warm and noisy audience must be replaced by the gentle reader; but the first voice is still that of Bob Elliott.

In *The Shape of Utopia*, speaking of our modern distrust of utopia, he said,

> If the word is to be redeemed, it will have to be by someone who has followed utopia into the abyss which yawns behind the Grand Inquisitor's vision, and who then has clambered out on the other side.[1]

That is my starting point, that startling image; and my motto is:

Usà puyew usu wapiw!

We shall be returning to both, never fear; what I am about here is returning.

In the first chapter of *The Shape of Utopia*, Bob points out that in the

---

1 Robert C. Elliott, *The Shape of Utopia* (Chicago: University of Chicago Press, 1970).

great participatory festivals such as Saturnalia, Mardi Gras, or Christmas, the age of peace and equality, the Golden Age, may be lived in an interval set apart for it, a time outside of daily time. But to bring perfect *communitas* into the structure of ordinary society would be a job only Zeus could handle; or, "if one does not believe in Zeus's good will, or even in his existence," says Bob, it becomes a job for the mind of man.

> Utopia is the application of man's reason and his will to the myth [of the Golden Age], man's effort to work out imaginatively what happens – or might happen – when the primal longings embodied in the myth confront the principle of reality. In this effort man no longer merely dreams of a divine state in some remote time: he assumes the role of creator.[2]

Now, the Golden Age, or Dream Time, is remote only from the rational mind. It is not accessible to euclidean reason; but on the evidence of all myth and mysticism, and the assurance of every participatory religion, it is, to those with the gift or discipline to perceive it, right here, right now. Whereas it is of the very essence of the rational or Jovian utopia that it is *not* here and *not* now. It is made by the reaction of will and reason against, away from, the here-and-now, and it is, as More said in naming it, nowhere. It is pure structure without content; pure model; goal. That is its virtue. Utopia is uninhabitable. As soon as we reach it, it ceases to be utopia. As evidence of this sad but ineluctable fact, may I point out that we in this room, here and now, are inhabiting utopia.

I was told as a child, and like to believe, that California was named "The Golden State" not just for the stuff Sutter found but for the wild poppies on its hills and the wild oats of summer. To the Spanish and Mexicans I gather it was the boondocks; but to the Anglos it has been a true utopia: the Golden Age made accessible by willpower, the wild paradise to be tamed by reason; the place where you go free of the old bonds and cramps, leaving behind your farm and your galoshes, casting aside your rheumatism and your inhibitions, taking up a new "life style" in a not-here-not-now where everybody gets rich quick in the movies or finds the meaning of life or anyhow gets a good tan hang-gliding. And the wild oats and the poppies still come up pure gold in cracks in the cement that we have poured over utopia.

---

2 Ibid.

In "assuming the role of creator," we seek what Lao Tzu calls "the profit of what is not," rather than participating in what is. To reconstruct the world, to rebuild or rationalize it, is to run the risk of losing or destroying what in fact is.

After all, California was not empty when the Anglos came. Despite the efforts of the missionaries, it was still the most heavily populated region in North America.

What the Whites perceived as a wilderness to be "tamed" was in fact better known to human beings than it has ever been since: known and named. Every hill, every valley, creek, canyon, gulch, gully, draw, point, cliff, bluff, beach, bend, good-sized boulder, and tree of any character had its name, its place in the order of things. An order was perceived, of which the invaders were entirely ignorant. Each of those names named, not a goal, not a place to get to, but a place where one is: a center of the world. There were centers of the world all over California. One of them is a bluff on the Klamath River. Its name was Katimin. The bluff is still there, but it has no name, and the center of the world is not there. The six directions can meet only in lived time, in the place people call home, the seventh direction, the center.

But we leave home, shouting Avanti! and Westward Ho!, driven by our godlike reason, which chafes at the limited, intractable, unreasonable present, and yearns to free itself from the fetters of the past.

"People are always shouting they want to create a better future," says Milan Kundera, in *The Book of Laughter and Forgetting*.

> It's not true. The future is an apathetic void of no interest to anyone. The past is full of life, eager to irritate us, provoke and insult us, tempt us to destroy or repaint it. The only reason people want to be masters of the future is to change the past.[3]

And at the end of the book he talks to the interviewer about forgetting: forgetting is

> the great private problem of man: death as the loss of the self. But what is this self? It is the sum of everything we remember. Thus, what

---

3 Milan Kundera, *The Book of Laughter and Forgetting* (London: Faber & Faber Ltd, 1982).

terrifies us about death is not the loss of the future but the loss of the past.[4]

And so, Kundera says, when a big power wants to deprive a smaller one of its national identity, of its self-consciousness, it uses what he calls the "method of organized forgetting."

And when a future-oriented culture impinges upon a present-centered one, the method becomes a compulsion. Things are forgotten wholesale. What are the names "Costanoan," "Wappo"? They are what the Spanish called the people around the Bay Area and in the Napa Valley, but what those people called themselves we do not know: the names were forgotten even before the people were wiped out. There was no past. Tabula rasa.

One of our finest methods of organized forgetting is called discovery. Julius Caesar exemplifies the technique with characteristic elegance in his *Gallic Wars*. "It was not certain that Britain existed," he says, "until I went there."

To whom was it not certain? But what the heathen know doesn't count. Only if godlike Caesar sees it can Britannia rule the waves.

Only if a European discovered or invented it could America exist. At least Columbus had the wit, in his madness, to mistake Venezuela for the outskirts of Paradise. But he remarked on the availability of cheap slave labor in Paradise.

The first chapter of *California: An Interpretive History*, by Professor Walton Bean, contains this paragraph:

> The survival of a Stone Age culture in California was not the result of any hereditary biological limitations on the potential of the Indians as a "race." They had been geographically and culturally isolated. The vast expanse of oceans, mountains, and deserts had sheltered California from foreign stimulation as well as from foreign conquest...

(being isolated from contact and protected from conquest are, you will have noticed, characteristics of utopia),

> ... and even within California the Indian groups were so settled that they had little contact with each other. On the positive side, there was

---

4 Ibid.

something to be said for their culture just as it was ... The California Indians had made a successful adaptation to their environment and they had learned to live without destroying each other.[5]

Professor Bean's excellent book is superior to many of its kind in the area of my particular interest: the first chapter. Chapter One of the American history – South or North America, national or regional – is usually short. Unusually short. In it, the "tribes" that "occupied" the area are mentioned and perhaps anecdotally described. In Chapter Two, a European "discovers" the area; and with a gasp of relief the historian plunges into a narration of the conquest, often referred to as settlement or colonization, and the acts of the conquerors. Since history has traditionally been defined by historians as the written record, this imbalance is inevitable. And in a larger sense it is legitimate; for the non-urban peoples of the Americas had no history, properly speaking, and therefore are visible only to the anthropologist, not to the historian, except as they entered into White history.

The imbalance is unavoidable, legitimate, and also, I believe, very dangerous. It expresses too conveniently the conquerors' wish to deny the value of the cultures they destroyed, and dehumanize the people they killed. It partakes too much of the method of organized forgetting. To call this "the New World" – there's a Caesarian birth!

The words "holocaust" and "genocide" are fashionable now; but not often are they applied to American history. We were not told in school in Berkeley that the history of California had the final solution for its first chapter. We were told that the Indians "gave way" before the "march of progress."

In the introduction to *The Wishing Bone Cycle*, Howard A. Norman says:

The Swampy Cree have a conceptual term which I've heard used to describe the thinking of a porcupine as he backs into a rock crevice:

Usà puyew usu wapiw.

"He goes backward, looks forward." The porcupine consciously goes backward in order to speculate safely on the future, allowing him to look

---

5 Walton Bean, *California: An Interpretive History* (New York: McGraw-Hill, 1968).

out at his enemy or the new day. To the Cree, it's an instructive act of self-preservation.[6]

The opening formula for a Cree story is "an invitation to listen, followed by the phrase, 'I go backward, look forward, as the porcupine does.'"[7]

In order to speculate safely on an inhabitable future, perhaps we would do well to find a rock crevice and go backward. In order to find our roots, perhaps we should look for them where roots are usually found. At least the Spirit of Place is a more benign one than the exclusive and aggressive Spirit of Race, the mysticism of blood that has cost so much blood. With all our self-consciousness, we have very little sense of where we live, where we are right here right now. If we did, we wouldn't muck it up the way we do. If we did, our literature would celebrate it. If we did, our religion might be participatory. If we did – if we really lived here, now, in this present – we might have some sense of our future as a people. We might know where the center of the world is.

> ... Ideally, at its loftiest and most pure, the utopia aspires to (if it has never reached) the condition of the idyll as Schiller describes it – that mode of poetry which would lead man, not back to Arcadia, but forward to Elysium, to a state of society in which man would be at peace with himself and the external world.[8]

> The California Indians had made a successful adaptation to their environment and they had learned to live without destroying each other.[9]

It was Arcadia, of course; it was not Elysium. I heed Victor Turner's warning not to confuse archaic or primitive societies with the true *communitas*, "which is a dimension of all societies, past and present."[10] I am not proposing a return to the Stone Age. My intent is not reactionary, nor even conservative, but simply subversive. It seems that the utopian imagination is trapped, like capitalism and industrialism and the human population, in

---

6 Howard A. Norman, introduction to *The Wishing Bone Cycle* (New York: Stonehill Publishing Co., 1979).

7 Ibid.

8 Elliott..

9 Bean.

10 Victor W. Turner, *The Ritual Process: Structure and Anti-Structure* (Chicago: Aldine Publishing Co., 1969).

a one-way future consisting only of growth. All I'm trying to do is figure
how to put a pig on the tracks.

Go backward. Turn and return.

If the word [utopia] is to be redeemed, it will have to be by someone
who has followed utopia into the abyss which yawns behind the Grand
Inquisitor's vision.[11]

The utopia of the Grand Inquisitor

is the product of "the euclidean mind" (a phrase Dostoyevsky often
used), which is obsessed by the idea of regulating all life by reason and
bringing happiness to man whatever the cost.[12]

The single vision of the Grand Inquisitor perceives the condition of man
in a way stated with awful clarity by Yevgeny Zamyatin, in *We*:

There were two in paradise, and the choice was offered to them: happiness without freedom, or freedom without happiness. No other choice.[13]

No other choice. Hear now the voice of Urizen!

Hidden, set apart in my stern counsels
Reserved for days of futurity,
I have sought for a joy without pain,
For a solid without fluctuation . . .

Lo, I unfold my darkness and on
This rock place with strong hand the book
Of eternal brass, written in my solitude.

Laws of peace, of love, of unity,
Of pity, compassion, forgiveness.
Let each choose one habitation,
His ancient infinite mansion,

---

11 Elliott.
12 Ibid.
13 Quoted in Elliott.

One command, one joy, one desire,
One curse, one weight, one measure,
One King, one God, one Law.[14]

In order to believe in utopia, Bob Elliott said, we must believe

> that through the exercise of their reason men can control and in major
> ways alter for the better their social environment ... One must have
> faith of a kind that our history has made nearly inaccessible.[15]

"When the Way is lost," Lao Tzu observed in a rather similar historical
situation a few thousand years earlier,

> there is benevolence. When benevolence is lost there is justice. When
> justice is lost there are the rites. The rites are the end of loyalty and good
> faith, the beginning of disorder.[16]

"Prisons," said William Blake, "are built with stones of Law."[17] And coming
back round to the Grand Inquisitor, we have Milan Kundera restating the
dilemma of Happiness versus Freedom:

> Totalitarianism is not only hell, but also the dream of paradise – the
> age-old dream of a world where everybody would live in harmony,
> united by a single common will and faith, without secrets from one
> another ... If totalitarianism did not exploit these archetypes, which are
> deep inside us all and rooted deep in all religions, it could never attract
> so many people, especially during the early phases of its existence. Once
> the dream of paradise starts to turn into reality, however, here and there
> people begin to crop up who stand in its way, and so the rulers of
> paradise must build a little gulag on the side of Eden. In the course of
> time this gulag grows ever bigger and more perfect, while the adjoining
> paradise gets ever smaller and poorer.[18]

---

14 William Blake, *The Book of Urizen*.
15 Elliott.
16 Lao Tzu, *Tao Teh Ching*.
17 William Blake, *The Marriage of Heaven and Hell*, Book III, *Proverbs of Heaven and Hell*.
18 Kundera.

The purer, the more euclidean the reason that builds a utopia, the greater is its self-destructive capacity. I submit that our lack of faith in the benevolence of reason as the controlling power is well founded. We must test and trust our reason, but to have *faith* in it is to elevate it to godhead. Zeus the Creator takes over. Unruly Titans are sent to the salt mines, and inconvenient Prometheus to the reservation. Earth itself comes to be the wart on the walls of Eden.

The rationalist utopia is a power trip. It is a monotheocracy, declared by executive decree, and maintained by willpower; as its premise is progress, not process, it has no habitable present, and speaks only in the future tense. And in the end reason itself must reject it.

"O that I had never drank the wine nor eat the bread
Of dark mortality, nor cast my view into futurity, nor turned
My back darkening the present, clouding with a cloud,
And building arches high and cities, turrets and towers and domes
Whose smoke destroyed the pleasant garden, and whose running
    kennels
Choked the bright rivers . . .

Then go, O dark futurity! I will cast thee forth from these
Heavens of my brain, nor will I look upon futurity more.
I cast futurity away, and turn my back upon that void
Which I have made, for lo! futurity is in this moment . . ."

So Urizen spoke . . .

Then, glorious bright, exulting in his joy,
He sounding rose into the heavens, in naked majesty,
In radiant youth . . .[19]

That is certainly the high point of this paper. I wish we could follow Urizen in his splendid vertical jailbreak, but it is a route reserved to the major poets and composers. The rest of us must stay down here on the ground, walking in circles, proposing devious side trips, and asking impertinent questions. My question now is: Where is the place Coyote made?

---

19 William Blake, *Vala, or the Four Zoas.*

In a paper about teaching utopia, Professor Kenneth Roemer says:

The importance of this question was forced upon me several years ago
in a freshman comp course at the University of Texas at Arlington. I
asked the class to write a paper in response to a hypothetical situation: if
you had unlimited financial resources and total local, state, and national
support, how would you transform Arlington, Texas, into utopia? A few
minutes after the class had begun to write, one of the students – a
mature and intelligent woman in her late thirties – approached my desk.
She seemed embarrassed, even upset. She asked, "What if I believe that
Arlington, Texas, *is* utopia?"[20]

What do you do with *her* in Walden Two?

Utopia has been euclidean, it has been European, and it has been
masculine. I am trying to suggest, in an evasive, distrustful, untrustworthy
fashion, and as obscurely as I can, that our final loss of faith in that radiant
sandcastle may enable our eyes to adjust to a dimmer light and in it perceive
another kind of utopia. As this utopia would not be euclidean, European,
or masculinist, my terms and images in speaking of it must be tentative
and seem peculiar. Victor Turner's antitheses of structure and *communitas*
are useful to my attempt to think about it: structure in society, in his terms,
is cognitive, *communitas* existential; structure provides a model, *communitas*
a potential; structure classifies, *communitas* reclassifies; structure is expressed
in legal and political institutions, *communitas* in art and religion.

Communitas breaks in through the interstices of structure, in liminality;
at the edges of structure, in marginality; and from beneath structure, in
inferiority. It is almost everywhere held to be sacred or "holy," possibly
because it transgresses or dissolves the norms that govern structured
or institutionalized relationships and is accompanied by experiences of
unprecedented potency.[21]

Utopian thought has often sought to institutionalize or legislate the experience of *communitas*, and each time it has done so it has run up against
the Grand Inquisitor.

---

20 Kenneth Roemer, "Using Utopia to Teach the Eighties," *World Future Society Bulletin* (July –
August 1980).
21 Turner.

The activities of a machine are determined by its structure, but the relation is reversed in organisms – organic structure is determined by its processes.[22]

That is Fritjof Capra, providing another useful analogy. If the attempt to provide a structure that will ensure *communitas* is impaled on the horns of its own dilemma, might one not abandon the machine model and have a go at the organic – permitting process to determine structure? But to do so is to go even further than the Anarchists, and to risk not only being called but being in fact regressive, politically naive, Luddite, and anti-rational. Those are real dangers (though I admit that the risk of being accused of not being in the Main Current of Western Thought is one I welcome the opportunity to run). What kind of utopia can come out of these margins, negations, and obscurities?* Who will even recognize it as a utopia? It won't look the way it ought to. It may look very like some kind of place Coyote made after having a conversation with his own dung.

The symbol which Trickster embodies is not a static one.

Paul Radin speaking. You will recall that the quality of static perfection is an essential element of the non-inhabitability of the euclidean utopia (a point that Bob Elliott discusses with much cogency). And he never was in Eden, because coyotes live in the New World. Driven forth by the angel with the flaming sword, Eve and Adam lifted their sad heads and saw Coyote, grinning.

The symbol which Trickster embodies is not a static one. It contains

---

22 Fritjof Capra, *The Turning Point* (London: Wildwood House).

*When I was struggling with the writing of this piece, I had not read the four volumes of Robert Nichols' *Daily Lives in Nghsi-Altai* (New York: New Directions, 1977–79). I am glad that I had not, because my thoughts could not then have so freely and fecklessly coincided, collided, and intersected with his. My paper would have been written in the consciousness of the existence of Nghsi-Altai, as Pierre Menard's *Quixote* was written in the consciousness of the existence of Cervantes' *Quixote*, and might have been even more different from what it is than Menard's *Quixote* from Cervantes'. But it can be and I hope will be *read* in the consciousness of the existence of Nghsi-Altai; and the fact that Nghsi-Altai is in some respects the very place I was laboriously trying to get to, and yet lies in quite the opposite direction, can only enlarge the use and meaning of my work. Indeed, if this note leads some readers to go find Nghsi-Altai for themselves, the whole thing will have been worthwhile.

within itself the promise of differentiation, the promise of god and man. For this reason every generation occupies itself with interpreting Trickster anew. No generation understands him fully but no generation can do without him ... for he represents not only the undifferentiated and distant past, but likewise the undifferentiated present within every individual ... If we laugh at him, he grins at us. What happens to him happens to us.[23]

Non-European, non-euclidean, non-masculinist: they are all negative definitions, which is all right, but tiresome; and the last is unsatisfactory, as it might be taken to mean that the utopia I'm trying to approach could only be imagined by women – which is possible – or only inhabited by women – which is intolerable. Perhaps the word I need is yin.

Utopia has been yang. In one way or another, from Plato on, utopia has been the big yang motorcycle trip. Bright, dry, clear, strong, firm, active, aggressive, lineal, progressive, creative, expanding, advancing, and hot.

Our civilization is now so intensely yang that any imagination of bettering its injustices or eluding its self-destructiveness must involve a reversal.

> The ten thousand things arise together
> and I watch their return.
> They return each to its root.
> Returning to one's roots is known as stillness.
> Returning to one's destiny is known as the constant.
> Knowledge of the constant is known as discernment.
> To ignore the constant
> is to go wrong, and end in disorder.[24]

To attain the constant, to end in order, we must return, go round, go inward, go yinward. What would a yin utopia be? It would be dark, wet, obscure, weak, yielding, passive, participatory, circular, cyclical, peaceful, nurturant, retreating, contracting, and cold.

Now on the subject of heat and cold: a reference in *The Shape of Utopia*

---

23 Paul Radin, *The Trickster* (New York: Philosophical Library, 1956).
24 Lao Tzu, Book I, Chapter 16.

sent me to a 1960 lecture by M. Lévi-Strauss, "The Scope of Anthropology," which so influenced my efforts to think out this paper that I wish to quote from it at some length, with apologies to those of you to whom the passage[25] is familiar. He is speaking of "primitive" societies.

> Although they exist in history, these societies seem to have worked out or retained a certain wisdom which makes them desperately resist any structural modification which might afford history a point of entry into their lives. The societies which have best protected their distinctive character appear to be those concerned above all with persevering in their existence.

Persevering in one's existence is the particular quality of the organism; it is not a progress towards achievement, followed by stasis, which is the machine's mode, but an interactive, rhythmic, and unstable process, which constitutes an end in itself.

> The way in which they exploit the environment guarantees them a modest standard of living as well as the conservation of natural resources. Though various, their rules of marriage reveal to the demographer's eye a common function; to set the fertility rate very low, and to keep it constant. Finally, a political life based upon consent, and admitting of no decisions but those arrived at unanimously, would seem designed to preclude the possibility of calling on that driving force of collective life which takes advantage of the contrast between power and opposition, majority and minority, exploiter and exploited.

Lévi-Strauss is about to make his distinction between the "hot" societies, which have appeared since the Neolithic Revolution, and in which "differentiations between castes and between classes are urged without cease, in order that social change and energy may be extracted from them," and the "cold" societies, self-limited, whose historical temperature is pretty near zero.

The relevance of this beautiful piece of anthropological thinking to my subject is immediately proven by Lévi-Strauss himself, who in the next

---

25 Claude Lévi-Strauss, *The Scope of Anthropology* (London: Jonathan Cape, 1968). Also included in *Structural Anthropology II* (New York: Basic Books, 1976). The version here is my own amalgam of the two translations.

paragraph thanks Heaven that anthropologists are not expected to predict man's future, but says that if they were, instead of merely extrapolating from our own "hot" society, they might propose a progressive integration of the best of the "hot" with the best of the "cold."

If I understand him, this unification would involve carrying the Industrial Revolution, already the principal source of social energy, to its logical extreme: the completed Electronic Revolution. After this, change and progress would be strictly cultural and, as it were, machine-made.

> With culture having integrally taken over the burden of manufacturing progress, society . . ., placed outside and above history, could once more assume that regular and as it were crystalline structure, which the surviving primitive societies teach us is not antagonistic to the human condition.

The last phrase, from that austere and somber mind, is poignant.

As I understand it, Lévi-Strauss suggests that to combine the hot and the cold is to transfer mechanical operational modes to machines while retaining organic modes for humanity. Mechanical progress; biological rhythm. A kind of superspeed electronic yang train, in whose yin pullmans and dining cars life is serene and the rose on the table does not even tremble. What worries me in this model is the dependence upon cybernetics as the integrating function. Who's up there in the engineer's seat? Is it on auto? Who wrote the program – old Nobodaddy Reason again? Is it another of those trains with no brakes?

It may simply be the bad habits of my mind that see in this brief utopian glimpse a brilliant update of an old science-fiction theme: the world where robots do the work while the human beings sit back and play. These were always satirical works. The rule was that either an impulsive young man wrecked the machinery and saved humanity from stagnation, or else the machines, behaving with impeccable logic, did away with the squashy and superfluous people. The first and finest of the lot, E. M. Forster's "The Machine Stops," ends on a characteristic double chord of terror and promise: the machinery collapses, the crystalline society is shattered with it, but outside there are free people – how civilized, we don't know, but outside and free.

We're back to Kundera's wart on the walls of Eden – the exiles from paradise in whom the hope of paradise lies, the inhabitants of the gulag who are the only free souls. The information systems of the train are marvelous, but the tracks run through Coyote country.

> In ancient times the Yellow Emperor first used benevolence and righteousness and meddled with the minds of men. Yao and Shun followed him and worked till there was no more hair on their shins ... in the practice of benevolence and righteousness, taxed their blood and breath in the establishment of laws and standards. But still some would not submit to their rule, and had to be exiled, driven away ... The world coveted knowledge, ... there were axes and saws to shape things, ink and plumblines to trim them, mallets and gouges to poke holes in them, and the world, muddled and deranged, was in great confusion.[26]

That is Chuang Tzu, the first great Trickster of philosophy, sending a raspberry to the Yellow Emperor, the legendary model of rational control. Things were hot in Chuang Tzu's day, too, and he proposed a radical cooling-off. The best understanding, he said, "rests in what it cannot understand. If you do not understand this, then Heaven the Equalizer will destroy you."[27]*

Having copied out this sentence, I obeyed, letting my understanding rest in what it could not understand, and went to the *I Ching*. I asked that book please to describe a yin utopia for me. It replied with Hexagram 30, the doubled trigram Fire, with a single changing line in the first place taking me to Hexagram 56, the Wanderer. The writing of the rest of this paper and the revisions of it were considerably influenced by a continuing rumination of those texts.

If utopia is a place that does not exist, then surely (as Lao Tzu would say) the way to get there is by the way that is not a way. And in the same vein, the nature of the utopia I am trying to describe is such that if it is to come, it must exist already.

I believe that it does:† most clearly as an element in such deeply

---

26 *The Complete Works of Chuang Tzu*, trans. Burton Watson (New York: Columbia University Press, 1968).
27 Ibid.
* "Heaven the Equalizer" was translated by James Legge as "the Lathe of Heaven," a fine phrase, from which I have got considerable mileage; but Joseph Needham has gently pointed out to me that when Chuang Tzu was writing the Chinese had not yet invented the lathe. Fortunately we now have Burton Watson's wonderfully satisfying translation to turn to.
† In Nghsi-Altai – partly.

unsatisfactory utopian works as Hudson's *A Crystal World* or Aldous Huxley's *Island*. Indeed Bob Elliott ended his book on utopia with a discussion of *Island*. Huxley's "extraordinary achievement," he says, "is to have made the old utopian goal – the central human goal – thinkable once more."[28] Those are the last words of the book. It is very like Bob that they should be not the closing but the opening of a door.

The major utopic element in my novel *The Dispossessed* is a variety of pacifist anarchism, which is about as yin as a political ideology can get. Anarchism rejects the identification of civilization with the state, and the identification of power with coercion; against the inherent violence of the "hot" society it asserts the value of such antisocial behavior as the general refusal of women to bear arms in war, and other coyote devices. In these areas anarchism and Taoism converge both in matter and manner, and so I came there to play my fictional games. The structure of the book may suggest the balance-in-motion and rhythmic recurrence of the Tai Chi, but its excess yang shows: though the utopia was (both in fact and in fiction) founded by a woman, the protagonist is a man; and he dominates it in, I must say, a very masculine fashion. Fond as I am of him, I'm not going to let him talk here. I want to hear a different voice. This is Lord Dorn, addressing the Council of his country, on June 16, 1906. He is talking not to, but about, us.

> With them the son and the father are of different civilizations and are strangers to each other. They move too fast to see more than the surface glitter of a life too swift to be real. They are assailed by too many new things ever to find the depths in the old before it has gone by. The rush of life past them they call progress, though it is too rapid for them to move with it. Man remains the same, baffled and astonished, with a heap of new things around him but gone before he knows them. Men may live many sorts of lives, and this they call "opportunity," and believe opportunity good without ever examining any one of those lives to know if it is good. We have fewer ways of life and most of us never know but one. It is a rich way, and its richness we have not yet exhausted . . . They cannot be blamed for seeing nothing good in us that will be destroyed by them. The good we have they do not understand, or even see.[29]

---

28 Elliott.

29 Austin Tappan Wright, *Islandia* (New York: Alfred A. Knopf, 1942).

Now, this speech might have been made in the council of any non-Western nation or people at the time of its encounter with Europeans in numbers. This could be a Kikuyu talking, or a Japanese – and certainly Japan's decision to Westernize was in the author's mind – and it is almost painfully close to the observations of Black Elk, Standing Bear, Plenty-Coups, and other native North American spokesmen.

Islandia is not a hot but a warm society: it has a definite though flexible class hierarchy, and has adopted some elements of industrial technology; it certainly has and is conscious of its history, though it has not yet entered into world history, mainly because, like California, it is geographically marginal and remote. In this central debate at the Council of Islandia, the hinge of the book's plot and structure, a deliberate choice is made to get no hotter: to reject the concept of progress as a wrong direction, and to accept persevering in one's existence as a completely worthy social goal.

In how many other utopias is this choice rationally propounded, argued, and made?

It is easy to dismiss *Islandia* as a mere fantasy of the Golden Age, naively escapist or regressive. I believe it is a mistake to do so, and that the options it offers are perhaps more realistic and more urgent than those of most utopias.

Here is M. Lévi-Strauss once more, this time on the subject of viruses:

The reality of a virus is almost of an intellectual order. In effect, its organism is reduced practically to the genetic formula that it injects into simple or complex beings, thus forcing their cells to betray their characteristic formula in order to obey its own and to manufacture beings like itself.

In order for our civilization to appear, the previous and simultaneous existence of other civilizations was necessary. And we know, since Descartes, that its originality consists essentially of a method which, because of its intellectual nature, is not suited to generating other civilizations of flesh and blood, but one which can impose its formula on them and force them to become like it. In comparison with these civilizations – whose living art expresses their corporeal quality because it relates to very intense beliefs and, in its conception as much as in its execution, to a certain state of equilibrium between man and nature – does our own civilization correspond to an animal or a viral type?[30]

---

30 Lévi-Strauss, "Art in 1985," in *Structural Anthropology II*.

This is the virus that Lord Dorn saw carried by the most innocent tourist from Europe or the United States: a plague against which his people had no immunity. Was he wrong?

Any small society that tried to make Lord Dorn's choice has, in fact, been forcibly infected; and the big, numerous civilizations – Japan, India, and now China – have either chosen to infect themselves with the viral fever or have failed to make any choice, all too often mixing the most exploitive features of the hot world with the most passive of the cold in a way that almost guarantees the impossibility of their persevering in their own existence or allowing local nature to continue in health. I wanted to speak of *Islandia* because I know no other utopian work that takes for its central intellectual concern this matter of "Westernization" or "progress," which is perhaps the central fact of our times. Of course the book provides no answer or solution; it simply indicates the way that cannot be gone. It is an enantiodromia, a *reculer pour mieux sauter*, a porcupine backing into a crevice. It goes sideways. That's very likely why it gets left out of the survey courses in Utopian Lit. But side trips and reversals are precisely what minds stuck in forward gear most need, and in its very quality of forswearing "futurity," of standing aside – and of having been left aside – *Islandia* is, I suggest, a valuable as well as an endearing book.

It is to some degree a Luddite book as well; and I am forced now to ask: Is it our high technology that gives our civilization its invasive, self-replicating, mechanical forward drive? In itself, any technology is "infectious" only as other useful or impressive elements of culture are; ideas, institutions, fashions too, may be self-replicating and irresistibly imitable. Obviously, technology is an essential element of all cultures and very often, in the form of potsherds or bits of styrofoam, all they leave behind in time. It is far too basic to all civilization to be characterized in itself as either yin or yang, I think. But at this point, here and now, the continuously progressing character of our technology, and the continuous change that depends upon it – "the manufacture of progress," as Lévi-Strauss called it – is the principal vehicle of the yang, or "hotness," of our society.

One need not smash one's typewriter and go bomb the laundromat, after all, because one has lost faith in the continuous advance of technology as the way towards utopia. Technology remains, in itself, an endless creative source. I only wish that I could follow Lévi-Strauss in seeing it as leading from the civilization that turns men into machines to "the civilization that will turn machines into men."[31] But I cannot. I do not see how even the almost ethereal technologies promised by electronics and information theory can offer more than the promise of the simplest tool: to make life materially easier, to enrich us. That is a great promise and gain! But if this enrichment of one type of civilization occurs only at the cost of the destruction of all other species and their inorganic matrix of earth, water, and air, and at increasingly urgent risk to the existence of all life on the planet, then it seems fairly clear to me that to count upon technological advance for *anything but* technological advance is a mistake. I have not been convincingly shown, and seem to be totally incapable of imagining for myself, how any further technological advance of any kind will bring us any closer to being a society predominantly concerned with preserving its existence; a society with a modest standard of living, conservative of natural resources, with a low constant fertility rate and a political life based upon consent; a society that has made a successful adaptation to its environment and has learned to live without destroying itself or the people next door. But that is the society I want to be able to imagine – I must be able to imagine, for one does not get on without hope.

What are we offered by way of hope? Models, plans, blueprints, wiring diagrams. Prospects of ever more inclusive communications systems linking virus to virus all over the globe – no secrets, as Kundera says. Little closed orbiting test-tubes full of viruses, put up by the L-5 Society, in perfect obedience to our compulsion to, as they say, "build the future" – to be Zeus, to have power over what happens, to control. Knowledge is power, and we want to know what comes next, we want it all mapped out.

Coyote country has not been mapped. The way that cannot be gone is not in the road atlas, or is every road in the atlas.

In the *Handbook of the Indians of California*, A. L. Kroeber wrote, "The California Indians ... usually refuse pointblank to make even an attempt [to draw a map], alleging utter inability."[32]

The euclidean utopia is mapped; it is geometrically organized, with the parts labeled a, a', b: a diagram or model, which social engineers can follow and reproduce. Reproduction, the viral watchword.

In the *Handbook*, discussing the so-called Kuksu Cult or Kuksu Society – a clustering of rites and observances found among the Yuki, Pomo,

31 Lévi-Strauss, *Scope of Anthropology*.
32 Alfred L. Kroeber, *Handbook of the Indians of California*, Smithsonian Institution, Bureau of American Ethnology Bulletin no. 78 (Washington, D.C., 1925).

Maidu, Wintu, Miwok, Costanoan, and Esselen peoples of Central California – Kroeber observed that our use of the terms "the cult" or "a society," our perception of a general or abstract entity, Kuksu, falsifies the native perception:

> The only societies were those of the town unit. They were not branches, because there was no parent stem. Our method, in any such situation, religious or otherwise, is to constitute a central and superior body. Since the day of the Roman empire and the Christian church, we hardly think of a social activity except as it is coherently organized into a definite unit definitely subdivided.
>
> But it must be recognized that such a tendency is not an inherent and inescapable one of all civilization. If we are able to think socially only in terms of an organized machine, the California native was just as unable to think in those terms.
>
> When we recall with how slender a machinery and how rudimentary an organization the whole business of Greek civilization was carried out, it becomes easily intelligible that the . . . Californian could dispense with almost all endeavors in this direction, which to us seem vital.[33]

Copernicus told us that the earth was not the center. Darwin told us that man is not the center. If we listened to the anthropologists we might hear them telling us, with appropriate indirectness, that the White West is not the center. The center of the world is a bluff on the Klamath River, a rock in Mecca, a hole in the ground in Greece, nowhere, its circumference everywhere.

Perhaps the utopist should heed this unsettling news at last. Perhaps the utopist would do well to lose the plan, throw away the map, get off the motorcycle, put on a very strange-looking hat, bark sharply three times, and trot off looking thin, yellow, and dingy across the desert and up into the digger pines.

I don't think we're ever going to get to utopia again by going forward, but only roundabout or sideways; because we're in a rational dilemma, an either/or situation as perceived by the binary computer mentality, and neither the either nor the or is a place where people can live. Increasingly often in these increasingly hard times I am asked by people I respect and

---

33 Ibid.

admire, "Are you going to write books about the terrible injustice and misery of our world, or are you going to write escapist and consolatory fantasies?" I am urged by some to do one – by some to do the other. I am offered the Grand Inquisitor's choice. Will you choose freedom without happiness, or happiness without freedom? The only answer one can make, I think, is: No.

Back round once more. *Usà puyew usu wapiw!*

> If the word [utopia] is to be redeemed, it will have to be by someone who has followed utopia into the abyss which yawns behind the Grand Inquisitor's vision, and who then has clambered out on the other side.[34]

Sounds like Coyote to me. Falls into things, traps, abysses, and then clambers out somehow, grinning stupidly. Is it possible that we are in fact no longer confronting the Grand Inquisitor? Could he be the Father Figure whom we have set up before us? Could it be that by turning around we can put him behind us, and leave him staring like Ozymandias King of Kings out across the death camps, the gulags, the Waste Land, the uninhabitable kingdom of Zeus, the binary-option, single-vision country where one must choose between happiness and freedom?

If so, then we are in the abyss behind him. Not out. A typical Coyote predicament. We have got ourselves into a really bad mess and have got to get out; and we have to be sure that it's the other side we get out to; and when we do get out, we shall be changed.

I have no idea who we will be or what it may be like on the other side, though I believe there are people there. They have always lived there. It's home. There are songs they sing there; one of the songs is called "Dancing at the edge of the world." If we, clambering up out of the abyss, ask questions of them, they won't draw maps, alleging utter inability; but they may point. One of them might point in the direction of Arlington, Texas. I live there, she says. See how beautiful it is!

This is the New World! we will cry, bewildered but delighted. We have discovered the New World!

Oh, no, Coyote will say. No, this is the old world. The one I made.

You made it for us! we will cry, amazed and grateful.

I wouldn't go so far as to say that, says Coyote.

---

34 Elliott.

A Left-Handed Commencement Address

○

1983

I want to thank the Mills College Class of '83 for offering me a rare chance: to speak aloud in public in the language of women.

I know there are men graduating, and I don't mean to exclude them, far from it. There is a Greek tragedy where the Greek says to the foreigner, "If you don't understand Greek, please signify by nodding." Anyhow, commencements are usually operated under the unspoken agreement that everybody graduating is either male or ought to be. That's why we are all wearing these twelfth-century dresses that look so great on men and make women look either like a mushroom or a pregnant stork. Intellectual tradition is male. Public speaking is done in the public tongue, the national or tribal language; and the language of our tribe is the men's language. Of course women learn it. We're not dumb. If you can tell Margaret Thatcher from Ronald Reagan, or Indira Gandhi from General Somoza, by anything they say, tell me how. This is a man's world, so it talks a man's language. The words are all words of power. You've come a long way, baby, but no way is long enough. You can't even get there by selling yourself out: because there is theirs, not yours.

Maybe we've had enough words of power and talk about the battle of life. Maybe we need some words of weakness. Instead of saying now that I hope you will all go forth from this ivory tower of college into the Real World and forge a triumphant career or at least help your husband to and keep our country strong and be a success in everything – instead of talking power, what if I talked like a woman right here in public? It won't sound right. It's going to sound terrible. What if I said what I hope for you is first, if – only if – you want kids, I hope you have them. Not hordes of them. A couple, enough. I hope they're beautiful. I hope you and they have enough to eat, and a place to be warm and clean in, and friends, and work you like doing. Well, is that what you went to college for? Is that all? What about success?

Success is somebody else's failure. Success is the American Dream we can keep dreaming because most people in most places, including thirty million of ourselves, live wide awake in the terrible reality of poverty. No, I do not wish you success. I don't even want to talk about it. I want to talk about failure.

Because you are human beings, you are going to meet failure. You are going to meet disappointment, injustice, betrayal, and irreparable loss. You will find you're weak where you thought yourself strong. You'll work for possessions and then find they possess you. You will find yourself – as I know you already have – in dark places, alone, and afraid.

What I hope for you, for all my sisters and daughters, brothers and sons, is that you will be able to live there, in the dark place. To live in the place that our rationalizing culture of success denies, calling it a place of exile, uninhabitable, foreign.

Well, we're already foreigners. Women as women are largely excluded from, alien to, the self-declared male norms of this society, where human beings are called Man, the only respectable god is male, and the only direction is up. So, that's their country; let's explore our own. I'm not talking about sex; that's a whole other universe, where every man and woman is on their own. I'm talking about society, the so-called man's world of institutionalized competition, aggression, violence, authority, and power. If we want to live as women, some separatism is forced upon us: Mills College is a wise embodiment of that separatism. The war-games world wasn't made by us or for us; we can't even breathe the air there without masks. And if you put the mask on you'll have a hard time getting it off. So how about going on doing things our own way, as to some extent you did here at Mills? Not *for* men and the male power hierarchy – that's their game. Not *against* men, either – that's still playing by their rules. But *with* any men who are with us: that's our game. Why should a free woman with a college education either fight Machoman or serve him? Why should she live her life on his terms?

Machoman is afraid of our terms, which are not all rational, positive, competitive, etc. And so he has taught us to despise and deny them. In our society, women have lived, and have been despised for living, the whole side of life that includes and takes responsibility for helplessness, weakness, and illness, for the irrational and the irreparable, for all that is obscure, passive, uncontrolled, animal, unclean – the valley of the shadow, the deep, the depths of life. All that the Warrior denies and refuses is left to us and

127

the men who share it with us and therefore, like us, can't play doctor, only nurse, can't be warriors, only civilians, can't be chiefs, only indians. Well, so that is our country. The night side of our country. If there is a day side to it, high sierras, prairies of bright grass, we only know pioneers' tales about it, we haven't got there yet. We're never going to get there by imitating Machoman. We are only going to get there by going our own way, by living there, by living through the night in our own country.

So what I hope for you is that you live there not as prisoners, ashamed of being women, consenting captives of a psychopathic social system, but as natives. That you will be at home there, keep house there, be your own mistress, with a room of your own. That you will do your work there, whatever you're good at, art or science or tech or running a company or sweeping under the beds, and when they tell you that it's second-class work because a woman is doing it, I hope you tell them to go to hell and while they're going, to give you equal pay for equal time. I hope you live without the need to dominate, and without the need to be dominated. I hope you are never victims, but I hope you have no power over other people. And when you fail, and are defeated, and in pain, and in the dark, then I hope you will remember that darkness is your country, where you live, where no wars are fought and no wars are won, but where the future is. Our roots are in the dark; the earth is our country. Why did we look up for blessing – instead of around, and down? What hope we have lies there. Not in the sky full of orbiting spy-eyes and weaponry, but in the earth we have looked down upon. Not from above, but from below. Not in the light that blinds, but in the dark that nourishes, where human beings grow human souls.

The Sentimental Agents
by Doris Lessing

1983

Doris Lessing's *Canopus in Argos* series has had some queer reviews. Some
academic critics, unwilling to recognize experiment in content rather than
form, dismiss her greatest experimental venture as "mere science fiction,"
not to be taken seriously. But among science-fiction readers and reviewers,
where the books might have been greeted with intelligent interest, the
attitude seems to be: Lessing is not One of Us, therefore we will not take
her seriously. Some feminist critics denounce her for departing from the
single issue of feminism. And then there are her adorers, for whom she can
do no wrong. None of these reviewers does her novels justice.

Doris Lessing, *The Sentimental Agents* (New York: Alfred A. Knopf, 1983;
London: Jonathan Cape Ltd, 1983).

Neither will I. I am much too angry at her. But perhaps this review will
move a reader to begin or to continue the series, of which *The Sentimental
Agents* is the fifth book – and that's what I'm after. Doris Lessing deserves
to be read! How many novelists are there writing now who can make you
really angry? How many refuse triviality, self-imitation, and the safe line,
whether it panders to the know-it-all snob or the know-nothing slob?
How many novelists take any risks at all? If you are thirsty for the dry taste
of courage, try Lessing.

But don't start with this one. Start with the first of the series, *Shikasta*,
or the second, *The Marriages Between Zones Three, Four, and Five* (which I
think very much the best so far). In this latest one, all the faults and few
of the strengths of Lessing's style survive the ordeal of an effort at satirical
playfulness by the most humorless major writer alive. She takes the themes
of Orwell's brief, beautiful *Animal Farm* and clomps around all over them
page after page, so gracelessly and so tastelessly that one ends up cheering

for the targets of her satire. She sets up feeble men of straw and knocks them over, braying, "Look! What fools! What knaves!" She loads every die she throws; she propagandizes steadily throughout a novel the intent of which is to satirize propaganda; she preaches against preaching and rants about ranting. The keenest novelistic observer of the political human being since the Koestler of *Darkness at Noon*, she generalizes marvelously, but as soon as she embodies the idea in a character, she overmanipulates, and all we see is a puppet kicking on strings. She bravely discards verisimilitude and even probability, but she discards compassionate insight along with them, replacing it not with irony but with judgmentalism. We must endure even her judgments on music; on a planet somewhere across the universe, we are informed that Tchaikovsky is a complainer and that the tune of "We Shall Overcome" is dismal. Finally, her confusion of emotion with sentimentality is a moral disaster.

And all this is presented as the wisdom of Canopus. I have not found much wisdom in the apparent heroes of the saga, Johor and the other agents of Canopus. They are arrogant, anthropocentric, authoritarian, forever smiling pityingly, forever talking down to everybody else, bearing the galactic version of the White Man's Burden with stifled but audible moans of self-pity through a universe populated by lesser breeds without the law ...And they are immortal. They are as self-righteous as the tiresome old Laputans of Robert Heinlein's novels, though less talkative. In fact, when it comes to real information, they stop talking. They smile pityingly.

Can it be that Lessing is playing her own double agent? Are we meant to dislike these saintly "agents," meant to distrust their wisdom as they distrust our rhetoric, meant to question the "Necessity" they invoke as they dismiss our inadequate concepts of virtue, freedom, justice, compassion? Are we expected to protest the Orders from Above that everyone in the book obeys unprotesting (or if they don't they rue the day)? If so, Lessing is risking even more than I thought, and is undercutting her book as she writes it, in a fashion and to an extent that few fancy critics of formal preciosities or *auteurs* of self-deconstructed anti-novels would dare contemplate. But then she is asking too much of her readers, to carry on so strained a duplicity in book after book.

It's time the people from Canopus stopped looking down from the heights, all head, no body. Any redneck preacher or hard-line Freudian can spout this stuff about subduing our "animal" nature and the "beast" in us (as if it were *animals* that made the mess we're in!). Surely Canopus, or Lessing, can do better than that? We don't need the soppy pseudo-reassurances of an *E. T.* – but neither do we need condemnations, preachifyings, and mystifications in the name of Reason. If Canopus knows what it is we do need, in the mess we've made, it's time they spoke. Put up or shut up, Johor!

Whose Lathe?

●

1984

This piece was written for the "Forum" section of my regional major news-paper, The Oregonian, *in May of 1984. The arguments made are local and specific; the problem addressed is national and general. Any author who boasts about freedom of the press in the United States should, perhaps, make certain that none of his or her books has been banned, dropped from a reading list as immoral or anti-religious or "secular humanist" (that bogey includes almost all science fiction), or weeded out or locked away by a public librarian or school librarian under pressure. The trouble is, it's not a matter the author is likely to hear about. I would not have known that one of my books was to have a censorship hearing in Washougal, Washington, a town twenty minutes' drive from my city, if a librarian in that school district had not alerted me the night before the hearing. Little as I wish to, I have to assume that censorship has been and is being imposed on my books, and on all literature, in school districts, schools, and libraries all over the country, and that there is nothing I can do about it except protest against it whenever and wherever I can; a protest I know other writers, and readers, will share.*

In a small town near Portland late this spring, a novel, *The Lathe of Heaven,* was the subject of a hearing concerning its suitability for use in a senior-high-school literature class. I took a lively interest in the outcome, because I wrote the novel.

The case against the book was presented first. The man who was asking that it be withdrawn stated his objections to the following elements in the book: fuzzy thinking and poor sentence structure; a mention of homo-sexuality; a character who keeps a flask of brandy in her purse, and who remarks that her mother did not love her. (It seemed curious to me that he did not mention the fact that this same character is a Black woman whose lover/husband is a White man. I had the feeling that this was really what he hated in the book, and that he was afraid to say so; but that was only my feeling.)

He also took exception to what he described as the author's advocacy of non-Christian religions and/or of non-separation of Church and State (his arguments on this point, or these points, were not clear to me).

Finally, during discussion, he compared the book to junk food, apparently because it was science fiction.

The English Department of the school then presented a carefully prepared, spirited defense of the book, including statements by students who had read it. Some liked it, some didn't like it, most objected to having it, or any other book, banned.

In discussion, teachers pointed out that since it is the policy of the Washougal School District to assign an alternative book to any student who objects on any grounds to reading an assigned one, the attempt to prevent a whole class from reading a book was an attempt to change policy, replacing free choice by censorship.

When the Instructional Materials Committee of the district voted on the motion to ban the book, the motion was defeated twenty votes to five. The hearing was public and was conducted in the most open and democratic fashion. I did not speak, as I felt the teachers and students had spoken eloquently for me.

Crankish attacks on the freedom to read are common at present. When backed and coordinated by organized groups, they become sinister. In this case, I saw something going on that worried me a good deal because it did not seem to be coming from an outside pressure group, but from elements of the educational establishment itself: this was the movement to change policy radically by instituting, or "clarifying," guidelines or criteria for the selection/elimination of books used in the schools. The motion on which this committee of the school district voted was actually that the book be withdrawn "while guidelines and policies for the district are worked out." Those guidelines and policies were the real goal, I think, of the motion.

Guidelines? That sounds dull. Innocent. Useful. Of course we have to be sure about the kinds of books we want our kids to read in school. Don't we?

Well, do we? The dangerous vagueness of the term "guidelines and policies for the district" slides right past such questions as: Who are "we"? Who decides what the children read? Does "we" include you? Me?

Teachers? Librarians? Students? Are fifteen-to-eighteen-year-olds ever "we," or are they always "they"?

And what are the guidelines to be? On what criteria or doctrines are they to be based?

The people concerned with schools in Oregon try, with ever decreasing budgets, to provide good, sound food in the school cafeterias, knowing that for some students that's the only real meal they get. They try, with ever decreasing budgets, to provide beautiful, intelligent books in classes and school libraries, knowing that for many students those are the only books they read. To provide the best: everyone agrees on that (even the people who vote against school levies). But we don't and we can't agree on what books are the best. And therefore what is vital is that we provide variety, abundance, plenty – not books that reflect one body of opinion or doctrine, not books that one group or sect thinks good, but the broadest, richest range of intellectual and artistic material possible.

Nobody is forced to read any of it. There is that very important right to refuse and choose an alternative.

When a bad apple turns up, it can be taken out of the barrel on a case-by-case, book-by-book basis – investigated, defended, prosecuted, and judged, as in the hearing on my *Lathe of Heaven*.* But this can't be done wholesale by using "guidelines," instructions for censorship. There is no such thing as a moral filter that lets good books through and keeps bad books out. Such criteria of "goodness" and "badness" are a moralist's dream but a democrat's nightmare.

Censorship, here or in Russia or wherever, is absolutely antidemocratic and elitist. The censor says: You don't know enough to choose, but we do, so you will read what we choose for you and nothing else. The democrat says: The process of learning is that of learning how to choose. Freedom isn't given, it's earned. Read, learn, and earn it.

I fear censorship in this Uriah Heepish guise of "protecting our children," "stricter criteria," "moral guidance," "a more definite policy," and so on. I hope administrators, teachers, librarians, parents, and students will resist it. Its advocates are people willing to treat others not only as if they were not free but were not even worthy of freedom.

---

* Currently (1987) a textbook written for Oregon schools called *Let's Oregonize* is going through this process on the state level. The arguments against it were brought by environmentalists and others who found it tendentious and biased towards certain industries and interests. From my point of view it certainly sounds like a rather bad apple. But it is getting a scrupulously fair hearing.

Theodora

●

1985

Written as the introduction to the Yolla Bolly Press edition of The Inland Whale, *Theodora Kroeber's retellings of Native American stories.*

Some people lead several lives all at once; my mother lived several lives one at a time. Her names reflect this serial complexity: Theodora Covel Kracaw Brown Kroeber Quinn. The last four are the names of men: Kracaw her father's name (and the source of her lifelong nickname Krakie), Brown, Kroeber, and Quinn her three husbands. Covel is a family name on her mother's side, used as a girl's middle name for several generations. Her first name came from a novel her mother liked, *Theodora Goes Wild*. She was Theo to some, Dora to none.

The (auto)biographical note about the author on the jacket of the first edition of *The Inland Whale* reads in part:

> Theodora Kroeber was born in Denver and spent her early years in the
> mining camp of Telluride, Colorado. She earned a B.A. in psychology and
> economics and an M.A. in clinical (then called "abnormal") psychology
> at the University of California. Offered a position in a boys' reformatory,
> she got married instead and had three sons and a daughter. When the
> children were grown and raising their own families, she began to write.
> Part of the background for her writing comes from Indians, rivers, and
> deserts encountered while accompanying her husband, A. L. Kroeber,
> the noted anthropologist, on professional journeys and field trips.

The bit about the boys' reformatory is a characteristically graceful piece of legerdemain: Theodora took her master's degree in 1920 and married Clifton Brown that same year; three years later, with two baby sons, she was widowed; in 1925 she met Alfred Kroeber; they married, and in 1926 and 1929 her other two children were born. Where the boys' reformatory comes in this crowded decade I can't quite figure out. Although she wrote two biographies notable for their exhaustive research and scrupulous selection of fact, Theodora's native gift was for the brilliant shortcut that reveals an emotional or dramatic truth, the event turned legend – not raw fact, but cooked fact, fact made savory and digestible. She was a great cook both of foods and of words.

The Inland Whale was written in the late 1950s, when, as she says, her children were off having children, and she and Alfred were enjoying the freedom of his long emeritus career, during which he taught at Harvard and Columbia and was a resident of various think tanks – well-traveled, unhurried, productive years. Work, writing, was pretty much like breathing to Alfred Kroeber; he just quietly did it all the time. With time and energy now to spare, Theodora soon found her own breath. First she wrote a couple of essays with Alfred (interesting pre-computer attempts at counting word frequency in poetry), then some children's stories (often a woman's way into literature – threatening to no one, including herself). Then a first novel. And then this book.

I don't know the genesis of the book, but would guess that separate stories, which she had tried retelling for their own sake and the work's sake, began to make a whole, a shape in her mind. Perhaps she set out to write a book of stories about women, but I think it more likely that the pattern became apparent and the connections imperative as she worked and reworked and re-reworked the material – for she was a hard writer, a merciless reviser. The coherence of the book and the clarity of her prose are the result of the kind of distillation that makes fine liquors, the kind of pressure that makes diamonds. She strove for a vivid simplicity, but she was never artless.

People ask if she told stories like these to her children. She read to us, but it is her aunt Betsy and my father whose storytelling I remember. Only a few times do I recall her making the "breakthrough into performance," as Dell Hymes calls it. Once when she was eighty or so, six or eight kids and grandkids at table, John Quinn presiding, one of us asked her about her experiences as a child of nine on a visit to San Francisco when the great earthquake of 1906 struck. All the storytelling power of her books got unleashed, and none of us will forget that hour. But usually it was conversational give-and-take that she wanted and created among family and friends. And one sees her valuation of written narrative as "higher" or more "finished" than oral – the conventional and almost universal judgment of her time both in literature and anthropology – in her notes to *The Inland Whale.*

Still, it is very like her to have chosen from all the stories of the peoples of California nine stories about women, at a time when even in anthropology the acts of women were easy to dismiss as secondary, women being subsumed (oddly enough) in Man. From her mother Phebe and other strong women of her late-frontier Western childhood, Theodora had a firm heritage of female independence and self-respect. Her sense of female solidarity was delicate and strong. She made her daughter feel a lifelong welcome, giving me the conviction that I had done the right thing in being born a woman – a gift many woman-children are denied. But also she would say that she "liked men better than women"; her temperament inclined her to the conventional supporting roles of wife and mother; and she detested the direct opposition of a woman's will to a man's. She must have thought her loving empire was endangered by feminism, for her intolerance of what she called "women's lib" went beyond her general distrust of ideologies. But all the same, in her life as a writer, I think she was a true feminist.

Look for Native American women in White literature before 1960: if you find any at all, you generally find something called a "squaw." There are no squaws in *The Inland Whale* – only human beings. This is not freedom from racist stereotyping only, but also freedom from masculinist prejudice, and a deliberate search for the feminine. Theodora kept telling me to write about women, not men, years before I (the "women's libber") was able to do so. She did so herself from the start, not only because the feminists of her mother's generation had freed us both, but also because she was true to her being, her perceptions, her female humanity. In all her different lives she was entirely woman.

The book was written and published, and *Ishi* was begun, while Alfred was alive. After his death came her life as widow, soon famous in her own right for her great book *Ishi*; and then a new life, and new directions in writing, as Mrs. John Quinn. She never wrote till she was over fifty and she never stopped writing till she died at eighty-three. I wish she had started earlier: we might have had more books from her; her novels might have found a publisher; and she wouldn't have had to wait for validation and self-confidence till a time in life when most artists are at ease with their craft and are getting the recognition they deserve. I know she regretted having started writing so late. But not bitterly. She wasn't a regretter, or a blamer. She kept going on, out of an old life, into a new one. So I imagine she goes now.

Science Fiction and the Future

●

1985

In February of 1985 the Oregon Museum of Science and Industry invited me to participate on a panel, Science Fiction and the Future, and the following was my prepared statement for that discussion.

We know where the future is. It's in front of us. Right? It lies before us – a great future lies before us – we stride forward confidently into it, every commencement, every election year. And we know where the past is. Behind us, right? So that we have to turn around to see it, and that interrupts our progress ever forward into the future, so we don't really much like to do it.

It seems that the Quechua-speaking peoples of the Andes see all this rather differently. They figure that because the past is what you know, you can see it – it's in front of you, under your nose. This is a mode of perception rather than action, of awareness rather than progress. Since they're quite as logical as we are, they say that the future lies behind – behind your back, over your shoulder. The future is what you *can't* see, unless you turn around and kind of snatch a glimpse. And then sometimes you wish you hadn't, because you've glimpsed what's sneaking up on you from behind ... So, as we drag the Andean peoples into our world of progress, pollution, soap operas, and satellites, they are coming backwards – looking over their shoulders to find out where they're going.

I find this an intelligent and appropriate attitude. At least it reminds us that our talk about "going forward into the future" is a metaphor, a piece of mythic thinking taken literally, perhaps even a bluff, based on our macho fear of ever being inactive, receptive, open, quiet, still. Our unquiet clocks make us think that we make time, that we control it. We plug in the timer and make time happen. But in fact the future comes, or is there, whether we rush forward to meet it in supersonic jets with nuclear warheads, or sit on a peak and watch the llamas graze. Morning comes whether you set the alarm or not.

The future is not mere space. This is where I part company with a whole variety of science fiction, the imperialistic kind, as seen in all the Space Wars and Star Wars novels and films and the whole branch of sf that reduces technology to hi-tech. In such fictions, space and the future are synonymous: they are a place we are going to get to, invade, colonize, exploit, and suburbanize.

If we do "get to" space, it's not unlikely that that's how we'll behave there. It is possible that we will "conquer" space. But it is not possible that we will "conquer" the future, because there is no way we can get there. The future is the part of the spacetime continuum from which – in the body and in ordinary states of consciousness – we are excluded. We can't even see it. Except for little glimpses over the shoulder.

When we look at what we can't see, what we do see is the stuff inside our heads. Our thoughts and our dreams, the good ones and the bad ones. And it seems to me that when science fiction is really doing its job that's exactly what it's dealing with. Not "the future." It's when we confuse our dreams and ideas with the non-dream world that we're in trouble, when we think the future is a place we own. Then we succumb to wishful thinking and escapism, and our science fiction gets megalomania and thinks that instead of being fiction it's prediction, and the Pentagon and the White House begin to *believe* it, and we get True Believers conquering the future by means of SDI.

As a science-fiction writer I personally prefer to stand still for long periods, like the Quechua, and look at what is, in fact, in front of me: the earth; my fellow beings on it; and the stars.

Prospects for Women in Writing

●

1986

I was invited to sit on a panel called Women in the Arts, at the Conference on Women in the Year 2000, held in Portland in September of 1986. Each panelist was asked to make a ten-minute statement about the prospects for women in her particular field.

It's only been about two hundred years since women gained access to literacy and began to empower themselves with that great power, the written word. And they have written. The works of women acknowledged as "great" – Austen, the Brontës, Dickinson, Eliot, Woolf – make a high road for other women writers to follow, so wide and clear that even the conscious or unconscious misogyny of most critics and teachers of literature hasn't been able to hide or close it.

There is less sexism in book and magazine publishing than in any field I know about. Of course most publishers are men, but most publishers now aren't even human: they're corporations. Many editors and other human beings in publishing are women or unmacho men. And thirty to fifty percent of living authors are women. With talent and obstinacy, then, a woman can and will get her writing published; with talent, obstinacy, and luck, her writing will be widely read and taken notice of. But.

As Tillie Olsen has demonstrated in *Silences*, although thirty to fifty percent of books are written by women, what is called "literature" remains eighty-eight to ninety percent male, decade after decade. No matter how successful, beloved, influential her work was, when a woman author dies, nine times out of ten she gets dropped from the lists, the courses, the anthologies, while the men get kept. If she had the nerve to have children, her chances of getting dropped are higher still. So we get Anthony Trollope coming out the ears while Elizabeth Gaskell is ignored, or endless studies of Nathaniel Hawthorne while Harriet Beecher Stowe is taught as a footnote to history. Most women's writing – like most work by women in any field – is called unimportant, secondary, by masculinist teachers and critics of both sexes; and literary styles and genres are constantly redefined to keep women's writing in second place. So if you want your writing to be taken seriously, don't marry and have kids, and above all, don't die. But if you have to die, commit suicide. They approve of that.

To find out what women writers are up against, if you want the useful blues, read Tillie Olsen, and if you want to get cheerfully enraged, read Joanna Russ's *How to Suppress Women's Writing* or Dale Spender's wonderful *Man Made Language*.

To try to summarize my own experience: The more truly your work comes from your own being, body and soul, rather than fitting itself into male conventions and expectations of what to write about and how to write it, the less it will suit most editors, reviewers, grant givers, and prize committees. But among all those are women and men to whom the real thing, the art, comes first; and you have to trust them. You have to trust yourself. And you have to trust your readers.

The writer only does half the job. It takes two to make a book. Many more women buy and read books than men. And in the last fifteen years there has been an increasing sense of strength and mutual validation among women writers and readers, a resistance to the male control over reading, a refusal to join men in sneering at what women want to write and read. Get hold of *The Norton Anthology of Literature by Women* and read it and then tell me women can't show men how to write and what to write about! The English profs keep sweeping our work under the rug, but that rug is about three feet off the floor by now, and things are coming out from under it and eating the English profs. Housework is woman's work, right? Well, it's time to shake the rugs.

Who's afraid of Virginia Woolf? Every little macho dodo, from Hemingway to Mailer. There is no more subversive act than the act of writing from a woman's experience of life using a woman's judgment. Woolf knew that and said it in 1930. Most of us forgot it and had to rediscover it all over again in the sixties. But for a whole generation now, women have been writing, publishing, and reading one another, in artistic and scholarly and feminist fellowship. If we go on doing that, by the year 2000 we will – *for the first time ever* – have kept the perceptions, ideas, and judgments of women alive in consciousness as an active, creative force in society for more than one generation. And our daughters and granddaughters won't have to start from zero the way we did. To keep women's words, women's works, alive and powerful – that's what I see as our job as writers and readers for the next fifteen years, and the next fifty.

Bryn Mawr Commencement Address

1986

Thinking about what I should say to you made me think about what we learn in college; and what we unlearn in college; and then how we learn to unlearn what we learned in college and relearn what we unlearned in college, and so on. And I thought how I have learned, more or less well, three languages, all of them English; and how one of these languages is the one I went to college to learn. I thought I was going to study French and Italian, and I did, but what I learned was the language of power – of social power; I shall call it the father tongue.

This is the public discourse, and one dialect of it is speech-making – by politicians, commencement speakers, or the old man who used to get up early in a village in Central California a couple of hundred years ago and say things very loudly on the order of "People need to be getting up now, there are things we might be doing, the repairs on the sweathouse aren't finished and the tar-weed is in seed over on Bald Hill; this is a good time of day for doing things, and there'll be plenty of time for lying around when it gets hot this afternoon." So everybody would get up grumbling slightly, and some of them would go pick tarweed – probably the women. This is the effect, ideally, of the public discourse. It makes something happen, makes somebody – usually somebody else – do something, or at least it gratifies the ego of the speaker. The difference between our politics and that of a native Californian people is clear in the style of the public discourse. The difference wasn't clear to the White invaders, who insisted on calling any Indian who made a speech a "chief," because they couldn't comprehend, they wouldn't admit, an authority without supremacy – a non-dominating authority. But it is such an authority that I possess for the brief – we all hope it is decently brief – time I speak to you. I have no right to speak to you. What I have is the responsibility you have given me to speak to you.

The political tongue speaks aloud – and look how radio and television

144

have brought the language of politics right back where it belongs – but the dialect of the father tongue that you and I learned best in college is a written one. It doesn't speak itself. It only lectures. It began to develop when printing made written language common rather than rare, five hundred years ago or so, and with electronic processing and copying it continues to develop and proliferate so powerfully, so dominatingly, that many believe this dialect – the expository and particularly the scientific discourse – is the *highest* form of language, the true language, of which all other uses of words are primitive vestiges.

And it is indeed an excellent dialect. Newton's *Principia* was written in it in Latin, and Descartes wrote Latin and French in it, establishing some of its basic vocabulary, and Kant wrote German in it, and Marx, Darwin, Freud, Boas, Foucault – all the great scientists and social thinkers wrote it. It is the language of thought that seeks objectivity.

I do not say it is the language of rational thought. Reason is a faculty far larger than mere objective thought. When either the political or the scientific discourse announces itself as the voice of reason, it is playing God, and should be spanked and stood in the corner. The essential gesture of the father tongue is not reasoning but distancing – making a gap, a space, between the subject or self and the object or other. Enormous energy is generated by that rending, that forcing of a gap between Man and World. So the continuous growth of technology and science fuels itself; the Industrial Revolution began with splitting the world-atom, and still by breaking the continuum into unequal parts we keep the imbalance from which our society draws the power that enables it to dominate every other culture, so that everywhere now everybody speaks the same language in laboratories and government buildings and headquarters and offices of business, and those who don't know it or won't speak it are silent, or silenced, or unheard.

You came here to college to learn the language of power – to be empowered. If you want to succeed in business, government, law, engineering, science, education, the media, if you want to succeed, you have to be fluent in the language in which "success" is a meaningful word.

White man speak with forked tongue; White man speak dichotomy. His language expresses the values of the split world, valuing the positive and devaluing the negative in each redivision: subject/object, self/other, mind/body, dominant/submissive, active/passive, Man/Nature, man/

woman, and so on. The father tongue is spoken from above. It goes one way. No answer is expected, or heard.

In our Constitution and the works of law, philosophy, social thought, and science, in its everyday uses in the service of justice and clarity, what I call the father tongue is immensely noble and indispensably useful. When it claims a privileged relationship to reality, it becomes dangerous and potentially destructive. It describes with exquisite accuracy the continuing destruction of the planet's ecosystem by its speakers. This word from its vocabulary, "ecosystem," is a word unnecessary except in a discourse that excludes its speakers from the ecosystem in a subject/object dichotomy of terminal irresponsibility.

The language of the fathers, of Man Ascending, Man the Conqueror, Civilized Man, is not your native tongue. It isn't anybody's native tongue. You didn't even hear the father tongue your first few years, except on the radio or TV, and then you didn't listen, and neither did your little brother, because it was some old politician with hairs in his nose yammering. And you and your brother had better things to do. You had another kind of power to learn. You were learning your mother tongue.

Using the father tongue, I can speak of the mother tongue only, inevitably, to distance it – to exclude it. It is the other, inferior. It is primitive: inaccurate, unclear, coarse, limited, trivial, banal. It's repetitive, the same over and over, like the work called women's work; earthbound, housebound. It's vulgar, the vulgar tongue, common, common speech, colloquial, low, ordinary, plebeian, like the work ordinary people do, the lives common people live. The mother tongue, spoken or written, expects an answer. It is conversation, a word the root of which means "turning together." The mother tongue is language not as mere communication but as relation, relationship. It connects. It goes two ways, many ways, an exchange, a network. Its power is not in dividing but in binding, not in distancing but in uniting. It is written, but not by scribes and secretaries for posterity; it flies from the mouth on the breath that is our life and is gone, like the outbreath, utterly gone and yet returning, repeated, the breath the same again always, everywhere, and we all know it by heart. John have you got your umbrella I think it's going to rain. Can you come play with me? If I told you once I told you a hundred times. Things here just aren't the same without Mother, I will now sign your affectionate brother James. Oh what am I going to do? So I said to her I said if he thinks she's going to stand for that but then there's his arthritis poor thing and no work. I love you. I hate you. I hate liver. Joan dear did you feed the sheep, don't just stand around mooning. Tell me what they said, tell me what you did. Oh how my feet do hurt. My heart is breaking. Touch me here, touch me again. Once bit twice shy. You look like what the cat dragged in. What a beautiful night. Good morning, hello, goodbye, have a nice day, thanks. God damn you to hell you lying cheat. Pass the soy sauce please. Oh shit. Is it grandma's own sweet pretty dear? What am I going to tell her? There there don't cry. Go to sleep now, go to sleep . . . Don't go to sleep!

It is a language always on the verge of silence and often on the verge of song. It is the language stories are told in. It is the language spoken by all children and most women, and so I call it the mother tongue, for we learn it from our mothers and speak it to our kids. I'm trying to use it here in public where it isn't appropriate, not suited to the occasion, but I want to speak it to you because we are women and I can't say what I want to say about women in the language of capital M Man. If I try to be objective I will say, "This is higher and that is lower," I'll make a commencement speech about being successful in the battle of life, I'll lie to you; and I don't want to.

Early this spring I met a musician, the composer Pauline Oliveros, a beautiful woman like a grey rock in a streambed; and to a group of us, women, who were beginning to quarrel over theories in abstract, objective language – and I with my splendid Eastern-women's-college training in the father tongue was in the thick of the fight and going for the kill – to us, Pauline, who is sparing with words, said after clearing her throat, "Offer your experience as your truth." There was a short silence. When we started talking again, we didn't talk objectively, and we didn't fight. We went back to feeling our way into ideas, using the whole intellect not half of it, talking with one another, which involves listening. We tried to offer our experience to one another. Not claiming something: offering something.

How, after all, can one experience deny, negate, disprove, another experience? Even if I've had a lot more of it, *your* experience is your truth. How can one being prove another being wrong? Even if you're a lot younger and smarter than me, *my* being is my truth. I can offer it; you don't have to take it. People can't contradict each other, only words can: words separated from experience for use as weapons, words that make the wound, the split between subject and object, exposing and exploiting the object but disguising and defending the subject.

People crave objectivity because to be subjective is to be embodied, to be a body, vulnerable, violable. Men especially aren't used to that; they're trained not to offer but to attack. It's often easier for women to trust one another, to try to speak our experience in our own language, the language we talk to each other in, the mother tongue; so we empower one another.

But you and I have learned to use the mother tongue only at home or safe among friends, and many men learn not to speak it at all. They're taught that there's no safe place for them. From adolescence on, they talk a kind of degraded version of the father tongue with each other – sports scores, job technicalities, sex technicalities, and TV politics. At home, to women and children talking mother tongue, they respond with a grunt and turn on the ball game. They have let themselves be silenced, and dimly they know it, and so resent speakers of the mother tongue; women babble, gabble all the time ... Can't listen to that stuff.

Our schools and colleges, institutions of the patriarchy, generally teach us to listen to people in power, men or women speaking the father tongue; and so they teach us not to listen to the mother tongue, to what the powerless say, poor men, women, children: not to hear that as valid discourse.

I am trying to unlearn these lessons, along with other lessons I was taught by my society, particularly lessons concerning the minds, work, works, and being of women. I am a slow unlearner. But I love my unteachers – the feminist thinkers and writers and talkers and poets and artists and singers and critics and friends, from Wollstonecraft and Woolf through the furies and glories of the seventies and eighties – I celebrate here and now the women who for two centuries have worked for our freedom, the unteachers, the unmasters, the unconquerors, the unwarriors, women who have at risk and at high cost offered their experience as truth. "Let us NOT praise famous women!" Virginia Woolf scribbled in a margin when she was writing *Three Guineas*, and she's right, but still I have to praise these women and thank them for setting me free in my old age to learn my own language.

The third language, my native tongue, which I will never know though I've spent my life learning it: I'll say some words now in this language. First a name, just a person's name, you've heard it before. Sojourner Truth. That name is a language in itself. But Sojourner Truth spoke the unlearned language; about a hundred years ago, talking it in a public place, she said, "I have been forty years a slave and forty years free and would be here forty years more to have equal rights for all." Along at the end of her talk she said, "I wanted to tell you a mite about Woman's Rights, and so I came out and said so. I am sittin' among you to watch; and every once and awhile I will come out and tell you what time of night it is." She said, "Now I will do a little singing. I have not heard any singing since I came here."[1]

Singing is one of the names of the language we never learn, and here for Sojourner Truth is a little singing. It was written by Joy Harjo of the Creek people and is called "The Blanket Around Her."[2]

maybe it is her birth
which she holds close to herself
or her death
which is just as inseparable
and the white wind
that encircles her is a part
just as
the blue sky
hanging in turquoise from her neck

oh woman
remember who you are
woman
it is the whole earth

So what am I talking about with this "unlearned language" – poetry, literature? Yes, but it can be speeches and science, any use of language when it is spoken, written, read, heard as art, the way dancing is the body moving as art. In Sojourner Truth's words you hear the coming together, the marriage of the public discourse and the private experience, making a power, a beautiful thing, the true discourse of reason. This is a wedding and welding back together of the alienated consciousness that I've been calling the father tongue and the undifferentiated engagement that I've been calling the mother tongue. This is their baby, this baby talk, the language you can spend your life trying to learn.

We learn this tongue first, like the mother tongue, just by hearing it or reading it; and even in our overcrowded, underfunded public high schools they still teach *A Tale of Two Cities* and *Uncle Tom's Cabin*; and in

---

1 Sojourner Truth, in *The Norton Anthology of Literature by Women*, ed. Sandra M. Gilbert and Susan Gubar (New York: W. W. Norton & Co., 1985).
2 Joy Harjo, "The Blanket Around Her," in *That's What She Said: Contemporary Poetry and Fiction by Native American Women*, ed. Rayna Green (Bloomington: Indiana University Press, 1984).

college you can take four solid years of literature, and even creative writing courses. But. It is all taught as if it were a dialect of the father tongue.

Literature takes shape and life in the body, in the womb of the mother tongue: always: and the Fathers of Culture get anxious about paternity. They start talking about legitimacy. They steal the baby. They ensure by every means that the artist, the writer, is male. This involves intellectual abortion by centuries of women artists, infanticide of works by women writers, and a whole medical corps of sterilizing critics working to purify the Canon, to reduce the subject matter and style of literature to something Ernest Hemingway could have understood.

But this is our native tongue, this is our language they're stealing: we can read it and we can write it, and what we bring to it is what it needs, the woman's tongue, that earth and savor, that relatedness, which speaks dark in the mother tongue but clear as sunlight in women's poetry, and in our novels and stories, our letters, our journals, our speeches. If Sojourner Truth, forty years a slave, knew she had the right to speak that speech, how about you? Will you let yourself be silenced? Will you listen to what men tell you, or will you listen to what women are saying? I say the Canon has been spiked, and while the Eliots speak only to the Lowells and the Lowells speak only to God, Denise Levertov comes stepping westward quietly, speaking to us.[3]

There is no savor
more sweet, more salt

than to be glad to be
what, woman,

and who, myself,
I am, a shadow

that grows longer as the sun
moves, drawn out

on a thread of wonder.
If I bear burdens

---

3 Denise Levertov, "Stepping Westward," in *Norton Anthology*.

they begin to be remembered
as gifts, goods, a basket

of bread that hurts
my shoulders but closes me

in fragrance. I can
eat as I go.

As I've been using the word "truth" in the sense of "trying hard not to lie," so I use the words "literature," "art," in the sense of "living well, living with skill, grace, energy" – like carrying a basket of bread and smelling it and eating as you go. I don't mean only certain special products made by specially gifted people living in specially privileged garrets, studios, and ivory towers – "High" Art; I mean also all the low arts, the ones men don't want. For instance, the art of making order where people live. In our culture this activity is not considered an art, it is not even considered work. "Do you work?" – and she, having stopped mopping the kitchen and picked up the baby to come answer the door, says, "No, I don't work." People who make order where people live are by doing so stigmatized as unfit for "higher" pursuits; so women mostly do it, and among women, poor, uneducated, or old women more often than rich, educated, and young ones. Even so, many people want very much to keep house but can't, because they're poor and haven't got a house to keep, or the time and money it takes, or even the experience of ever having seen a decent house, a clean room, except on TV. Most men are prevented from housework by intense cultural bias; many women actually hire another woman to do it for them because they're scared of getting trapped in it, ending up like the woman they hire, or like that woman we all know who's been pushed so far over by cultural bias that she can't stand up, and crawls around the house scrubbing and waxing and spraying germ killer on the kids. But even on her kneebones, where you and I will never join her, even she has been practicing as best she knows how a great, ancient, complex, and necessary art. That our society devalues it is evidence of the barbarity, the aesthetic and ethical bankruptcy, of our society.

As housekeeping is an art, so is cooking and all it involves – it involves, after all, agriculture, hunting, herding . . . So is the making of clothing and all it involves . . . And so on; you see how I want to revalue the word "art" so that when I come back as I do now to talking about words it is in the context of the great arts of living, of the woman carrying the basket of bread, bearing gifts, goods. Art not as some ejaculative act of ego but as a way, a skillful and powerful way of being in the world. I come back to words because words are my way of being in the world, but meaning by language as art a matter infinitely larger than the so-called High forms. Here is a poem that tries to translate six words by Hélène Cixous, who wrote *The Laugh of the Medusa*; she said, "Je suis là où ça parle," and I squeezed those six words like a lovely lemon and got out all the juice I could, plus a drop of Oregon vodka.

> I'm there where
> it's talking
> Where that speaks I
> am in that talking place
>   Where
> that says
> my being is
>   Where
> my being there
> is speaking
> I am
>   And so
> laughing
> in a stone ear

The stone ear that won't listen, won't hear us, and blames us for its being stone . . . Women can babble and chatter like monkeys in the wilderness, but the farms and orchards and gardens of language, the wheatfields of art – men have claimed these, fenced them off: No Trespassing, it's a man's world, they say. And I say,

> oh woman
> remember who you are
> woman
> it is the whole earth

We are told, in words and not in words, we are told by their deafness, by their stone ears, that our experience, the life experience of women, is not valuable to men – therefore not valuable to society, to humanity. We are valued by men only as an element of their experience, as things experienced; anything we may say, anything we may do, is recognized only if said or done in their service.

One thing we incontestably do is have babies. So we have babies as the male priests, lawmakers, and doctors tell us to have them, when and where to have them, how often, and how to have them; so that is all under control. But we are *not to talk about* having babies, because that is not part of the experience of men and so nothing to do with reality, with civilization, and no concern of art. – A rending scream in another room. And Prince Andrey comes in and sees his poor little wife dead bearing his son – Or Levin goes out into his fields and thanks his God for the birth of his son – And we know how Prince Andrey feels and how Levin feels and even how God feels, but we don't know what happened. Something happened, something was done, which we know nothing about. But what was it? Even in novels by women we are only just beginning to find out what it is that happens in the other room – what women do.

Freud famously said, "What we shall never know is what a woman wants." Having paused thoughtfully over the syntax of that sentence, in which WE are plural but "a woman" apparently has no plural, no individuality – as we might read that a cow must be milked twice a day or a gerbil is a nice pet – WE might go on then to consider whether WE know anything about, whether WE have ever noticed, whether WE have ever asked a woman what she *does* – what women do.

Many anthropologists, some historians, and others have indeed been asking one another this question for some years now, with pale and affrighted faces – and they are beginning also to answer it. More power to them. The social sciences show us that speakers of the father tongue are capable of understanding and discussing the doings of the mothers, if they will admit the validity of the mother tongue and listen to what women say.

But in society as a whole the patriarchal mythology of what "a woman" does persists almost unexamined, and shapes the lives of women. "What are you going to do when you get out of school?" "Oh, well, just like any other woman, I guess I want a home and family" – and that's fine, but what is this home and family just like other women's? Dad at work, mom home, two kids eating apple pie? This family, which our media and now our government declare to be normal and impose as normative, this nuclear family now accounts for seven percent of the arrangements women live in in America. Ninety-three percent of women don't live that way. They don't do that. Many wouldn't if you gave it to them with bells on. Those who want that, who believe it's their one true destiny – what's their chance of achieving it? They're on the road to Heartbreak House.

But the only alternative offered by the patriarchal mythology is that of the Failed Woman – the old maid, the barren woman, the castrating bitch, the frigid wife, the lezzie, the libber, the Unfeminine, so beloved of misogynists both male and female.

Now indeed there are women who want to be female men; their role model is Margaret Thatcher, and they're ready to dress for success, carry designer briefcases, kill for promotion, and drink the Right Scotch. They want to buy into the man's world, whatever the cost. And if that's true desire, not just compulsion born of fear, O.K.; if you can't lick 'em join 'em. My problem with that is that I can't see it as a good life even for men, who invented it and make all the rules. There's power in it, but not the kind of power I respect, not the kind of power that sets anybody free. I hate to see an intelligent woman voluntarily double herself up to get under the bottom line. Talk about crawling! And when she talks, what can she talk but father tongue? If she's the mouthpiece for the man's world, what has she got to say for herself?

Some women manage it – they may collude, but they don't sell out as women; and we know that when they speak for those who, in the man's world, are the others: women, children, the poor . . .

But it is dangerous to put on Daddy's clothes, though not, perhaps, as dangerous as it is to sit on Daddy's knees.

There's no way you can offer your experience as your truth if you deny your experience, if you try to be a mythical creature, the dummy woman who sits there on Big Daddy's lap. Whose voice will come out of her prettily hinged jaw? Who is it says yes all the time? Oh yes, yes, I will. Oh I don't know, you decide. Oh I can't do that. Yes hit me, yes rape me, yes save me, oh yes. That is how A Woman talks, the one in What-we-shall-never-know-is-what-A-Woman-wants.

A Woman's place, need I say, is in the home, plus at her volunteer work or the job where she's glad to get sixty cents for doing what men get paid a dollar for but that's because she's always on pregnancy leave or childcare?

No! A Woman is home caring for her children! even if she can't. Trapped in this well-built trap, A Woman blames her mother for luring her into it, while ensuring that her own daughter never gets out; she recoils from the idea of sisterhood and doesn't believe women have friends, because it probably means something unnatural, and anyhow, A Woman is afraid of women. She's a male construct, and she's afraid women will deconstruct her. She's afraid of everything, because she can't change. Thighs forever thin and shining hair and shining teeth and she's my Mom, too, all seven percent of her. And she never grows old.

There are old women – little old ladies, as people always say; little bits, fragments of the great dummy statue goddess A Woman. Nobody hears if old women say yes or no, nobody pays them sixty cents for anything. Old men run things. Old men run the show, press the buttons, make the wars, make the money. In the man's world, the old man's world, the young men run and run and run until they drop, and some of the young women run with them. But old women live in the cracks, between the walls, like roaches, like mice, a rustling sound, a squeaking. Better lock up the cheese, boys. It's terrible, you turn up a corner of civilization and there are all these old women running around on the wrong side –

I say to you, you know, you're going to get old. And you can't hear me. I squeak between the walls. I've walked through the mirror and am on the other side, where things are all backwards. You may look with a good will and a generous heart, but you can't see anything in the mirror but your own face; and I, looking from the dark side and seeing your beautiful young faces, see that that's how it should be.

But when you look at yourself in the mirror, I hope you see yourself. Not one of the myths. Not a failed man – a person who can never succeed because success is basically defined as being male – and not a failed goddess, a person desperately trying to hide herself in the dummy Woman, the image of men's desires and fears. I hope you look away from those myths and into your own eyes, and see your own strength. You're going to need it. I hope you don't try to take your strength from men, or from a man. Secondhand experience breaks down a block from the car lot. I hope you'll take and make your own soul; that you'll feel your life for yourself pain by pain and joy by joy; that you'll feed your life, eat, "eat as you go" – you who nourish, be nourished!

If being a cog in the machine or a puppet manipulated by others isn't what you want, you can find out what you want, your needs, desires, truths, powers, by accepting your own experience as a woman, as this woman, this body, this person, your hungry self. On the maps drawn by men there is an immense white area, terra incognita, where most women live. That country is all yours to explore, to inhabit, to describe.

But none of us lives there alone. Being human isn't something people can bring off alone; we need other people in order to be people. We need one another.

If a woman sees other women as Medusa, fears them, turns a stone ear to them, these days, all her hair may begin to stand up on end hissing, *Listen, listen, listen!* Listen to other women, your sisters, your mothers, your grandmothers – if you don't hear them how will you ever understand what your daughter says to you?

And the men who can talk, converse with you, not trying to talk through the dummy Yes-Woman, the men who can accept your experience as valid – when you find such a man love him, honor him! But don't obey him. I don't think we have any right to obedience. I think we have a responsibility to freedom.

And especially to freedom of speech. Obedience is silent. It does not answer. It is contained. Here is a disobedient woman speaking, Wendy Rose of the Hopi and Miwok people, saying in a poem called "The Parts of a Poet,"[4]

> parts of me are pinned
> to earth, parts of me
> undermine song, parts
> of me spread on the water,
> parts of me form a rainbow
> bridge, parts of me follow
> the sandfish, parts of me
> are a woman who judges.

Now this is what I want: I want to hear your judgments. I am sick of the silence of women. I want to hear you speaking all the languages, offering your experience as your truth, as human truth, talking about working, about making, about unmaking, about eating, about cooking, about feeding, about taking in seed and giving out life, about killing, about feeling,

---

4 Wendy Rose, "The Parts of a Poet," in *That's What She Said.*

about thinking; about what women do; about what men do; about war, about peace; about who presses the buttons and what buttons get pressed and whether pressing buttons is in the long run a fit occupation for human beings. There's a lot of things I want to hear you talk about.

This is what I don't want: I don't want what men have. I'm glad to let them do their work and talk their talk. But I do not want and will not have them saying or thinking or telling us that theirs is the only fit work or speech for human beings. Let them not take our work, our words, from us. If they can, if they will, let them work with us and talk with us. We can all talk mother tongue, we can all talk father tongue, and together we can try to hear and speak that language which may be our truest way of being in the world, we who speak for a world that has no words but ours.

I know that many men and even women are afraid and angry when women do speak, because in this barbaric society, when women speak truly they speak subversively – they can't help it: if you're underneath, if you're kept down, you break out, you subvert. We are volcanoes. When we women offer our experience as our truth, as human truth, all the maps change. There are new mountains.

That's what I want – to hear you erupting. You young Mount St. Helenses who don't know the power in you – I want to hear you. I want to listen to you talking to each other and to us all: whether you're writing an article or a poem or a letter or teaching a class or talking with friends or reading a novel or making a speech or proposing a law or giving a judgment or singing the baby to sleep or discussing the fate of nations, I want to hear you. Speak with a woman's tongue. Come out and tell us what time of night it is! Don't let us sink back into silence. If we don't tell our truth, who will? Who'll speak for my children, and yours?

So I end with the end of a poem by Linda Hogan of the Chickasaw people, called "The Women Speaking."[5]

Daughters, the women are speaking.
They arrive
over the wise distances
on perfect feet.
Daughters, I love you.

---

5 Linda Hogan, "The Women Speaking," in ibid.

Heroes

●

1986

For Elizabeth Arthur and Joy Johannessen

For thirty years I've been fascinated by books about the early explorations of the Antarctic, and particularly by the books written by men who were on the expeditions: Scott, Shackleton, Cherry-Garrard, Wilson, Byrd, and so on, all of them not only men of courage and imagination but excellent writers, vivid, energetic, exact, and powerful. As an American I wasn't exposed to the British idolization of Scott that now makes it so chic to sneer at him, and I still feel that I am competent to base my judgment of his character, or Shackleton's, or Byrd's, on their own works and witness, without much reference to the various biases of biographers.

They were certainly heroes to me, all of them. And as I followed them step by frostbitten-toed step across the Ross Ice Barrier and up the Beardmore Glacier to the awful place, the white plateau, and back again, many times, they got into my toes and my bones and my books, and I wrote *The Left Hand of Darkness*, in which a Black man from Earth and an androgynous extraterrestrial pull Scott's sledge through Shackleton's blizzards across a planet called Winter. And fifteen years or so later I wrote a story, "Sur," in which a small group of Latin Americans actually reach the South Pole a year before Amundsen and Scott, but decide not to say anything about it, because if the men knew that they had got there first – they are all women – it wouldn't do. The men would be so let down. "We left no footprints, even," says the narrator.

Now, in writing that story, which was one of the pleasantest experiences of my life, I was aware that I was saying some rather hard things about heroism, but I had no desire or intention to debunk or devalue the actual explorers of Antarctica. What I wanted was to join them, fictionally. I had been along with them so many times in their books; why couldn't a few

of us, my kind of people, housewives, come along with them in my book
. . . or even come before them?

These simple little wishes, when they become what people call "ideas"
– as in "Where do you get the *ideas* for your stories?" – and when they
find themselves in an appropriate nutrient medium such as prose, may
begin to grow, to get yeasty, to fizz. Whatever the "idea" of that story was,
it has continued to ferment in the dark vats of my mental cellars and is
now quite heady, with a marked nose and a complicated aftertaste, like a
good '69 Zinfandel.

I wasn't aware of this process until recently, when I was watching the
Public Broadcasting series about Shackleton (as well conceived, cast, and
produced as the series about Scott and Amundsen was shoddy). There were
Ernest Shackleton and his three friends struggling across the abomination
of desolation towards the Pole, two days before they had to turn back only
ninety-seven miles short of that geometrical *bindu* which they desired
so ardently to attain. And the voice-over spoke words from Shackleton's
journal: "Man can only do his best. The strongest forces of Nature are
arrayed against us." And I sat there and thought, Oh, what nonsense!

That startled me. I had been feeling just as I had always felt for those
cold, hungry, tired, brave men, and commiserating them for the bitter
disappointment awaiting them – and yet Shackleton's words struck me as
disgustingly false, as silly. Why? I had to think it out; and this paper is the
process of thinking it out.

"Man can only do his best" – well, all right. They were all men, of
course, and a long way from the suffragists back home; they honestly believed that "man" includes women, or would have said they did if they had
ever thought about it, which I doubt they ever did. I am sure they would
have laughed heartily at the proposal that their expedition include women.
But still, Man can only do his best; or, to put it in my dialect, people can
only do their best; or, as King Yudhisthira says in the great and bitter end
of the *Mahabharata*, "By nothing that I do can I attain a goal beyond my
reach." That king whose dog's name is Dharma knows what he is talking
about. As did those English explorers, with their clear, fierce sense of duty.

But how about "The strongest forces of Nature are arrayed against us"?
Here's the problem. What did you expect, Ernest? Indeed, what did you
ask for? Didn't you set it up that way? Didn't you arrange, with vast trouble
and expense, that the very strongest "forces of Nature" would be "arrayed
against" you and your tiny army?

What is false is the military image; what is foolish is the egoism; what is pernicious is the identification of "Nature" as enemy. We are asked to believe that the Antarctic continent became aware that four Englishmen were penetrating her virgin whiteness and so unleashed upon them the punishing fury of her revenge, the mighty weaponry of wind and blizzard, and so forth and so on. Well, I don't believe it. I don't believe that Nature is either an enemy, or a woman, to humanity. Nobody has ever thought so but Man; and the thought is, to one not Man, no longer acceptable even as a poetic metaphor. Nobody, nothing, "arrayed" any "forces" against Shackleton except Shackleton himself. He created an obstacle to conquer or an enemy to attack; attacked; and was defeated – by what? By himself, having himself created the situation in which his defeat could occur.

Had he reached the Pole he would have said, "I have conquered, I have achieved," in perfectly self-justified triumph. But, forced to retreat, he does not say, "I am defeated"; he blames it on that which is not himself, Nature. If Man wins the battle he starts, he takes the credit for winning, but if he doesn't win, he doesn't lose; "forces arrayed against" him defeat him. Man does not, cannot fail. And Shackleton, speaking for Man, refuses the responsibility for a situation for which he was responsible from beginning to end.

In an even more drastic situation for which he was even more responsible, in his last journal entry Scott wrote:

> We took risks, we knew we took them; things have come out against us, and therefore we have no cause for complaint, but bow to the will of Providence, determined still to do our best to the last.

I have seriously tried to find those words false and silly; I can't do it. Their beauty is no accident.

"Things have come out against us" sounds rather like a projection of fault (like the "forces arrayed against us") but lacks any note of accusation or blame; the underlying image is that of gambling, trusting to luck. "Providence," which is how Scott referred to God, does seem to come in as the "Other," a will opposed to Scott's will as Nature was opposed to Shackleton's; but something you call by the name of Providence is not something you perceive as an opponent or an enemy – indeed, the connotations are maternal: nurturing, sheltering, providing. The man may be speaking like a child, but not like a spoiled child. He takes responsibility for the risks taken, and beyond hope finds duty unalterable: "to do our best to the last." Like Yudhisthira, he knew what "the last" meant. Nothing in me finds this contemptible, and I can't imagine ever finding it contemptible. But I don't know. I have found so many things silly that just a few years ago seemed fine . . . Time to bottle the wine: if you leave it too long in the wood it sours and is lost. I don't want to go sour. All I want to do is lose the hero myths so that I can find what is worth admiration.

All right: what I admire in Shackleton, at that moment on the Barrier, is that he turned back. He gave up; he admitted defeat; and he saved his men. Unfortunately he also saved his pride by posturing a bit, playing hero. He couldn't admit that his weakness was his strength; he did the right thing, but said the wrong one. So I go on loving Shackleton, but with the slightest shade of contempt for his having boasted.

But Scott, who did nearly everything wrong, why have I no such contempt for Scott? Why does he remain worthy in my mind of that awful beauty and freedom, my Antarctica? Evidently because he admitted his failure completely – living it through to its end, death. It is as if Scott realized that his life was a story he had to tell, and he had to get the ending right.

This statement may be justly seen as frivolous, trivializing. The death of five people isn't "just a story."

But then, what is a story? And what does one live for? To stay alive, certainly; but only that?

In Amundsen's practical, realistic terms, the deaths of Scott and his four companions were unnecessary, preventable. But then, in what terms was Amundsen's polar journey necessary? It had no justification but nationalism/egoism – "Yah! I'm going to get there first!"

When Scott's party stopped for the last time, the rocks they had collected for the Museum of Natural History were still heavy on the sledge. That is very moving; but I will not use the scientific motives of Scott's expedition to justify his polar journey. It was a mere race too, with no goal but winning. It was when he lost the race that it became a real journey to a real end. And this reality, this value to others, lies in the account he kept.

Amundsen's relation of his polar run is interesting, informative, in some respects admirable. Scott's journal is all that and very much more than that. I would rank it with Woolf's or Pepys's diaries, as a personal record of inestimable value, written by an artist.

Scott's temperament was not very well suited to his position as leader;

his ambition and intensity drove him to lead, but his inflexibility, vanity, and unpredictability could make his leadership a disaster, for example in his sudden decision to take four men, not three, on the last lap to the Pole, thus oversetting all the meticulous arrangements for supplies. Scott arranged his own defeat, his death, and the death of the four men he was responsible for. He "asked for it." And there were certainly self-destructive elements in his personality. But it would be merely glib to say that he "wanted to fail," and it would miss what I see as the real heroism: what he made of his failure. He took complete responsibility for it. He witnessed truly. He kept on telling the story.

"Unless a grain of wheat fall into the ground and die, it abideth alone; but if it die, it bringeth forth much fruit."

His self-sacrifice was not, I think, deliberate; but his behavior was sacrificial, rather than heroic. And it was as that unheroic creature, a writer, that he gathered, garnered, saved what could be saved from defeat, suffering, and death. Because he was an artist, his testimony turns mere waste and misery into that useful thing, tragedy.

His companion Edward Wilson, whose paintings are perhaps the finest visual record of Antarctica, kept a diary of the polar journey too. Wilson was a far sweeter, more generous man than Scott, and his diary is very moving, but it has not the power of Scott's – it is not a work of art; it records, but it does not ultimately take responsibility for what happens. Self-absorbed, willful, obsessed, controlling, Scott was evidently an artist born. He should never have been entrusted with a polar expedition, no doubt. But he was; and he had so fierce a determination to tell his story to the end that he wrote it even as he lay in the tent on the ice dying of cold, starvation, and gangrene among his dead. And so Antarctica is ours. He won it for us.

The Carrier Bag Theory of Fiction

1986/1988

In the temperate and tropical regions where it appears that hominids evolved into human beings, the principal food of the species was vegetable. Sixty-five to eighty percent of what human beings ate in those regions in Paleolithic, Neolithic, and prehistoric times was gathered; only in the extreme Arctic was meat the staple food. The mammoth hunters spectacularly occupy the cave wall and the mind, but what we actually did to stay alive and fat was gather seeds, roots, sprouts, shoots, leaves, nuts, berries, fruits, and grains, adding bugs and mollusks and netting or snaring birds, fish, rats, rabbits, and other tuskless small fry to up the protein. And we didn't even work hard at it – much less hard than peasants slaving in somebody else's field after agriculture was invented, much less hard than paid workers since civilization was invented. The average prehistoric person could make a nice living in about a fifteen-hour work week.

Fifteen hours a week for subsistence leaves a lot of time for other things. So much time that maybe the restless ones who didn't have a baby around to enliven their life, or skill in making or cooking or singing, or very interesting thoughts to think, decided to slope off and hunt mammoths. The skillful hunters then would come staggering back with a load of meat, a lot of ivory, and a story. It wasn't the meat that made the difference. It was the story.

It is hard to tell a really gripping tale of how I wrested a wild-oat seed from its husk, and then another, and then another, and then another, and then another, and then I scratched my gnat bites, and Ool said something funny, and we went to the creek and got a drink and watched newts for a while, and then I found another patch of oats . . . No, it does not compare, it cannot compete with how I thrust my spear deep into the titanic hairy flank while Oob, impaled on one huge sweeping tusk, writhed screaming, and blood spouted everywhere in crimson torrents, and Boob was crushed

163

to jelly when the mammoth fell on him as I shot my unerring arrow straight through eye to brain.

That story not only has Action, it has a Hero. Heroes are powerful. Before you know it, the men and women in the wild-oat patch and their kids and the skills of the makers and the thoughts of the thoughtful and the songs of the singers are all part of it, have all been pressed into service in the tale of the Hero. But it isn't their story. It's his.

When she was planning the book that ended up as *Three Guineas*, Virginia Woolf wrote a heading in her notebook, "Glossary"; she had thought of reinventing English according to a new plan, in order to tell a different story. One of the entries in this glossary is *heroism*, defined as "botulism." And *hero*, in Woolf's dictionary, is "bottle." The hero as bottle, a stringent reevaluation. I now propose the bottle as hero.

Not just the bottle of gin or wine, but bottle in its older sense of container in general, a thing that holds something else.

If you haven't got something to put it in, food will escape you – even something as uncombative and unresourceful as an oat. You put as many as you can into your stomach while they are handy, that being the primary container; but what about tomorrow morning when you wake up and it's cold and raining and wouldn't it be good to have just a few handfuls of oats to chew on and give little Oom to make her shut up, but how do you get more than one stomachful and one handful home? So you get up and go to the damned soggy oat patch in the rain, and wouldn't it be a good thing if you had something to put Baby Oo Oo in so that you could pick the oats with both hands? A leaf a gourd a shell a net a bag a sling a sack a bottle a pot a box a container. A holder. A recipient.

> The first cultural device was probably a recipient ... Many theorizers feel that the earliest cultural inventions must have been a container to hold gathered products and some kind of sling or net carrier.

So says Elizabeth Fisher in *Women's Creation* (McGraw-Hill, 1975).* But no, this cannot be. Where is that wonderful, big, long, hard thing, a bone, I believe, that the Ape Man first bashed somebody with in the movie and then, grunting with ecstasy at having achieved the first proper murder, flung up into the sky, and whirling there it became a space ship thrusting

---

* London: Wildwood House Ltd 1980.

its way into the cosmos to fertilize it and produce at the end of the movie a lovely fetus, a boy of course, drifting around the Milky Way without (oddly enough) any womb, any matrix at all? I don't know. I don't even care. I'm not telling that story. We've heard it, we've all heard all about all the sticks and spears and swords, the things to bash and poke and hit with, the long, hard things, but we have not heard about the thing to put things in, the container for the thing contained. That is a new story. That is news.

And yet old. Before – once you think about it, surely long before – the weapon, a late, luxurious, superfluous tool; long before the useful knife and ax; right along with the indispensable whacker, grinder, and digger – for what's the use of digging up a lot of potatoes if you have nothing to lug the ones you can't eat home in – with or before the tool that forces energy outward, we made the tool that brings energy home. It makes sense to me. I am an adherent of what Fisher calls the Carrier Bag Theory of human evolution.

This theory not only explains large areas of theoretical obscurity and avoids large areas of theoretical nonsense (inhabited largely by tigers, foxes, and other highly territorial mammals); it also grounds me, personally, in human culture in a way I never felt grounded before. So long as culture was explained as originating from and elaborating upon the use of long, hard objects for sticking, bashing, and killing, I never thought that I had, or wanted, any particular share in it. ("What Freud mistook for her lack of civilization is woman's lack of *loyalty* to civilization," Lillian Smith observed.) The society, the civilization they were talking about, these theoreticians, was evidently theirs; they owned it, they liked it; they were human, fully human, bashing, sticking, thrusting, killing. Wanting to be human too, I sought for evidence that I was; but if that's what it took, to make a weapon and kill with it, then evidently I was either extremely defective as a human being, or not human at all.

That's right, they said. What you are is a woman. Possibly not human at all, certainly defective. Now be quiet while we go on telling the Story of the Ascent of Man the Hero.

Go on, say I, wandering off towards the wild oats, with Oo Oo in the sling and little Oom carrying the basket. You just go on telling how the mammoth fell on Boob and how Cain fell on Abel and how the bomb fell on Nagasaki and how the burning jelly fell on the villagers and how the missiles will fall on the Evil Empire, and all the other steps in the Ascent of Man.

If it is a human thing to do to put something you want, because it's useful, edible, or beautiful, into a bag, or a basket, or a bit of rolled bark or leaf, or a net woven of your own hair, or what have you, and then take it home with you, home being another, larger kind of pouch or bag, a container for people, and then later on you take it out and eat it or share it or store it up for winter in a solider container or put it in the medicine bundle or the shrine or the museum, the holy place, the area that contains what is sacred, and then next day you probably do much the same again — if to do that is human, if that's what it takes, then I am a human being after all. Fully, freely, gladly, for the first time.

Not, let it be said at once, an unaggressive or uncombative human being. I am an aging, angry woman laying mightily about me with my handbag, fighting hoodlums off. However I don't, nor does anybody else, consider myself heroic for doing so. It's just one of those damned things you have to do in order to be able to go on gathering wild oats and telling stories.

It is the story that makes the difference. It is the story that hid my humanity from me, the story the mammoth hunters told about bashing, thrusting, raping, killing, about the Hero. The wonderful, poisonous story of Botulism. The killer story.

It sometimes seems that that story is approaching its end. Lest there be no more telling of stories at all, some of us out here in the wild oats, amid the alien corn, think we'd better start telling another one, which maybe people can go on with when the old one's finished. Maybe. The trouble is, we've all let ourselves become part of the killer story, and so we may get finished along with it. Hence it is with a certain feeling of urgency that I seek the nature, subject, words of the other story, the untold one, the life story.

It's unfamiliar, it doesn't come easily, thoughtlessly to the lips as the killer story does; but still, "untold" was an exaggeration. People have been telling the life story for ages, in all sorts of words and ways. Myths of creation and transformation, trickster stories, folktales, jokes, novels . . .

The novel is a fundamentally unheroic kind of story. Of course the Hero has frequently taken it over, that being his imperial nature and uncontrollable impulse, to take everything over and run it while making stern decrees and laws to control his uncontrollable impulse to kill it. So the Hero has decreed through his mouthpieces the Lawgivers, first, that the proper shape of the narrative is that of the arrow or spear, starting *here* and going straight *there* and THOK! hitting its mark (which drops dead); second, that the central concern of narrative, including the novel, is conflict; and third, that the story isn't any good if he isn't in it.

I differ with all of this. I would go so far as to say that the natural, proper, fitting shape of the novel might be that of a sack, a bag. A book holds words. Words hold things. They bear meanings. A novel is a medicine bundle, holding things in a particular, powerful relation to one another and to us.

One relationship among elements in the novel may well be that of conflict, but the reduction of narrative to conflict is absurd. (I have read a how-to-write manual that said, "A story should be seen as a battle," and went on about strategies, attacks, victory, etc.) Conflict, competition, stress, struggle, etc., within the narrative conceived as carrier bag / belly / box / house / medicine bundle, may be seen as necessary elements of a whole which itself cannot be characterized either as conflict or as harmony, since its purpose is neither resolution nor stasis but continuing process.

Finally, it's clear that the Hero does not look well in this bag. He needs a stage or a pedestal or a pinnacle. You put him in a bag and he looks like a rabbit, like a potato.

That is why I like novels: instead of heroes they have people in them.

So, when I came to write science-fiction novels, I came lugging this great heavy sack of stuff, my carrier bag full of wimps and klutzes, and tiny grains of things smaller than a mustard seed, and intricately woven nets which when laboriously unknotted are seen to contain one blue pebble, an imperturbably functioning chronometer telling the time on another world, and a mouse's skull; full of beginnings without ends, of initiations, of losses, of transformations and translations, and far more tricks than conflicts, far fewer triumphs than snares and delusions; full of space ships that get stuck, missions that fail, and people who don't understand. I said it was hard to make a gripping tale of how we wrested the wild oats from their husks, I didn't say it was impossible. Who ever said writing a novel was easy?

If science fiction is the mythology of modern technology, then its myth is tragic. "Technology," or "modern science" (using the words as they are usually used, in an unexamined shorthand standing for the "hard" sciences and high technology founded upon continuous economic growth), is a heroic undertaking, Herculean, Promethean, conceived as triumph, hence ultimately as tragedy. The fiction embodying this myth will be, and has been, triumphant (Man conquers earth, space, aliens, death, the future, etc.) and tragic (apocalypse, holocaust, then or now).

If, however, one avoids the linear, progressive, Time's-(killing)-arrow mode of the Techno-Heroic, and redefines technology and science as primarily cultural carrier bag rather than weapon of domination, one pleasant side effect is that science fiction can be seen as a far less rigid, narrow field, not necessarily Promethean or apocalyptic at all, and in fact less a mythological genre than a realistic one.

It is a strange realism, but it is a strange reality.

Science fiction properly conceived, like all serious fiction, however funny, is a way of trying to describe what is in fact going on, what people actually do and feel, how people relate to everything else in this vast sack, this belly of the universe, this womb of things to be and tomb of things that were, this unending story. In it, as in all fiction, there is room enough to keep even Man where he belongs, in his place in the scheme of things; there is time enough to gather plenty of wild oats and sow them too, and sing to little Oom, and listen to Ool's joke, and watch newts, and still the story isn't over. Still there are seeds to be gathered, and room in the bag of stars.

The Fisherwoman's Daughter

1988

I read the first version of this paper at Brown University and at Miami University in Ohio, and revised it heavily to read at Wesleyan College in Georgia. Then I wrote it all over again to read at Portland State University. I have a feeling I read it somewhere else, but can't reconstruct where. When I went to Tulane to be a Mellon Fellow – to be precise, a quarter of a Mellon – I re-wrote it again, and that version, which I pretended was definitive, appeared in Tulane's series of Mellon papers, under the title "A Woman Writing." Asked to give the talk in a benefit series in San Francisco, I decided to include more about my mother, whose writing life was lived in the Bay Area; and that led to another full revision.

In preparing the manuscript of this book, I came to the immense folder containing the five – in places identical, in places widely differing – typescripts of the talk; and I thought, "If I have to rewrite that thing once more I will die." So I merely included the latest version, without rereading it. My ruthless editor would have none of that. "Pusillanimous woman," she said, "what about all the bits you left out?" "What about them?" I snarled. "I think if we just put them together it will work," said she. "Show me," said I, craftily. So she did. I hope it does.

What pleases me most about the piece, after so much work on it, is that I can look on it at last as a collaboration. The responses from the various audiences I read it to, both questions in the lecture hall and letters afterward, guided and clarified my thinking and saved me from many follies and omissions. The present re-collation and editing has given me back the whole thing – not shapely and elegant, but a big crazy quilt. And that was my working title for it when I first began gathering material: "Crazy Quilt." That name hints again at collaboration, which is what I saw myself as doing as I pieced together the works and words of so many other writers – ancestors, strangers, friends.

"'So of course,' wrote Betty Flanders, pressing her heels rather deeper in the sand, 'there was nothing for it but to leave.'"

That is the first sentence of Virginia Woolf's *Jacob's Room*.[1] It is a woman writing. Sitting on the sand by the sea, writing. It's only Betty Flanders, and she's only writing a letter. But first sentences are doors to worlds. This world of Jacob's room, so strangely empty at the end of the book when the mother stands in it holding out a pair of her son's old shoes and saying, "What am I to do with these?" – this is a world in which the first thing one sees is a woman, a mother of children, writing.

On the shore, by the sea, outdoors, is that where women write? Not at a desk, in a writing room? Where does a woman write, what does she look like writing, what is my image, your image, of a woman writing? I asked my friends: "A woman writing: what do you see?" There would be a pause, then the eyes would light up, seeing. Some sent me to paintings, Fragonard, Cassatt, but mostly these turned out to be paintings of a woman reading or with a letter, not actually writing or reading the letter but looking up from it with unfocused eyes: Will he never never return? Did I remember to turn off the pot roast? . . . Another friend responded crisply, "A woman writing is taking dictation." And another said, "She's sitting at the kitchen table, and the kids are yelling."

And that last is the image I shall pursue. But first let me tell you my own first answer to my question: Jo March. From the immediacy, the authority, with which Frank Merrill's familiar illustrations of *Little Women*[2] came to my mind as soon as I asked myself what a woman writing looks like, I know that Jo March must have had real influence upon me when I was a young scribbler. I am sure she has influenced many girls, for she is not, like most "real" authors, either dead or inaccessibly famous; nor, like so many artists in books, is she set apart by sensitivity or suffering or general superlativity; nor is she, like most authors in novels, male. She is close as a sister and common as grass. As a model, what does she tell scribbling girls? I think it worthwhile to follow the biography of Jo March the Writer until we come to that person of whom, as a child and until quite recently, I knew almost nothing: Louisa May Alcott.

We first meet Jo as a writer when sister Amy vengefully burns her

---

1 Virginia Woolf, *Jacob's Room* (London: The Hogarth Press).

2 The edition of *Little Women* I used was my mother's and is now my daughter's. It was published in Boston by Little, Brown, undated, around the turn of the century, and Merrill's fine drawings have also been reproduced in other editions.

manuscript, "the loving work of several years. It seemed a small loss to others, but to Jo it was a dreadful calamity." How could a book, several years' work, be "a small loss" to anyone? That horrified me. How could they ask Jo to forgive Amy? At least she nearly drowns her in a frozen lake before forgiving her. At any rate, some chapters later Jo is

> very busy in the garret. . . seated on the old sofa, writing busily, with her papers spread out on a trunk before her . . . Jo's desk up here was an old tin kitchen . . .

– the *OED* says, "New England: a roasting pan." So Jo's room of her own at this stage is a garret furnished with a sofa, a roasting pan, and a rat. To any twelve-year-old, heaven.

> Jo scribbled away till the last page was filled, when she signed her name with a flourish . . . Lying back on the sofa she read the manuscript carefully through, making dashes here and there, and putting in many exclamation points, which looked like little balloons; then she tied it up with a smart red ribbon and sat a minute looking at it with a sober, wistful expression, which plainly showed how earnest her work had been.

I am interested here by the counterplay of a deflating irony – the scribbling, the dashes, the balloons, the ribbon – and that wistful earnestness.

Jo sends her story to a paper, it is printed, and she reads it aloud to her sisters, who cry at the right places. Beth asks, "Who wrote it?"

> The reader suddenly sat up, cast away the paper, displaying a flushed countenance, and with a funny mixture of solemnity and excitement, replied, in a loud voice, "Your sister."

The March family makes a great fuss, "for these foolish, affectionate people made a jubilee of every little household joy" – and there again is deflation, a writer's first publication reduced to a "little household joy." Does it not debase art? And yet does it not also, by refusing the heroic tone, refuse to inflate art into something beyond the reach of any "mere girl"?

So Jo goes on writing; here she is some years later, and I quote at length, for this is the central image.

Every few weeks she would shut herself up in her room, put on her scribbling suit, and "fall into a vortex," as she expressed it, writing away at her novel with all her heart and soul, for till that was finished she could find no peace. Her "scribbling suit" consisted of a black woolen pinafore on which she could wipe her pen at will, and a cap of the same material, adorned with a cheerful red bow . . . This cap was a beacon to the inquiring eyes of her family, who during these periods kept their distance, merely popping in their heads semi-occasionally to ask, with interest, "Does genius burn, Jo?" They did not always venture even to ask this question, but took an observation of the cap, and judged accordingly. If this expressive article of dress was drawn low upon the forehead, it was a sign that hard work was going on; in exciting moments it was pushed rakishly askew; and when despair seized the author it was plucked wholly off and cast upon the floor. At such times the intruder silently withdrew; and not until the red bow was seen gayly erect upon the gifted brow, did anyone dare address Jo.

She did not think herself a genius by any means; but when the writing fit came on, she gave herself up to it with entire abandon, and led a blissful life, unconscious of want, care, or bad weather, while she sat safe and happy in an imaginary world, full of friends almost as real and dear to her as any in the flesh. Sleep forsook her eyes, meals stood untasted, day and night were all too short to enjoy the happiness which blessed her only at such times, and made these hours worth living, even if they bore no other fruit. The divine afflatus usually lasted a week or two, and then she emerged from her vortex, hungry, sleepy, cross, or despondent.

This is a good description of the condition in which the work of art is done. This is the real thing – domesticated. The cap and bow, the facetious turns and the disclaimers, deflate without degrading, and allow Alcott to make a rather extraordinary statement: that Jo is doing something very important and doing it entirely seriously and that there is nothing unusual about a young woman's doing it. This passion of work and this happiness which blessed her in doing it are fitted without fuss into a girl's commonplace life at home. It may not seem much; but I don't know where else I or many other girls like me, in my generation or my mother's or my daughters', were to find this model, this validation.

Jo writes romantic thrillers and they sell; her father shakes his head and says, "Aim at the highest and never mind the money," but Amy remarks, "The money is the best part of it." Working in Boston as a governess-seamstress, Jo sees that "money conferred power: money and power, therefore, she resolved to have; not to be used for herself alone," our author's author hastily adds, "but for those whom she loved more than self... She took to writing sensation stories." Her first visit to the editorial office of the *Weekly Volcano* is handled lightly, but the three men treat her as a woman who has come to sell herself – true Lévi-Straussians, to whom what a woman does is entirely subsumed in woman as commodity. Refusing shame, Jo writes on, and makes money by her writing; admitting shame, she does not "tell them at home."

Jo soon found that her innocent experience had given her but few glimpses of the tragic world which underlies society; so, regarding it in a business light, she set about supplying her deficiencies with characteristic energy ... She searched newspapers for accidents, incidents, and crimes; she excited the suspicions of public librarians by asking for works on poisons; she studied faces in the street, and characters good, bad, and indifferent all about her ... Much describing of other people's passions and feelings set her to studying and speculating about her own – a morbid amusement, in which healthy young minds do not voluntarily indulge –

but which one might think appropriate, even needful, to the young novelist? However, "wrongdoing always brings its own punishment, and when Jo most needed hers, she got it."

Her punishment is administered by the Angel in the House, in the form of Professor Bhaer. Knowing that she is soiling her pure soul, he attacks the papers she writes for: "I do not like to think that good young girls should see such things." Jo weakly defends them, but when he leaves she rereads her stories, three months' work, and burns them. Amy doesn't have to do it for her any more; she can destroy herself. Then she sits and wonders: "I almost wish I hadn't any conscience, it's so inconvenient!" A cry from the heart of Bronson Alcott's daughter. She tries a pious tale and a children's story, which don't sell, and gives up: she "corked up her inkstand."

Beth dies, and trying to replace her, Jo tries "to live for others" – finally driving her mother to say, "Why don't you write? That always used to make you happy." So she does, and she writes both well and successfully – until Professor Bhaer returns and marries her, evidently the only way to make her stop writing. She has his two boys to bring up, and then her two boys, and then all those Little Men in the next volume; at the end of *Little Women*, in the chapter called "Harvest Time," she says, "I haven't given up the hope that I may write a good book yet, but I can wait."

The harvest seems indefinitely deferred. But, in Rachel Blau Du Plessis' phrase,[3] Jo writes beyond the ending. In the third volume, *Jo's Boys*, she has gone back in middle age to writing, and is rich and famous. There is realism, toughness, and comedy in the descriptions of her managing the household, mothering the teenagers, writing her chapters, and trying to avoid the celebrity hunters. In fact this, like the whole story of Jo the Writer, is quite close to Louisa Alcott's own story, with one large difference. Jo marries and has children. Lu did not.

And yet she undertook the responsibility for a family, some of whom were as improvident and self-centered as any baby. There is a heartbreaking note in her journal[4] for April 1869, when she was suffering a "bad spell" of mercury poisoning (the calomel given her to cure fever when she was a nurse in the Civil War made her sick the rest of her life):

Very poorly. Feel quite used up. Don't care much for myself, as rest is heavenly, even with pain; but the family seems so panic-stricken and helpless when I break down, that I try to keep the mill going. Two short tales for L., $50; two for Ford, $20; and did my editorial work, though two months are unpaid for. Roberts wants a new book, but am afraid to get into a vortex lest I fall ill.

Alcott used the same word Jo used for her passions of writing; here are a couple of journal passages comparable to the "vortex" passage in *Little Women*.

August 1860 – "Moods" [a novel]. Genius burned so fiercely that for four weeks I wrote all day and planned nearly all night, being quite possessed by my work. I was perfectly happy, and seemed to have no wants.

3 Rachel Blau Du Plessis, *Writing Beyond the Ending: Narrative Strategies of Twentieth-Century Women Writers* (London: Harvester Press Ltd, 1986).
4 Louisa May Alcott, *Life, Letters, and Journals* (Boston: Roberts Brothers, 1890).

February 1861 – Another turn at "Moods," which I remodeled. From the 2d to the 25th I sat writing, with a run at dusk; could not sleep, and for three days was so full of it I could not stop to get up. Mother made me a green silk cap with a red bow, to match the old green and red party wrap, which I wore as a "glory cloak." Thus arrayed sat in a grove of manuscripts, "living for immortality" as May said. Mother wandered in and out with cordial cups of tea, worried because I couldn't eat. Father thought it fine, and brought his reddest apples and hardest cider for my Pegasus to feed upon … It was very pleasant and queer while it lasted …

And it is pleasant to see how the family whose debts she slaved to pay off, and which she strove so to protect and keep in comfort, tried to protect and help her in return.

Like so many women of her century, then, Lu Alcott had a family, though she did not marry. "Liberty is a better husband than love to many of us," she wrote, but in fact she had very little liberty, in the sense of freedom from immediate, personal responsibilities. She even had a baby – her sister May's. Dying from complications of childbirth, May asked the beloved older sister, then forty-eight, to bring up little Lu; which she did until her death eight years later.

All this is complex, more complex, I think, than one tends to imagine; for the Victorian script calls for a clear choice – either books or babies for a woman, not both. And Jo *seems* to make that choice. I was annoyed at myself when I realized that I had forgotten Jo's survival as a writer – that my memory, except for one nagging scrap that led me to look up *Jo's Boys* at last, had followed the script. That, of course, is the power of the script: you play the part without knowing it.

Here is a classic – a scriptural – description of a writing woman, the mother of children, one of whom is just now in the process of falling down the stairs.

Mrs Jellyby was a pretty, very diminutive, plump woman, of from forty to fifty, with handsome eyes, though they had a curious habit of seeming to look a long way off … [She] had very good hair, but was too much occupied with her African duties to brush it … We could not help noticing that her dress didn't nearly meet up the back, and that the open space was railed across with a latticework of stay-laces – like a summer-house.

The room, which was strewn with papers and nearly filled by a great writing-table covered with similar litter, was, I must say, not only very untidy, but very dirty. We were obliged to take notice of that with our sense of sight, even while, with our sense of hearing, we followed the poor child who had tumbled downstairs: I think into the back kitchen, where somebody seemed to stifle him. But what principally struck us was a jaded and unhealthy-looking, though by no means plain girl, at the writing-table, who sat biting the feather of her pen, and staring at us. I suppose nobody ever was in such a state of ink.[5]

I will, with difficulty, restrain myself from reading you the rest of *Bleak House*. I love Dickens and will defend his Mrs. Jellyby and her correspondence with Borrioboola-Gha as an eternal send-up of those who meddle with foreign morals while remaining oblivious to the misery under their nose. But I observe also that he uses a woman to make this point, probably because it was, and is, safe: few readers would question the assumption that a woman should put family before public responsibility, or that if she does work outside the "private sphere" she will be neglectful of her house, indifferent to the necks of her children, and incompetent to fasten her clothing. Mrs. Jellyby's daughter is saved from her enforced "state of ink" by marriage, but Mrs. Jellyby will get no help from her husband, a man so inert that their marriage is described as the union of mind and matter. Mrs. Jellyby is a joy to me, she is drawn with so much humor and good nature; and yet she troubles me, because behind her lurks the double standard. Nowhere among Dickens' many responsible, intelligent women is there one who does real artistic or intellectual work, to balance Mrs. Jellyby and reassure us that it isn't what she does but how she does it that is deplorable. And yet the passage just quoted is supposed to have been written by a woman – the character Esther Summerson. Esther herself is a problem. How does she write half Dickens' novel for him while managing Bleak House and getting smallpox and everything else? We never catch her at it. As a woman writing, Esther is invisible. She is not in the script.

There may be a sympathetic portrait of a woman writer with children in a novel written by a man. I have read versions of this paper in Rhode

---

5 Charles Dickens, *Bleak House*.

Island, Ohio, Georgia, Louisiana, Oregon, and California, and asked each audience please to tell me if they knew of any such. I wait in hope. Indeed, the only sympathetic picture of a woman novelist in a man's novel that I know is the protagonist of *Diana of the Crossways*. Meredith shows her writing novels for her living, doing it brilliantly, and finding her freedom in her professionalism. But, self-alienated by a disastrous infatuation, she begins to force her talent and can't work – the script apparently being that love is incidental for a man, everything for a woman. At the end, well off and happily married, she is expecting a baby, but not, it appears, a book. All the same, Diana still stands, nearly a century later, quite alone at her crossways.

Invisibility as a writer is a condition that affects not only characters but authors, and even the children of authors. Take Elizabeth Barrett Browning, whom we have consistently put to bed with a spaniel, ignoring the fact that when she wrote *Aurora Leigh* she was the healthy mother of a healthy four-year-old – ignoring, in fact, the fact that she wrote *Aurora Leigh*, a book about being a woman writer, and how difficult one's own true love can make it for one.

Here is a woman who had several children and was a successful novelist, writing a letter to her husband about a hundred and fifty years ago, or maybe last night:

> If I *am* to write, I must have a room to myself, which shall be *my* room. All last winter I felt the need of some place where I could go and be quiet. I could not [write in the dining room] for there was all the setting of tables and clearing up of tables and dressing and washing of children, and everything else going on, and . . . I never felt comfortable there, though I tried hard. Then if I came into the parlor where you were, I felt as if I were interrupting you, and you know you sometimes thought so too.[6]

What do you mean? Not at all! Silly notion! Just like a woman!

Fourteen years and several more children later, that woman wrote *Uncle Tom's Cabin* – most of it at the kitchen table.

A room of one's own – yes. One may ask why Mr. Harriet Beecher Stowe got a room to himself to write in, while the woman who wrote the

---

6 Harriet Beecher Stowe, 1841, quoted in Tillie Olsen, *Silences* (London: Virago Press, 1980).

most morally effective American novel of the nineteenth century got the kitchen table. But then one may also ask why she accepted the kitchen table. Any self-respecting man would have sat there for five minutes and then stalked out shouting, "Nobody can work in this madhouse, call me when dinner's ready!" But Harriet, a self-respecting woman, went on getting dinner with the kids all underfoot *and* writing her novels. The first question, to be asked with awe, is surely, How? But then, Why? *Why* are women such patsies?

The quick-feminist-fix answer is that they are victims of and/or accomplices with the patriarchy, which is true but doesn't really get us anywhere new. Let us go to another woman novelist for help. I stole the Stowe quotation (and others) from Tillie Olsen's *Silences*, a book to which this paper stands in the relation of a loving but undutiful daughter – Hey, Ma, that's a neat quotation, can I wear it? This next one I found for myself, in the *Autobiography* of Margaret Oliphant, a fascinating book, from the generation just after Stowe. Oliphant was a successful writer very young, married, had three kids, went on writing, was left a widow with heavy debts and the three kids plus her brother's three kids to bring up, did so, went on writing ... When her second book came out, she was still, like Jo March, a girl at home.

> I had a great pleasure in writing, but the success and the three editions had no particular effect upon my mind ... I had nobody to praise me except my mother and [brother] Frank, and their applause – well, it was delightful, it was everything in the world – it was life – but it did not count. They were part of me, and I of them, and we were all in it.[7]

I find that extraordinary. I cannot imagine any male author saying anything like that at all. There is a key here – something real that has been neglected, been hidden, been denied.

> ... The writing ran through everything. But then it was also subordinate to everything, to be pushed aside for any little necessity. I had no table even to myself, much less a room to work in, but sat at the corner of the family table with my writing-book, with everything going on as if I had

---

[7] This and the subsequent connected passages are from the *Autobiography and Letters of Mrs. Margaret Oliphant*, edited by Mrs. Harry Coghill (Leicester: Leicester University Press, The Victorian Library, 1974).

been making a shirt instead of writing a book . . . My mother sat always
at needlework of some kind, and talked to whoever might be present,
and I took my share in the conversation, going on all the same with my
story, the little groups of imaginary persons, these other talks evolving
themselves quite undisturbed.

How's that for an image, the group of imaginary people talking in the
imaginary room in the real room among the real people talking, and all of
it going on perfectly quiet and unconfused . . . But it's shocking. She can't
be a real writer. Real writers writhe on solitary sofas in cork-lined rooms,
agonizing after *le mot juste* – don't they?

My study, all the study I have ever attained to, is the little second
drawing-room where all the life of the house goes on . . .

– you recall that she was bringing up six children? –

. . . and I don't think I have ever had two hours undisturbed (except at
night when everybody is in bed) during my whole literary life. Miss
Austen, I believe, wrote in the same way, and very much for the same
reason; but at her period the natural flow of life took another form. The
family were half ashamed to have it known that she was not just a young
lady like the others, doing her embroidery. Mine were quite pleased
to magnify me and to be proud of my work, but always with a hidden
sense that it was an admirable joke . . .

– perhaps artists cast off their families and go to the South Sea Islands
because they want to be perceived as heroes and their families think they
are funny? –

. . . a hidden sense that it was an admirable joke, and no idea that any
special facilities or retirement was necessary. My mother would have felt
her pride much checked, almost humiliated, if she had conceived that
I stood in need of any artificial aids of that description. That would at
once have made the work unnatural to her eyes, and also to mine.

Oliphant was a proud Scotswoman, proud of her work and her strength;
yet she wrote nonfiction potboilers rather than fight her male editors and

publishers for better pay for her novels. So, as she says bitterly, "Trollope's worst book was better paid than my best." Her best is said to be *Miss Marjoribanks*, but I have never yet been able to get a copy of it; it was disappeared, along with all her other books. Thanks to publishers such as Virago we can now get Oliphant's *Hester*, a stunning novel, and *Kirsteen* and a few others, but they are still taught, so far as I know, only in women's studies courses; they are not part of the Canon of English Literature, though Trollope's potboilers are. No book by a woman who had children has ever been included in that august list.

I think Oliphant gives us a glimpse of why a novelist might not merely endure writing in the kitchen or the parlor amidst the children and the housework, but might endure it willingly. She seems to feel that she profited, that her writing profited, from the difficult, obscure, chancy connection between the art work and the emotional/manual/managerial complex of skills and tasks called "housework," and that to sever that connection would put the writing itself at risk, would make it, in her word, unnatural.

The received wisdom of course is just the opposite: that any attempt to combine art work with housework and family responsibility is impossible, unnatural. And the punishment for unnatural acts, among the critics and the Canoneers, is death.

What is the ethical basis of this judgment and sentence upon the housewife-artist? It is a very noble and austere one, with religion at its foundation: it is the idea that the artist must sacrifice himself to his art. (I use the pronoun advisedly.) His responsibility is to his work alone. It is a motivating idea of the Romantics, it guides the careers of poets from Rimbaud to Dylan Thomas to Richard Hugo, it has given us hundreds of hero figures, typical of whom is James Joyce himself and his Stephen Dedalus. Stephen sacrifices all "lesser" obligations and affections to a "higher" cause, embracing the moral irresponsibility of the soldier or the saint. This heroic stance, the Gauguin Pose, has been taken as the norm – as natural to the artist – and artists, both men and women, who do not assume it have tended to feel a little shabby and second-rate.

Not, however, Virginia Woolf. She observed factually that the artist needs a small income and a room to work in, but did not speak of heroism. Indeed, she said, "I doubt that a writer can be a hero. I doubt that a hero can be a writer." And when I see a writer assume the full heroic posture, I incline to agree. Here, for example, is Joseph Conrad:

For twenty months I wrestled with the Lord for my creation ... mind and will and conscience engaged to the full, hour after hour, day after day ... a lonely struggle in a great isolation from the world. I suppose I slept and ate the food put before me and talked connectedly on suitable occasions, but I was never aware of the even flow of daily life, made easy and noiseless for me by a silent, watchful, tireless affection.[8]

A woman who boasted that her conscience had been engaged to the full in such a wrestling match would be called to account by both women and men; and women are now calling men to account. What "put food" before him? What made daily life so noiseless? What in fact was this "tireless affection," which sounds to me like an old Ford in a junkyard but is apparently intended as a delicate gesture towards a woman whose conscience was engaged to the full, hour after hour, day after day, for twenty months, in seeing to it that Joseph Conrad could wrestle with the Lord in a very relatively great isolation, well housed, clothed, bathed, and fed?

Conrad's "struggle" and Jo March/Lu Alcott's "vortex" are descriptions of the same kind of all-out artistic work; and in both cases the artist is looked after by the family. But I feel an important difference in their perceptions. Where Alcott receives a gift, Conrad asserts a right; where she is taken into the vortex, the creative whirlwind, becoming part of it, he wrestles, struggles, seeking mastery. She is a participant; he is a hero. And her family remain individuals, with cups of tea and timid inquiries, while his is depersonalized to "an affection."

Looking for a woman writer who might have imitated this heroic infantilism, I thought of Gertrude Stein, under the impression that she had used Alice Toklas as a "wife" in this utilitarian sense; but that, as I should have guessed, is an anti-lesbian canard. Stein certainly took hero-artist poses and indulged an enormous ego, but she played fair; and the difference between her domestic partnership and that of Joyce or Conrad is illuminating. And indeed, lesbianism has given many artists the network of support they need – for there is a heroic aspect to the practice of art; it is lonely, risky, merciless work, and every artist needs some kind of moral support or sense of solidarity and validation.

The artist with the least access to social or aesthetic solidarity or approbation has been the artist-housewife. A person who undertakes

---

8 Joseph Conrad, quoted in Olsen.

responsibility both to her art and to her dependent children, with no "tire-less affection" or even tired affection to call on, has undertaken a full-time double job that can be simply, practically, destroyingly impossible. But that isn't how the problem is posed – as a recognition of immense practical difficulty. If it were, practical solutions would be proposed, beginning with childcare. Instead the issue is stated, even now, as a moral one, a matter of ought and ought not. The poet Alicia Ostriker puts it neatly: "That women should have babies rather than books is the considered opinion of Western civilization. That women should have books rather than babies is a variation on that theme."[9]

Freud's contribution to this doctrine was to invest it with such a weight of theory and mythology as to make it appear a primordial, unquestion-able fact. It was of course Freud who, after telling his fiancée what it is a woman wants, said that what we shall never know is what a woman wants. Lacan is perfectly consistent in following him, if I as a person without discourse may venture to say so. A culture or a psychology predicated upon man as human and woman as other cannot accept a woman as artist. An artist is an autonomous, choice-making self: to be such a self a woman must unwoman herself. Barren, she must imitate the man – imperfectly, it goes without saying.[*]

Hence the approbation accorded Austen, the Brontës, Dickinson, and Plath, who though she made the mistake of having two children com-pensated for it by killing herself. The misogynist Canon of Literature can include these women because they can be perceived as incomplete women, as female men.

Still, I have to grit my teeth to criticize the either-books-or-babies doctrine, because it has given real, true comfort to women who could not or chose not to marry and have children, and saw themselves as "having"

---

9 Alicia Ostriker, *Writing Like a Woman*, Michigan Poets on Poetry Series (Ann Arbor: University of Michigan Press, 1983).

* A particularly exhilarating discussion of this issue is the essay "Writing and Motherhood" by Susan Rubin Suleiman, in *The (M)other Tongue: Essays in Feminist Psychoanalytic Interpretation*, edited by Garner, Kahane, and Springnether (Ithaca: Cornell University Press, 1985). Suleiman gives a short history of the nineteenth-century books-or-babies theory and its refinement in the twentieth century by such psychologists as Helene Deutsch, remarking that "it took psychoanaly-sis to transform moral obligation into a psychological 'law,' equating the creative impulse with the procreative one and decreeing that she who has a child feels no need to write books." Suleiman presents a critique of the feminist reversal of this theory (she who has a book feels no need to have children) and analyzes current French feminist thinking on the relationship between writing and femininity/motherhood.

books instead. But though the comfort may be real, I think the doctrine false. And I hear that falseness when a Dorothy Richardson tells us that other women can have children but nobody else can write *her* books. As if "other women" could have had *her* children – as if books came from the uterus! That's just the flip side of the theory that books come from the scrotum. This final reduction of the notion of sublimation is endorsed by our chief macho dodo writer, who has announced that "the one thing a writer needs to have is balls." But he doesn't carry the theory of penile authorship to the extent of saying that if you "get" a kid you can't "get" a book and so fathers can't write. The analogy collapsed into identity, the you-can't-create-if-you-procreate myth, is applied to women only.

I've found I have to stop now and say clearly what I'm not saying. I'm not saying a writer ought to have children, I'm not saying a parent ought to be a writer, I'm not saying any woman *ought* to write books *or* have kids. Being a mother is one of the things a woman can do – like being a writer. It's a privilege. It's not an obligation, or a destiny. I'm talking about mothers who write because it is almost a taboo topic – because women have been told that they *ought not* to try to be both a mother and a writer because both the kids and the books will *pay* – because it can't be done – because it is unnatural.

This refusal to allow both creation and procreation to women is cruelly wasteful: not only has it impoverished our literature by banning the housewives, but it has caused unbearable personal pain and self-mutilation: Woolf obeying the wise doctors who said she must not bear a child; Plath who put glasses of milk by her kids' beds and then put her head in the oven.

A sacrifice, not of somebody else but of oneself, is demanded of women artists (while the Gauguin Pose demands of men artists only that they sacrifice others). I am proposing that this ban on a woman artist's full sexuality is harmful not only to the woman but to the art.

There is less censure now, and more support, for a woman who wants both to bring up a family and work as an artist. But it's a small degree of improvement. The difficulty of trying to be responsible, hour after hour day after day for maybe twenty *years*, for the well-being of children and the excellence of books, is immense: it involves an endless expense of energy and an impossible weighing of competing priorities. And we don't know much about the process, because writers who are mothers haven't talked much about their motherhood – for fear of boasting? for fear of being trapped in the Mom trap, discounted? – nor have they talked much about their writing as in any way connected with their parenting, since the heroic myth demands that the two jobs be considered utterly opposed and mutually destructive.

But we heard a hint of something else from Oliphant; and here (thanks, Tillie) is the painter Käthe Kollwitz:

> I am gradually approaching the period in my life when work comes first. When both the boys were away for Easter, I hardly did anything but work. Worked, slept, ate, and went for short walks. But above all I worked.
>
> And yet I wonder whether the "blessing" isn't missing from such work. No longer diverted by other emotions, I work the way a cow grazes.

That is marvelous – "I work the way a cow grazes." That is the best description of the "professional" at work I know.

> Perhaps in reality I accomplish a little more. The hands work and work, and the head imagines it's producing God knows what, and yet, formerly, when my working time was so wretchedly limited, I was more productive, because I was more sensual; I lived as a human being must live, passionately interested in everything ... Potency, potency is diminishing. [10]

This *potency* felt by a woman is a potency from which the Hero-Artist has (and I choose my words carefully) cut himself off, in an egoism that is ultimately sterile. But it is a potency that has been denied by women as well as men, and not just women eager to collude with misogyny.

Back in the seventies Nina Auerbach wrote that Jane Austen was able to write because she had created around her "a child-free space." Germ-free I knew, odor-free I knew, but child-free? And Austen? who wrote in the parlor, and was a central figure to a lot of nieces and nephews? But I tried to accept what Auerbach said, because although my experience didn't fit it, I was, like many women, used to feeling that my experience was faulty, not right – that it was *wrong*. So I was probably wrong to keep on writing

---

10 Käthe Kollwitz, *Diaries and Letters*, quoted in Olsen.

in what was then a fully child-filled space. However, feminist thinking evolved rapidly to a far more complex and realistic position, and I, stumbling along behind, have been enabled by it to think a little for myself.

The greatest enabler for me was always, is always, Virginia Woolf. And I quote now from the first draft of her paper "Professions for Women,"[11] where she gives her great image of a woman writing.

> I figure her really in an attitude of contemplation, like a fisher-woman, sitting on the bank of a lake with her fishing rod held over its water. Yes that is how I see her. She was not thinking; she was not reasoning; she was not constructing a plot; she was letting her imagination down into the depths of her consciousness while she sat above holding on by a thin but quite necessary thread of reason.

Now I interrupt to ask you to add one small element to this scene. Let us imagine that a bit farther up the bank of the lake sits a child, the fisherwoman's daughter. She's about five, and she's making people out of sticks and mud and telling stories with them. She's been told to be very quiet please while Mama fishes, and she really is very quiet except when she forgets and sings or asks questions; and she watches in fascinated silence when the following dramatic events take place. There sits our woman writing, our fisherwoman, when –

> suddenly there is a violent jerk; she feels the line race through her fingers.
>
> The imagination has rushed away; it has taken to the depths; it has sunk heaven knows where – into the dark pool of extraordinary experience. The reason has to cry "Stop!", the novelist has to pull on the line and haul the imagination to the surface. The imagination comes to the top in a state of fury.
>
> Good heavens she cries – how dare you interfere with me – how dare you pull me out with your wretched little fishing line? And I – that is, the reason – have to reply, "My dear you were going altogether too far. Men would be shocked." Calm yourself I say, as she sits panting on

11 The talk, known in its revised form as "Professions for Women" and so titled in the Essays, was given on January 21, 1931, to the London National Society for Women's Service, and can be found complete with all deletions and alternate readings in Mitchell Leaska's editing of Woolf's *The Pargiters* (London: The Hogarth Press, 1978).

the bank – panting with rage and disappointment. We have only got to
wait fifty years or so. In fifty years I shall be able to use all this very queer
knowledge that you are ready to bring me. But not now. You see I go
on, trying to calm her, I cannot make use of what you tell me – about
women's bodies for instance – their passions – and so on, because the
conventions are still very strong. If I were to overcome the conventions
I should need the courage of a hero, and I am not a hero.

   I doubt that a writer can be a hero. I doubt that a hero can be a
writer.

   ... Very well, says the imagination, dressing herself up again in her
petticoat and skirts, we will wait. We will wait another fifty years. But it
seems to me a pity.

It seems to me a pity. It seems to me a pity that more than fifty years have
passed and the conventions, though utterly different, still exist to protect
men from being shocked, still admit only male experience of women's
bodies, passions, and existence. It seems to me a pity that so many women,
including myself, have accepted this denial of their own experience and
narrowed their perception to fit it, writing as if their sexuality were limited
to copulation, as if they knew nothing about pregnancy, birth, nursing,
mothering, puberty, menstruation, menopause, except what men are
willing to hear, nothing except what men are willing to hear about housework, childwork, lifework, war, peace, living, and dying as experienced in
the female body and mind and imagination. "Writing the body," as Woolf
asked and Hélène Cixous asks, is only the beginning. We have to rewrite
the world.

   White writing, Cixous calls it, writing in milk, in mother's milk. I like
that image, because even among feminists, the woman writer has been
more often considered in her sexuality as a lover than in her sexuality
as pregnant-bearing-nursing-childcaring. Mother still tends to get disappeared. And in losing the artist-mother we lose where there's a lot to gain.
Alicia Ostriker thinks so. "The advantage of motherhood for a woman
artist," she says – have you ever heard anybody say that before? the *advantage*
of motherhood for an artist? –

   The advantage of motherhood for a woman artist is that it puts her
   in immediate and inescapable contact with the sources of life, death,
   beauty, growth, corruption ... If the woman artist has been trained to

believe that the activities of motherhood are trivial, tangential to the main issues of life, irrelevant to the great themes of literature, she should untrain herself. The training is misogynist, it protects and perpetuates systems of thought and feeling which prefer violence and death to love and birth, and it is a lie.

. . . "We think back through our mothers, if we are women," declares Woolf, but through whom can those who are themselves mothers . . . do their thinking? . . . we all need data, we need information, . . . the sort provided by poets, novelists, artists, from within. As our knowledge begins to accumulate, we can imagine what it would signify to all women, and men, to live in a culture where childbirth and mothering occupied the kind of position that sex and romantic love have occupied in literature and art for the last five hundred years, or . . . that warfare has occupied since literature began.[12]

My book *Always Coming Home* was a rash attempt to imagine such a world, where the Hero and the Warrior are a stage adolescents go through on their way to becoming responsible human beings, where the parent-child relationship is not forever viewed through the child's eyes but includes the reality of the mother's experience. The imagining was difficult, and rewarding.

Here is a passage from a novel where what Woolf, Cixous, and Ostriker ask for is happening, however casually and unpretentiously. In Margaret Drabble's *The Millstone*,[13] Rosamund, a young scholar and freelance writer, has a baby about eight months old, Octavia. They share a flat with a friend, Lydia, who's writing a novel. Rosamund is working away on a book review:

> I had just written and counted my first hundred words when I remembered Octavia; I could hear her making small happy noises . . .
>
> I was rather dismayed when I realized she was in Lydia's room and that I must have left the door open, for Lydia's room was always full of nasty objects like aspirins, safety razors and bottles of ink; I rushed along to rescue her and the sight that met my eyes when I opened the door was enough to make anyone quake. She had her back to the door and was sitting in the middle of the floor surrounded by a sea of

---

12 Ostriker.
13 Margaret Drabble, *The Millstone* (London: Weidenfeld and Nicolson Ltd, 1965).

torn, strewed, chewed paper. I stood there transfixed, watching the neat small back of her head and her thin stalk-like neck and flowery curls: suddenly she gave a great screech of delight and ripped another sheet of paper. "Octavia," I said in horror, and she started guiltily, and looked round at me with a charming deprecating smile: her mouth, I could see, was wedged full of wads of Lydia's new novel.

I picked her up and fished the bits out and laid them carefully on the bedside table with what was left of the typescript; pages 70 to 123 seemed to have survived. The rest was in varying stages of dissolution: some pages were entire but badly crumpled, some were in large pieces, some in small pieces, and some, as I have said, were chewed up. The damage was not, in fact, as great as it appeared at first sight to be, for babies, though persistent, are not thorough: but at first sight it was frightful ... In a way it was clearly the most awful thing for which I had ever been responsible, but as I watched Octavia crawl around the sitting room looking for more work to do, I almost wanted to laugh. It seemed so absurd, to have this small living extension of myself, so dangerous, so vulnerable, for whose injuries and crimes I alone had to suffer ... It really was a terrible thing ... and yet in comparison with Octavia being so sweet and so alive it did not seem so very terrible ...

Confronted with the wreckage, Lydia is startled, but not deeply distressed:

... and that was it, except for the fact that Lydia really did have to rewrite two whole chapters as well as doing a lot of boring sellotaping, and when it came out it got bad reviews anyway. This did succeed in making Lydia angry.

I have seen Drabble's work dismissed with the usual list of patronizing adjectives reserved for women who write as women, not imitation men. Let us not let her be disappeared. Her work is deeper than its bright surface. What is she talking about in this funny passage? Why does the girl-baby eat not her mother's manuscript but another woman's manuscript? Couldn't she at least have eaten a manuscript by a man? – no, no, that's not the point. The point, or part of it, is that babies eat manuscripts. They really do. The poem not written because the baby cried, the novel put aside because of a pregnancy, and so on. Babies eat books. But they spit out wads of them that can be taped back together; and they are only babies for a couple of years, while writers live for decades; and it is terrible, but not very terrible. The manuscript that got eaten *was* terrible; if you know Lydia you know the reviewers were right. And that's part of the point too – that the supreme value of art depends on other equally supreme values. But that subverts the hierarchy of values; "men would be shocked . . ."

In Drabble's comedy of morals the absence of the Hero-Artist is a strong ethical statement. Nobody lives in a great isolation, nobody sac-rifices human claims, nobody even scolds the baby. Nobody is going to put their head, or anybody else's head, into an oven: not the mother, not the writer, not the daughter – these three and one who, being women, do not separate creation and destruction into *I create I You are destroyed*, or vice versa. Who are responsible, take responsibility, for both the baby and the book.*

But I want now to turn from fiction to biography and from general to personal; I want to talk a bit about my mother, the writer.

Her maiden name was Theodora Kracaw; her first married name was Brown; her second married name, Kroeber, was the one she used on her books; her third married name was Quinn. This sort of many-namedness doesn't happen to men; it's inconvenient, and yet its very cumbersomeness reveals, perhaps, the being of a woman writer as not one simple thing – the author – but a multiple, complex process of being, with various responsi-bilities, one of which is to her writing.

Theodora put her personal responsibilities first – chronologically. She brought up and married off her four children before she started to write. She took up the pen, as they used to say – she had the most amazing left-handed scrawl – in her mid-fifties. I asked her once, years later, "Did you want to write, and put it off intentionally, till you'd got rid of us?"

---

* My understanding of this issue has been much aided by Carol Gilligan's *In a Different Voice* (Cambridge: Harvard University Press, 1982), as well as by Jean Baker Miller's modestly revolutionary *Toward a New Psychology of Women* (Boston: Beacon Press, 1976[†]). Gilligan's thesis, stated very roughly, is that our society brings up males to think and speak in terms of their rights, females in terms of their responsibilities, and that conventional psychologies have implicitly evaluated the "male" image of a hierarchy of rights as "superior" (hierarchically, of course) to the "female" image of a network of mutual responsibilities. Hence a man finds it (relatively) easy to assert his "right" to be free of relationships and dependents, à la Gauguin, while women are not granted and do not grant one another any such right, preferring to live as part of an intense and complex network in which freedom is arrived at, if at all, mutually. Coming at the matter from this angle, one can see why there are no or very few "Great Artists" among women, when the "Great Artist" is defined as inherently superior to and not responsible towards others.
† London: Allen Lane, 1978.

And she laughed and said, "Oh, no, I just wasn't *ready*." Not an evasion or a dishonest answer, but not, I think, the whole answer.

She was born in 1897 in a wild Colorado mining town, and her mother boasted of having been *born* with the vote – in Wyoming, which ratified woman suffrage along with statehood – and rode a stallion men couldn't ride; but still, the Angel in the House was very active in those days, the one whose message is that a woman's needs come after everybody else's. And my mother really came pretty close to incarnating that Angel, whom Woolf called "the woman men wish women to be." Men fell in love with her – all men. Doctors, garage mechanics, professors, roach exterminators. Butchers saved sweetbreads for her. She was also, to her daughter, a demanding, approving, nurturing, good-natured, loving, lively mother – a first-rate mother. And then, getting on to sixty, she became a first-rate writer.

She started out, as women so often do, by writing some books for children – not competing with men, you know, staying in the "domestic sphere." One of these, *A Green Christmas*, is a lovely book that ought to be in every six-year-old's stocking. Then she wrote a charming and romantic autobiographical novel – still on safe, "womanly" ground. Next she ventured into Native American territory with *The Inland Whale*; and then she was asked to write the story of an Indian called Ishi, the only survivor of a people massacred by the North American pioneers, a serious and risky subject requiring a great deal of research, moral sensitivity, and organizational and narrative skill.

So she wrote it, the first best seller, I believe, that University of California Press ever published. *Ishi* is still in print in many languages, still used, I think, in California schools, still deservedly beloved. It is a book entirely worthy of its subject, a book of very great honesty and power.

So, if she could write that in her sixties, what might she have written in her thirties? Maybe she really "wasn't ready." But maybe she listened to the wrong angel, and we might have had many more books from her. Would my brothers and I have suffered, have been cheated of anything, if she had been writing them? I think my aunt Betsy and the household help we had back then would have kept things going just fine. As for my father, I don't see how her writing could have hurt him or how her success could have threatened him. But I don't know. All I do know is that once she started writing (and it was while my father was alive, and they collaborated on a couple of things), she never stopped; she had found the work she loved.

Once, not long after my father's death, when *Ishi* was bringing her the validation of praise and success she very much needed, and while I was still getting every story I sent out rejected with monotonous regularity, she burst into tears over my latest rejection slip and tried to console me, saying that she wanted rewards and success for me, not for herself. And that was lovely, and I treasured her saying it then as I do now. That she didn't really mean it and I didn't really believe it made no difference. Of course she didn't want to sacrifice her achievement, her work, to me – why on earth should she? She shared what she could of it with me by sharing the pleasures and anguishes of writing, the intellectual excitement, the shoptalk – and that's all. No angelic altruism. When I began to publish, we shared that. And she wrote on; in her eighties she told me, without bitterness, "I wish I had started sooner. Now there isn't time." She was at work on a third novel when she died.

As for myself: I have flagrantly disobeyed the either-books-or-babies rule, having had three kids and written about twenty books, and thank God it wasn't the other way around. By the luck of race, class, money, and health, I could manage the double-tightrope trick – and especially by the support of my partner. He is not my wife; but he brought to marriage an assumption of mutual aid as its daily basis, and on that basis you can get a lot of work done. Our division of labor was fairly conventional; I was in charge of house, cooking, the kids, and novels, because I wanted to be, and he was in charge of being a professor, the car, the bills, and the garden, because he wanted to be. When the kids were babies I wrote at night; when they started school I wrote while they were at school; these days I write as a cow grazes. If I needed help he gave it without making it into a big favor, and – this is the central fact – he did not ever begrudge me the time I spent writing, or the blessing of my work.

That is the killer: the killing grudge, the envy, the jealousy, the spite that so often a man is allowed to hold, trained to hold, against anything a woman does that's not done in his service, for him, to feed his body, his comfort, his kids. A woman who tries to work against that grudge finds the blessing turned into a curse; she must rebel and go it alone, or fall silent in despair. Any artist must expect to work amid the total, rational indifference of everybody else to their work, for years, perhaps for life: but no artist can work well against daily, personal, vengeful resistance. And that's exactly what many women artists get from the people they love and live with.

I was spared all that. I was free – born free, lived free. And for years that personal freedom allowed me to ignore the degree to which my writing was controlled and constrained by judgments and assumptions which I thought were my own, but which were the internalized ideology of a male supremacist society. Even when subverting the conventions, I disguised my subversions from myself. It took me years to realize that I chose to work in such despised, marginal genres as science fiction, fantasy, young adult, precisely because they were excluded from critical, academic, canonical supervision, leaving the artist free; it took ten more years before I had the wits and guts to see and say that the exclusion of the genres from "literature" is unjustified, unjustifiable, and a matter not of quality but of politics. So too in my choice of subjects: until the mid-seventies I wrote my fiction about heroic adventures, high-tech futures, men in the halls of power, men – men were the central characters, the women were peripheral, secondary. Why don't you write about women? my mother asked me. I don't know how, I said. A stupid answer, but an honest one. I did not know how to write about women – very few of us did – because I thought that what men had written about women was the truth, was the true way to write about women. And I couldn't.

My mother could not give me what I needed. When feminism began to reawaken, she hated it, called it "those women's libbers"; but it was she who had steered me years and years before to what I would and did need, to Virginia Woolf. "We think back through our mothers," and we have many mothers, those of the body and those of the soul. What I needed was what feminism, feminist literary theory and criticism and practice, had to give me. And I can hold it in my hands – not only *Three Guineas*, my treasure in the days of poverty, but now all the wealth of *The Norton Anthology of Literature by Women* and the reprint houses and the women's presses. Our mothers have been returned to us. This time, let's hang on to them.

And it is feminism that has empowered me to criticize not only my society and myself but – for a moment now – feminism itself. The books-or-babies myth is not only a misogynist hang-up, it can be a feminist one. Some of the women I respect most, writing for publications that I depend on for my sense of women's solidarity and hope, continue to declare that it is "virtually impossible for a heterosexual woman to be a feminist," as if heterosexuality were heterosexism; and that social marginality, such as that of lesbian, childless, Black, or Native American women, "appears to be necessary" to form the feminist. Applying these judgments to myself, and believing that as a woman writing at this point I have to be a feminist to be worth beans, I find myself, once again, excluded – disappeared.

The rationale of the exclusionists, as I understand it, is that the material privilege and social approbation our society grants the heterosexual wife, and particularly the mother, prevent her solidarity with less privileged women and insulate her from the kind of anger and the kind of ideas that lead to feminist action. There is truth in this; maybe it's true for a lot of women; I can oppose it only with my experience, which is that feminism has been a life-saving *necessity* to women trapped in the wife/ mother "role." What do the privilege and approbation accorded the housewife-mother by our society in fact consist of? Being the object of infinite advertising? Being charged by psychologists with total answerability for children's mental well-being, and by the government with total answerability for children's welfare, while being regularly equated with apple pie by sentimental warmongers? As a social "role," motherhood, for any woman I know, simply means that she does everything everybody else does plus bringing up the kids.

To push mothers back into "private life," a mythological space invented by the patriarchy, on the theory that their acceptance of the "role" of mother invalidates them for public, political, artistic responsibility, is to play Old Nobodaddy's game, by his rules, on his side.

In *Writing Beyond the Ending*, Du Plessis shows how women novelists write about the woman artist: they make her an ethical force, an activist trying "to change the life in which she is also immersed."[14] To have and bring up kids is to be about as immersed in life as one can be, but it does not always follow that one drowns. A lot of us can swim.

Again, whenever I give a version of this paper, somebody will pick up on this point and tell me that I'm supporting the Superwoman syndrome, saying that a woman *should* have kids write books be politically active and make perfect sushi. I am not saying that. We're all asked to be Superwoman; I'm not asking it, our society does that. All I can tell you is that I believe it's a lot easier to write books while bringing up kids than to bring up kids while working nine to five plus housekeeping. But that is what our society, while sentimentalizing over Mom and the Family, demands of most women – unless it refuses them any work at all and

---

14 Du Plessis.

dumps them onto welfare and says, Bring up your kids on food stamps, Mom, we might want them for the army. Talk about superwomen, those are the superwomen. Those are the mothers up against the wall. Those are the marginal women, without either privacy or publicity; and it's because of them more than anyone else that the woman artist has a responsibility to "try to change the life in which she is also immersed."

And now I come back round to the bank of that lake, where the fisherwoman sits, our woman writer, who had to bring her imagination up short because it was getting too deeply immersed … The imagination dries herself off, still swearing under her breath, and buttons up her blouse, and comes to sit beside the little girl, the fisherwoman's daughter. "Do you like books?" she says, and the child says, "Oh, yes. When I was a baby I used to eat them, but now I can read. I can read all of Beatrix Potter by myself, and when I grow up I'm going to write books, like Mama."

"Are you going to wait till your children grow up, like Jo March and Theodora?"

"Oh, I don't think so," says the child. "I'll just go ahead and do it."

"Then will you do as Harriet and Margaret and so many Harriets and Margarets have done and are still doing, and hassle through the prime of your life trying to do two full-time jobs that are incompatible with each other in practice, however enriching their interplay may be both to the life and the art?"

"I don't know," says the little girl. "Do I have to?"

"Yes," says the imagination, "if you aren't rich and you want kids."

"I might want one or two," says reason's child. "But why do women have two jobs where men only have one? It isn't reasonable, is it?"

"Don't ask me!" snaps the imagination. "I could think up a dozen better arrangements before breakfast! But who listens to me?"

The child sighs and watches her mother fishing. The fisherwoman, having forgotten that her line is no longer baited with the imagination, isn't catching anything, but she's enjoying the peaceful hour; and when the child speaks again she speaks softly. "Tell me, Auntie. What is the one thing a writer has to have?"

"I'll tell you," says the imagination. "The one thing a writer has to have is not balls. Nor is it a child-free space. Nor is it even, speaking strictly on the evidence, a room of her own, though that is an amazing help, as is the goodwill and cooperation of the opposite sex, or at least the local, in-house representative of it. But she doesn't have to have that. The one thing a writer has to have is a pencil and some paper. That's enough, so long as she knows that she and she alone is in charge of that pencil, and responsible, she and she alone, for what it writes on the paper. In other words, that she's free. Not wholly free. Never wholly free. Maybe very partially. Maybe only in this one act, this sitting for a snatched moment being a woman writing, fishing the mind's lake. But in this, responsible; in this, autonomous; in this, free."

"Auntie," says the little girl, "can I go fishing with you now?"

Things Not Actually Present:
On *The Book of Fantasy* and J. L. Borges

1988

In 1988 Xanadu Press published The Book of Fantasy, *a translation of the* Antologia de la literatura fantástica, *which Jorge Luis Borges, Adolfo Bioy Casares, and Silvina Ocampo first published in Buenos Aires in 1940. Asked to contribute a foreword to the English edition, I did so with pleasure. I have revised it so that I could include it in this collection, wanting to render some small homage to Borges.*

There are two books that I look on as esteemed and cherished great-aunts or grandmothers, wise and mild though sometimes rather dark of counsel, to be turned to when my judgment hesitates. One of these books provides facts, of a peculiar sort. The other does not. The *I Ching* or *Book of Changes* is the visionary elder who has outlived fact, the ancestor so old she speaks a different tongue. Her counsel is sometimes appallingly clear, sometimes very obscure indeed. "The little fox crossing the river wets its tail," she says, smiling faintly, or, "A dragon appears in the field," or, "Biting upon dried gristly meat." One retires to ponder long over such advice.

The other Auntie is younger, and speaks English. Indeed she speaks more English than anybody else. She offers fewer dragons and much more dried gristly meat. And yet *A New English Dictionary on Historical Principles*, or the OED as she is known to her family, is also a Book of Changes. Most wonderful in its transmutations, it is not the Book of Sand, yet is inexhaustible; not an Aleph, yet all we have said and can ever say is in it, if we can but find it.

"Auntie!" I say, magnifying glass in hand, because my edition, the Compact Auntie, is compressed into two volumes of print no larger than grains of sand, "Auntie! Please tell me about fantasy, because I want to talk about a Book of Fantasy, but I am not sure what I am talking about."

"Fantasy, or Phantasy," Auntie replies, clearing her throat, "is from the Greek *phantasia*, lit. 'a making visible.'" She explains that *phantasia* is related to the verbs *phantasein*, "to make visible," or in Late Greek, "to imagine, have visions," and *phainein*, "to show." And she summarizes the earliest meanings of the word *fantasy* in English: an appearance, a phantom, the mental process of sensuous perception, the faculty of imagination, a false notion, a caprice, a whim.

Then, though she eschews the casting of yarrow stalks or coins polished with sweet oil, being after all an Englishwoman, she begins to tell the Changes – the mutations of a word moving through the minds of people moving through the centuries. She shows how *fantasy*, which to the Schoolmen of the late Middle Ages meant "the mental apprehension of an object of perception," that is, the mind's very act of linking itself to the phenomenal world, came in time to signify just the reverse: an hallucination, or a phantasm, or the habit of deluding oneself. And then the word, doubling back on its tracks like a hare, came to mean the imagination itself, "the process, the faculty, or the result of forming mental representations of things not actually present." Though seemingly very close to the Scholastic use of the word, this definition of *fantasy* leads in quite the opposite direction, often going so far as to imply that the imagination is extravagant, or visionary, or merely fanciful.

So the word *fantasy* remains ambiguous, standing between the false, the foolish, the delusory, the shallows of the mind, and the mind's deep connection with the real. On this threshold it sometimes faces one way, masked and costumed, frivolous, an escapist; then it turns, and we glimpse as it turns the face of an angel, bright truthful messenger, arisen Urizen.

Since the compilation of my *Oxford English Dictionary*, the tracks of the word have been complicated still further by the comings and goings of psychologists. Their technical uses of *fantasy* and *phantasy* have influenced our sense and use of the word; and they have also given us the handy verb "to fantasise." If you are fantasising, you may be daydreaming, or you might be using your imagination therapeutically as a means of discovering reasons Reason does not know, discovering yourself to yourself.

But Auntie does not acknowledge the existence of that verb. Into her Supplement (through the tradesmen's door) she admits only *fantasist*, and defines the upstart, politely but with a faint curl of the lip, as "one who 'weaves' fantasies." She illustrates the word with quotations from Oscar Wilde and H. G. Wells. Evidently she means that fantasists are writers, but is not quite willing to admit it.

Indeed, in the early twentieth century, the days of victorious Realism, fantasists were often apologetic about what they did, offering it as mere word weaving – fancywork – a sort of bobble-fringing to *real* literature, or passing it off as being "for children" and therefore beneath the notice of critics, professors, and dictionary makers.

Writers of fantasy are often less modest now that what they do is recognized as literature, or at least as a genre of literature, or at least as a subliterary genre, or at least as a commercial product. For fantasies are rife and many-colored on the bookshelves. The head of the fabled unicorn is laid upon the lap of Mammon, and the offering is acceptable to Mammon. Fantasy has, in fact, become quite a business.

But when one night in Buenos Aires in 1937 three friends sat talking together about fantastic literature, it was not yet a business.

Nor was it even known as fantastic literature when one night in a villa in Geneva in 1818 three friends sat talking together and telling ghost stories. They were Mary Shelley, her husband Percy, and Lord Byron – and Claire Clairmont was probably with them, and the strange young Dr. Polidori – and they told awful tales, and Mary was frightened. "We will each," cried Byron, "write a ghost story!" So Mary went away and thought about it, fruitlessly, until a few nights later she had a nightmare in which a "pale student" used strange arts and machineries to arouse from unlife the "hideous phantasm of a man."

And so, alone of the friends, she wrote her ghost story, *Frankenstein, or The Modern Prometheus*, which is the first great modern fantasy. There are no ghosts in it; but fantasy, as the OED observed, is more than ghoulie-mongering.

Because ghosts haunt one corner of the vast domain of fantastic literature, both oral and written, people familiar with that corner of it call the whole thing ghost stories, or horror stories; just as others call it Fairyland after the part of it they love best or despise most, and others call it science fiction, and others call it stuff and nonsense. But the nameless being given life by Frankenstein's or Mary Shelley's arts and machineries is neither ghost nor fairy; science fictional he may be; stuff and nonsense he is not. He is a creature of fantasy, archetypal, deathless. Once raised he will not sleep again, for his pain will not let him sleep, the unanswered moral questions that woke with him will not let him rest in peace.

When there began to be money in the fantasy business, plenty of money was made out of him in Hollywood, but even that did not kill him.

Very likely his story was mentioned on that night in 1937 in Buenos

Aires when Silvina Ocampo and her friends Borges and Bioy Casares fell to talking, so Casares tells us, "about fantastic literature . . . discussing the stories which seemed best to us. One of us suggested that if we put together the fragments of the same type we had listed in our notebooks, we would have a good book."

So that, charmingly, is how *The Book of Fantasy* came to be: three friends talking. No plans, no definitions, no business, except the intention of "having a good book."

In the making of such a book by such makers, certain definitions were implied by the exclusion of certain stories, and by inclusion other definitions were ignored; so, perhaps for the first time, horror story and ghost story and fairy tale and science fiction all came together between the same covers. Thirty years later the anthologists enlarged the collection considerably for a new edition, and Borges suggested further inclusions to the editors of the first English-language edition shortly before his death.

It is an idiosyncratic selection, completely eclectic; in fact it is a wild mishmash. Some of the stories will be familiar to most readers, others are exotic and peculiar. A piece we might think we know almost too well, such as "The Cask of Amontillado," regains its essential strangeness when read among works and fragments from the Orient and South America and distant centuries, by Kafka, Swedenborg, Yeats, Cortazar, Akutagawa, Niu Chiao, James Joyce . . . The inclusion of a good many late-nineteenth- and early-twentieth-century writers, especially British ones, reflects, I imagine, particularly the taste of Borges, himself a member and perpetuator of the international tradition of fantasy that included Kipling and Wells.

Perhaps I should not say "tradition," since it has no name as such and little recognition in critical circles, and is distinguished in college English departments mainly by being ignored. But I believe there is a company of fantasists that Borges belonged to even as he transcended it, and that he honored even as he transformed it. As he included these writers in the *Book of Fantasy*, we may see it as a notebook of sources and affiliations and elective affinities for him and his fellow editors, and for their generation of Latin American writers, which preceded the ones we call magical realists.

By saying that fantasy is for children (which some of it is) and dismissing it as commercial and formulaic (which some of it is), critics feel justified in ignoring it all. Yet looking at such writers as Italo Calvino, Gabriel Garcia Marquez, Philip K. Dick, Salman Rushdie, José Saramago, it is possible to believe that our narrative fiction has for years been going, slowly and vaguely and massively, not in the wash and slap of fad and fashion but as a deep current, in one direction – towards rejoining the "ocean of story," fantasy.

Fantasy is, after all, the oldest kind of narrative fiction, and the most universal.

Fiction as we currently think of it, the novel and short story as they have existed since the eighteenth century, offers one of the very best means of understanding people different from oneself, short of experience. Fiction is often really much more useful than lived experience; it takes much less time, costs nothing (from the library), and comes in a manageable, orderly form. You can understand it. Experience just steamrollers over you and you begin to see what happened only years and years later, if ever. Fiction is much better than reality at providing useful factual, psychological, and moral understanding.

But realistic fiction is culture-specific. If it's your culture, your decade, fine; but if the story takes place in another century or another country, reading it with understanding involves an act of displacement, of translation, which many readers are unable or unwilling to make. The lifeways, the language, the morals and mores, the unspoken assumptions, all the details of ordinary life that are the substance and strength of realistic fiction, may be obscure, uninterpretable to the reader of another time and place. So writers who want their story to be understood not only by their contemporary compatriots but also by people of other lands and times, may seek a way of telling it that is more universally comprehensible; and fantasy is such a way.

Fantasies are often set in ordinary life, but the material of fantasy is a more permanent, universal reality than the social customs realism deals with. The substance of fantasy is psychic stuff, human constants: situations and imageries we recognize without having to learn or know anything at all about New York now, or London in 1850, or China three thousand years ago.

A dragon appears in the field . . .

American readers and writers of fiction may yearn for the pure veracity of Jewett or Dreiser, as the English may look back with longing to the fine solidities of Arnold Bennett; but the societies in and for which those novelists wrote were limited and homogeneous enough to be described in a language that could seriously pretend to describe, in Trollope's phrase, "the way we live now." The limits of that language – shared assumptions of class, culture, education, ethics – both focus and shrink the scope of the fiction. Society in the decades around the second millennium, global, multilingual, enormously irrational, undergoing incessant radical change, is not describable in a language that assumes continuity and a common experience of life. And so writers have turned to the global, intuitional language of fantasy to describe, as accurately as they can, the way "we" live "now."

So it is in so much contemporary fiction that the most revealing and accurate descriptions of our daily life are shot through with strangeness, or displaced in time, or set upon imaginary worlds, or dissolved into the phantasmagoria of drugs or of psychosis, or rise from the mundane suddenly into the visionary and as simply descend from it again.

So it may be that the central ethical dilemma of our age, the use or nonuse of annihilating power, was posed most cogently in fictional terms by the purest of fantasists. Tolkien began *The Lord of the Rings* in 1937 and finished it about ten years later. During those years, Frodo withheld his hand from the Ring of Power, but the nations did not.

So it is that Italo Calvino's *Invisible Cities* may serve as a better guidebook to our world than any Michelin or Fodor's.

So it is that the magical realists of South America, and their counterparts in India and elsewhere, are valued for their revelatory and entire truthfulness to the history of their lands and people.

And so it is that Jorge Luis Borges, a writer in a marginal country, a marginal continent, who chose to identify himself with a marginal tradition, not the mainstream of modernist realism that flowed so full in his youth and maturity, remains a writer central to our literature.

His own poems and stories, his images of reflections, libraries, labyrinths, forking paths, his books of tigers, of rivers, of sand, of mysteries, of changes, are everywhere honored, because they are beautiful; because they are nourishing; and because they fulfill the most ancient, urgent function of words (even as the *I Ching* and the *Oxford English Dictionary* do): to form for us "mental representations of things not actually present," so that we can form a judgment of what world we live in and where we might be going in it, what we can celebrate, what we must fear.

Prides:
An Essay on Writing Workshops

✺

1989

This piece was a contribution to a volume edited by Paul M. Wrigley and Debbie Cross as a benefit for the Susan Petrey Fund and Clarion West Writers Workshop in 1989. This version is different here and there, updated, but the illustrations are the same.

Sometimes I worry about workshops. I've taught quite a few – Clarion West four times; in Australia; at Haystack on the Oregon coast and at the Malheur Field Station in the Oregon desert; at the Indiana and Bennington Writers Conferences, at the Writing Centers in D.C., and at Portland State University; and many times at the beloved and much-missed Flight of the Mind. And I still teach workshops sometimes, though sometimes I think I should stop. Not only because I am getting old and lazy, but because I'm two-minded about workshops, not single-minded. I worry, are they a good thing – yes? no?

I always come down on the Yes side – lightly, but with both feet.

A workshop can certainly do harm as well as good.

The most harmless harm it can do is waste time. This happens when people come to it expecting to teach or be taught how to write. If you think you can teach people how to write you're wasting their time and if they think you can teach them how to write they're wasting yours, and vice (as it were) versa.

People attending workshops are not learning how to write.[*] What they are learning or doing (as I understand it) will come up later on.

A more harmful harm that can infect the workshop is the ego trip.

---

[*] I use the verb "to write" here to mean writing literary and/or commercially saleable prose. Writing in the sense of how to compose a sentence, why and how to punctuate, etc., can indeed be taught and learned – usually, or at least hopefully, in grade school and high school. It is definitely a prerequisite to writing in the other sense; yet some people come to writing workshops without these skills. They believe that art does not need craft. They are mistaken.

Classes in literary writing and writers' conferences, years ago, were mostly ego trips – the Great author and his disciples. A good deal of that still goes on at "prestigious" universities and creative writing programs featuring pickled big names. It was the system of mutual group criticism, the Clarion system, now used almost everywhere writing is taught, that freed the pedagogy of writing from hierarchical authority and authorial hierarchy.

But even in a mutual-criticism workshop the instructor can go on an ego trip. I have known an instructor who ran an amateur Esalen, playing mind games and deliberately disintegrating participants' personalities without the faintest idea of how to put them back together. I have known an instructor who ran a little Devil's Island, punishing the participants for writing by trashing their work, except for a favorite trusty or two who got smarmed over. I have known an instructor – oh, many, too many – who ran a little Paris Island, where a week of systematic misogyny was supposed to result in a "few good men." I have known instructors who seemed to be running for a popularity prize, and instructors who just ran away, leaving their students to flounder, not showing up from Monday until Friday, when they came to collect their check.

Such self-indulgence can do real and permanent damage, particularly when the instructor is famous and respected, and the participant is – and they all are more or less – insecure and vulnerable. To offer one's work for criticism is an act of trust requiring real courage. It must be respected as such. I know several people who after a brutal dismissal by a writer they admired stopped writing for years, one of them forever. Certainly a writing instructor has a responsibility to defend the art, and the right to set very high standards, but nobody has the right to stop a person from trying to learn. The defense of excellence has nothing whatever to do with bullying.

Ego-tripping by participants can also be destructive to the work of other individuals or of the whole group, unless the instructor is savvy enough to refuse to play games with the troublemaker, who is usually either a manipulative bully or a passive bully, a psychopathically demanding person. I was slow to learn that as the instructor I must refuse to collude with these people. I am still not good at handling them, but have found that if I ask other participants to help me they do so, often with a skill, kindness, and psychological sensitivity that never cease to amaze me.

Perhaps all workshops should have a sign on the door: Do Not Feed the Ego! But then on the other side of the door should be a sign: Do Not Feed the Altruist! Because the practice of any art is impeded by both egoism and altruism. What's needed is concentration on the work.

I shall now go out on a limb, hunch my shoulders, clack my beak, stare fiercely, and announce that I think there are two types of workshop that are to some extent intrinsically harmful. Both types tend to corrupt the work. They do it differently, but are alike in using writing not as an end but as a means. I will call them commercial and establishmentarian.

Commercially oriented workshops and conferences range from the modest kind where everybody is dying to meet the New York editor and the agent who sells in six figures and nothing is talked about but "markets," "good markets for paragraphs," "good markets for religious and uplift," and so on – to the fancy kind where everybody sneers at little old ladies who write paragraphs, but would kill to meet the same editor and the same agent, and where nothing is talked about but "markets," "meeting contacts," "finding an agent with some smarts," "series sales," and so on. All these matters of business are of legitimate, immediate, and necessary interest to a writer. Writers need to learn their trade, and how to negotiate the increasingly difficult marketplace. The trade can be taught and learned just as the craft can. But a workshop where the trade is the principal focus of interest is not a writing workshop. It is a business class.

If success in selling is my primary interest, I am not primarily a writer, but a salesperson. If I teach success in selling as the writer's primary objective, I am not teaching writing; I'm teaching, or pretending to teach, the production and marketing of a commodity.

Establishmentarian workshops and programs, on the other hand, eschew low talk of marketing. *Sell* is a four-letter word at such places. You go to them to be in the right place, where you will meet the right people. The purpose of such programs, most of which are in the eastern half of the United States, is to feed an in-group or elite, the innermost members of which go to the innermost writers' colonies and get the uppermost grants by recommending one another.

If being perceived as a successful writer is my primary interest, I am not primarily a writer, but a social climber: a person using certain paraliterary ploys to attain a certain kind of prestige. If I teach these techniques in a workshop, I am not teaching writing, but methods of joining an elite.

It is to be noticed that membership in the elite may, not incidentally, improve one's chances to sell work in the marketplace. There's always a well-kept road between the marketplace and the really nice part of town.

Papa Hemingway said that writers write for money and Papa Freud said that artists work for fame, money, and the love of women. I'll leave out the love of women, though it would be much more fun to talk about. Fame and money – success and power. If you agree with the Papas, there are workshops for you, but this is not the essay for you. I think both Papas were talking through their hats. I don't think writers write for either fame or money, though they love them when they can get them. Writers don't write "for" anything, not even for art's sake. They write. Singers sing, dancers dance, writers write. The whole question of what a thing is "for" has no more to do with art than it has to do with babies, or forests, or galaxies.

In a money economy, artists must sell their work or be supported by gifts while doing it. Since our national government is hysterically suspicious of all artists, and most arts foundations are particularly stingy to writers, North American writers must be directly concerned with the skills of marketing and grant-getting. They need to learn their trade. There are many guidebooks and organizations to help them learn it. But the trade is not the art. Writers and teachers of writing who put saleability before quality degrade the writer and the work. Writing workshops that put marketing and contact-making before quality degrade the art.

If you don't agree with me, that's fine. Just keep out of my workshop.

Finally, one more cause of time-wasting: workshop codependency, the policy of encouraging eternal returners, workshop junkies, people who go to retreats and groups year after year but don't write anything the rest of the year . . . and the policy of giving a grant simply because the applicant has received other grants to attend other workshops and writers' colonies.

A friend who was at one of the very elite New England artist colonies told me about a woman there who *had no address*. She lived at colonies and conferences. She had published two short stories in the last ten years. She was a professional, all right, but her profession was not writing.

Junkies always bring an old manuscript to the workshop, and when it gets criticized, they tell us about the great writers at greater workshops who said how great it was. If the instructor demands new work from junkies, they are outraged – "But I've been working on this since 1950!" Bearded with moss and in garments green, indistinct in the twilight, they will be hauling out that same damned unfinished manuscript twenty years from now and whining, "But *Longfellow* said it was *tremendously sensitive!*"

But then, I am a workshop junky too: I keep doing them. Why?

So, to the positive side. Maybe nobody can teach anybody how to write, but, just as techniques for attaining profit and prestige can be taught in the commercial and establishmentarian programs, so realistic expectations, useful habits, respect for the art, and respect for oneself as a writer can be acquired in work-centered workshops.

What the instructor has to give is, I think, above all, experience – whether rationalized and verbalized or just shared by being there, being a writer, reading the work, talking about the work.

What most participants need most is to learn to think of themselves as writers.

For the young, this is all too often no problem at all. Many teenagers, college-agers, having no idea what being a fiction writer entails, assume they can write novels and screenplays and play drums in a band and pass their GREs and fifteen other things at the same time, no sweat. This blithe attitude is healthy, it is endearing, and it means they do not belong in a serious workshop (or, in my opinion, in a writing program ending in a degree of any kind). The very young cannot, except in rare cases, make the commitment that is required.

With many adults the problem is the opposite – lack of confidence. Women, particularly women with children, or in middle age and older, may find it enormously difficult to take seriously anything they do that isn't done "for other people" – the altruism trap. Men brought up to consider themselves as wage earners and ordinary joes may in the same way find it hard to take the leap to considering themselves seriously as writers. And this is why, though peer groups of amateur and semiamateur writers are a wonderful development of the last decades, and though the functioning of the workshop is strictly egalitarian, the workshop has an instructor: a central figure who is a professional, a real, indubitable, published writer, able to share professionalism and lend reality-as-a-writer to everyone in the circle.

And thus it is important that instructors should not be writing teachers but writers teaching: people who have published professionally and actively in the field of the workshop.

And it is important that they should be women as often as they are men. (If they are Gethenians, this latter requirement is no problem; otherwise it should be a central concern of the workshop managers.)

Instructors are not only symbols and gurus. They are directly useful. Their assignments, directions, discussions, exercises, criticisms, responses, and fits of temperament allow the participants to discover that they can meet a deadline, write a short story overnight, try a new form, take a risk, discover gifts they didn't know they had. The instructor directs their practice.

Practice is an interesting word. We think of practicing as beginner's stuff, playing scales, basic exercises. But the practice of an art is the doing of that art – it *is* the art. When the participants have been practicing writing with a bunch of other practicing writers for a week, they can feel with some justification that they are, in fact, writers.

So perhaps the essence of a workshop that works is the group itself. The instructor facilitates the formation of the group, but the circle of people is the source of energy. It is, by the way, important that it be literally, in so far as possible, a circle. This is the Teepee Theory of Workshopping. A circle of units is not a hierarchy. It is one shape made of many, one whole, one thing.

Participants who participate, who write, read, criticize, and discuss, are learning a great deal. First of all, they're learning to take criticism, learning that they *can* take criticism. Negative, positive, aggressive, constructive, valuable, stupid, they can take it. Most of us can, but we don't think we can till we do; and the fear of it can be crippling. To find that you have been roundly criticized and yet have gone on writing – that frees up a lot of energy.

Participants are also learning to read other people's writing and criticize it responsibly. For a good many, this is the first real reading they've ever done: reading not as passive absorption, as in reading junk for relaxation and escape; reading not as detached intellectual analysis, as in English 102; but reading as the intensely active and only partially intellectual process of *collaboration with a text.* A workshop in which one person learned to read that way would have justified itself. But if the group forms, everybody begins reading each other's work that way; and often real reading is so exciting to those new to it that it leads to the overvaluation of texts that is one of the minor hazards of a lively workshop.

Learning to read gives people a whole new approach to writing. They have learned to read what they write. They can turn their critico-collaborative skills onto their own work and so be enabled to revise, to revise constructively, without dreading revision as a destructive process, or a never-ending one, as many inexperienced writers do.

I spoke of the psychological acuteness and sensitivity I have learned to count on and call on in workshop groups. I think it rises from the fact that the people feel that they are working hard together at hard work, and that they have experienced honesty and trust as absolutely essential to getting the work done. So they will use all their skills to achieve that honesty and trust. If the group works as a group, everyone in it, including the instructor, is strengthened by its community and exhilarated by its energy.

This is such a rare and valuable experience that it's no wonder good workshops almost always spin off into small peer groups that may go on working together for months or years.

And it's one reason why I go on teaching. I come home from a workshop and I write.

The Writer, that noble heroic figure gazing at a blank page who is such an awful bore in books and movies because he doesn't get to bash holes in marble or slash brushes over canvas or conduct gigantic orchestras or die playing Hamlet – he only gets to gaze, and drink, and mope, and crumple up sheets of paper and throw them at a wastebasket, which is just as boring as what he does in real life, which is he sits there, and he sits there, and he sits there, and if you say anything he jumps and shouts WHAT? – the Writer, I say, is not only boring, but lonely, even when, perhaps especially when her family (she has changed sex, like Orlando) is with her, asking where is my blue shirt? when is dinner? The Writer is liable to feel like a little, tiny person all alone in a desert where the sand is words. Giant figures of Best-Sellers and Great Authors loom over her like statues – Look on my works, ye puny, and despair! – This lonely, sitting-there person may find that in a work-centered workshop she can draw on the kind of group support and collaborative rivalry, the pooled energy, that actors, dancers, and musicians, all performing artists, draw on all the time.

And so long as ego-tripping is discouraged, the process of the workshop, depending on mutual aid, stimulation, emulation, honesty, and trust, can produce an unusually pure and clear form of that energy.

The participant may be able to carry some of that energy home, not having learned "how to write," but having learned what it is to write.

I think of a good workshop as a pride of lions at a waterhole. They all hunt zebras all night and then they all eat the zebra, growling a good deal, and then they all come to the waterhole to drink together. Then in the heat of the day they lie around rumbling and swatting flies and looking benevolent. It is something to have belonged, even for a week, to a pride of lions.

Indian Uncles
by Ursula Kroeber Le Guin

●

1991

From a talk given for the Emeriti Lectures at the Department of Anthropology of the University of California at Berkeley, November 4, 1991. I rewrote the piece for a celebration of the hundredth anniversary of the department, November 16, 2001.

Because I was talking to people who knew my background (some of them perhaps better than I did) and all the people I mentioned, I did no explaining; therefore a few explanations are in order:

Alfred L. Kroeber, my father, founded that department in 1901, and taught in it till he retired in 1947. He married Theodora Kracaw Brown, my mother, in 1925. We lived in Berkeley near the campus.

In 1911 a "wild" Indian appeared in a small northern California town. He spoke a language the remaining local Indians did not know, and had evidently lived his entire life in hiding, with the remnant of his people, from the whites. A linguist from the university, T. T. Waterman, was able to talk a little with him, and brought him down to the museum of anthropology, then in San Francisco. He lived there from then on, learning the ways of the new world he had entered and teaching the ways of his own lost world to the scientists and to visitors to the museum. His people did not name themselves to others, so he was called Ishi, which means "man" in his own Yahi language. I relate below how my mother became Ishi's biographer. Her books about him are Ishi in Two Worlds and Ishi, Last of His Tribe. His story is, I think, essential reading to anyone who thinks they know, or wants to learn, how the West was won, and who Americans are.

Many, many people have asked me, eager and expectant, "Wasn't it wonderful to know Ishi?"

And I'm floored every time. All I can do is disappoint them by explaining that Ishi died thirteen years before I was born. I can't remember even hearing his name until the late fifties, when a biography of him became first a subject of family conversation and then the consuming object of my mother's work and thought for several years.

But my father, in my recollection, didn't talk about Ishi. He talked very little about the past; he didn't reminisce. As a man twenty years older than his wife, a father of grandfather age, he may well have determined never to be a garrulous old bore bleating about the good old days. But also by temperament he didn't live in the past, but in the present, in the moment, right up to his death at eighty-four. I wish he had reminisced more, because he had done so many interesting things in interesting places, and was a fine storyteller. But getting his own past out of him was like pulling hen's teeth. Once he did describe to us what he did during the 1906 Fire in San Francisco (it's in my mother's biography of him), and while he was in the remembering vein I asked him what he *felt* during the earthquake and after. He worked on his pipe for a while, lighting matches and making neat little piles of them, and then he said, "Exhilaration."

I don't mean to suggest that he was one of those yup-nope men. He was a highly conversable person, but he was too interested in what was happening now to look back much. I longed to know something about his first wife, Henrietta Rothschild, of San Francisco, but I didn't know how to ask and he didn't know how to answer, or there was too much old grief buried there and he wasn't going to dig it up and display it. There is a modesty of grief, and he was a modest man.

That may also be why he didn't talk about Ishi. So much old grief, old pain, still sharp. Not the cheap guilt trips the psychodramatizers pull out of their cheap hats: emotionally stunted scientist exploiting noble savage – Dr. Treves and the Elephant Man, Dr. Kroeber and Ishi – that is not what happened. It has happened, as we all know, and as he knew. But not in this case. Perhaps just the opposite.

The idea that objective observation can be performed only by an observer totally free of subjectivity involves an ideal of inhuman purity which we now recognize as being, fortunately, unattainable. But the dilemma of the subjective practitioner of objectivity persists, and presents itself to anthropologists in its most acute and painful form: the relationship between observer and observed when both of them are human. Novelists, people who write about people, have the same moral problem, the problem of exploitation, but we rarely face it in so stark a form. I'm awed at the courage of any scientist who admits it in all its intractability.

Looking at it from my naive, outsider's standpoint, it seems to me that most of the Boasians had a pretty strict take on it. I know my father distrusted whites – amateurs or professionals – who claimed emotional or spiritual identification with Indians. He saw such claims as sentimental and co-optative. To him the term *going native* was one of disapproval. His friendships with Indians were that: friendships. Beginning in collaborative work, based on personal liking and respect, they involved neither patronization nor co-optation.

With Ishi, a man almost unimaginably vulnerable in his tragic solitude, dependent by necessity, yet strong, generous, clear-minded, and affectionate, an extraordinary person in every way, this relationship of friendship must have been unusually complex and intense.

My father was consciously, consistently loyal to the ideal of objective science, but it was the passions of personal grief and personal loyalty that dictated his message from New York trying to prevent the autopsy of Ishi's body – "Tell them as far as I am concerned science can go to hell. We propose to stand by our friends."

His message came too late. A contemporary anthropologist has said that if he felt so strongly about the matter, why didn't he get on an airplane and come West and see about it? One would think that an anthropologist might be aware that in 1916 there was a certain lack of airplanes to get on. A telegram was the only means he had to try to prevent the desecration.

I know little of the circumstances of the subsequent grotesque division of the body, which reminds me of the way kings and emperors were buried in bits, the head in Vienna, the heart in Habsburg, other pieces in other parts of the empire. Saints the same – an arm here, a finger there, a toe in a reliquary . . . It would appear that to the European, dismembering a body and keeping bits of it around is a sign of respect. This is definitely a strain on our American cultural relativism. I leave it to you anthropologists to work it out.

Kroeber accepted defeat and got on with the work to be done. I do not think his silence was indifference but the muteness of undesired complicity and the dumbness of the bereaved. He had lost his friend. He had lost a person whom he loved and was responsible for, and lost him to the same sickness that had killed his wife a few years earlier, tuberculosis, the "White Sickness." Over and over he had worked with individuals who were among the last of their people. One way or another his people and their white sicknesses had destroyed them. He was silent because neither he nor his science had a vocabulary for his knowledge. And if he couldn't find the right words, he wouldn't use the wrong ones.

Not long after Ishi's death, my father took leave from anthropology, was psychoanalyzed, and practiced analysis for some years. But I don't think Freud had quite the words he needed, either. The scope of his work and writing widened with the years, but at the very end of his life he returned to Californian ethnology, using his long-accumulated expertise to support Californian tribes in their suit against the U.S. government for restoration and reparation of their lands, spending months of testimony and cross-examination in a federal courtroom. My brother Ted, who drove him to many of these sessions, recalls the judge's attempts to give the old man a break now and then, and Alfred's patient but urgent determination to get the job done.

He wrote as little about Ishi as possible. When asked about Ishi, he answered. When it was suggested he should write a biography of Ishi, he declined. Robert Heizer took the excellent expedient of offering the task to my mother, who had never known Ishi, never been his friend, was not an anthropologist, was not a man, and could be trusted to find the right words if anybody could.

I was in the Lowie Museum here with Alfred Kroeber's little great-granddaughter, ten years ago, and she showed me the headphones at the Ishi exhibit, where you can hear Ishi telling a story. I put them on and heard his voice for the first time. I broke into tears. For a moment. It seems the only appropriate response.

Some of you may have hoped to hear more about the family or about my father's colleagues and students, who were certainly a large element in our family life. I am afraid I share Alfred's incapacity for reminiscence. I am much better at making things up than at remembering them. The two Indian friends of my father's that I can say something about, because as a child I did really relate to them, are the Papago Juan Dolores and the Yurok Robert Spott. But here I run into the moral problem we storytellers share with you anthropologists: the exploitation of real people. People should not *use* other people. My memories of these two Native American friends are hedged with caution and thorned with fear. What, after all, did I or do I understand about them? When I knew them, what did I know about them, about their political or their individual situation? Nothing. Not their people's history, not their personal history, not their contributions to anthropology – nothing.

I was a little kid, youngest of the family. We always went up to the Napa Valley in June as soon as school was out. My parents had bought a forty-acre ranch there for two thousand dollars. We settled in and set up the packed-dirt croquet court, and Juan – a killer croquet player – always got there in time for his birthday.

I was amazed to learn that Juan Dolores, a grown-up, actually didn't know what day he was born on. Birthdays were important. Mine and my brothers' and my parents' were celebrated with cake and ice cream and candles and ribbons and presents, and it was a matter of great moment that one was now seven. How could it *not matter* to a person? In pondering this first discovery of the difference between Western time and Indian time, I was perhaps composting the soil from which the cultural relativism of my fictions would grow and flourish. But Juan (we kids called him Wahn, we didn't know Spanish Hwahn) – Juan had to have a birth date in order to fill out the papers for his social security or his pension from the university or something; bureaucrats, like me, believe in birthdays. So he and my father chose him a birthday. Now, that was nifty, sitting around and deciding when you wanted to be born. They picked St. John's Eve, Midsummer Night. And thereafter, Juan's birthday was celebrated with cake, candles, and all the rest: a festival of this small tribe, celebrated soon after their annual migration sixty miles to the north, marking both the summer solstice and the ritual visit of the Papago.

The Papago stayed for a month or longer. The top front bedroom of the old house in the Valley is still called Juan's Room by the elders of the tribe. During those visits he and my father may have worked together. I paid no attention to that. All I remember about Juan's visits is using him. The use of grown-ups by children is one of the numerous exceptions to my absolute rule that people should not use other people. Weaker people, of course, get to use stronger ones; they have to. But the limits of use are best set by the strong, not by the weak. Juan was not very good at setting limits, at least when it came to children. He let us get away with murder. We got him to make a drum for us, and as I recall we insisted that it be a Plains Indian drum, because that was a *real* Indian drum, no matter that he was a real non-Plains Indian. In any case he made a marvelous drum, and we beat on it for years.

We picked up phrases like "Lo! the poor Indian!" and, from some magazine article, a title, "The Vanishing Red Man." With what is called the cruelty of children, we used these phrases; we called Juan Lo, the Vanishing Papago. Hello, Lo! You haven't vanished yet! I think he thought it was funny too; I think if he hadn't, we'd have known it, and shut up. I hope so. We weren't cruel, we were ignorant, foolish. Children are ignorant and foolish. But they learn. If they are given a chance to learn.

There's a lot of poison oak in those hills, and we were all covered with calamine lotion all the time. Juan boasted that Indians never got poison oak. My brothers challenged him – Indians don't *ever* get poison oak? Never? Prove it! Dare you! – Juan went down on a hundred-degree day into a twelve-foot thicket of poison oak by the creek and cut it all down with a machete. We have a tiny Kodak picture: a sea of poison oak, one small, bald, dark head just visible in it, shining with sweat. He got tired, but he didn't get poison oak. Decades later when I read in Sarah Winnemucca's autobiography how she nearly died as a child from her first exposure, I modified Juan's claim: *some* Indians never get poison oak. It may have been that he was determined not to.

He was, I think, a strong, determined man; the intellectual work he did is proof of it; which makes his endless patience with us kids even more beautiful. This memory is not my own but of my mother's telling: Juan's first summer visit, long before he had a birthday, was the summer I learned to walk, 1931 I suppose. This infant would stagger over to Juan and say "Go-go?" And whatever he was doing, writing or reading or talking or working, Juan would excuse himself and gravely accompany me across the yard and up the driveway on a great journey of a hundred yards or so, I holding on to him firmly by one finger. Now that part I do seem to remember; perhaps it's just my mother's vivid telling; but I know which finger it was, the first of his left hand, a strong, thick, dark finger that entirely and warmly filled my hand.

In the forties when he was living in Oakland, Juan was mugged, robbed, and badly beaten. When he came for a visit at our Berkeley house after he got out of the hospital, I was afraid to come downstairs. I had heard that "his head was broken," and imagined horrors. I finally was ordered down, and said hello, and sneaked a look. He wasn't horrible. He was tired, and old, and sad. I was too ashamed and shy to show him my affection. I didn't know I loved him. Children brought up in great security, tribal or familial, aren't very aware of love, as I suppose fish aren't very aware of water. That's the way it ought to be, love as air, love as the human element. But I see

Juan now, a gentle, intellectual man, living in exile and poverty, licensed by bigotry to be a prey of bullies – the world was full of such people in the 1940s. It is full of such people now. I wish I had had the sense to take his hand.

The first time Robert Spott came to stay with us in the Valley, his major problem must have been getting enough to eat. My memory of Yurok table manners is that if anybody speaks during a meal, everybody puts down their fork or soupspoon or whatever, swallows, and stops eating till the conversation is done. Only when speech is over does eating resume. Such a custom might arise among a rather formal people who had plenty to eat and plenty of time to eat it in. (With that idea in mind, as a novelist, I once invented some people living on an Ice Age planet where food, warmth, and leisure were often hard to come by: to them it was extremely bad manners to speak at all during a meal. Eat now, talk later – first things first. This is probably far too logical for a real custom.) And I may well have misunderstood or misremembered; my brother Karl's recollection of correct Yurok table manners is that having taken a bite, one puts one's spoon or hand down on the table until quite done chewing; and that also, when the host stops eating, the guest stops. In any case, there was Robert, and us four kids and Aunt Betsy and my parents and probably some other odd relatives or ethnologists or refugees around the dinner table, and we were a talkative and discursive and argumentative lot, with the kids encouraged to take a responsible part in the conversation. So every time anybody said anything, which was constantly, poor Robert laid down his fork, swallowed, and looked up with courteous and undivided attention, while we gobbled and babbled on. And as my father ate with extreme, neat rapidity, Robert must have had to stop eating before he had had anything much to eat at all. I believe he learned eventually to imitate our uncouthness.

I often felt uncouth around Robert Spott. He had tremendous personal dignity and authority. I believed for years that he was a – what my linguistic nephew informs me is now pronounced shawman, but which I continue to pronounce shayman, since my father did, and it doesn't sound so New Agey. My brother Ted's memory, more enlightened than mine by six years, is that Robert's mother was the shaman, and that she and perhaps other women of his people trained him, not specifically as a shaman or doctor but in the knowledge of tribal and religious customs.

They demanded this learning of him, a heavy and lifelong commitment, because there was no other fit candidate and the knowledge would die with them if he did not accept it. I have it in my head that Robert accepted the burden only with reluctance. Ted tells me that Robert served as an advocate for his people in Sacramento, taking on the then seemingly hopeless struggle to preserve Yurok culture and values against white contempt and exploitation – a task that might daunt anyone. At the time, I understood nothing of that grim political work, and may have romanticized it by mythologizing Robert as an unwilling shaman. A girl does tend to spin romances about a handsome, stately, stern, dark man who doesn't say much.

Robert was grave, serious; we took no liberties with him. Was it a cultural or a temperamental difference, or both, that Juan Dolores was long-suffering with us brats, and Robert Spott was aloof and instructive? I can still blush when I remember myself rather unusually holding the table, chattering away breakneck, telling some event of the day, and being abruptly silenced by Robert. I had far exceeded the conversational limit proper to a well-bred Yurok girl, which I imagine may be a word or two. Robert laid down his fork and swallowed, and when I paused for breath, he spoke to the adults on a subject of interest to adults. My culture told me that it is rude to interrupt people, and I was resentful; but I shut up. Children have to be stupid, or to have been culturally stupidized, not to recognize genuine authority. My resentment was an attempt to justify my embarrassment. Robert had introduced me to a very Yurok moral sentiment, shame. Not guilt, there was nothing to be guilty about; just shame. You blush resentfully, you hold your tongue, and you figure it out. I have Robert to thank in part for my deep respect for shame as a social instrument. Guilt I believe to be counterproductive, but shame can be immensely useful; if, for example, any member of Congress was acquainted in any form with shame – well, never mind.

Both Juan and Robert are associated in my mind with the moving of great rocks. Blue boulders of serpentine, dug from the reddish dirt above the road. The menfolk and my great-aunt Betsy built a drylaid wall of them. The end rock nearest the house, a beautiful blue-green monster, is still called by all members of the tribe Juan's Rock, though some of them may not know why. He selected it and directed and labored in the levering and rolling of it from above the driveway down to its present place. No one got killed or even maimed, though the women worried and lamented in the kitchen, and I was told two thousand times to *keep uphill* from that rock.

Then, or before that – there was definitely some competition between the two men, some matter of my rock is bigger than your rock – Robert built us a marvelous outdoor fireplace. It is both technically and in fact a sacred place. It is built as a Yurok meditation shelter is built, and so oriented; but the fire burns where the meditator would sit, and so he completed the half circle of the shelter with a half circle of flat stones for people to sit on around the fire. And there my people have sat for seventy years, to eat, and tell stories, and watch the summer stars.

There is a photograph of my father and Robert, one listening, the other telling, with lifted hand and faraway gaze. They are sitting on those fireplace stones. Robert and Alfred talked together sometimes in English, sometimes in Yurok. It was perhaps unusual for the daughter of a first-generation German immigrant from New York to hear him talking Yurok, but I didn't know that. I didn't know anything. I thought everybody spoke Yurok. But I knew where the center of the world was.

The Writer On, and At, Her Work

1991/1995

Written for Janet Sternburg's 1995 anthology The Writer on Her Work, *volume 2,* New Essays in New Territory.

Her work
is never done.
She has been told that
and observed it for herself.
  Her work
spins unrelated filaments
into a skein: the whorl
or wheel turns the cloudy mass
into one strong thread,
over, and over, and over.
  Her work
weaves unrelated elements
into a pattern: the shuttle
thrown across the warp
makes roses, mazes, lightning,
over, and over, and over.
  Her work
brings out of dirt and water
a whole thing, a hole where
the use of the pot is,
a container for the thing
contained, a holy thing, a holder,
a saver,
happening on the clayey wheel
between her and her clayey hands,
over, and over, and over.

Her work
is with pots and baskets,
bags, cans, boxes, carryalls,
pans, jars, pitchers, cupboards, closets,
rooms, rooms in houses, doors,
desks in the rooms in the houses,
drawers and pigeonholes in the desks,
secret compartments
in which lie for generations
secret letters.
   Her work
is with letters,
with secret letters.
Letters that were not written
for generations.
She must write them
over, and over, and over.

   She works with her body,
a day-laborer.
She labors, she travails,
sweating and complaining,
She is her instrument,
whorl, shuttle, wheel.
She is the greasy wool and the raw clay
and the wise hands
that work by day
for the wages of the worker.
   She works within her body,
a night creature.
She runs between the walls.
She is hunted down and eaten.
She prowls, pounces, kills, devours.
She flies on soundless wings.
Her eyes comprehend the darkness.
The tracks she leaves are bloody,
and at her scream
everything holds still,

hearing that other wisdom.

Some say any woman working
is a warrior.
I resist that definition.
A fighter in necessity, sure,
a wise fighter,
but a professional?
One of los Generales?
Seems to me she has better things
to do than be a hero.
Medals were made for flatter chests.
They sort of dangle off her tits
and look embarrassing.
The uniforms don't fit.
If she shoots from the hip,
she hears the freudians applauding –
See? See? they say,
See? See? She wants one!
(She wants mine!
She can't have it!
She can't can she Daddy?
            No, son.)
Others say she's a goddess,
The Goddess, transcendent,
knowing everything by nature,
the Archetype
at the typewriter.
Resist that definition.
    Her work, I really think her work
isn't fighting, isn't winning,
isn't being the Earth, isn't being the Moon.
Her work, I really think her work
is finding what her real work is
and doing it,
her work, her own work,
her being human,
her being in the world.

So, if I am
a writer, my work
is words. Unwritten letters.
    Words are my way of being
human, woman, me.
Word is the whorl that spins me,
the shuttle thrown though the warp of years
to weave a life, the hand
that shapes to use, to grace.
Word is my tooth,
my wing.
Word is my wisdom.

I am a bundle of letters
in a secret drawer
in an old desk.
What is in the letters?
What do they say?

I am kept here a prisoner by the evil Duke.

Georgie is much better now, and I have been canning peaches like mad.

I cannot tell my husband or even my sister, I cannot live without you, I think of you day and night, when will you come to me?

My brother Will hath gone to London and though I begg'd with all my heart to go with him nor he nor my Father would have it so, but laugh'd and said, Time the wench was married.

The ghost of a woman walks in this house. I have heard her weeping in the room that was used as a nursery.

If I only knew that my letters were reaching you, but there is no way to get information at any of the bureaus, they will not say where you have been sent.

Don't grieve for me. I know what I am doing.

Bring the kids and they can all play together and we can sit and talk till we're blue in the face.

Did he know about her cousin Roger and the shotgun?

I don't know if it's any good but I've been working on it since September.

How many of us will it take to hang him?

I am taking the family to America, the land of Freedom.

I have found a bundle of old letters in a secret compartment in my desk.

Letters of words of stories:
they tell stories.
The writer tells stories, the stories,
over, and over, and over.

Man does, they say, and Woman is.
Doing and being. Do and be.
O.K., I be writing, Man.
I be telling.
("Je suis la où ça parle,"
says la belle Hélène.)
I be saying and parlaying.
I be being
this way. How do I do being?
Same way I be doing.
I would call it working
or else, it doesn't matter, playing.

The writer at her work
is playing.
Not chess not poker not monopoly,
none of the war games –
Even if she plays by all their rules
and wins – wins what?
Their funny money? –

not playing hero,
not playing god –
well, but listen, making things
is a kind of godly business, isn't it?
All right, then, playing god,
Aphrodite the Maker, without whom
"nothing is born into the shining
borders of light, nor is anything lovely or lovable made,"
Spider Grandmother, spinning,
Thought Woman, making it all up,
Coyote Woman, playing –
playing it, a game,
without a winner or a loser,
a game of skill, a game of make
believe.

Sure it's a gamble,
but not for money.
Sorry Ernie this ain't stud.
The stakes
are a little higher.

     The writer at her work
is odd, is peculiar, is particular,
certainly, but not, I think,
singular.
She tends to the plural.

I for example am Ursula; Miss
Ursula Kroeber;
Mrs. then Ms. Le Guin;
Ursula K. Le Guin; this latter is
"the writer," but who were,
who are, the others?
She is the writer
at their work.

     What are they doing,

those plurals of her?
Lying in bed.
Lazy as hound dogs.
She-Plural is lying in bed
in the morning early.
Long before light, in winter;
in summer "the morning people
are chirping on the roof."
And like the sparrows
her thoughts go hopping
and flying and trying out words.
And like the light of morning
her thought impalpably touches
shape, and reveals it,
brings seeing from dimness,
being from inexhaustible chaos.
That is the good time.
That is the time when this she-plural writer
finds what is to be written.
In the first light,
seeing with the eyes
of the child waking,
lying between sleep and the day
in the body of dream,
in the body of flesh
that has been/is
a fetus, a baby, a child, a girl, a woman, a lover, a mother,
has contained other bodies,
incipient beings, minds unawakened, not to awaken,
has been sick, been damaged, been healed,
been old, is born and dying, will die,
in the mortal, inexhaustible
body
of her work:

    That is the good time.

Spinning the fleece of the sun, that cloudy mass,

weaving a glance and a gesture,
shaping the clay of emotion:
housekeeping. Patterning.
Following patterns.
Lying there
in the dreamtime
following patterns.

   So then you have to cut it out –
take a deep breath,
the first cut, the blank page! –
and sew it together (drudgery,
toil in the sacred sweatshop),
the garment, the soul-coat,
the thing made of words,
cloth of the sunfleece,
the new clothes of the Emperor.

(Yes, and some kid comes along
and yaps, "But he hasn't any clothes on!"
Muzzle the brat
till it learns
that none of us has any clothes on,
that our souls are naked,
dressed in words only,
in charity only,
the gift of the others.
Any fool can see through it.
Only fools say so.)

   Long ago when I was Ursula
writing, but not "the writer,"
and not very plural yet,
and worked with the owls not the sparrows,
being young, scribbling at midnight:

I came to a place
I couldn't see well in the darkness,

where the road turned
and divided, it seemed like,
going different ways.
I was lost.
I didn't know which way.
It looked like one roadsign said To Town
and the other didn't say anything.

So I took the way that didn't say.
I followed
myself.
"I don't care," I said,
terrified.
"I don't care if nobody ever reads it!
I'm going *this* way."

And I found myself
in the dark forest, in silence.

You maybe have to find yourself,
yourselves,
in the dark forest.
Anyhow, I did then. And still now,
always. At the bad time.

   When you find the hidden catch
in the secret drawer
behind the false panel
inside the concealed compartment
in the desk in the attic
of the house in the dark forest,
and press the spring firmly,
a door flies open to reveal
a bundle of old letters,
and in one of them
is a map
of the forest
that you drew yourself

before you ever went there.

   The Writer At Her Work:
I see her walking
on a path through a pathless forest,
or a maze, a labyrinth.
As she walks she spins,
and the fine thread falls behind her
following her way,
telling
where she is going,
where she has gone.
Telling the story.
The line, the thread of voice,
the sentences saying the way.

   The Writer On Her Work:
I see her, too, I see her
lying on it.
Lying, in the morning early,
rather uncomfortable.
Trying to convince herself
that it's a bed of roses,
a bed of laurels,
or an innerspring mattress,
or anyhow a futon.
But she keeps twitching.

There's a *lump*, she says.
There's something
like a *rock* – like a *lentil* –
I can't sleep.

There's something
the size of a split pea
that I haven't written.
That I haven't written right.
I can't sleep.

She gets up
and writes it.
Her work
is never done.

Dogs, Cats, and Dancers:
Thoughts About Beauty

●

1992

*An earlier version of this piece was published in 1992 in the "Reflections"
section of Allure magazine, where it was retitled "The Stranger Within." I
have fiddled around with it a good bit since then.*

Dogs don't know what they look like. Dogs don't even know what size
they are. No doubt it's our fault, for breeding them into such weird shapes
and sizes. My brother's dachshund, standing tall at eight inches, would
attack a Great Dane in the full conviction that she could tear it apart.
When a little dog is assaulting its ankles the big dog often stands there
looking confused – "Should I eat it? Will it eat me? I *am* bigger than it,
aren't I?" But then the Great Dane will come and try to sit in your lap and
mash you flat, under the impression that it is a Peke-a-poo.

My children used to run at sight of a nice deerhound named Teddy,
because Teddy was so glad to see them that he wagged his whiplash tail so
hard that he knocked them over. Dogs don't notice when they put their
paws in the quiche. Dogs don't know where they begin and end.

Cats know exactly where they begin and end. When they walk slowly
out the door that you are holding open for them, and pause, leaving their
tail just an inch or two inside the door, they know it. They know you have
to keep holding the door open. That is why their tail is there. It is a cat's
way of maintaining a relationship.

Housecats know that they are small, and that it matters. When a cat
meets a threatening dog and can't make either a horizontal or a vertical escape, it'll suddenly triple its size, inflating itself into a sort of weird
fur blowfish, and it may work, because the dog gets confused again – "I
thought that was a cat. Aren't I bigger than cats? Will it eat me?"

Once I met a huge, black, balloonlike object levitating along the sidewalk making a horrible moaning growl. It pursued me across the street.
I was afraid it might eat me. When we got to our front steps it began to

shrink, and leaned on my leg, and I recognized my cat, Leonard; he had been alarmed by something across the street.

Cats have a sense of appearance. Even when they're sitting doing the wash in that silly position with one leg behind the other ear, they know what you're sniggering at. They simply choose not to notice. I knew a pair of Persian cats once; the black one always reclined on a white cushion on the couch, and the white one on the black cushion next to it. It wasn't just that they wanted to leave cat hair where it showed up best, though cats are always thoughtful about that. They knew where they looked best. The lady who provided their pillows called them her Decorator Cats.

A lot of us humans are like dogs: we really don't know what size we are, how we're shaped, what we look like. The most extreme example of this ignorance must be the people who design the seats on airplanes. At the other extreme, the people who have the most accurate, vivid sense of their own appearance may be dancers. What dancers look like is, after all, what they do.

I suppose this is also true of fashion models, but in such a limited way – in modeling, what you look like *to a camera* is all that matters. That's very different from really living in your body the way a dancer does. Actors must have a keen self-awareness and learn to know what their body and face are doing and expressing, but actors use words in their art, and words are great illusion makers. A dancer can't weave that word screen around herself. All a dancer has to make her art from is her appearance, position, and motion.

The dancers I've known have no illusions or confusions about what space they occupy. They hurt themselves a lot – dancing is murder on feet and pretty tough on joints – but they never, ever step in the quiche. At a rehearsal I saw a young man of the troupe lean over like a tall willow to examine his ankle. "Oh," he said, "I have an owie on my almost perfect body!" It was endearingly funny, but it was also simply true: his body is almost perfect. He knows it is, and knows where it isn't. He keeps it as nearly perfect as he can, because his body is his instrument, his medium, how he makes a living, and what he makes art with. He inhabits his body as fully as a child does, but much more knowingly. And he's happy about it.

I like that about dancers. They're so much happier than dieters and exercisers. Guys go jogging up my street, thump thump thump, grim faces, glazed eyes seeing nothing, ears plugged by earphones – if there was a quiche on the sidewalk, their weird gaudy running shoes would squish right through it. Women talk endlessly about how many pounds last week, how many pounds to go. If they saw a quiche they'd scream. If your body isn't perfect, punish it. No pain no gain, all that stuff. Perfection is "lean" and "taut" and "hard" – like a boy athlete of twenty, a girl gymnast of twelve. What kind of body is that for a man of fifty or a woman of any age? "Perfect"? What's perfect? A black cat on a white cushion, a white cat on a black one . . . A soft brown woman in a flowery dress . . . There are a whole lot of ways to be perfect, and not one of them is attained through punishment.

Every culture has its ideal of human beauty, and especially of female beauty. It's amazing how harsh some of these ideals are. An anthropologist told me that among the Inuit people he'd been with, if you could lay a ruler across a woman's cheekbones and it didn't touch her nose, she was a knockout. In this case, beauty is very high cheekbones and a very flat nose. The most horrible criterion of beauty I've yet met is the Chinese bound foot: feet dwarfed and crippled to be three inches long increased a girl's attractiveness, therefore her money value. Now that's serious no pain no gain.

But it's all serious. Ask anybody who ever worked eight hours a day in three-inch heels. Or I think of when I was in high school in the 1940s: the white girls got their hair crinkled up by chemicals and heat so it would curl, and the black girls got their hair mashed flat by chemicals and heat so it wouldn't curl. Home perms hadn't been invented yet, and a lot of kids couldn't afford these expensive treatments, so they were wretched because they couldn't follow the rules, the rules of beauty.

Beauty always has rules. It's a game. I resent the beauty game when I see it controlled by people who grab fortunes from it and don't care who they hurt. I hate it when I see it making people so self-dissatisfied that they starve and deform and poison themselves. Most of the time I just play the game myself in a very small way, buying a new lipstick, feeling happy about a pretty new silk shirt. It's not going to make me beautiful, but it's beautiful itself, and I like wearing it.

People have decorated themselves as long as they've been people. Flowers in the hair, tattoo lines on the face, kohl on the eyelids, pretty silk shirts – things that make you feel good. Things that suit you. Like a white pillow suits a lazy black cat . . . That's the fun part of the game.

One rule of the game, in most times and places, is that it's the young who are beautiful. The beauty ideal is always a youthful one. This is partly simple realism. The young *are* beautiful. The whole lot of 'em. The older I get, the more clearly I see that and enjoy it.

But it gets harder and harder to enjoy facing the mirror. Who is that old lady? Where is her *waist*? I got resigned, sort of, to losing my dark hair and getting all this limp grey stuff instead, but now am I going to lose even that and end up all pink scalp? I mean, enough already. Is that another mole or am I turning into an Appaloosa? How large can a knuckle get before it becomes a kneejoint? I don't want to see, I don't want to know.

And yet I look at men and women my age and older, and their scalps and knuckles and spots and bulges, though various and interesting, don't affect what I think of them. Some of these people I consider to be very beautiful, and others I don't. For old people, beauty doesn't come free with the hormones, the way it does for the young. It has to do with bones. It has to do with who the person is. More and more clearly it has to do with what shines through those gnarly faces and bodies.

I know what worries me most when I look in the mirror and see the old woman with no waist. It's not that I've lost my beauty – I never had enough to carry on about. It's that that woman doesn't look like me. She isn't who I thought I was.

My mother told me once that, walking down a street in San Francisco, she saw a blonde woman coming towards her in a coat just like hers. With a shock, she realized she was seeing herself in a mirrored window. But she wasn't a blonde, she was a redhead! – her hair had faded slowly, and she'd always thought of herself, seen herself, as a redhead ... till she saw the change that made her, for a moment, a stranger to herself.

We're like dogs, maybe: we don't really know where we begin and end. In space, yes; but in time, no.

All little girls are supposed (by the media, anyhow) to be impatient to reach puberty and to put on "training bras" before there's anything to train, but let me speak for the children who dread and are humiliated by the changes adolescence brings to their body. I remember how I tried to feel good about the weird heavy feelings, the cramps, the hair where there hadn't been hair, the fat places that used to be thin places. They were supposed to be good because they all meant that I was Becoming a Woman. And my mother tried to help me. But we were both shy, and maybe both a little scared. Becoming a woman is a big deal, and not always a good one.

When I was thirteen and fourteen I felt like a whippet suddenly trapped inside a great lumpy Saint Bernard. I wonder if boys don't often feel something like that as they get their growth. They're forever being told that they're supposed to be big and strong, but I think some of them miss being slight and lithe. A child's body is very easy to live in. An adult body isn't. The change is hard. And it's such a tremendous change that it's no wonder a lot of adolescents don't know who they are. They look in the mirror – that is me? Who's me?

And then it happens again, when you're sixty or seventy.

Cats and dogs are smarter than us. They look in the mirror, once, when they're a kitten or a puppy. They get all excited and run around hunting for the kitten or the puppy behind the glass . . . and then they get it. It's a trick. A fake. And they never look again. My cat will meet my eyes in the mirror, but never his own.

Who I am is certainly part of how I look and vice versa. I want to know where I begin and end, what size I am, and what suits me. People who say the body is unimportant floor me. How can they believe that? I don't want to be a disembodied brain floating in a glass jar in a sci-fi movie, and I don't believe I'll ever be a disembodied spirit floating ethereally about. I am not "in" this body, I *am* this body. Waist or no waist.

But all the same, there's something about me that doesn't change, hasn't changed, through all the remarkable, exciting, alarming, and disappointing transformations my body has gone through. There is a person there who isn't only what she looks like, and to find her and know her I have to look through, look in, look deep. Not only in space, but in time.

I am not lost until I lose my memory.

There's the ideal beauty of youth and health, which never really changes, and is always true. There's the ideal beauty of movie stars and advertising models, the beauty-game ideal, which changes its rules all the time and from place to place, and is never entirely true. And there's an ideal beauty that is harder to define or understand, because it occurs not just in the body but where the body and the spirit meet and define each other. And I don't know if it has any rules.

One way I can try to describe that kind of beauty is to think of how we imagine people in heaven. I don't mean some literal Heaven promised by a religion as an article of belief; I mean just the dream, the yearning wish we have that we could meet our beloved dead again. Imagine that "the circle is unbroken," you meet them again "on that beautiful shore." What do they look like?

People have discussed this for a long time. I know one theory is that everybody in heaven is thirty-three years old. If that includes people who die as babies, I guess they grow up in a hurry on the other side. And if they die at eighty-three, do they have to forget everything they've learned for fifty years? Obviously, one can't get too literal with these imaginings. If you do, you run right up against that old, cold truth: you can't take it with you.

But there is a real question there: How do we remember, how do we *see,* a beloved person who is dead?

My mother died at eighty-three, of cancer, in pain, her spleen enlarged so that her body was misshapen. Is that the person I see when I think of her? Sometimes. I wish it were not. It is a true image, yet it blurs, it clouds, a truer image. It is one memory among fifty years of memories of my mother. It is the last in time. Beneath it, behind it is a deeper, complex, ever-changing image, made from imagination, hearsay, photographs, memories. I see a little red-haired child in the mountains of Colorado, a sad-faced, delicate college girl, a kind, smiling young mother, a brilliantly intellectual woman, a peerless flirt, a serious artist, a splendid cook – I see her rocking, weeding, writing, laughing – I see the turquoise bracelets on her delicate, freckled arm – I see, for a moment, all that at once, I glimpse what no mirror can reflect, the spirit flashing out across the years, beautiful.

That must be what the great artists see and paint. That must be why the tired, aged faces in Rembrandt's portraits give us such delight: they show us beauty not skin-deep but life-deep. In Brian Lanker's album of photographs *I Dream a World*, face after wrinkled face tells us that getting old can be worth the trouble if it gives you time to do some soul making. Not all the dancing we do is danced with the body. The great dancers know that, and when they leap, our soul leaps with them – we fly, we're free. And the poets know that kind of dancing. Let Yeats say it:

O chestnut tree, great-rooted blossomer,
Are you the leaf, the blossom or the bole?
O body swayed to music, O brightening glance,
How can we know the dancer from the dance?

Introducing Myself

●

1992

Written in the early nineties as a performance piece, performed a couple of times, and slightly updated for this volume.

I am a man. Now you may think I've made some kind of silly mistake about gender, or maybe that I'm trying to fool you, because my first name ends in *a*, and I own three bras, and I've been pregnant five times, and other things like that that you might have noticed, little details. But details don't matter. If we have anything to learn from politicians it's that details don't matter. I am a man, and I want you to believe and accept this as a fact, just as I did for many years.

You see, when I was growing up at the time of the Wars of the Medes and Persians and when I went to college just after the Hundred Years War and when I was bringing up my children during the Korean, Cold, and Vietnam Wars, there were no women. Women are a very recent invention. I predate the invention of women by decades. Well, if you insist on pedantic accuracy, women have been invented several times in widely varying localities, but the inventors just didn't know how to sell the product. Their distribution techniques were rudimentary and their market research was nil, and so of course the concept just didn't get off the ground. Even with a genius behind it an invention has to find its market, and it seemed like for a long time the idea of women just didn't make it to the bottom line. Models like the Austen and the Brontë were too complicated, and people just laughed at the Suffragette, and the Woolf was way too far ahead of its time.

So when I was born, there actually were only men. People were men. They all had one pronoun, his pronoun; so that's who I am. I am the generic he, as in, "If anybody needs an abortion he will have to go to another state," or "A writer knows which side his bread is buttered on." That's me, the writer, him. I am a man.

Not maybe a first-rate man. I'm perfectly willing to admit that I may be in fact a kind of second-rate or imitation man, a Pretend-a-Him. As a him, I am to a genuine male him as a microwaved fish stick is to a whole grilled Chinook salmon. I mean, after all, can I inseminate? Can I belong to the Bohemian Club? Can I run General Motors? Theoretically I can, but you know where theory gets us. Not to the top of General Motors, and on the day when a Radcliffe woman is president of Harvard University you wake me up and tell me, will you? Only you won't have to, because there aren't any more Radcliffe women; they were found to be unnecessary and abolished. And then, I can't write my name with pee in the snow, or it would be awfully laborious if I did. I can't shoot my wife and children and some neighbors and then myself. Oh to tell you the truth I can't even drive. I never got my license. I chickened out. I take the bus. That is terrible. I admit it, I am actually a very poor imitation or substitute man, and you could see it when I tried to wear those army surplus clothes with ammunition pockets that were trendy and I looked like a hen in a pillowcase. I am shaped wrong. People are supposed to be lean. You can't be too thin, everybody says so, especially anorexics. People are supposed to be lean and taut, because that's how men generally are, lean and taut, or anyhow that's how a lot of men start out and some of them even stay that way. And men are people, people are men, that has been well established, and so people, real people, the right kind of people, are lean. But I'm really lousy at being people, because I'm not lean at all but sort of podgy, with actual fat places. I am untaut. And then, people are supposed to be tough. Tough is good. But I've never been tough. I'm sort of soft and actually sort of tender. Like a good steak. Or like Chinook salmon, which isn't lean and tough but very rich and tender. But then salmon aren't people, or anyhow we have been told that they aren't, in recent years. We have been told that there is only one kind of people and they are men. And I think it is very important that we all believe that. It certainly is important to the men.

What it comes down to, I guess, is that I am just not manly. Like Ernest Hemingway was manly. The beard and the guns and the wives and the little short sentences. I do try. I have this sort of beardoid thing that keeps trying to grow, nine or ten hairs on my chin, sometimes even more; but what do I do with the hairs? I tweak them out. Would a man do that? Men don't tweak. Men shave. Anyhow white men shave, being hairy, and I have even less choice about being white or not than I do about being a man or not. I am white whether I like being white or not. The doctors can do nothing for me. But I do my best not to be white, I guess, under the circumstances, since I don't shave. I tweak. But it doesn't mean anything because I don't really have a real beard that amounts to anything. And I don't have a gun and I don't have even one wife and my sentences tend to go on and on and on, with all this syntax in them. Ernest Hemingway would have died rather than have syntax. Or semicolons. I use a whole lot of half-assed semicolons; there was one of them just now; that was a semicolon after "semicolons," and another one after "now."

And another thing. Ernest Hemingway would have died rather than get old. And he did. He shot himself. A short sentence. Anything rather than a long sentence, a life sentence. Death sentences are short and very, very manly. Life sentences aren't. They go on and on, all full of syntax and qualifying clauses and confusing references and getting old. And that brings up the real proof of what a mess I have made of being a man: I am not even young. Just about the time they finally started inventing women, I started getting old. And I went right on doing it. Shamelessly. I have allowed myself to get old and haven't done one single thing about it, with a gun or anything.

What I mean is, if I had any real self-respect wouldn't I at least have had a face-lift or some liposuction? Although liposuction sounds to me like what they do a lot of on TV when they are young or youngish, though not when they are old, and when one of them is a man and the other a woman, though not under any other circumstances. What they do is, this young or youngish man and woman take hold of each other and slide their hands around on each other and then they perform liposuction. You are supposed to watch them while they do it. They move their heads around and flatten out their mouth and nose on the other person's mouth and nose and open their mouths in different ways, and you are supposed to feel sort of hot or wet or something as you watch. What I feel is like I'm watching two people doing liposuction, and *this* is why they finally invented women? Surely not.

As a matter of fact I think sex is even more boring as a spectator sport than all the other spectator sports, even baseball. If I am required to watch a sport instead of doing it, I'll take show jumping. The horses are really good-looking. The people who ride them are mostly these sort of nazis, but like all nazis they are only as powerful and successful as the horse they are riding, and it is after all the horse who decides whether to jump that five-barred gate or stop short and let the nazi fall off over its neck.

Only usually the horse doesn't remember it has the option. Horses aren't awfully bright. But in any case, show jumping and sex have a good deal in common, though you usually can only get show jumping on American TV if you can pick up a Canadian channel, which is not true of sex. Given the option, though I often forget that I have an option, I certainly would *watch* show jumping and *do* sex. Never the other way round. But I'm too old now for show jumping, and as for sex, who knows? I do; you don't.

Of course golden oldies are supposed to jump from bed to bed these days just like the horses jumping the five-barred gates, bounce, bounce, bounce, but a good deal of this super sex at seventy business seems to be theory again, like the woman CEO of General Motors and the woman president of Harvard. Theory is invented mostly to reassure people in their forties, that is men, who are worried. That is why we had Karl Marx, and why we still have economists, though we seem to have lost Karl Marx. As such, theory is dandy. As for practice, or praxis as the Marxists used to call it apparently because they liked *x*'s, you wait till you are sixty or seventy and then you can tell me about your sexual practice, or praxis, if you want to, though I make no promises that I will listen, and if I do listen I will probably be extremely bored and start looking for some show jumping on the TV. In any case you are not going to hear anything from me about my sexual practice or praxis, then, now, or ever.

But all that aside, here I am, old, when I wrote this I was sixty years old, "a sixty-year-old smiling public man," as Yeats said, but then, he *was* a man. And now I am over seventy. And it's all my own fault. I get born before they invent women, and I live all these decades trying so hard to be a good man that I forget all about staying young, and so I didn't. And my tenses get all mixed up. I just am young and then all of a sudden I was sixty and maybe eighty, and what next?

Not a whole lot.

I keep thinking there must have been something that a real man could have done about it. Something short of guns, but more effective than Oil of Olay. But I failed. I did nothing. I absolutely failed to stay young. And then I look back on all my strenuous efforts, because I really did try, I tried hard to be a man, to be a good man, and I see how I failed at that. I am at best a bad man. An imitation phony second-rate him with a ten-hair beard and semicolons. And I wonder what was the use. Sometimes I think I might just as well give the whole thing up. Sometimes I think I might just as well exercise my option, stop short in front of the five-barred gate, and let the nazi fall off onto his head. If I'm no good at pretending to be a man and no good at being young, I might just as well start pretending that I am an old woman. I am not sure that anybody has invented old women yet; but it might be worth trying.

Off the Page: Loud Cows,
A Talk and a Poem about Reading Aloud

1992/1994

"Off the Page" was a talk for a conference on Women and Language held by graduate students of the Department of Linguistics at the University of California in Berkeley, in April 1998. In getting it ready for this book, I didn't change the informality of the language, since the piece not only is about reading aloud to a live audience but was written for performance. The audience was by no means all women, but they were more receptive to uncomforting remarks about gender equality than most academic groups. I have performed the poem "Loud Cows" at that meeting, in New York, and elsewhere, and it appears as a frontispiece in The Ethnography of Reading, *edited by Jonathan Boyarin.*

What happened to stories and poems after the invention of printing is a strange and terrible thing. Literature lost its voice. Except on the stage, it was silenced. Gutenberg muzzled us.

By the time I got born the silence of literature was considered an essential virtue and a sign of civilization. Nannies and grannies told stories aloud to babies, and "primitive" peoples spoke their poems, poor illiterate jerks, but the real stuff, literature, was literally letters, letterpress, little black noiseless marks on paper. And libraries were temples of the goddess of silence attended by vigilant priestesses going *Shhhh.*

If you listen to the first Caedmon tape of poets reading, which was a landmark, you'll hear T. S. Eliot going *adduh, adduh* in this dull grey mutter, and Elizabeth Bishop going *gnengnengne* in a low flat whine. They were good poets who'd been taught poetry was to be seen not heard, and thought the music in their verse should be a secret between the poet and the reader – like the music that people who know how to read music hear when they read a score. Nobody was playing the music of poetry out loud.

Until Dylan Thomas. You know the Caedmon tape of him reading at Columbia in 1952? I was there at that reading, and you can hear me – in the passionate silence of the audience listening to that passionate voice. Not a conspiracy of silence, but a participatory silence, a community collaboration in letting him let the word loose aloud. I left that reading two feet above the ground, and it changed my understanding of the art forever.

So then there were the Beat poets, all posing and using and screwed up by testosterone, but at least audible, and Ginsberg's "Howl," which from the title on is a true performance piece that will not lie down quietly on the paper and be good. And ever since then, our poets have been noisy. Now God knows there are too many open-mike readings in the world; but better drivel at an open mike than silence from a closed mouth. And we have the voices of all recent poets on tape, so we can hear their word on their breath, with their heartbeat in it. Whereas of the greatest English writer of the twentieth century we have one tiny BBC recording: about ninety seconds of Virginia Woolf's voice reading a little essay. But in it you hear an invaluable hint of the rhythm that she said was where all the words began for her, the mysterious rhythm of her own voice.

It wasn't till the seventies, I think, that publishers realized they could sell more books by sending the author to two hundred cities in eight days to sign them – and then realized that people like not only to see the author sit and grin and write its name, but also to hear the author stand up and read its story. So now you here in Berkeley have Black Oak and Cody's, and we in Portland have Powell's and the Looking Glass, and Seattle has Elliott Bay Books running two readings a day every day of the week, and people come. They come to be read to. Some of them want books signed and some of them want to ask weird questions, but most of them want to be read to. To hear the word.

One reason I think this is a restoration of an essential function of literature is that it is reciprocal: a social act. The audience is part of the performance. A lecture isn't reciprocal, it's a talking-to. There were professors at Harvard when I was there who would give you a C if you *breathed* during a lecture. But the hush during a performance is alive and responsive, as at the theater. Nothing kills a play like a dead audience. This response is recognized and called for in all oral literatures. Zunis listening to a narrative recital say a word, *eeso,* meaning yes, OK, about once a minute and whenever appropriate. In oral cultures generally, kids are taught to make these soft response-noises; if they don't, it's assumed they weren't listening and they're sent out in disgrace. Any Baptist preacher who doesn't hear Yes Lord! and Amen! pretty often knows he's lost the congregation. In poetry readings, big groups or small, the convention is mostly a little soft groan or *hahh* at a striking line or at the end. In prose readings the response convention is even subtler, except for laughter, but there are audible responses which the reader counts on just as the actor does.

I learned that once for all at a reading I did in Santa Barbara. They had no lights on the audience, so I was facing this black chasm, and no sound came out of it. Total silence. Reading to pillows. Despair. Afterwards the students came around all warm and affectionate and said they'd loved it, but it was too late, I was a wreck. They'd been so laid back or so respectful or something they hadn't given me any response, and so they hadn't been working with me; and you can't do it alone.

It was men who first got poetry off the page, but the act was of great importance to women. Women have a particular stake in keeping the oral functions of literature alive, since misogyny wants women to be silent, and misogynist critics and academics do not want to hear the woman's voice in literature, in any sense of the word. There is solid evidence for the fact that when women speak more than 30 percent of the time, men perceive them as dominating the conversation; well, similarly, if, say, two women in a row get one of the big annual literary awards, masculine voices start talking about feminist cabals, political correctness, and the decline of fairness in judging. The 30 percent rule is really powerful. If more than one woman out of four or five won the Pulitzer, the PEN/Faulkner, the Booker – if more than one woman in ten were to win the Nobel literature prize – the ensuing masculine furor would devalue and might destroy the prize. Apparently, literary guys can only compete with each other. Put on a genuinely equal competitive footing with women, they get hysterical. They just have to have their voices heard 70 percent of the time.

Well, when feminism got reborn, it urged literary women to raise their voices, to yell unladylikely, to shoot for parity. So ever since, we have been grabbing the mike and letting loose. And it was this spirit of *hey, let's make a lot of noise* that carried me into experimenting with performance poetry. Not performance art, where you take your clothes off and dip yourself in chocolate or anything exciting like that, I'm way too old for that to work at all well and also I am a coward. But just letting my own voice loose, getting it off the page. Making female noises, shrieking and squeaking and being *shrill*, all those things that annoy people with longer vocal cords. Another case where the length of organs seems to be so important to men.

I read this piece, "Loud Cows," on tape at first but then didn't know what to do with the tape, so I do it live; and it's never twice the same, and though it has been printed, it really needs you, the audience, to be there, going *eeso, eeso!* So I'll end up now by performing it, in the hope of sending you away from this great conference with the memory of seeing an old woman mooing loudly in public.

LOUD COWS

It's allowed. It is allowed, we are allowedSILENCE!

It is allowed. It IS allowed. It IS allowedSILENCE!!

it *used* to be allowed.

SI – EE – LENTSSSSS.

I-EE AM THE AWE – THOR.

REEEED MEEE IN SI-EE-LENT AWE.

> but it's aloud.
> it *is* aloud.

A word is a noise a word is a noise
A word is a NOISE a NOISE a NOISE –

> AWWWWW.

The word is aloud. The word is a loud thing.
The loud word is allowed, aloud to be, the loud word allows to be, it allows as how.

but
GUNS have si-len-cers.
Gumments have sssi-len-sssers.
So do Private SseC-tors.
Words are to be-hayve.
To lie sigh-lent-ly on pages being good.

To keep their covers over them.
Words are to be clean.
To be neat.
To be seen   not   heard.

Words are the children of the fathers who saySILENCE!
who say BANG! you're dead!

But:
the word is longer than daddy and louder than bang.
And all that silent words forbid DO NOT TRESPASS KEEP OUT
SILENCE!
And all that silent words forbid,
loud words allow to be.

All, all walls fall.

I say aloud: All walls all fall.
   It is aloud, it is allowed to be loud,
   and I say it is aloud LOUDly
   loudness allowing us to BE us – SO –

MOOOOOOOOOOOOOO**VE OH**-ver –

here come the LOUD COWS right NOW!

Mooooooooving throooooooough the silences

Mooooooooing in the Libraries

LOUD COWS in the sacred groves *(sssssh! don't wake daddy!)*

MOOO-OOOO-OOOOVE along there,

MOOOOOOVe along,
                    JUMP! over the

                    moooOOOOOOO**ON!**

LOUD cows LOUD COWS
Loud SOWS LOUD SOWS now
   mouthing sounds**HEY!**

IT IS ALOUD!

Reading Young, Reading Old:
Mark Twain's *Diaries of Adam and Eve*

●

1995

This piece was written as a preface to the Diaries of Adam and Eve *in the Oxford edition of the complete works of Mark Twain, 1996, edited by Shelley Fisher Fishkin. It appears here substantially as it did there (minus two paragraphs about the illustrations reproduced in the Oxford edition).*

Every tribe has its myths, and the younger members of the tribe generally get them wrong. My tribal myth of the great Berkeley Fire of 1923 went this way: when my mother's mother-in-law, who lived near the top of Cedar Street, saw the flames sweeping over the hill straight towards the house, she put her Complete Works of Mark Twain in Twenty-Five Volumes into her Model A and went away from that place.

Because I was going to put that story in print, I made the mistake of checking it first with my brother Ted. In a slow, mild sort of way, Ted took it all to pieces. He said, well, Lena Brown never had a Model A. As a matter of fact, she didn't drive. The way I remember the story, he said, some fraternity boys came up the hill and got her piano out just before the fire reached that hill. And a bearskin rug, and some other things. But I don't remember, he said, that anything was said about the Complete Works of Mark Twain.

He and I agreed, however, that fraternity boys who would choose to rescue a piano and a bear rug from a house about to be engulfed by a fiery inferno might well have also selected the Works of Mark Twain. And the peculiarity of their selection may be illuminated by the fact that the piano ended up in the fraternity house. But after the fire or during it, Lena Brown somehow rescued the bear rug and the Complete Works from her rescuers; because Ted remembers the bear; and I certainly, vividly remember the Complete Works.

I also remain convinced that she was very fond of them, that she *would have* rescued them rather than her clothes and silver and checkbook.

And maybe she really did. At any rate, when she died she left them to the family, and my brothers and I grew up with them, a full shelf of lightweight, middle-sized books in slightly pebbly and rather ratty red bindings. They are no longer, alas, in the family, but I have tracked down the edition in a library. As soon as I saw the row of red books I said Yes! with the startled joy one would feel at seeing an adult one had loved as a child, alive and looking just as he did fifty years ago. Our set was, to the best of my knowledge, the 1917 Authorized Uniform Edition, published by Harper & Brothers, and copyright by the Mark Twain Company.

The only other complete works I recall around the house was my great-aunt Betsy's Dickens. I was proud of both sets. Complete works and uniform editions are something you don't often see any more except in big libraries, but ordinary people used to own them and be proud of them. They have a majesty about them. Physically they are imposing, the uniform row of bindings, the gold-stamped titles; but the true majesty of a complete works is spiritual. It is a great mental edifice, a house of many mansions, into which a reader can enter at any of the doors, or a young reader can climb in the windows, and wander about, experiencing magnanimity.

My great-aunt was very firm about not letting us get into Dickens yet. She said nobody under eighteen had any business reading Dickens. We would merely misunderstand him and so spoil the pleasure we would otherwise take in him the rest of our lives. She was right, and I am grateful. At sixteen, I whined till she let me read *David Copperfield*, but she warned me about Steerforth, lest I fall in love with him as she had done, and break my heart. When Betsy died she left me her Dickens. We had him re-bound, for he had got a bit shabby traveling around the West with her for fifty or sixty years. When I take a book from that set I think how, wherever she went, she had this immense refuge and resource with her, reliable as not much else in her life was.

Except for Dickens, nobody told us not to read anything, and I burrowed headlong into every book on the shelves. If it was a story, I read it. And there stood that whole row of pebbly red books, all full of stories.

Obviously I got to *Tom Sawyer* very soon, and *Huck Finn*; and my next-older brother, Karl, showed me the sequels, which we judged pretty inferior, critical brats that we were. After *The Prince and the Pauper*, I got into *Life on the Mississippi*, and *Roughing It* – my prime favorite for years

– and the stories, and the whole Complete Works in fact, one red book after another, snap, munch, gulp, snap, munch, gulp.

I didn't much like the *Connecticut Yankee*. The meaning of the book went right over my head. I just thought the hero was a pigheaded, loud-mouthed show-off. But a little thing like not liking a book didn't keep me from reading it. Not then. It was like Brussels sprouts. Nobody could like them, but they existed, they were food, you ate them. Eating and reading were a central, essential part of life. Eating and reading can't all be Huck and corn on the cob, some of it has to be Brussels sprouts and the Yankee. And there were plenty of good bits in the *Yankee*. The only one of the row of red books I ever stuck at was *Joan of Arc*. I just couldn't swallow her. She wouldn't go down. And I believe our set was lacking the *Christian Science* volume, because I don't remember even having a go at that. If it had been there, I would have chewed at it, the way kids do, the way Eskimo housewives soften walrus hide, though I might not have been able to swallow it either.

My memory is that it was Karl who discovered *Adam's and Eve's Diaries* and told me to read them. I have always followed Karl's advice in reading, even after he became an English professor, because he never led me astray before he was a professor. I never would have got into *Tom Brown's School Days* for instance, if he hadn't told me you can skip the first sixty pages, and it must have been Karl who told me to stick with *Candide* till I got to the person with one buttock, who would make it all worthwhile. So I found the right pebbly red book and read both the Diaries. I loved them instantly and permanently.

And yet when I reread them this year, it was the first time for about fifty years. Not having the Complete Works with me throughout life, I have over the years reread only my favorites of the books, picked up here and there, and the stories contained in various collections. And none of those collections contained the Diaries.

This five-decade gap in time makes it irresistible to try to compare my reading of the Diaries as a child with my reading of them now.

The first thing to be said is that, when I reread them, there did not seem to have been any gap at all. What's fifty years? Well, when it comes to some of the books one read at five or at fifteen, it's an abyss. Many books I loved and learned from have fallen into it. I absolutely cannot read *The Swiss Family Robinson* and am amazed that I ever did – talk about chewing walrus hide! – but the Diaries give me a curious feeling of constancy, almost of immortality: because they haven't changed at all. They are just as fresh and surprising as when I read them first. Nor am I sure that my reading of them is very different from what it was back then.

I will try to follow that then-and-now response through three aspects of the Diaries: humor, gender, and religion.

Though it seems that children and adults have different senses of humor, they overlap so much I wonder if people don't just use the same apparatus differently at different ages. At about the age I first came on the Diaries, ten or eleven, I was reading the stories of James Thurber with sober, pious attention. I knew they were funny, that grown-ups laughed aloud reading them, but they didn't make me laugh. They were wonderful, mysterious tales of human behavior, like all the folktales and stories in which people did the amazing, terrifying, inexplicable things that grown-ups do. The various night wanderings of the Thurber family in "The Night the Bed Fell Down" were no more and no less strange to me than the behavior of the Reed family in the first chapter of *Jane Eyre*. Both were fascinating descriptions of life – eyewitness accounts, guidebooks to the world awaiting me. I was much too interested to laugh.

When I did laugh at Thurber was when he played with words. The man who came with the reeves and the cook who was alarmed by the doom-shaped thing on top of the refrigerator were a source of pure delight to me, then as now. The accessibility of Mark Twain's humor to a child surely has much to do with the way he plays with language, the deadpan absurdities, the marvelous choices of word. The first time I ever read the story about the blue jay trying to fill the cabin with acorns, I nearly died. I lay on the floor gasping and writhing with joy. Even now I feel a peaceful cheer come over me when I think of that blue jay. And it's all in the way he tells it, as they say. The story is the way the story is told.

Adam's Diary is funny, when it is funny, because of the way Adam writes it.

This made her sorry for the creatures which live in there, which she calls fish, for she continues to fasten names on to things that don't need them and don't come when they are called by them, which is a matter of no consequence to her, as she is such a numskull anyway; so she got a lot of them out and brought them in last night and put them in my

249

bed to keep warm, but I have noticed them now and then all day, and I don't see that they are any happier there than they were before, only quieter.

Now that is a pure Mark Twain tour de force sentence, covering an immense amount of territory in an effortless, aimless ramble that seems to be heading nowhere in particular and ends up with breathtaking accuracy at the gold mine. Any sensible child would find that funny, perhaps not following all its divagations but delighted by the swing of it, by the word *numskull*, by the idea of putting fish in the bed; and as that child grew older and reread it, its reward would only grow; and if that grown-up child had to write an essay on the piece and therefore earnestly studied and pored over this sentence, she would end up in unmitigated admiration of its vocabulary, syntax, pacing, sense, and rhythm, above all the beautiful timing of the last two words; and she would, and she does, still find it funny.

Twain's humor is indestructible. Trying to make a study of the rhythms of prose last year, I analyzed a paragraph from "The Jumping Frog" – laboring over it, dissecting it, counting beats, grouping phrases, reducing it to a mere drum-score – and even after all that mauling, every time I read it, it was as fresh-flowing and lively and amusing as ever, or more so. The prose itself is indestructible. It is all of a piece. It is a living person speaking. Mark Twain put his voice on paper with a fidelity and vitality that makes electronic recordings seem crude and quaint.

I wonder if this is why we trust him, even though he lets us down so often. Lapses such as the silly stuff about Niagara in Adam's Diary – evidently worked in to make it suit a publication about the Falls – would make me distrust most writers. But Mark Twain's purity is unmistakable and incorruptible, which is why the lapses stick out so, and yet are forgivable. I have heard a great pianist who made a great many mistakes in playing; the mistakes were of no account because the music was true. Though Mark Twain forces his humor sometimes, always his own voice comes back, comes through; and his own voice is one of hyperbole and absurdity and wild invention and absolute accuracy and truth.

So all in all my response to the humor of the Diaries is very much what it was fifty years ago. This is partly because a good deal of the humor is perfectly childish. I mean that as praise. There is no meanness in it, no nudging and winking, nothing snide. Now, as then, I find Adam very funny, but so obtuse I often want to kick him rather than laugh at him. Eve isn't quite as funny, but I don't get as cross with her, so it's easier to laugh.

I read the Diaries before I had any personal interest, as you might say, in gender. I had noticed that there were males and females and had learned from a useful Germanic book how babies occurred, but the whole thing was entirely remote and theoretical, about as immediately interesting to me as the Keynesian theory of economics. "Latency," one of Freud's fine imaginative inventions, was more successful than most; children used to have years of freedom before they had to start working their hormones into the kind of lascivious lather that is now expected of ten-year-olds. Anyhow, in the 1940s gender was not a subject of discussion. Men were men (running things or in uniform, mostly), women were women (housekeeping or in factories, mostly), and that was that. Except for a few subversives like Virginia Woolf nobody publicly questioned the institutions and assumptions of male primacy. It was the century's low point architecturally in the Construction of Gender, reduced in those years to something about as spacious and comfortable as a broom closet.

But the Diaries date from the turn of the nineteenth century, a time of revolutionary inquiry into gender roles, the first age of feminism, the period of the woman suffrage movement and of the "New Woman" – who was precisely the robust and joyously competent Eve that Mark Twain gives us.

I see now in the Diaries, along with a tenderness and a profound delicacy of feeling about women, a certain advocacy. Mark Twain is always on the side of the underdog; and though he believed it was and must be a man's world, he knew that women were the underdogs in it. This fine sense of justice is what gives both the Diaries their moral complexity.

There was an element of discomfort in them for me as a child, and I think it lies just here, in that complexity and a certain degree of self-contradiction.

It is not Adam's superiority of brains or brawn that gives him his absolute advantage over Eve, but his blockish stupidity. He does not notice, does not listen, is uninterested, indifferent, dumb. He will not relate to her; she must relate herself – in words and actions – to him, and relate him to the rest of Eden. He is entirely satisfied with himself as he is; she must adapt her ways to him. He is immovably fixed at the center of his own attention. To live with him she must agree to be peripheral to him, contingent, secondary.

The degree of social and psychological truth in this picture of life in Eden is pretty considerable. Milton thought it was a fine arrangement; it appears Mark Twain didn't, since he shows us at the end of both Diaries that although Eve has not changed much, she has changed Adam profoundly. She always was awake. He slowly, finally wakes up, and does her, and therefore himself, justice. But isn't it too late, for her?

All this I think I followed pretty well, and was fascinated and somewhat troubled by, though I could not have discussed it, when I read the Diaries as a child. Children have a seemingly innate passion for justice; they don't have to be taught it. They have to have it beaten out of them, in fact, to end up as properly prejudiced adults.

Mark Twain and I both grew up in a society that cherished a visionary ideal of gender by pairs: the breadwinning, self-reliant husband and the home-dwelling, dependent wife. He the oak, she the ivy; power his, grace hers. He works and earns; she "doesn't work," but keeps his house, bears and brings up his children, and furnishes him the aesthetic and often the spiritual comforts of life. Now at this latter end of the century, the religio-political conservative's vision of what men and women do and should do is still close to that picture, though even more remote from most people's experience than it was fifty or a hundred years ago. Do Twain's Adam and Eve essentially fit this powerful stereotype, or do they vary it significantly?

I think the variations are significant, even if the text fudges them in the end. Mark Twain is not supporting a gender ideal, but investigating what he sees as real differences between women and men, some of them fitting into that ideal, some in conflict with it.

Eve is the intellectual in Eden, Adam the redneck. She is wildly curious and wants to learn everything, to name everything. Adam has no curiosity about anything, certain that he knows all he needs to know. She wants to talk, he wants to grunt. She is sociable, he is solitary. She prides herself on being scientific, though she settles for her own pet theory without testing it; her method is purely intuitive and rational, without a shadow of empiricism. He thinks she ought to test her ideas, but is too lazy to do it himself. He goes over Niagara Falls in a barrel, he doesn't say why; apparently because a man does such things. Far more imaginative and influenced by the imagination than he, she does dangerous things only when she doesn't know they're dangerous. She rides tigers and talks to the serpent. She is rebellious, adventurous, and independent; he does not question authority. She is the innocent troublemaker. Her loving anarchism ruins his mindless, self-sufficient, authoritarian Eden – and saves him from it.

Does it save her?

This spirited, intelligent, anarchic Eve reminds me of H. G. Wells's Ann Veronica, an exemplary New Woman of 1909. Yet Ann Veronica's courage and curiosity finally lead her not to independence but to wifehood, seen as the proper and sufficient fulfillment of feminine being. We are ominously close to the Natasha Syndrome, the collapse of a vivid woman character into a brood sow as soon as she marries and has children. Once she has won Adam over, once the children come, does Eve stop asking and thinking and singing and naming and venturing? We don't know. Tolstoy gives us a horrible glimpse of Natasha married; Wells tries to convince us Ann Veronica is going to be just fine; but Mark Twain tells us nothing about what Eve becomes. She falls silent. Not a good sign. After the Fall we have only Adam's voice, puzzling mightily over what kind of animal Cain is. Eve tells us only that she would love Adam even if he beat her – a very bad sign. And, forty years later, she says, "He is strong, I am weak, I am not so necessary to him as he is to me – life without him would not be life; how could I endure it?"

I don't know whether I am supposed to believe her, or can believe her. It doesn't sound like the woman I knew. Eve, weak? Rubbish! Adam's usefulness as a helpmeet is problematical, a man who, when she tells him they'll have to work for their living, decides "She will be useful. I will superintend" – a man who thinks his son is a kangaroo. Eve did need him in order to have children, and since she loves him she would miss him; but where is the evidence that she couldn't survive without him? He would presumably have survived without her, in the brutish way he survived before her. But surely it is their *interdependence* that is the real point?

I want, now, to read the Diaries as a subtle, sweet-natured send-up of the Strong Man-Weak Woman arrangement; but I'm not sure it's possible to do so, or not entirely. It may be both a send-up and a capitulation.

And Adam has the last word. "Wheresoever she was, *there* was Eden." But the poignancy of those words is utterly unexpected, a cry from the heart. It made me shiver as a child; it does now.

I was raised as irreligious as a jackrabbit, and probably this is one reason

Mark Twain made so much sense to me as a child. Descriptions of church-going interested me as the exotic rites of a foreign tribe, and nobody described churchgoing better than Mark Twain did. But God, as I encountered him in my reading, seemed only to cause unnecessary complications, making people fall into strange postures and do depressing things; he treated Beth March abominably, and did his best to ruin Jane Eyre's life before she traded him in for Rochester. I didn't read any of the books in which God is the main character until a few years later. I was perfectly content with books in which he didn't figure at all.

Could anybody but Mark Twain have told the story of Adam and Eve without mentioning Jehovah?

As a heathen child I was entirely comfortable with his version. I took it for granted that it was the sensible one.

As an ancient heathen I still find it sensible, but can better appreciate its originality and courage. The nerve of the man, the marvelous, stunning independence of that mind! In pious, prayerful, censorious, self-righteous Christian America of 1896, or 1996 for that matter, to show God as an unnecessary hypothesis, by letting Eve and Adam cast themselves out of Eden without any help at all from him, and really none from the serpent either – to put sin and salvation, love and death in our own hands, as our own, strictly human business, our responsibility – now that's a free soul, and a brave one.

What luck for a child to meet such a soul when she is young. What luck for a country to have a Mark Twain in its heart.

All Happy Families

1997

At one of those times when I wanted to be writing a story but didn't have one to write, I got to thinking again about the opening words of Anna Karenina, *which are so often quoted as if they were true, and decided the time had come to write down my thoughts, since I had nothing better to do. They were published, after a while, in the* Michigan Quarterly Review.

I used to be too respectful to disagree with Tolstoy, but after I got into my sixties my faculty of respect atrophied. Besides, at some point in the last forty years I began to question Tolstoy's respect for his wife. Anybody can make a mistake in marriage, of course. But I have an impression that no matter whom he married Tolstoy would have respected her only in certain respects, though he expected her to respect him in all respects. In this respect, I disapprove of Tolstoy; which makes it easier to disagree with him in the first place, and in the second place, to say so.

There has been a long gap between the first and second places – years. But there was a period of as many years even before the first place, before I achieved the point of disagreement, the ability to disapprove. During all those years, from when I was fourteen or so and first read him, till I was in my forties, I was, as it were, married to Tolstoy, his loyal wife. Though fortunately not expected to copy his manuscripts six times over by hand, I read and reread his books with joy and zeal. I respected him without ever asking if or wondering whether he, as it were, respected me. When E. M. Forster, in an essay on Tolstoy, told me that he didn't, I replied, He has that right!

And if E. M. Forster had asked, What gives him that right? I would have answered simply, genius.

But E. M. Forster didn't ask; which is just as well, since he probably would have asked what I meant by genius.

I think what I meant by genius was that I thought Tolstoy actually knew what he was talking about – unlike the rest of us.

However, at some point, around forty or so, I began to wonder if he really knew what he was talking about any better than anybody else, or if what he knew better than anybody else was *how* to talk about it. The two things are easily confused.

So then, quietly, in my private mind, surrounded by the soft, supportive mutterings of feminists, I began to ask rude questions of Tolstoy. In public I remained a loyal and loving wife, entirely respectful of his opinions as well as his art. But the unspoken questions were there, the silent disagreement. And the unspoken, as we know, tends to strengthen, to mature and grow richer over the years, like an undrunk wine. Of course it may just go to Freudian vinegar. Some thoughts and feelings go to vinegar very quickly, and must be poured out at once. Some go on fermenting in the bottle, and burst out in an explosion of murderous glass shards. But a good, robust, well-corked feeling only gets deeper and more complicated, down in the cellar. The thing is knowing when to uncork it.

It's ready. I'm ready. The great first sentence of the first chapter of the great book – not the greatest book, but perhaps the second greatest – is, yes, we can say it in unison: "All happy families are alike; unhappy families are each unhappy in their own way." Translations vary, but not significantly.

People quote that sentence so often that it must satisfy them; but it does not, it never quite did, satisfy me. And twenty years ago or so, I began admitting my dissatisfaction to myself. These happy families he speaks of so confidently in order to dismiss them as all alike – where are they? Were they very much commoner in the nineteenth century? Did he know numerous happy families among the Russian nobility, or middle class, or peasantry, all of them alike? This seems so unlikely that I wondered if perhaps he knew a few happy families, which is not impossible; but that those few were all alike seems deeply, very deeply implausible. Was his own family happy, either the one he grew up in or the one he fathered? Did he know one family, one single family, that could, over a substantial period of time, as a whole and in each of its component members, honestly be called happy? If he did he knew one more than most of us do.

I'm not just showing off my sexagenarian cynicism, proud though I may be of it. I admit that a family can be happy, in the sense that almost all the members of it are in good health, good spirits, and good temper with one another, for quite a long time – a week, a month, even longer. And if we go into the comparative mode, then certainly some families are far happier than others, on the whole and for years on end – because there are so many extremely unhappy families. Many people I have talked with about such matters were in one way or another unhappy as children; and perhaps most people, though they stay deeply attached to their relatives and recall joyous times with them, would not describe their family as happy. "We had some real good times," they say.

I grew up in a family that on the whole seems to have been happier than most families; and yet I find it false – an intolerable cheapening of reality – simply to describe it as happy. The enormous cost and complexity of that "happiness," its dependence upon a whole substructure of sacrifices, repressions, suppressions, choices made or forgone, chances taken or lost, balancings of greater and lesser evils – the tears, the fears, the migraines, the injustices, the censorships, the quarrels, the lies, the angers, the cruelties it involved – is all that to be swept away, brushed under the carpet by the brisk broom of a silly phrase, "a happy family"?

And why? In order to imply that happiness is easy, shallow, ordinary; a common thing not worth writing a novel about? Whereas unhappiness is complex, deep, difficult to attain, unusual; unique indeed; and so a worthy subject for a great, a unique novelist?

Surely that is a silly idea. But silly or not, it has been imposingly in-fluential among novelists and critics for decades. Many a novelist would wither in shame if the reviewers caught him writing about happy people, families like other families, people like other people; and indeed many critics are keenly on the watch for happiness in novels in order to dismiss it as banal, sentimental, or (in other words) for women.

How the whole thing got gendered, I don't know, but it did. The gendering supposes that male readers have strong, tough, reality-craving natures, while feeble female readers crave constant reassurance in the form of little warm blobs of happiness – fuzzy bunnies.

This is true of some women. Some women have never experienced any glimpse of happiness in their whole life better than a stuffed fuzzy bunny and so they surround themselves with stuffed fuzzy bunnies, fictional or actual. In this they may be luckier than most men, who aren't allowed stuffed fuzzy bunnies, only girls in bunny suits. In any case, who can blame them, the men or the women? Not me. Anybody who has been privileged to know real, solid, nonfuzzy happiness, and then lets some novelist or critic buffalo them into believing that they shouldn't read about it because

257

it's commoner than unhappiness, inferior to unhappiness, less interesting than unhappiness, – where does my syntax lead me? Into judgmentalism. I shall extricate myself in silence.

The falseness of Tolstoy's famous sentence is nowhere shown more clearly than in Tolstoy's novels, including the one it's the first sentence of. Dolly's family, which is the unhappy one we are promised, is in my opinion a moderately, that is to say a realistically happy one. Dolly and her children are kind and contented, often merry together, and the husband and wife definitely have their moments, for all his stupid skirt-chasing. In the greater novel, the Rostovs when we meet them might well be described as a happy family – rich, healthy, generous, kind, full of passions and counterpassions, full of vitality, energy, and love. But the Rostovs are not "like" anybody; they are idiosyncratic, unpredictable, incomparable. And, like most human beings, they can't hang on to their happiness. The old Count wastes his children's heritage and the Countess worries herself sick; Moscow burns; Natasha falls in love with a cold fish, nearly runs away with a cretin, marries and turns into a mindless brood sow; Petya is killed pointlessly in the war at sixteen. Jolly good fun! Fuzzy bunnies everywhere!

Tolstoy knew what happiness is – how rare, how imperiled, how hard-won. Not only that, he had the ability to describe happiness, a rare gift, which gives his novels much of their extraordinary beauty. Why he denied his knowledge in the famous sentence, I don't know. He did a good deal of lying and denying, perhaps more than many lesser novelists do. He had more to lie about; and his cruel theoretical Christianity led him into all kinds of denials of what in his fiction he saw and showed to be true. So maybe he was just showing off. It sounded good. It made a great first sentence.

My next essay will be about whether or not I want to be told to call a stranger Ishmael.

The Operating Instructions

●

2000

I wrote this piece in 2000 as a talk to a group of people interested in local literacy and literature.

A poet has been appointed ambassador. A playwright is elected president. Construction workers stand in line with officer managers to buy a new novel. Adults seek moral guidance and intellectual challenge in stories about warrior monkeys, one-eyed giants, and crazy knights who fight windmills. Literacy is considered a beginning, not an end.

. . . Well, maybe in some other country, but not this one. In America the imagination is generally looked on as something that might be useful when the TV is out of order. Poetry and plays have no relation to practical politics. Novels are for students, housewives, and other people who don't work. Fantasy is for children and primitive peoples. Literacy is so you can read the operating instructions.

I think the imagination is the single most useful tool humankind possesses. It beats the opposable thumb. I can imagine living without my thumbs, but not without my imagination.

I hear voices agreeing with me. "Yes, yes!" they cry – "the creative imagination is a tremendous plus in business! We value creativity, we *reward* it!" In the marketplace, the word *creativity* has come to mean the generation of ideas applicable to practical strategies to make larger profits. This reduction has gone on so long that the word *creative* can hardly be degraded further. I don't use it any more, yielding it to capitalists and academics to abuse as they like. But they can't have *imagination*.

Imagination is not a means of making money. It has no place in the vocabulary of profit making It is not a weapon, though all weapons originate from it, and the use, or nonuse, of all weapons depends on it: as do all tools and their uses. The imagination is a fundamental way of thinking, an essential means of becoming and remaining human. It is a tool of the mind.

Therefore we have to learn to use it. Children have imagination to start with, as they have body, intellect, the capacity for language: all things essential to their humanity, things they need to learn how to use, how to use well. Such teaching, training, and practice should begin in infancy and go on throughout life. Young human beings need exercises in imagination as they need exercise in all the basic skills of life, bodily and mental: for growth, for health, for competence, for joy. This need continues as long as the mind is alive.

When children are taught to hear and learn the central literature of their people, or, in literate cultures, to read and understand it, their imagination is getting a very large part of the exercise it needs.

Nothing else does as well, not even the other arts. We are a wordy species. Words are the wings both intellect and imagination fly on. Music, dance, visual arts, crafts of all kinds, all are central to human development and well-being, and no art or skill is ever useless learning; but to train the mind to take off from immediate reality and return to it with new understanding and new strength, there is nothing like poem and story.

Through story, every culture defines itself and teaches its children how to be people and members of their people – Hmong, !Kung, Hopi, Quechua, French, Californian . . . We are those who arrived at the Fourth World . . . We are Joan's nation . . . We are the sons of the Sun . . . We came from the sea . . . We are the people who live at the center of the world.

A people that doesn't live at the center of the world, as defined and described by its poets and storytellers, is in a bad way. The center of the world is where you live. You can breathe the air there. You know how things are done there, how things are done rightly, done well.

A child who doesn't know where the center is – where home is, *what* home is – that child is in a very bad way.

Home isn't Mom and Dad and Sis and Bud. Home isn't where they have to let you in. It's not a place at all. Home is imaginary.

Home, imagined, comes to be. It is real, realer than any other place, but you can't get to it unless your people show you how to imagine it – whoever your people are. They may not be your relatives. They may never have spoken your language. They may have been dead for a thousand years. They may be nothing but words printed on paper, ghosts of voices, shadows of minds. But they can guide you home. They are your human community.

All of us have to learn how to invent our lives, make them up, imagine them. We need to be taught these skills; we need guides to show us how. If we don't, our lives get made up for us by other people.

Human beings have always joined in groups to imagine how best to live and help one another carry out the plan. The essential function of human community is to arrive at some agreement on what we need, what life ought to be, what we want our children to learn, and then collaborate in learning and teaching so that we and they can go on the way we think is the right way.

Small communities with strong traditions are usually clear about the way they want to go, and good at teaching it. But tradition may crystallize imagination to the point of fossilizing it as dogma and forbidding new ideas. Larger communities, such as cities, open up room for people to imagine alternatives, learn from people of different traditions, and invent their own ways to live.

As alternatives proliferate, however, those who take the responsibility of teaching find little social and moral consensus on what they should be teaching – what we need, what life ought to be. In our time of huge populations exposed continuously to reproduced voices, images, and words used for commercial and political profit, there are too many people who want to and can invent us, own us, shape and control us through seductive and powerful media. It's a lot to ask of a child to find a way through all that, alone.

Nobody can do anything very much, really, alone.

What a child needs, what we all need, is to find some other people who have imagined life along lines that make sense and allow some freedom, and listen to them. Not hear passively, but listen.

Listening is an act of community, which takes space, time, and silence.

Reading is a means of listening.

Reading is not as passive as hearing or viewing. It's an act: you do it. You read at your pace, your own speed, not the ceaseless, incoherent, gabbling, shouting rush of the media. You take in what you can and want to take in, not what they shove at you so fast and hard and loud that you're overwhelmed. Reading a story, you may be told something, but you're not being sold anything. And though you're usually alone when you read, you are in communion with another mind. You aren't being brainwashed or co-opted or used; you've joined in an act of the imagination.

I know no reason why the media could not create a similar community of the imagination, as theater has often done in societies of the past, but they're not doing it. They are so controlled by advertising and profiteering that the best people who work in them, the real artists, if they resist the pressure to sell out, get drowned out by the endless rush for novelty, by the greed of the entrepreneurs.

Much of literature remains free of such co-optation simply because a lot of books were written by dead people, who by definition are not greedy.

And many living poets and novelists, though their publishers may be crawling abjectly after bestsellers, continue to be motivated less by the desire for gain than by the wish to do what they'd probably do for nothing if they could afford it, that is, practice their art – make something well, get something right. Books remain comparatively, and amazingly, honest and reliable.

They may not be "books," of course, they may not be ink on wood pulp but a flicker of electronics in the palm of a hand. Incoherent and commercialized and worm-eaten with porn and hype and blather as it is, electronic publication offers those who read a strong new means of active community. The technology is not what matters. Words are what matter. The sharing of words. The activation of imagination through the reading of words.

The reason literacy is important is that literature *is* the operating instructions. The best manual we have. The most useful guide to the country we're visiting, life.

The Question I Get Asked Most Often

2000/2003

This was a talk, first given for Portland Arts and Lectures in October 2000, then for Seattle Arts and Lectures in April 2002. I have revised it slightly for publication. It has not been published before, though bits of it can be found in my book Steering the Craft *and elsewhere in my writings about writing. As a talk, it was called "Where Do You Get Your Ideas From?" – but in my previous collection of talks and essays,* The Language of the Night, *there's a different essay with that title (there being many answers to the question). So I have retitled it.*

The question fiction writers get asked most often is: Where do you get your ideas from? Harlan Ellison has been saying for years that he gets ideas for his stories from a mail-order house in Schenectady.

When people ask "Where do you get your ideas from?" what some of them really want to know is the e-mail address of that company in Schenectady.

That is: they want to be writers, because they know writers are rich and famous; and they know that there are secrets that writers know; and they know if they can just learn those secrets, that mystical address in Schenectady, they will be Stephen King.

Writers, as I know them, are poor, they are infamous, and they couldn't keep a secret if they had one. Writers are wordy people. They talk, they blab, they yadder. They whine all the time to each other about what they're writing and how hard it is, they teach writing workshops and write writing books and give talks about writing, like this. Writers tell all. If they could tell beginners where to get ideas from, they would. In fact they do, all the time. Some of them actually get somewhat rich and famous by doing it.

What do the how-to-write writers say about getting ideas? They say stuff like: Listen to conversations, note down interesting things you hear or read about, keep a journal, describe a character, imagine a dresser drawer and describe what's in it – Yeah, yeah, but that's all *work*. Anybody can do *work*. I wanna be a writer. What's the address in Schenectady?

Well, the secret to writing is writing. It's only a secret to people who don't want to hear it. Writing is how you be a writer.

So why did I want to try to answer this foolish question, Where do you get your ideas from? Because underneath the foolishness is a real question, which people really yearn to have answered – a big question.

Art is craft: all art is always and essentially a work of craft: but in the true work of art, before the craft and after it, is some essential, durable core of being, which is what the craft works on, and shows, and sets free. The statue in the stone. How does the artist find that, see it, before it's visible? That is a real question.

One of my favorite answers is this: Somebody asked Willie Nelson how he thought of his tunes, and he said, "The air is full of tunes, I just reach up and pick one."

Now that is not a secret. But it is a sweet mystery.

And a true one. A true mystery. That's what it is. For a fiction writer, a storyteller, the world is full of stories, and when a story is there, it's there, and you just reach up and pick it.

Then you have to be able to let it tell itself.

First you have to be able to wait. To wait in silence. Wait in silence, and listen. Listen for the tune, the vision, the story. Not grabbing, not pushing, just waiting, listening, being ready for it when it comes. This is an act of trust. Trust in yourself, trust in the world. The artist says, the world will give me what I need and I will be able to use it rightly.

Readiness – not grabbiness, not greed – readiness: willingness to hear, to listen, listen carefully, to see clearly, see accurately – to let the words be right. Not almost right. Right. To know how to make something out of the vision, that's the craft: that's what practice is for. Because being ready doesn't mean just sitting around, even if it looks like that's what writers mostly do. Artists practice their art continually, and writing is an art that involves a lot of sitting. Scales and finger exercises, pencil sketches, endless unfinished and rejected stories ... The artist who practices knows the difference between practice and performance, and the essential connection between them. The gift of those seemingly wasted hours and years is patience and readiness, a good ear, a keen eye, and a skilled hand, a rich vocabulary and grammar. The Lord knows where talent comes from, but craft comes from practice.

With those tools, those instruments, with that hard-earned mastery, that craftiness, artists do their best to let the "idea" – the tune, the vision, the story – come through clear and undistorted. Clear of ineptitude, awkwardness, amateurishness. Undistorted by convention, fashion, opinion.

This is a very radical job, this dealing with the ideas you get if you are an artist and take your job seriously, this shaping a vision into the medium of words. It's what I like best to do in the world, and craft is what I like to talk about when I talk about writing, and I could happily go on and on about it. But I'm trying to talk about where the vision, the stuff you work on, the "idea" comes from. So:

The air is full of tunes.

A piece of rock is full of statues.

The earth is full of visions.

The world is full of stories.

As an artist, you trust that. You trust that that is so. You know it is so. You know that whatever your experience, it will give you the material, the "ideas" for your work. (From here on I'll leave out music and fine arts and stick to storytelling, which is the only thing I truly know anything about, though I do think all the arts are one at the root.)

All right, these "ideas" – what does that word mean? "Idea" is a short-hand way of saying: the material, the subject, subjects, the matter of a story. What the story is about. What the story *is*.

Idea is a strange word for an imagined matter, not abstract but intensely concrete, not intellectual but embodied. However, *idea* is the word we're stuck with. And it's not wholly off center, because the imagination is a rational faculty.

"I got the idea for that story from a dream I had . . ." "I haven't had a good story idea all year . . ." "Here am I sitting after half the morning, crammed with ideas, and visions, and so on, and can't dislodge them, for lack of the right rhythm . . ."

That last sentence was written in 1926 by Virginia Woolf, in a letter to a writer friend; and I will come back in the end to it, because what she says about rhythm goes deeper than anything I have ever thought or read about where art comes from. But before I can talk about rhythm I have to talk about experience and imagination.

Where do writers get their ideas from? From experience. That's obvious.

And from imagination. That's less obvious.

Fiction results from imagination working on experience. We shape experience in our minds so that it makes sense. We force the world to be coherent – to tell us a story.

Not only fiction writers do this; we all do it; we do it constantly, continually, in order to survive. People who can't make the world into a story go mad. Or, like infants or (perhaps) animals, they live in a world that has no history, no time but now.

The minds of animals are a great, sacred, present mystery. I do think animals have languages, but they are entirely truthful languages. It seems that we are the only animals who can *lie*. We can think and say what is not so and never was so, or what has never been, yet might be. We can invent; we can suppose; we can imagine. All that gets mixed in with memory. And so we're the only animals who tell stories.

An ape can remember and extrapolate from her experience: once I stuck a stick in that ant hill and the ants crawled on it, so if I put this stick in that ant hill again, maybe the ants will crawl on it again, and I can lick them off again, yum. But only we human beings can imagine – can tell the story about the ape who stuck a stick in an anthill and it came out covered with gold dust and a prospector saw it and that was the beginning of the great gold rush of 1877 in Rhodesia.

That story is not true. It is fiction. Its only relation to reality is the fact that some apes do stick sticks in anthills and there was a place once called Rhodesia. But there was no gold rush in 1877 in Rhodesia. I made it up. I am human, therefore I lie. All human beings are liars; that is true; you must believe me.

Fiction: imagination working on experience. A great deal of what we consider our experience, our memory, our hard-earned knowledge, our history, is in fact fiction. But never mind that. I'm talking about real fiction – stories, novels. They all come from the writer's experience of reality worked upon, changed, filtered, distorted, clarified, transfigured, by imagination.

"Ideas" come from the world through the head.

The interesting part of this process to me is the passage through the head, the action of the imagination on the raw material. But that's the part of the process that a great many people disapprove of.

I wrote a piece years ago called "Why Are Americans Afraid of

Dragons?" In it I talked about how so many Americans distrust and despise not only the obviously imaginative kind of fiction we call fantasy, but all fiction, often rationalizing their fear and contempt with financial or religious arguments: reading novels is a waste of valuable time, the only true book is the Bible, and so on. I said that many Americans have been taught "to repress their imagination, to reject it as something childish or effeminate, unprofitable, and probably sinful. They have learned to fear [the imagination]. But they have never learned to discipline it at all."

I wrote that in 1974. The millennium has come and gone and we still fear dragons.

If you fear something you may try to diminish it. You infantilize it. Fantasy is for children – kiddylit – can't take it seriously. But fantasy also has shown that it can make money. Gotta take *that* seriously. So when the first Harry Potter book, which combined two very familiar conventions, the British school story and the orphan-child-of-great-gifts, hit the big time, many reviewers praised it lavishly for its originality. By which they showed their absolute ignorance of both traditions the book follows – the small one of the school story, and the great one, a tradition that descends from the *Mahabharata* and the *Ramayana*, the *Thousand and One Nights* and *Beowulf* and the Tale of Monkey and medieval romance and Renaissance epic, through Lewis Carroll and Kipling to Tolkien, to Borges and Calvino and Rushdie and the rest of us: a tradition, a form of literature which really cannot be dismissed as "entertainment," "great fun for the kiddies," or "well at least they're reading *something*."

Critics and academics have been trying for forty years to bury the greatest work of imaginative fiction in English. They ignore it, they condescend to it, they stand in large groups with their backs to it – because they're afraid of it. They're afraid of dragons. They have Smaugophobia. "Oh those awful Orcs," they bleat, flocking after Edmund Wilson. They know if they acknowledge Tolkien they'll have to admit that fantasy can be literature, and that therefore they'll have to redefine what literature is. And they're too damned lazy to do it.

What the majority of our critics and teachers call "literature" is still modernist realism. All other forms of fiction – westerns mysteries science fiction fantasy romance historical regional you name it – is dismissed as "genre." Sent to the ghetto. That the ghetto is about twelve times larger than the city, and currently a great deal livelier, so what? Magic realism, though – that bothers them; they hear Gabriel Garcia Marquez gnawing quietly at the foundations of the ivory tower, they hear all these crazy Indians (American ones and Indian ones) dancing up in the attic of the *New York Times Book Review*. They think maybe if they just call it all post-modernism it will go away.

To think that realistic fiction is by definition superior to imaginative fiction is to think imitation is superior to invention. In mean moments I have wondered if this unstated but widely accepted, highly puritanical proposition is related to the recent popularity of the memoir and the personal essay.

But that has been a genuine popularity, a real preference, not a matter of academic canonizing: people really do want to read memoir and personal essay, and writers want to write it. I've felt rather out of step. I like history and biography, sure, but when family and personal memoir seems to be the dominant narrative form – well, I have searched my soul for prejudice, and found it. I prefer invention to imitation. I love novels. I love made-up stuff.

Our high valuation of story drawn directly from personal experience may be a logical extension of our high value for realism in fiction. If faithful imitation of actual experience is fiction's greatest virtue, then memoir is more virtuous than fiction can ever be. The memoir writer's imagination, subordinated to the hard facts, serves to connect the facts aesthetically and to draw from them a moral or intellectual lesson, but is understood to be forbidden to invent. Emotion will certainly be roused, but imagination may scarcely be called upon. Recognition, rather than discovery, is the reward.

True recognition is a true reward. The personal essay is a noble and difficult discipline. I'm not knocking it. I admire it with considerable awe. But I'm not at home in it.

I keep looking for dragons in this country, and not finding any. Or only finding them in disguise.

Some of the most praised recent memoirs have been about growing up in poverty. Hopeless poverty, cruel fathers, incompetent mothers, abused children, misery, fear, loneliness . . . But is this the property of nonfiction? Poverty, cruelty, incompetence, dysfunctional families, injustice, degrada-tion – that is the very stuff of the fireside tale, the folktale, stories of ghosts and vengeance beyond the grave – and of *Jane Eyre*, and *Wuthering Heights*, and *Huckleberry Finn*, and *Cien Años de Soledad* . . . The ground of our experience is dark, and all our inventions start in that darkness. From it, some of them leap forth in fire.

The imagination can transfigure the dark matter of life. And in many personal essays and autobiographies, that's what I begin to miss, to crave: transfiguration. To recognize our shared, familiar misery is not enough. I want to *recognize something I never saw before*. I want the vision to leap out at me, terrible and blazing – the fire of the transfiguring imagination. I want the true dragons.

Experience is where the ideas come from. But a story isn't a mirror of what happened. Fiction is experience translated by, transformed by, trans-figured by the imagination. Truth includes but is not coextensive with fact. Truth in art is not imitation, but reincarnation.

In a factual history or memoir, the raw material of experience, to be valuable, has to be selected, arranged, and shaped. In a novel, the process is even more radical: the raw materials are not only selected and shaped but fused, composted, recombined, reworked, reconfigured, reborn, and at the same time allowed to find their own forms and shapes, which may be only indirectly related to rational thinking. The whole thing may end up looking like pure invention. A girl chained to a rock as a sacrifice to a monster. A mad captain and a white whale. A ring that confers absolute power. A dragon.

But there's no such thing as pure invention. It all starts with experience. Invention is recombination. We can work only with what we have. There are monsters and leviathans and chimeras in the human mind; they are psychic facts. Dragons are one of the truths about us. We have no other way of expressing that particular truth about us. People who deny the existence of dragons are often eaten by dragons. From within.

Another way we have recently taken of showing our deep distrust of the imagination, our puritanical lust to control it and limit it, is in the way we tell stories electronically, on TV and in media such as electronic games and CD-ROMs.

Reading is active. To read a story is to participate actively in the story. To read is to tell the story, tell it to yourself, reliving it, rewriting it with the author, word by word, sentence by sentence, chapter by chapter . . . If you want proof, just watch an eight-year-old reading a story she likes. She is concentratedly, tensely, fiercely alive. She is as intense as a hunting cat. She is a tiger eating.

Reading is a most mysterious act. It absolutely has not been replaced and will not be replaced by any kind of viewing. Viewing is an entirely different undertaking, with different rewards.

A reader reading *makes* the book, brings it into meaning, by translating arbitrary symbols, printed letters, into an inward, private reality. Reading is an act, a creative one. Viewing is relatively passive. A viewer watching a film does not make the film. To watch a film is to be taken into it – to participate in it – be made part of it. Absorbed by it. Readers eat books. Film eats viewers.

This can be wonderful. It's wonderful to be eaten by a good movie, to let your eyes and ears take your mind into a reality you could never otherwise know. However, passivity means vulnerability; and that's what a great deal of media storytelling exploits.

Reading is an active transaction between the text and the reader. The text is under the control of the reader – she can skip, linger, interpret, misinterpret, return, ponder, go along with the story or refuse to go along with it, make judgments, revise her judgments; she has time and room to genuinely interact. A novel is an active, ongoing collaboration between the writer and the reader.

Viewing is a different transaction. It isn't collaborative. The viewer consents to participate and hands over control to the filmmaker or pro- grammer. Psychically there is no time or room outside an audiovisual narrative for anything but the program. For the viewer, the screen or mon- itor temporarily becomes the universe. There's very little leeway, and no way to control the constant stream of information and imagery – unless one refuses to accept it, detaches oneself emotionally and intellectually, in which case it appears essentially meaningless. Or one can turn the program off.

Although there's a lot of talk about transactional viewing and *interactive* is a favorite word of programmers, the electronic media are a paradise of control for programmers and a paradise of passivity for viewers. There is nothing in so-called interactive programs except what the programmer put in them; the so-called choices lead only to subprograms chosen by the programmer, no more a choice than a footnote is – do you read it or don't you? The roles in role-playing games are fixed and conventional; there are no characters in games, only personae. (That's why teenagers love them; teenagers need personae. But they have to shed those perso- nae eventually, if they're going to become persons.) Hypertext offers the storyteller a wonderful complexity, but so far hypertext fiction seems to be like Borges's garden of forking paths that lead only to other forking paths, fascinating, like fractals, and ultimately nightmarish. Interactivity in the sense of the viewer controlling the text is also nightmarish, when interpreted to mean that the viewer can rewrite the novel. If you don't like the end of *Moby Dick* you can change it. You can make it happy. Ahab kills the whale. Ooowee.

Readers can't kill the whale. They can only reread until they understand why Ahab collaborated with the whale to kill himself. Readers don't control the text: they genuinely interact with it. Viewers are either controlled by the program or try to control it. Different ball games. Different universes.

When I was working on this talk, a 3-D animated version of *The Little Prince* came out on CD-ROM. The blurb said it "offers more than just the story of the Little Prince. You can, for example, catch an orbiting planet in the Little Prince's universe and learn all about the planet's secrets and its inhabitants."

In the book the prince visits several planets, with extremely interesting inhabitants, and his own tiny planet has an immense secret – a rose – the rose he loves. Do these CD guys think Saint-Exupéry was stingy with his planets? Or are they convinced that stuffing irrelevant information into a work of art enriches it?

Ah, but there is more: you can "enter the Fox Training Game and after you've 'tamed' the fox that the Little Prince meets, he will give you a gift."

Do you remember the fox, in *The Little Prince*? He insists that the little prince tame him. Why? the prince asks, and the fox says that if he is tamed he will always love the wheat fields, because they're the color of the little prince's hair. The little prince asks how to tame him, and the fox says he has to do it by being very patient, sitting down "at a little distance from me in the grass. I shall look at you out of the corner of my eye, and you will say nothing. Words are the source of misunderstanding. But you will sit a little closer to me every day . . ." And it should be at the same time every day, so that the fox will "know at what hour my heart is to be ready to greet you. One must observe the proper rites."

And so the fox is tamed, and when the little prince is about to leave, "Ah," said the fox, "I shall cry." So the little prince laments, "Being tamed didn't do you any good," but the fox says, "It has done me good, because of the color of the wheat fields." And when they part, the fox says, "I will make you a present of a secret . . . It is the time you wasted for your rose that makes your rose important . . . You become responsible, forever, for what you have tamed."

So, then, the child viewing the CD-ROM tames the fox, that is, presses buttons until the food pellet drops into the food dish – no, sorry, that's rats – the child selects the "right" choices from the program till informed that the fox is tamed. Somehow this seems different from imagining doing what the book says: coming back every day at the same time and sitting silently while a fox looks at you from the corner of its eye. Something essential has been short-circuited. Has been falsified. What do you think the fox's "gift" is, in the CD-ROM? I don't know, but if it was a twenty-four-carat gold ring with an emerald, it wouldn't top the fox's gift in the book, which is nine words – "You become responsible, forever, for what you have tamed."

The gift *The Little Prince* gives its readers is itself. It offers them absolutely nothing but a charming story with a few charming pictures, and the chance to face fear, grief, tenderness, and loss.

Which is why that story, written in the middle of a war by a man about to die in that war, is honored by children, adults, and even literary critics. Maybe the CD-ROM isn't as ghastly as it sounds; but it's hard not to see it as an effort to exploit, to tame something that, like a real fox, must be left wild: the imagination of an artist.

Antoine de Saint-Exupéry did crash-land in the desert once, in the 1930s, and nearly died. That is a fact. He did not meet a little prince from another planet there. He met terror, thirst, despair, and salvation. He wrote a splendid factual account of that experience in *Wind, Sand, and Stars*. But later, it got composted, transmuted, transfigured, into a fantastic story of a little prince. Imagination working on experience. Invention springing, like a flower, a rose, out of the desert sands of reality.

Thinking about the sources of art, about where ideas come from, we often give experience too much credit. Earnest biographers often fail to realize that novelists make things up. They seek a direct source for everything in a writer's work, as if every character in a novel were based on a person the writer knew, every plot gambit had to mirror a specific actual event. Ignoring the incredible recombinatory faculty of the imagination, this fundamentalist attitude short-circuits the long, obscure process by which experience becomes story.

Aspiring writers keep telling me they'll start writing when they've gathered experience. Usually I keep my mouth shut, but sometimes I can't control myself and ask them, ah, like Jane Austen? Like the Brontë sisters? Those women with their wild, mad lives cram full of gut-wrenching adventure working as stevedores in the Congo and shooting up drugs in Rio and hunting lions on Kilimanjaro and having sex in SoHo and all that stuff that writers have to do – well, that some writers have to do?

Very young writers usually *are* handicapped by their relative poverty of experience. Even if their experiences are the stuff of which fiction can be made – and very often it's exactly the experiences of childhood and adolescence that feed the imagination all the rest of a writer's life – they don't have *context*, they don't yet have enough to compare it with. They haven't had time to learn that other people exist, people who have had similar experiences, and different experiences, and that they themselves will have different experiences ... a breadth of comparison, a fund of empathic knowledge, crucial to the novelist, who after all is making up a whole world.

So fiction writers are slow beginners. Few are worth much till they're thirty or so. Not because they lack life experience, but because their imagination hasn't had time to context it and compost it, to work on what they've done and felt, and realize its value is where it's common to the human condition. Autobiographical first novels, self-centered and self-pitying, often suffer from poverty of imagination.

But many fantasies, works of so-called imaginative fiction, suffer from the same thing: imaginative poverty. The writers haven't actually used their imagination, haven't made up anything – they've just moved archetypes around in a game of wish fulfillment. A saleable game.

In fantasy, since the fictionality of the fiction, the inventions, the dragons, are all right out in front, it's easy to assume that the story has no relation at all to experience, that everything in a fantasy can be just the way the writer wants it. No rules, all cards wild. All the ideas in fantasy are just wishful thinking – right? Well, no. Wrong.

It may be that the further a story gets away from common experience and accepted reality, the less wishful thinking it can do, the more firmly its essential ideas must be grounded in common experience and accepted reality.

Serious fantasy goes into regions of the psyche that may be very strange territory, dangerous ground, places where wise psychologists tread cautiously: and for that reason, serious fantasy is usually both conservative and realistic about human nature. Its mode is usually comic not tragic – that is, it has a more or less happy ending – but, just as the tragic hero brings his tragedy on himself, the happy outcome in fantasy is *earned* by the behavior of the protagonist. Serious fantasy invites the reader on a wild journey of invention, through wonders and marvels, through mortal risks and dangers – all the time hanging on to a common, everyday, realistic morality. Generosity, reliability, compassion, courage: in fantasy these moral qualities are seldom questioned. They are accepted, and they are tested – often to the limit, and beyond.

The people who write the stuff on the book covers obsessively describe fantasy as "a battle between good and evil." That phrase describes serious fantasy only in the sense of Solzhenitsyn's saying: "The line between good and evil runs straight through every human heart." In serious fantasy, the real battle is moral and internal. We have met the enemy, as Pogo said, and he is us. To do good, heroes must know or learn that the "axis of evil" is within them.

In commercial fantasy the so-called battle of good and evil is a mere power struggle. Look at how they act: the so-called good wizards and the so-called bad ones are equally violent and irresponsible. This is about as far from Tolkien as you can get.

But why should moral seriousness matter, why do probability and consistency matter, when it's "all just made up"?

Well, moral seriousness is what makes a fantasy matter, because it's what's real in the story. A made-up story is inevitably trivial if nothing real is at stake, if mere winning, coming out on top, replaces moral choice. Easy wish fulfillment has a great appeal to children, who are genuinely powerless; but if it's all a story has to offer, in the end it's not enough.

In the same way, the purer the invention, the more important is its credibility, consistency, coherence. The rules of the invented realm must be followed to the letter. All magicians, including writers, are extremely careful about their spells. Every word must be the right word. A sloppy wizard is a dead wizard. Serious fantasists delight in invention, in the freedom to invent, but they know that careless invention kills the magic. Fantasy shamelessly flouts fact, but it is as deeply concerned with truth as the grimmest, greyest realism.

A related point: The job of the imagination, in making a story from experience, may be not to gussy it up, but to tone it down. The world is unbelievably strange, and human behavior is frequently so weird that no kind of narrative except farce or satire can handle it. I am thinking of a true story I heard about a man who rationed his daughters' toilet paper. He had three daughters and it infuriated him that they used so much toilet paper, so he tore all the toilet paper rolls into the little component squares, and made three piles of six squares on the bathroom counter, and each daughter was to use one pile each day. You see what I mean? In a case like this, the function of the imagination is to judge whether anything so bizarre belongs in the story without turning it into farce or mere gross-out.

The whole matter of "leaving it to the imagination" – that is, including elements of the story only by allusion and implication – is enormously important. Even journalists can't report the full event, but can only tell bits of it; both the realist and the fantasist leave out a tremendous amount, *suggesting* through imagery or metaphors just enough that the reader can imagine the event.

And the reader does just that. Story is a collaborative art. The writer's imagination works in league with the reader's imagination, calls on the reader to collaborate, to fill in, to flesh out, to bring their own experience to the work. Fiction is not a camera, and not a mirror. It's much more like a Chinese painting – a few lines, a few blobs, a whole lot of blank space. From which *we* make the travelers, in the mist, climbing the mountain towards the inn under the pines.

I have written fantastic stories closely based on actual experience, and realistic stories totally made up out of moonshine; some of my science fiction is full of accurate and carefully researched fact, while my stories about ordinary people doing ordinary things on the Oregon coast in 1990 contain large wetlands and quicksands of pure invention. I will refer to some of my own works in hopes of showing how fictional "ideas" arise from a combination of experience and imagination that is indissoluble and unpredictable and doesn't follow orders.

In my Earthsea books, particularly the first one, people sail around all the time on the sea in small boats. They do it quite convincingly, and many people understandably assume that I spent years sailing around on the sea in small boats.

My entire experience with sailboats was in my junior semester in Berkeley High School, when they let us take Sailing for gym credit. On a windy day in the Berkeley Marina, my friend Jean and I managed to overturn and sink a nine-foot catboat in three feet of water. We sang "Nearer

My God to Thee" as she went down, and then waded a half mile back to the boathouse. The boatman was incredulous. You *sank* it? he said. *How?*

That will remain one of the secrets of the writer.

All right, so all that sailing around that Ged does in Earthsea does not reflect experience – not *my* experience. Only my imagination, using that catboat, and *other people's* experience – novels I'd read – and some research (I do know why *Lookfar* is clinkerbuilt), and asking friends questions, and some trips on ocean liners. But basically, it's a fake.

So is all the snow and ice in *The Left Hand of Darkness.* I never even saw snow till I was seventeen and I certainly never pulled a sledge across a glacier. Except with Scott, and Shackleton, and those guys. In books. Where do you get your ideas from? From books, of course, from other people's books, what are books for? If I didn't read how could I write?

We writers all stand on each other's shoulders, we all use each other's ideas and skills and plots and secrets. Literature is a communal enterprise. That "anxiety of influence" stuff is just testosterone talking. Understand me: I don't mean plagiarism: I'm not talking about imitation, or copying, or theft. If I thought I had really deliberately used any other writer's writing, I certainly wouldn't stand here congratulating myself, I'd go hide my head in a paper bag (along with several eminent historians). What I mean is that stuff from other people's books gets into us just as our own experience does, and like actual experience gets composted and transmuted and transformed by the imagination, and comes forth entirely changed, our own, growing out of our own mind's earth.

So, I acknowledge with delight my endless debt to every storyteller I have ever read, factual or fictional, my colleagues, my collaborators – I praise them and honor them, the endless givers of gifts.

In my science fiction novel set on a planet populated by people whose gender arrangements are highly imaginative, the part about two people hauling a sledge across a glacier is as factually accurate as I could make it, down to the details of their gear and harness, how much weight they haul, how far they can get in a day, what different snow surfaces are like, and so on. None of this is from my direct experience; all of it is from the books I've read about the Antarctic ever since I was in my twenties. It is factual material woven into a pure fantasy. As a matter of fact, so is all the stuff about their gender arrangements; but that's a little too complicated to go into here.

Once I wanted to write a story from the point of view of a tree. The "idea" of the story came with the sight of an oak alongside the road to McMinnville. I was thinking as we drove by that when that oak was young, Highway 18 was a quiet country road. I wondered what the oak thought about the highway, the cars. Well, so, where do I get the experience of being a tree, on which my imagination is to work? Books don't help much here. Unlike Shackleton and Scott, oaks don't keep diaries. Personal observation is my only experiential material. I have seen a lot of oaks, been around oaks, been in some oaks, externally, climbing around; now I want to be in one internally, inside. What does it feel like to be an oak? Large, for one thing; lively, but quiet, and not very flexible, except at the tips, out there in the sunlight. And deep – very deep – roots going down in the dark . . . To live rooted, to be two hundred years in one place, unmoving, yet traveling immensely through the seasons, the years, through time . . . Well, you know how it's done. You did it as a kid, you still do it. If you don't do it, your dreams do it for you.

In dreams begins responsibility, said a poet. In dreams, in imagination, we begin to be one another. I am thou. The barriers go down.

Big stories, novels, don't come from just one stimulus but a whole clumping and concatenation of ideas and images, visions and mental perceptions, all slowly drawing in around some center which is usually obscure to me until long after the book's done and I finally say Oh, *that's* what that book's about. To me, two things are essential during the drawing-together, the clumping process, before I know much of anything about the story: I have to see the place, the landscape; and I have to know the principal people. By name. And it has to be the right name. If it's the wrong name, the character won't come to me. I won't know who they are. I won't be able to be them. They won't talk. They won't *do* anything. Please don't ask me how I arrive at the name and how I know when it's the right name; I have no idea. When I hear it, I know it. And I know where the person is. And then the story can begin.

Here is an example: my recent book *The Telling*. Unlike most of my stories, it started with something you really could call an idea – a fact I had learned. I have been interested most of my life in the Chinese philosophy called Taoism. At the same time that I finally also learned a little about the religion called Taoism, an ancient popular religion of vast complexity, a major element of Chinese culture for two millennia, I learned that it had been suppressed, almost entirely wiped out, by Mao Tse-tung. In one generation, one psychopathic tyrant destroyed a tradition two thousand years old. In my lifetime. And I knew nothing about it.

The enormity of the event, and the enormity of my ignorance, left me stunned. I had to think about it. Since the way I think is fiction, eventually I had to write a story about it. But how could I write a novel about China? My poverty of experience would be fatal. A novel set on an imagined world, then, about the extinction of a religion as a deliberate political act . . . counterpointed by the suppression of political freedom by a theocracy? All right, there's my theme, my idea if you will.

I'm impatient to get started, impassioned by the theme. So I look for the people who will tell me the story, the people who are going to live this story. And I find this uppity kid, this smart girl who goes from Earth to that world. I don't remember what her name was, she had five different names and none of them was the true name. I started the book five times, it got nowhere. I had to stop.

I had to sit patiently and say nothing, at the same time every day, while the fox looked at me from the corner of its eye, and slowly let me get a little bit closer.

And finally the woman whose story it was spoke to me. I'm Sutty, she said. Follow me. So I followed her; and she led me up into the high mountains; and she gave me the book.

I had a good idea, but I did not have a story. Critics talk as if stories were all idea, but intellect does not make story any more than ideology makes art. The story had to make itself, find its center, find its voice, Sutty's voice. Then, because I was waiting for it, it could give itself to me.

Or put it this way: I had a lot of stuff in my head, good stuff, clear ideas – but I couldn't pull it together, I couldn't dance with it, because I hadn't waited to catch the beat. I didn't have the rhythm.

This book takes its title from a letter from Virginia Woolf to her friend Vita Sackville-West. Vita had been pontificating about finding the right word, Flaubert's *mot juste,* and agonizing very Frenchly about style; and Virginia wrote back, very Englishly:

> As for the *mot juste,* you are quite wrong. Style is a very simple matter: it is all *rhythm.* Once you get that, you can't use the wrong words. But on the other hand here am I sitting after half the morning, crammed with ideas, and visions, and so on, and can't dislodge them, for lack of

the right rhythm. Now this is very profound, what rhythm is, and goes far deeper than words. A sight, an emotion, creates this wave in the mind, long before it makes words to fit it; and in writing (such is my present belief) one has to recapture this, and set this working (which has nothing apparently to do with words) and then, as it breaks and tumbles in the mind, it makes words to fit it. But no doubt I shall think differently next year.

Woolf wrote that eighty years ago, and if she did think differently next year, she didn't tell anybody. She says it lightly, but she means it: this is very profound. I have not found anything more profound, or more useful, about the source of story – where the ideas come from.

Beneath memory and experience, beneath imagination and invention – beneath *words,* as she says – there are rhythms to which memory and imagination and words all move; and the writer's job is to go down deep enough to begin to feel that rhythm, to find it, move to it, be moved by it, and let it move memory and imagination to find words.

She's full of ideas but she can't dislodge them, she says, because she can't find their rhythm – can't find the beat that will unlock them, set them moving forward into a story, get them telling themselves.

A wave in the mind, she calls it; and says that a sight or an emotion may create it – like a stone dropped into still water, and the circles go out from the center in silence, in perfect rhythm, and the mind follows those circles outward and outward till they turn to words . . . but her image is greater: her wave is a sea wave, traveling smooth and silent a thousand miles across the ocean till it strikes the shore, and crashes, breaks, and flies up in a foam of words. But the wave, the rhythmic impulse, is before words, "has nothing to do with words." So the writer's job is to recognize the wave, the silent swell, way out at sea, way out in the ocean of the mind, and follow it to shore, where it can turn or be turned into words, unload its story, throw out its imagery, pour out its secrets. And ebb back into the ocean of story.

What is it that prevents the ideas and visions from finding their necessary underlying rhythm, why couldn't Woolf "dislodge" them that morning? It could be a thousand things, distractions, worries; but very often I think what keeps a writer from finding the words is that she grasps at them too soon, hurries, grabs; she doesn't wait for the wave to come in and break. She wants to write because she's a writer; she wants to say this, and tell people that, and show people something else, things she knows, her ideas, her opinions, her beliefs, important ideas … but she doesn't wait for the wave to come and carry her beyond all the ideas and opinions, to where you *cannot use the wrong word*.

None of us is Virginia Woolf, but I hope every writer has had at least a moment when they rode the wave, and all the words were right.

As readers, we have all ridden that wave, and known that joy.

Prose and poetry — all art, music, dance — rise from and move with the profound rhythms of our body, our being, and the body and being of the world. Physicists read the universe as a great range of vibrations, of rhythms. Art follows and expresses those rhythms. Once we get the beat, the right beat, our ideas and our words dance to it, the round dance that everybody can join. And then I am thou, and the barriers are down. For a little while.

Rhythmic Pattern in *The Lord of the Rings*

●

2001

This piece, growing out of my attempts to study and consider the rhythms of prose and written for my own amusement, happily found a home in Karen Haber's anthology of writing on Tolkien, Meditations on Middle Earth, *published in 2001. I have added a brief note about the film version of the first book of the Trilogy, released late in the same year.*

Since I had three children, I've read Tolkien's Trilogy aloud three times. It's a wonderful book to read aloud or (consensus by the children) listen to. Even when the sentences are long, their flow is perfectly clear, and follows the breath; punctuation comes just where you need to pause; the cadences are graceful and inevitable. Like Dickens and Virginia Woolf, Tolkien must have heard what he wrote. The narrative prose of such novelists is like poetry in that it wants the living voice to speak it, to find its full beauty and power, its subtle music, its rhythmic vitality.

Woolf's vigorous, highly characteristic sentence rhythms are surely and exclusively prose: I don't think she ever uses a regular beat. Dickens and Tolkien both occasionally drop into metrics. Dickens's prose in moments of high emotional intensity tends to become iambic, and can even be scanned: "It is a far, far better thing that I do/than I have ever done." The hoity-toity may sneer, but this iambic beat is tremendously effective – particularly when the metric regularity goes unnoticed as such. If Dickens recognized it, it didn't bother him. Like most really great artists, he'd use any trick that worked.

Woolf and Dickens wrote no poetry. Tolkien wrote a great deal, mostly narratives and "lays," often in forms taken from the subjects of his scholarly interest. His verse often shows extraordinary intricacy of meter, alliteration, and rhyme, yet is easy and fluent, sometimes excessively so. His prose narratives are frequently interspersed with poems, and once at least in the Trilogy he quietly slips from prose into verse without signaling it typographically. Tom Bombadil, in *The Fellowship of the Ring*, speaks metrically. His name is a drumbeat, and his meter is made up of free, galloping dactyls and trochees, with tremendous forward impetus: Tum tata Tum tata, Tum ta Tum ta ... "You let them out again, Old Man Willow! What be you a-thinking of? You should not be waking. Eat earth! Dig deep! Drink water! Go to sleep! Bombadil is talking!" Usually Tom's speech is printed without line breaks, so unwary or careless silent readers may miss the beat until they *see* it as verse – as song, actually, for when his speech is printed as verse Tom is singing.

As Tom is a cheerfully archetypal fellow, profoundly in touch with, indeed representing the great, natural rhythms of day and night, season, growth and death, it's appropriate that he should talk in rhythm, that his speech should sing itself. And, rather charmingly, it's an infectious beat; it echoes in Goldberry's speech, and Frodo picks it up. "Goldberry!" he cries as they are leaving. "My fair lady, clad all in silver green! We have never said farewell to her, nor seen her since that evening!"

If there are other metric passages in the Trilogy, I've missed them. The speech of the elves and noble folk such as Aragorn has a dignified, often stately gait, but not a regular stress-beat. I suspected King Théoden of iambics, but he only drops into them occasionally, as all measured English speech does. The narrative moves in balanced cadences in passages of epic action, with a majestic sweep reminiscent of epic poetry, but it remains pure prose. Tolkien's ear was too good and too highly trained in prosody to let him drop into meter unknowingly.

Stress-units – metric feet – are the smallest elements of rhythm in literature, and in prose probably the only quantifiable ones. A while ago I got interested in the ratio of stresses to syllables in prose, and did some counting.

In poetry, by and large, one syllable out of every two or three has a beat on it: Tum ta Tum ta ta Tum Tum ta, and so on ... In narrative prose, that ratio goes down to one beat in two to four: ta Tum tatty Tum ta Tum tatatty, and so on ... In discursive and technical writing the ratio of unstressed syllables goes higher; textbook prose tends to hobble along clogged by a superfluity of egregiously unnecessary and understressed polysyllables.

Tolkien's prose runs to the normal narrative ratio of one stress every two to four syllables. In passages of intense action and feeling the ratio may get pretty close to 50 percent, like poetry, but still, except for Tom, it is irregular, it can't be scanned.

Stress-beat in prose is fairly easy to identify and count, though I doubt
any two readers of a prose passage would mark the stresses in exactly the
same places. Other elements of rhythm in narrative are less physical and far
more difficult to quantify, having to do not with an audible repetition, but
with the pattern of the narrative itself. These elements are longer, larger,
and very much more elusive.

Rhythm is repetition. Poetry can repeat anything – a stress-pattern, a
phoneme, a rhyme, a word, a line, a stanza. Its formality gives it endless
liberty to establish rhythmic structure.

What is repeatable in narrative prose? In oral narrative, which generally
maintains many formal elements, rhythmic structure may be established by
the repetition of certain key words, and by grouping events into similar,
accumulative semirepetitions: think of "The Three Bears" or "The Three
Little Pigs." European story uses triads; Native American story is more
likely to do things in fours. Each repetition both builds the foundation of
the climactic event, and advances the story.

Story moves, and normally it moves forward. Silent reading doesn't
need repetitive cues to keep the teller and the hearers oriented, and people
can read much faster than they speak. So people accustomed to silent
reading generally expect narrative to move along pretty steadily, without
formalities and repetitions. Increasingly, during the past century, readers
have been encouraged to look at a story as a road we're driving, well paved
and graded and without detours, on which we go as fast as we possibly
can, with no changes of pace and certainly no stops, till we get to – well
– to the end, and stop.

"There and Back Again": in Bilbo's title for *The Hobbit*, Tolkien has
already told us the larger shape of his narrative, the direction of his road.

The rhythm that shapes and directs his narrative is noticeable, was
noticeable to me, because it is very strong and very simple, as simple as a
rhythm can be: two beats. Stress, release. Inbreath, outbreath. A heartbeat.
A walking gait – but on so vast a scale, so capable of endlessly complex and subtle variation, that it carries the whole enormous narrative
straight through from beginning to end, from There to Back Again,
without faltering. The fact is, we *walk* from the Shire to the Mountain
of Doom with Frodo and Sam. One, two, left, right, on foot, all the way.
And back.

What are the elements that establish this long-distance walking pace?
What elements recur, are repeated with variations, to form the rhythms of

prose? Those that I am aware of are: Words and phrases. Images. Actions. Moods. Themes.

Words and phrases, repeated, are easy to identify. But Tolkien is not, after all, telling his story aloud; writing prose for silent, and sophisticated, readers, he doesn't use key words and stock phrases as storytellers do. Such repetitions would be tedious and faux-naive. I have not located any "refrains" in the Trilogy.

As for imagery, actions, moods, and themes, I find myself unable to separate them usefully. In a profoundly conceived, craftily written novel such as *The Lord of the Rings*, all these elements work together indissolubly, simultaneously. When I tried to analyze them out I just unraveled the tapestry and was left with a lot of threads, but no picture. So I settled for bunching them all together. I noted every repetition of any image, action, mood, or theme without trying to identify it as anything other than a repetition.

I was working from my impression that a dark event in the story was likely to be followed by a brighter one (or vice versa); that when the characters had exerted terrible effort, they then got to have a rest; that each action brought a reaction, never predictable in nature, because Tolkien's imagination is inexhaustible, but more or less predictable in kind, like day following night, and winter after fall.

This "trochaic" alternation of stress and relief is of course a basic device of narrative, from folktales to *War and Peace*; but Tolkien's reliance on it is striking. It is one of the things that make his narrative technique unusual for the mid-twentieth century. Unrelieved psychological or emotional stress or tension, and a narrative pace racing without a break from start to climax, characterize much of the fiction of the time. To readers with such expectations, Tolkien's plodding stress/relief pattern seemed and seems simplistic, primitive. To others it may seem a remarkably simple, subtle technique of keeping the reader going on a long and ceaselessly rewarding journey.

I wanted to see if I could locate the devices by which Tolkien establishes this master rhythm in the Trilogy; but the idea of working with the whole immense saga was terrifying. Perhaps some day I or a braver reader can identify the larger patterns of repetition and alternation throughout the narrative. I narrowed my scope to one chapter, the eighth of volume 1, "Fog on the Barrow Downs": some fourteen pages, chosen almost arbitrarily, though I did want a selection with some traveling in it, journey being such a large component of the story. I went through the chapter noting every major image, event, and feeling-tone and particularly noting recurrences or strong similarity of words, phrases, scenes, actions, feelings, and images. Very soon, sooner than I expected, repetitions began to emerge, including a positive/negative binary pattern of alternation or reversal.

These are the chief recurrent elements I listed (page references are to the George Allen & Unwin edition of 1954):

A vision or vista of a great expanse (three times: in the first paragraph; in the fifth paragraph; and on page 157, when the vision is temporal – back into history)

The image of a single figure silhouetted against the sky (four times: Goldberry, page 147; the standing stone, page 148; the barrow-wight, page 151; Tom, pages 153 and 154. Tom and Goldberry are bright figures in sunlight, the stone and the wraith are dark looming figures in mist)

Mention of the compass directions – frequent, and often with a benign or malign connotation

The question "Where are you?" three times (page 150, when Frodo loses his companions, calls, and is not answered; page 151, when the barrow-wight answers him; and Merry, on page 154, "Where did you get to, Frodo?" answered by Frodo's "I thought that I was lost" and Tom's "You've found yourself again, out of the deep water")

Phrases describing the hill country through which they ride and walk, the scent of turf, the quality of the light, the ups and downs, and the hilltops on which they pause: some benign, some malign

Associated images of haze, fog, dimness, silence, confusion, unconsciousness, paralysis (foreshadowed on page 148 on the hill of the standing stone, intensified on page 149 as they go on, and climaxing on page 150 on the barrow), which reverse to images of sunlight, clarity, resolution, thought, action (pages 151–153)

What I call reversal is a pulsation back and forth between polarities of feeling, mood, image, emotion, action – examples of the stress/release pulse that I think is fundamental to the structure of the book. I listed some of these binaries or polarities, putting the negative before the positive, though that is not by any means always the order of occurrence. Each such reversal or pulsation occurs more than once in the chapter, some three or four times.

darkness/daylight
resting/traveling on
vagueness/vividness of perception
confusion of thought/clarity
sense of menace/of ease
imprisonment or a trap/freedom
enclosure/openness
fear/courage
paralysis/action
panic/thoughtfulness
forgetting/remembering
solitude/companionship
horror/euphoria
cold/warmth

These reversals are not simple binary flips. The positive causes or grows from the negative state, and the negative from the positive. Each yang contains its yin, each yin contains its yang. (I don't use the Chinese terms lightly; I believe they fit with Tolkien's conception of how the world works.)

Directionality is extremely important all through the book. I believe there is no moment when we don't know, literally, where north is, and what direction the protagonists are going. Two of the wind rose points have a pretty clear and consistent emotional value: east has bad connotations, west is benign. North and south vary more, depending on where we are in time and space; in general I think north is a melancholy direction and south a dangerous one. In a passage early in the chapter, one of the three great "vistas" offers us the whole compass view, point by point: west, the Old Forest and the invisible, beloved Shire; south, the Brandywine River flowing "away out of the knowledge of the hobbits"; north, a "featureless and shadowy distance"; and east, "a guess of blue and a remote white glimmer . . . the high and distant mountains" – where their dangerous road will lead them.

The additional points of the Native American and the airplane compass – up and down – are equally firmly established. Their connotations are complex. Up is usually a bit more fortunate than down, hilltops better than valleys; but the Barrow Downs – hills – are themselves an unlucky place to be. The hilltop where they sleep under the standing stone is a bad place, but there is a *hollow* on it, as if to contain the badness. *Under* the barrow is the worst place of all, but Frodo gets there by climbing *up* a hill. As they wind their way downward, and northward, at the end of the chapter, they are relieved to be leaving the uplands; but they are going back to the danger of the Road.

Similarly, the repeated image of a figure silhouetted against the sky – above seen from below – may be benevolent or menacing.

As the narrative intensifies and concentrates, the number of characters dwindles abruptly to one. Frodo, afoot, goes on ahead of the others, seeing what he thinks is the way out of the Barrow Downs. His experience is increasingly illusory – two standing stones like "the pillars of a headless door," which he has not seen before (and will not see when he looks for them later) – a quickly gathering dark mist, voices calling his name (from the eastward), a hill which he must climb "up and up," having (ominously) lost all sense of direction. At the top, "It was wholly dark. 'Where are you?' he cried out miserably." This cry is unanswered.

When he sees the great barrow loom above him, he repeats the question, "angry and afraid" – "'Where are you?'" And this time he is answered, by a deep, cold voice out of the ground.

The key action of the chapter, inside the barrow, involves Frodo alone in extreme distress, horror, cold, confusion, and paralysis of body and will – pure nightmare. The process of reversal – of escape – is not simple or direct. Frodo goes through several steps or stages in undoing the evil spell.

Lying paralyzed in a tomb on cold stone in darkness, he *remembers* the Shire, Bilbo, his life. Memory is the first key. He thinks he has come to a terrible end, but refuses to accept it. He lies "thinking and getting a hold on himself," and as he does so, light begins to shine.

But what it shows him is horrible: his friends lying as if dead, and "across their three necks lay one long naked sword."

A song begins – a kind of limping, sick reversal of Tom Bombadil's jolly caroling – and he sees, unforgettably, "a long arm groping, walking on its fingers towards Sam . . . and towards the hilt of the sword that lay upon him."

He stops thinking, loses his hold on himself, forgets. In panic terror, he considers putting on the Ring, which has lain so far, all through the chapter, unmentioned in his pocket. The Ring, of course, is the central image of the whole book. Its influence is utterly baneful. Even to think of putting it on is to imagine himself abandoning his friends and justifying his cowardice – "Gandalf would admit that there had been nothing else he could do."

His courage and his love for his friends are stung awake by this *imagination*: he escapes temptation by immediate, violent (re)action: he seizes the sword and strikes at the crawling arm. A shriek, darkness, he falls forward over Merry's cold body.

With that touch, his memory, stolen from him by the fog-spell, returns fully: he remembers the house under the Hill – Tom's house. He remembers Tom, who is the earth's memory. With that he recollects himself.

Now he can remember the spell that Tom gave him in case of need, and he speaks it, calling at first "in a small desperate voice," and then, with Tom's name, loud and clear.

And Tom answers: the immediate, right answer. The spell is broken. "Light streamed in, the plain light of day."

Imprisonment, fear, cold, and solitude reverse to freedom, joy, warmth, and companionship . . . with one final, fine touch of horror: "As Frodo left the barrow for the last time he thought he saw a severed hand wriggling still, like a wounded spider, in a heap of fallen earth." (Yang always has a spot of yin in it. And Tolkien seems to have had no warm spot for spiders.)

This episode is the climax of the chapter, the maximum of stress, Frodo's first real test. Everything before it led towards it with increasing tension. It is followed by a couple of pages of relief and release. That the hobbits feel hungry is an excellent sign. After well-being has been restored, Tom gives the hobbits weapons, knives forged, he tells them rather somberly, by the Men of Westernesse, foes of the Dark Lord in dark years long ago. Frodo and his companions, though they don't know it yet, are of course themselves the foes of that lord in this age of the world. Tom speaks – riddlingly, and not by name – of Aragorn, who has not yet entered the story. Aragorn is a bridge figure between the past and the present time, and as Tom speaks, the hobbits have a momentary, huge, strange vision of the depths of time, and heroic figures, "one with a star on his brow" – a foreshadowing of their saga, and of the whole immense history of Middle Earth. "Then the vision faded, and they were back in the sunlit world."

Now the story proceeds with decreased immediate plot tension or suspense, but undecreased narrative pace and complexity. We are going back towards the rest of the book, as it were. Towards the end of the chapter the larger plot, the greater suspense, the stress they are all under, begin again to loom in the characters' minds. The hobbits have fallen into a frying pan and managed to get out of it, as they have done before and will do again, but the fire in Mount Doom still burns.

They travel on. They walk, they ride. Step by step. Tom is with them and the journey is uneventful, comfortable enough. As the sun is setting they reach the Road again at last, "running from South-west to North-east, and on their right it fell quickly down into a wide hollow." The portents are not too good. And Frodo mentions – not by name – the Black Riders, to avoid whom they left the Road in the first place. The chill of fear creeps back. Tom cannot reassure them: "Out east my knowledge fails." His dactyls, even, are subdued.

He rides off into the dusk, singing, and the hobbits go on, just the four of them, conversing a little. Frodo reminds them not to call him by his name. The shadow of menace is inescapable. The chapter that began with a hopeful daybreak vision of brightness ends in a tired evening gloom. These are the final sentences:

> Darkness came down quickly, as they plodded slowly downhill and up again, until at last they saw lights twinkling some distance ahead.
>
> Before them rose Bree-hill barring the way, a dark mass against misty stars; and under its western flank nestled a large village. Towards it they now hurried, desiring only to find a fire, and a door between them and the night.

These few lines of straightforward narrative description are full of rapid reversals: darkness/lights twinkling – downhill/up again – the rise of Bree-hill/the village under it (*west* of it) – a dark mass/misty stars – a fire/the night. They are like drumbeats. Reading the lines aloud I can't help thinking of a Beethoven finale, as in the Ninth Symphony: the absolute certainty and definition of crashing chord and silence, repeated, repeated again. Yet the tone is quiet, the language simple, and the emotions evoked are quiet, simple, common: a longing to end the day's journey, to be inside by the fire, out of the night.

After all, the whole Trilogy ends on much the same note. From darkness into the firelight. "Well," Sam says, "I'm back."

There and back again ... In this single chapter, certain of the great themes of the book, such as the Ring, the Riders, the Kings of the West, the Dark Lord, are struck once only, or only obliquely. Yet this small part of the great journey is integrally part of the whole in event and imagery: the barrow-wight, once a servant of the Dark Lord, appears even as Sauron himself will appear at the climax of the tale, looming, "a tall dark figure against the stars." And Frodo defeats him, through memory, imagination, and unexpected act.

The chapter itself is one "beat" in the immense rhythm of the book. Each of its events and scenes, however vivid, particular, and local, echoes or recollects or foreshadows other events and images, relating all the parts of the book by repeating or suggesting parts of the pattern of the whole.

I think it is a mistake to think of story as simply moving forward. The rhythmic structure of narrative is both journeylike and architectural. Great novels offer us not only a series of events, but a *place*, a landscape of the imagination which we can inhabit and return to. This may be particularly clear in the "secondary universe" of fantasy, where not only the action but the setting is avowedly invented by the author. Relying on the irreducible simplicity of the trochaic beat, stress/unstress, Tolkien constructs an inexhaustibly complex, stable rhythmic pattern in imagined space and time. The tremendous landscape of Middle Earth, the psychological and moral universe of *The Lord of the Rings*, is built up by repetition, semirepetition, suggestion, foreshadowing, recollection, echo, and reversal. Through it the story goes forward at its steady, human gait. There, and back again.

Note (2002): I enjoyed the film of *The Fellowship of the Ring* immensely, and feel an awed admiration for the scriptwriters who got so much of the story and the *feeling* of the story into the brevity of a movie. I was sorry not to see the barrow-wight's hand crawling towards Frodo, but they were very wise to leave out Tom – wise in all their omissions. Nothing was disappointing but the orcs, standard-issue slimy monsters with bad teeth, bah. I expected that the greatest difference between the book and the film might be a difference of pace; and it is. The film begins at a proper footpace, an old man jogging along in a pony cart ... but soon it's off at a dead run, galloping, rushing, leaping through landscapes, adventures, marvels, and perils, with barely a pause at Rivendell to discuss what to do next. Instead of the steady rhythm of breathing, you can't even catch your breath.

I don't know that the filmmakers had much choice about it. Movie audiences have been trained to expect whiz-bang pacing, an eye-dazzling ear-splitting torrent of images and action leaving no time for thought and little for emotional response. And the audience for a fantasy film is assumed to be young, therefore particularly impatient.

Watching once again the wonderful old film *Chushingura*, which takes four hours to tell the (comparatively) simple story of the Forty-seven Ronin, I marveled at the quiet gait, the silences, the seemingly aimless lingering on certain scenes, the restraint that slowly increases tension till it gathers tremendous force and weight. I wish a Tolkien film could move at a pace like that. If it was as beautiful and well written and well acted as this one is, I'd be perfectly happy if it went on for hours and hours . . . But that's a daydream.

And I doubt that any drama, no matter how un-whiz-bang, could in fact capture the singular gait that so deeply characterizes the book. The vast, idiosyncratic prose rhythms of *The Lord of the Rings*, like those of *War and Peace*, have no counterpart in Western theatrical writing.

So all I wish is that they'd slowed down the movie, every now and then, even just held still for a moment and let there be a rest, a beat of silence . . .

A Matter of Trust

●

2002

A talk given to a writing workshop in Vancouver, Washington, February 2002.

In order to write a story, you have to trust yourself, you have to trust the story, and you have to trust the reader.

Before you start writing, neither the story nor the reader even exists, and the only thing you have to trust is yourself. And the only way you can come to trust in yourself as a writer is to write. To commit yourself to that craft. To be writing, to have written, to work on writing, to plan to write. To read, to write, to practice your trade, to learn your job, until you know something about it, and know you know something about it.

This can be tricky. I have an eleven-year-old pen pal who has written half a story and is now demanding that I put him in touch with my agent and a publisher. It is my very disagreeable duty to tell him that he hasn't quite earned that much trust in himself as a writer, yet.

On the other hand I know some very good writers who never finish anything, or finish it and then destroy it with overrevising to meet real or imagined criticisms, because they don't trust themselves as writers, which means they can't trust their writing.

Confidence in yourself as a writer is pretty much the same as all other kinds of confidence, the confidence of a plumber or a school-teacher or a horseback rider: you earn it by doing, you build it up slowly, by working at it. And sometimes, particularly when you're new at the game, you fake it – you act like you know what you're doing, and maybe you can get away with it. Sometimes if you act as if you were blessed, you will be blessed. That too is part of trusting oneself. I think it works better for writers than it does for plumbers.

★

So much for trusting oneself. Now, to trust the story, what does that mean? To me, it means being willing not to have full control over the story as you write it.

Which would explain why it takes so long to learn to write. First you have to learn how to write English, and learn how to tell stories in general – techniques, practice, all that: so that you are in control. And then you have learn how to relinquish it.

Let me say here that many writers and teachers of writing would disagree strongly with what I'm saying. They'd say, you don't learn how to ride a horse, control the horse, make it do what you want it to do, and then take off its bridle and ride it bareback without reins – that's stupid. However, that is what I recommend. (Taoism is always stupid.) For me it's not enough to be a good rider, I want to be a centaur. I don't want to be the rider controlling the horse, I want to be both the rider and the horse.

How far to trust your story? It depends on the story, and your own judgment and experience are the only guide. The only generalizations I'm willing to make are these: Lack of control over a story, usually arising from ignorance of the craft or from self-indulgence, may lead to slackness of pace, incoherence, sloppy writing, spoiled work. Overcontrol, usually arising from self-consciousness or a competitive attitude, may lead to tightness, artificiality, self-conscious language, dead work.

Deliberate, conscious control, in the sense of knowing and keeping to the plan, the subject, the gait, and the direction of the work, is invaluable in the planning stage – before writing – and in the revision stage – after the first draft. During the actual composition it seems to be best if conscious intellectual control is relaxed. An insistent consciousness of the *intention* of the writing may interfere with the *process* of writing. The writer may get in the way of the story.

This is not as mystical as it sounds. All highly skilled work, all true craft and art, is done in a state where most aspects of it have become automatic through experience, through total familiarity with the medium, whether the medium is the sculptor's stone, or the drummer's drum, or the body of the dancer, or, for the writer, word sounds, word meanings, sentence rhythm, syntax, and so on. The dancer *knows* where her left foot goes, and the writer *knows* where the comma's needed. The only decisions a skilled artisan or artist makes while working are aesthetic ones. Aesthetic decisions are not rational; they're made on a level that doesn't coincide with rational consciousness. Thus, in fact, many artists feel they're in something like a trance state while working, and that in that state they don't make the decisions. The work tells them what needs doing and they do it. Perhaps it is as mystical as it sounds.

To go back to my horse metaphor, a good cowboy on a good horse rides with a loose rein and doesn't keep telling the horse what to do, because the horse knows. The cowboy knows where they're going, but the horse knows how to get them there.

I hope I don't sound like one of those bearers of glad tidings to writers who announce that there's nothing to it, just shut down your intellect and free up your right brain and emit words. I have enormous respect for my art as an art and my craft as a craft, for skill, for experience, for hard thought, for painstaking work. I hold those things in reverence. I respect commas far more than I do congressmen. People who say that commas don't matter may be talking about therapy or self-expression or other good things, but they're not talking about writing. They may be talking about getting started, leaping over timidity, breaking through emotional logjams; but they're still not talking about writing. If you want to be a dancer, find out how to use your feet. If you want to be a writer, find out where the comma goes. Then worry about all that other stuff.

Now, let's say I want to write a story. (Speaking for myself personally, that can be taken for granted; I always want to write a story; there never is anything I'd rather do than write a story.) In order to write that story, first I have learned how to write English, and how to write stories, by doing it quite regularly.*

I have also learned that what I need, once the story gets going, is to relinquish conscious control, get my damned intentions and theories and opinions out of the way, and let the story carry me. I need to trust it.

But as a rule, I can trust the story only if there has been a previous stage of some kind, a period of approach. This may well involve conscious planning, sitting and thinking about the setting, the events, the characters, maybe making notes. Or it may involve a long semiconscious gestation, during which events and characters and moods and ideas drift around half formed, changing forms, in a kind of dreamy limbo of the mind. And I do mean long. Years, sometimes. But then at other times, with other stories,

---

* And, of course, by reading stories. Reading – reading stories other writers wrote, reading voraciously but judgmentally, reading the best there is and learning from it how well, and how differently, stories can be told – this is so essential to being a writer that I tend to forget to mention it; so here it is in a footnote.

this approach stage is quite abrupt: a sudden vision or clear sense of the shape and direction of the story comes into the mind, and one is ready to write.

All these approach states or stages may occur at any time – at your desk, walking on the street, waking up in the morning, or when your mind ought to be on what Aunt Julia is saying, or the electricity bill, or the stew. You may have a whole grandiose James Joyce epiphany thing, or you may just think, *oh, yes, I see how that'll go.*

The most important thing I have to say about this preliminary period is don't rush it. Your mind is like a cat hunting; it's not even sure yet what it's hunting. It listens. Be patient like the cat. Very, very attentive, alert, but patient. Slow. Don't push the story to take shape. Let it show itself. Let it gather impetus. Keep listening. Make notes or whatever if you're afraid you'll forget something, but don't rush to the computer. Let the story drive you to it. When it's ready to go, you'll know it.

And if – like most of us – your life isn't all your own, if you haven't got time to write at that moment when you know the story's ready to be written, don't panic. It's just as tough as you are. It's yours. Make notes, think about your story, hang on to it and it will hang on to you. When you find or make the time to sit down to it, it will be there waiting for you.

Then comes the trancelike, selfless, rather terrifying, devouring work or play of composition, which is very difficult to talk about.

About planning and composition I want to make one observation: that it's delightful for a writer to be sheltered and shielded while at this intense work, given solitude and freedom from human responsibilities, like Proust in his padded cell, or the people who keep going to writers' colonies and having their lunch brought in a basket; delightful indeed, but dangerous, because it makes a luxury into a condition of work – a necessity. What you need as a writer is exactly what Virginia Woolf said: enough to live on and a room of your own. It's not up to other people to provide either of those necessities. It's up to you, and if you want to work, you figure how to get what you need to do it. What you live on probably has to come from daily work, not writing. How dirty your room gets is probably up to you. That the door of the room is shut, and when, and for how long, is also up to you. If you have work to do, you have to trust yourself to do it. A kind spouse is invaluable, a fat grant, an advance on spec, a session at a retreat may be a tremendous help: but it's your work, not theirs, and it has to be done on your terms, not theirs.

All right, so you shut the door, and you write down a first draft, at white heat, because that energy has been growing in you all through the prewriting stage and when released at last, is incandescent. You trust yourself and the story and you write.

So now it's written. You sit around and feel tired and good and look at the manuscript and savor all the marvelous, wonderful bits.

Then it cools down and you cool down, and arrive, probably somewhat chilled and rueful, at the next stage. Your story is full of ugly, stupid bits. You distrust it now, and that's as it should be. But you still have to trust yourself. You have to know that you can make it better. Unless you're a genius or have extremely low standards, composition is followed by critical, patient revision, with the thinking mind turned on.

I can trust myself to write my story at white heat without asking any questions of it – if I know my craft through practice – if I have a sense of where this story's going – and if when it's got there, I'm willing to turn right round and go over it and over it, word by word, idea by idea, testing and proving it till it goes right. Till all of it goes right.

Parenthetically: This is the period when it is most useful to have criticism from others – in a peer group or a class or from professional editors. Informed, supportive criticism is invaluable. I am a strong believer in the workshop as a way of gaining confidence and critical skills not only before you get published, but also for experienced professional writers. And a trustworthy editor is a pearl beyond price. To learn to trust your readers – and which readers to trust – is a very great step. Some writers never take it. I will return to that subject in a moment.

To sum up, I have to trust the story to know where it's going, and after I've written it I have to trust myself to find out where it or I got off track and how to get it all going in one direction in one piece.

And only after all that – usually long after – will I fully know and be able to say what, in fact, the story was about and why it had to go the way it went. Any work of art has its reasons which reason does not wholly understand.

When a story's finished, it's always less than your vision of it was before it was written. But it may also do more than you knew you were doing, say more than you realized you were saying. That's the best reason of all to trust it, to let it find itself.

To conceive a story or manipulate it to make it serve a purpose outside itself, such as an ambition to be famous, or an agent's opinion about what will sell, or a publisher's wish for instant profit, or even a noble end such as teaching or healing, is a failure of trust, of respect for the work. Of course almost all writers compromise here, to some extent. Writers are professionals in an age when capitalism pretends to be the arbiter of good; they have to write for the market. Only poets totally and sublimely ignore the market and therefore live on air – air and fellowships. Writers want to right wrongs, or bear witness to outrages, or convince others of what they see as truth. But in so far as they let such conscious aims control their work, they narrow its potential scope and power. That sounds like the doctrine of Art for Art's Sake. I don't offer it as a doctrine, but as a practical observation.*

Somebody asked James Clerk Maxwell in 1820 or so, What is the *use* of electricity? and Maxwell asked right back, What is the use of a baby?

What's the use of *To the Lighthouse*? What's the use of *War and Peace*? How would I dare try to define it, to limit it?

The arts function powerfully in establishing and confirming human community. Story, told or written, certainly serves to enlarge understanding of other people and of our place in the world as a whole. Such uses are intrinsic to the work of art, integral with it. But any limited, conscious, objective purpose is likely to obscure or deform that integrity.

Even if I don't feel my skill and experience are sufficient (and they are never sufficient), I must trust my gift, and therefore trust the story I write, know that its use, its meaning or beauty, may go far beyond anything I could have planned.

A story is a collaboration between teller and audience, writer and reader. Fiction is not only illusion, but collusion.

Without a reader there's no story. No matter how well written, if it isn't read it doesn't exist as a story. The reader makes it happen just as much as

* For example, read *War and Peace*. (If you have not read *War and Peace*, what are you waiting for?) The greatest of all novels is interrupted now and then by the voice of Count Tolstoy, telling us what we ought to think about history, great men, the Russian soul, and other matters. His opinions are far more interesting, convincing, and persuasive as we unconsciously absorb them *from the story* than when they appear as lectures. Tolstoy was a supremely and deservedly self-confident writer, and much of the power and beauty of his book lies in his perfect trust in his characters. They do what they must do, and all they must do: and it is enough. But the earnestness of his convictions seem to have weakened his confidence in his power to embody those ideas in his story; and those failures of trust are the only dull and unconvincing portions of the greatest of all novels.

the writer does. Writers are likely to ignore this fact, perhaps because they resent it.

The relationship of writer and reader is popularly seen as a matter of control and consent. The writer is The Master, who compels, controls, and manipulates the reader's interest and emotion. A lot of writers love this idea.

And lazy readers want masterful writers. They want the writer to do all the work while they just watch it happen, like on TV.

Most best-sellers are written for readers who are willing to be passive consumers. The blurbs on their covers often highlight the coercive, aggressive power of the text – compulsive page-turner, gut-wrenching, jolting, mind-searing, heart-stopping – what is this, electroshock torture?

From commercial writing of this type, and from journalism, come the how-to-write clichés, "Grab your readers with the first paragraph," "Hit them with shocker scenes," "Never give them time to breathe," and so on.

Now, a good many writers, particularly those entangled in academic programs in fiction, get their intellect and ego so involved in what they're saying and how they're saying it that they forget that they're saying it to anyone. If there's any use in the grab-'em-and-wrench-their-guts-out school of advice, it's that it at least reminds the writer that there is a reader out there to be grabbed and gutted.

But just because you realize your work may be seen by somebody other than the professor of creative writing, you don't have to go into attack mode and release the Rottweilers. There's another option. You can consider the reader, not as a helpless victim or a passive consumer, but as an active, intelligent, worthy collaborator. A colluder, a coillusionist.

Writers who choose to try to establish mutual trust believe it is possible to attract readers' attention without verbal assault and battery. Rather than grab, frighten, coerce, or manipulate a consumer, collaborative writers try to interest a reader. To induce or seduce people into moving with the story, participating in it, joining their imagination with it.

Not a rape: a dance.

Consider the story as a dance, the reader and writer as partners. The writer leads, yes; but leading isn't pushing; it's setting up a field of mutuality where two people can move in cooperation with grace. It takes two to tango.

Readers who have only been grabbed, bashed, gut-wrenched, and electroshocked may need a little practice in being interested. They may

298

need to learn how to tango. Once they've tried it, they'll never go back among the pit bulls.

Finally, there is the difficult question of "audience": In the mind of the writer planning or composing or revising the work, what is the presence of the potential reader or readers? Should the audience for the work dominate the writer's mind and guide the writing? Or should the writer while writing be utterly free of such considerations?

I wish there were a simple sound bite answer, but actually this is a terribly complicated question, particularly on the moral level.

Being a writer, conceiving a fiction, implies a reader. Writing is communication, though that's not all it is. One communicates *to* somebody. And what people want to read influences what people want to write. Stories are drawn out of writers by the spiritual and intellectual and moral needs of the writer's people. But all that operates on a quite unconscious level.

Once again it's useful to see the writer's work as being done in three stages. In the approach stage, it may be essential to think about your potential audience: who is this story for? For instance, is it for kids? Little kids? Young adults? Any special, limited audience calls for specific kinds of subject matter and vocabulary. All genre writing, from the average formula romance to the average *New Yorker* story, is written with an audience in mind – an audience so specific it can be called a market.

Only the very riskiest kind of fiction is entirely inconsiderate of the reader/market, saying, as it were, I will be told, and somebody, somewhere, will read me! Probably 99 percent of such stories end up, in fact, unread. And probably 98 percent of them are unreadable. The other 1 or 2 percent come to be known as masterpieces, usually very slowly, after the brave author has long been silent.

Consciousness of audience is limiting, both positively and negatively. Consciousness of audience offers choices, many of which have ethical implications – puritanism or porn? shock the readers or reassure them? do something I haven't tried or do my last book over? – and so on.

The limitations imposed by aiming at a specific readership may lead to very high art; all craft is a matter of rules and limitations, after all. But if consciousness of audience *as market* is the primary factor controlling your writing, you are a hack. There are arty hacks and artless hacks. Personally I prefer the latter.

All this has been about the approach stage, the what-am-I-going-to-write stage. Now that I know, dimly or exactly, who I'm writing for – anything from my granddaughter to all posterity – I start writing. And now, at the writing stage, consciousness of audience can be absolutely fatal. It is what makes writers distrust their story, stick, block, start over and over, never finish. Writers need a room of their own, not a room full of imaginary critics all watching over their shoulders saying "Is 'The' a good way to start that sentence?" An overactive internal aesthetic censor, or the external equivalent – what my agent or my editor is going to say – is like an avalanche of boulders across the story's way. During composition I have to concentrate entirely on the work itself, trusting and aiding it to find its way, with little or no thought of what or who it's for.

But when I get to the third stage, revision and rewriting, it reverses again: awareness that somebody's going to read this story, and of who might read this story, becomes essential.

What's the goal of revision? Clarity – impact – pace – power – beauty . . . all things that imply a mind and heart *receiving* the story. Revision clears unnecessary obstacles away so the reader can receive the story. That is why the comma is important. And why the right word, not the approximately right word, is important. And why consistency is important. And why moral implications are important. And all the rest of the stuff that makes a story readable, makes it live. In revising, you must trust yourself, your judgment, to work with the receptive intelligence of your potential readers.

You also may have to trust specific actual readers – spouse, friends, workshop peers, teachers, editors, agents. You may be pulled between your judgment and theirs, and it can be tricky to arrive at the necessary arrogance, or the necessary humility, or the right compromise. I have writer friends who simply cannot hear any critical suggestions; they drown them out by going into defensive explanation mode: *Oh, yes, but see, what I was doing* – are they geniuses or just buttheaded? Time will tell. I have writer friends who accept every critical suggestion uncritically, and end up with as many different versions as they have critics. If they meet up with bullying, manipulative agents and editors, they're helpless.

What can I recommend? Trust your story; trust yourself; trust your readers – but wisely. Trust watchfully, not blindly. Trust flexibly, not rigidly. The whole thing, writing a story, is a high-wire act – there you are out in midair walking on a spiderweb line of words, and down in the darkness people are watching. What can you trust but your sense of balance?

On the Frontier

2003

This brief meditation, written in 1996 for the journal Frontiers, *where it appeared as "Which Side Am I On, Anyway?" has been rewritten for this book.*

THE FRONTIER

A frontier has two sides. It is an interface, a threshold, a liminal site, with all the danger and promise of liminality.

The front side, the yang side, the side that calls itself the frontier, that's where you boldly go where no one has gone before, rushing forward like a stormfront, like a battlefront. Nothing before you is real. It is empty space. My favorite quotation from the great frontiersman Julius Caesar: "It was not certain that Britannia existed, until I went there." It does not exist, it is empty, and therefore full of dream and promise, the seven shining cities. And so you go there. Seeking gold, seeking land, annexing all before you, you expand your world.

The other side of the frontier, the yin side: that's where you live. You always lived there. It's all around you, it's always been. It is the real world, the true and certain world, full of reality.

And it is where they come. You were not certain they existed, until they came.

Coming from another world, they take yours from you, changing it, draining it, shrinking it into a property, a commodity. And as your world is meaningless to them until they change it into theirs, so as you live among them and adopt their meanings, you are in danger of losing your own meaning to yourself.

In the wake of the North American frontier is where my father the anthropologist did his fieldwork, among the wrecks of cultures, the ruins of languages, the broken or almost-broken continuities and communities, the shards of an infinite diversity smashed by a monoculture. A postfrontiersman, a white immigrant's son learning Indian cultures and languages in the first half of the twentieth century, he tried to save meaning. To learn and tell the stories that might otherwise be lost. The only means he had to do so was by translating, recording in his foreign language: the language of science, the language of the conqueror. An act of imperialism. An act of human solidarity.

My mother continued his work with her history of a survivor of the frontier, the native Californian Ishi. I admire her book as deeply as I admire its subject, but have always regretted the subtitle, *A Biography of the Last Wild Indian in North America*, for it contradicts the sense and spirit of the story she tells. Ishi was not wild. He did not come out of the wilderness, but out of a culture and tradition far more deeply rooted and soundly established than that of the frontiersmen who slaughtered his people to get their land. He did not live in a wilderness but in a dearly familiar world he and his people knew hill by hill, river by river, stone by stone. Who made those golden hills a wilderness of blood and mourning and ignorance?

If there are frontiers between the civilized and the barbaric, between the meaningful and the unmeaning, they are not lines on a map nor are they regions of the earth. They are boundaries of the mind alone.

MY FRONTIERS

Innate or acquired, a delight in learning unfamiliar (foreign, alien, "wild") significances and an unwillingness to limit value or significance to a single side of the frontier have shaped my writing.

North Americans have looked at their future as they looked at their Western lands: as an empty place (animals, Indians, aliens don't count) to be "conquered," "tamed," filled up with themselves and their doings: a meaningless blank on which to write their names. This is the same future one finds in much science fiction, but not in mine. In mine the future is already full; it is much older and larger than our present; and we are the aliens in it.

My fantasies explore the use of power as art and its misuse as domination; they play back and forth along the mysterious frontier between what we think is real and what we think is imaginary, exploring the borderlands.

Capitalism, which ceases to exist if it is not expanding its empire, establishes an ever-moving frontier, and its yang conquistadors forever pursue El Dorado. You cannot be too rich, they cry. My realistic fictions are mostly about people on the yin side of capitalism: housewives, waitresses, librarians, keepers of dismal little motels. The people who live, you might say, on the rez, in the broken world the conquistadors leave behind.

Living in a world that is valued only as gain, an ever-expanding world-as-frontier that has no worth of its own, no fullness of its own, you live in danger of losing your own worth to yourself. That's when you begin to listen to the voices from the other side, and to ask questions of failure and the dark.

I am a granddaughter of the American frontier. My mother's family moved and bought and farmed and failed and moved on, from Missouri to Wyoming to Colorado to Oregon to California and back. We followed yang; we found yin. I am grateful. My heritage is the wild oats the Spanish sowed on the hills of California, the cheatgrass the ranchers left in the counties of Harney and Malheur. Those are the crops my people planted, and I have reaped. There is my straw-spun gold.

Old Body, Not Writing

2003

Some bits of this went into a piece called "Writer's Block" for the New York Times *Syndicate, and a small part went into* Steering the Craft. *It is a rambling meditation that I came back to on and off over several years, when I wasn't writing what I wanted to be writing.*

Just now I'm not writing. That is, I'm writing here and now that I'm not writing, because I am unhappy about not writing. But if I have nothing to write I have nothing to write. Why can't I wait in patience till I do? Why is the waiting hard?

Because I am not as good at anything else and nothing else is as good. I would rather be writing than anything else.

Not because it is a direct pleasure in the physical sense, like a good dinner or sex or sunlight. Composition is hard work, involving the body not in satisfying activity and release but only in stillness and tension. It is usually accompanied by uncertainty as to the means and the outcome, and often surrounded by a kind of driving anxiety ("I have to finish this before I die and finishing it is going to kill me"). In any case, while actually composing, I'm in a kind of trance state that isn't pleasant or anything else. It has no qualities. It is unconsciousness of self. While writing I am unconscious of my existence or any existence except in the words as they sound and make rhythms and connect and make syntax and in the story as it happens.

Aha, then writing is an escape? (Oh the Puritan overtones in that word!) An escape from dissatisfactions, incompetences, woes? Yes, no doubt. And also a compensation for lack of control over life, for powerlessness. Writing, I'm in power, I control, I choose the words and shape the story. Don't I?

Do I? Who's I? Where's I while I write? Following the beat. The words. They're in control. It's the story that has the power. I'm what follows it, records it. That's my job, and the work is in doing my job right.

We use *escape* and *compensation* negatively, and so we can't use them to define the act of making, which is positive and irreducible to anything but itself. True making is truly satisfying. It is more truly satisfying than anything I know.

So when I have nothing to write I have nothing to escape to, nothing to compensate with, nothing to give control to, no power to share in, and no satisfaction. I have to just be here being old and worried and muddling and afraid that nothing makes sense. I miss and want that thread of words that runs through day and night leading me through the labyrinth of the years. I want a story to tell. What will give me one?

Having a clear time to write, often I sit and think hard, forcefully, powerfully, and make up interesting people and interesting situations from which a story could grow. I write them down, I work at them. But nothing grows. I am trying to make something happen, not waiting till it happens. I don't have a story. I don't have the person whose story it is.

When I was young, I used to know that I had a story to write when I found in my mind and body an imaginary person whom I could embody myself in, with whom I could identify strongly, deeply, bodily. It was so much like falling in love that maybe that's what it was.

That's the physical side of storytelling, and it's still mysterious to me. Since I was in my sixties it has happened again (with Teyeo and Havzhiva in *Four Ways to Forgiveness*, for example) to my great delight, for it's an active, intense delight, to be able to live in the character night and day, have the character living in me, and their world overlapping and interplaying with my world. But I didn't embody so deeply with anybody in *Searoad*, nor with most of my characters in the last ten or fifteen years. Yet writing *Tehanu* or "Sur" or "Hernes" was as exciting as anything I ever did, and the satisfaction was solid.

I still find embodying or identifying most intense when the character is a man — when the body is absolutely not my own. That reach or leap across gender has an inherent excitement in it (which is probably why it is like falling in love). My identification with women characters such as Tenar or Virginia or Dragonfly is different. There is an even more sexual aspect to it, but not genital sexuality. Deeper. In the middle of my body, where you center from in t'ai chi, where the chi is. That is where my women live in me.

This embodying business may be different for men and women (if other writers do it at all — how do I know?). But I incline to believe

Virginia Woolf was right in thinking that the real thing goes on way past gender. Norman Mailer may seriously believe that you have to have balls to be a writer. If you want to write the way he writes I suppose you do. To me a writer's balls are irrelevant if not annoying. Balls aren't where the action is. When I say the middle of the body I don't mean balls, prick, cunt, or womb. Sexualist reductionism is as bad as any other kind. If not worse.

When I had a hysterectomy, I worried about my writing, because sexualist reductionism had scared me. But I'm sure it wasn't as bad for me as losing his balls would be for a man like Norman Mailer. Never having identified my sex, my sexuality, or my writing with my fertility, I didn't have to trash myself. I was able, with some pain and fear but not dreadful pain and fear, to think about what the loss meant to me as a writer, a person in a body who writes.

What it felt like to me was that in losing my womb I had indeed lost some connection, a kind of easy, bodily imagination, that had to be replaced, if it could be replaced, by the mental imagination alone. For a while I thought that I could not embody myself in an imagined person as I used to. I thought I couldn't "be" anyone but me.

I don't mean that when I had a womb I believed that I carried characters around in it like fetuses. I mean that when I was young I had a complete, unthinking, bodily connection and emotional apprehension of my imagined people.

Now (perhaps because of the operation, perhaps through mere aging) I was obliged to make the connection deliberately in the mind. I had to reach out with a passion that was not simply physical. I had to "be" other people in a more radical, complete way.

This wasn't necessarily a loss. I began to see it might be a gain, forcing me to take the more risky way. The more intelligence the better, so long as the passion, the bodily emotional connection is made, is there.

Essays are in the head, they don't have bodies the way stories do: that's why essays can't satisfy me in the long run. But headwork is better than nothing, as witness me right now, making strings of words to follow through the maze of the day (a very simple maze: one or two choices, a food pellet for a reward). Any string of meaningfully connected words is better than none.

If I can find intensely felt meaning in the words or invest them with it, better yet – whether the meaning be intellectual, as now, or consist in their music, in which case I would, ¡ojalá! be writing poetry.

Best of all is if they find bodies and begin to tell a story.

Up there I said "be" somebody, "have the person," "find the person." This is the mystery.

I use the word *have* not in the sense of "having" a baby, but in the sense of "having" a body. To have a body is to be embodied. Embodiment is the key.

My plans for stories that don't become stories all lack that key, the person or people whose story it is, the heart, the soul, the embodied inwardness of a person or several people. When I am working on a story that isn't going to work, I make people up. I could describe them the way the how-to-write books say to do. I know their function in the story. I write about them – but I haven't found them, or they haven't found me. They don't inhabit me, I don't inhabit them. I don't *have* them. They are bodiless. So I don't have a story.

But as soon as I make this inward connection with a character, I know it body and soul, I *have* that person, I am that person. To have the person (and with the person, mysteriously, comes the name) is to have the story. Then I can begin writing directly, trusting the person knows where she or he is going, what will happen, what it's all about.

This is extremely risky, but it works for me, these days, more often than it used to. And it makes for a story that is without forced or extraneous elements, all of a piece, uncontrolled by intrusions of opinion, willpower, fear (of unpopularity, censorship, the editor, the market, whatever), or other irrelevancies.

So my search for a story, when I get impatient, is not so much looking for a topic or subject or nexus or resonance or place-time (though all that is or will be involved) as casting about in my head for a stranger. I wander about the mental landscape looking for somebody, an Ancient Mariner or a Miss Bates, who will (almost certainly not when I want them, not when I invite them, not when I long for them, but at the most inconvenient and impossible time) begin telling me their story and not let me go until it's told.

The times when nobody is in the landscape are silent and lonely. They can go on and on until I think nobody will ever be there again but one stupid old woman who used to write books. But it's no use trying to populate it by willpower. These people come only when they're ready, and they do not answer to a call. They answer silence.

Many writers now call any period of silence a "block."

Would it not be better to look on it as a clearing? A way to go till you get where you need to be?

If I want to write and have nothing to write I do indeed feel blocked, or rather chocked – full of energy but nothing to spend it on, knowing my craft but nothing to use it on. It is frustrating, wearing, infuriating. But if I fill the silence with constant noise, writing anything in order to be writing something, forcing my willpower to invent situations for stories, I may be blocking myself. It's better to hold still and wait and listen to the silence. It's better to do some kind of work that keeps the body following a rhythm but doesn't fill up the mind with words.

I have called this waiting "listening for a voice." It has been that, a voice. It was that in "Hernes," all through, when I'd wait and wait, and then the voice of one of the women would come and speak through me.

But it's more than voice. It's a bodily knowledge. Body is story; voice tells it.

The Critics, the Monsters, and the Fantasists

2003

There was a while when people kept telling me, you must read this wonderful book about a school for wizards, it's so original, there's never been
anything like it!

The first time this happened, I confess I thought they were telling me
to read my own *A Wizard of Earthsea*, which involves a school for wizards,
and has been in print since 1969. No such luck! I had to hear all about
Harry, and it was hard, at first. I felt ignoble envy. But I soon felt a growing
and less ignoble astonishment. Reviewers and critics were talking about
Rowling's book as if it were a unique, unprecedented phenomenon.

The true phenomenon was the huge, genuine popularity the book
earned before the best-seller machinery took over. It was a charmer, in
the wizardly sense of the word: it cast the narrative spell. Word-of-mouth
led adults to read it who had not read anything remotely like it since they
were ten, if then; and finding it new to their experience, they thought it
original.

But people who write about books are supposed to have some experience in reading. Those who praised *Harry Potter* for its originality were
demonstrating blank ignorance of the traditions to which it belongs – not
only a British subgenre, the "school story," but also a major world tradition,
the literature of fantasy. How could so many reviewers and literary critics
know so little about a major field of fiction, have so little background, so
few standards of comparison, that they believed a book that was typical
of a tradition, indeed quite conventional, even derivative, to be a unique
achievement?

The modernists are largely to blame. Edmund Wilson and his generation left a tradition of criticism that is, in its way, quite a little monster.
In this school for anti-wizards, no fiction is to be taken seriously except
various forms of realism, labeled "serious." The rest of narrative fiction is
labeled "genre" and is dismissed unread.

Following this rule, the universities taught generations of students to shun all "genres," including fantasy (unless it was written before 1900, wasn't written in English, and/or can be labeled magical realism). Students in English departments were also taught to flee most children's books, or books that appeal to both children and adults, as if they were ripe buboes. And in many universities this still holds. Academic professionalism is at stake – possibly tenure. To touch genre is to be defiled. Reviewers in the popular journals, most of whom come out of the universities, mostly still obey the rule. If the reality of what people read forces a periodical to review mysteries or science fiction, they keep the reviews separate, in purdah, under a coy title.

Nobody can rightly judge a novel without some knowledge of the standards, expectations, devices, tropes, and history of its genre (or genres, for increasingly they mix and interbreed). The knowledge and craft a writer brings to writing fantasy, the expectations and skills a reader brings to reading it, differ significantly from those they bring to realistic fiction – or to science fiction, or the thriller, or the mystery, or the western, or the romance, or the picture book, or the chapter-book for kids, or the novel for young adults.

There are of course broad standards of competence in narrative. It would be interesting to identify writers whose narrative gift transcends genre, to find out what it is that Jane Austen, Rudyard Kipling, and Patrick O'Brian have in common (arguably a great deal). But distinction is essential to criticism, and the critic should know when a standard is inappropriate to a genre.

It might be an entertaining and educative exercise in fiction courses to make students discover inappropriate standards by using them. For example: Judge *The Lord of the Rings* as if it were a late-twentieth century realistic novel. (Deficient in self-evident relevance, in sexual and erotic components, in individual psychological complexity, in explicit social references ... Exercise too easy, has been done a thousand times.)

Judge *Moby Dick* as science fiction. (Strong on technological information and on motivation, and when the story moves, it moves; but crippled by the author's foot-dragging and endless self-indulgence in pompous abstractions, fancy language, and rant.)

Judge *Pride and Prejudice* as a Western. (A pretty poor show all round. Women talking. Darcy is a good man and could be a first-rate rancher, even if he does use those fool little pancake saddles, but with a first name like Fitzwilliam, he'll never make it in Wyoming.)

And to reverse the whole misbegotten procedure: Judge modern realist fiction by the standards of fantasy. (A narrow focus on daily details of contemporary human affairs; trapped in representationalism, suffocatingly unimaginative, frequently trivial, and ominously anthropocentric.)

The mandarins of modernism and some of the pundits of postmodernism were shocked to be told that a fantasy trilogy by a professor of philology is the best-loved English novel of the twentieth century. Why were they surprised?

Until the eighteenth century in Europe, imaginative fiction *was* fiction. Realism in fiction is a recent literary invention, not much older than the steam engine and probably related to it. Whence the improbable claim that it is the only form of fiction deserving to be admired and loved?

The particular way we make distinctions between factual and fictional narrative is also quite recent, and though useful, inevitably unreliable. As soon as you tell a story, it turns into fiction (or, as Borges put it, all narrative is fiction). It appears that in trying to resist this ineluctable process, or deny it, we of the Scientific West have come to place inordinate value on fiction that pretends to be, or looks awfully like, fact.

But in doing so, we've forgotten how to read the fiction that most fully exploits fictionality.

I'm not saying people don't read fantasy; a whole lot of us *people* do; but our scholars and critics for the most part don't read it and don't know how to read it. I feel shame for them. Sometimes I feel rage. I want to say to the literature teacher who remains willfully, even boastfully ignorant of a major element of contemporary fiction: you are incompetent to teach or judge your subject. Readers and students who do know the field, meanwhile, have every right to challenge your ignorant prejudice. Rise, undergraduates of the English Departments! You have nothing to lose but your A on the midterm!

And to the reviewers, I want to say, O critic, if you should come upon a fantasy, and it should awaken an atrophied sense of wonder in you, calling with siren voice to your dear little Inner Child, and you should desire to praise its incomparable originality, it would be well to have read in the literature of fantasy, so that you can make some comparisons and bring some critical intelligence to bear. Otherwise you're going to look like a

Patent Office employee rushing out into the streets of Washington crying, "A discovery, amazing, unheard of! A miraculous invention, which is a circular disc, pierced with an axle, upon which vehicles may roll with incredible ease across the earth!"

I often wish I could indicate to such people that there are pleasant and easy ways to remedy their ignorance. I would like to ask them to read *The Lord of the Rings*, because to me the book is in itself a sufficient demonstration of the value of fantasy literature. But if they don't know how to read it, it will do more harm than good. They'll come away snarling *childish, primitive, escapist, simplistic,* and other mantras of the school for anti-wizards, having learned nothing.

The author of *The Lord of the Rings* was himself a scholar, and while wearing his professorial hat he wrote essays about the kind of fiction he wrote. Anybody who wants to be able to think about fantasy literature would do well to begin with them. The best introductory guide I know to the domain of fantasy is the essay in his book *The Monsters and the Critics* called – unfortunately – "On Fairy Stories."[1] (Why Tolkien, who came to have a murderous hatred of sweet little fairies of the Tinker Bell breed, used that phrase instead of the already acceptable words *fantasy* or *fantastic* literature, I don't know; but he did. All professors have a streak of madness.) At any rate, it is perfectly possible to disagree with Tolkien's explanation and justification of the nature of fantasy, but it is really not admissible to talk seriously about fantasy without knowing what he said. Critics and academics who refuse to recognize fantasy as literature must at the very least have read Tolkien, both as critic and as novelist, and be able to justify their opinion against both his opinion and his accomplishment.

Alas, many of them read Todorov instead. Todorov said many interesting things in his book on fantasy, but few of them have anything to do with fantasy. Anyone familiar with the literature he should have read can only admire his perverse ingenuity in getting off the subject.

But then, I wonder how many of the teachers and critics who so stoutly refuse to consider fantasy as literature have read Bakhtin or Borges? Or Kroeber or Attebery, to name two of the most informed and thoughtful contemporary writers about the field?

---

1 Tolkien, John Ronald Reuel: *The Monsters and the Critics and Other Essays*, ed. C. Tolkien, Houghton Mifflin, 1984.

I wonder how many of them have actually read a fantasy novel since they were nine or ten years old?

This essay designedly began by talking about a children's book, for in talking about fantasy, one can't exclude children's literature (something that evidently never occurred to Todorov).

The capacity of much fantasy literature to override age-boundaries, to me a most admirable power, is to the anti-wizards a degrading weakness. That a novel can be read by a ten-year-old implies to them that it must be faulty as an adult novel: out comes the mantra, *primitive escapist simplistic* – in a word, *childish*. "Oh, those awful orcs," Wilson squeals cutely, believing himself to be imitating a reader of fantasy. The modernists wanted so badly to be perceived as grown-ups that they left a legacy of contempt for children's literature, which is still rarely questioned. Scholars of kiddilit are relegated to a drab kindergarten annex to the canonical structure of Literature, an embarrassment to the architects of Importance.

To throw a book out of serious consideration because it was written for children, or because it is read by children, is in fact a monstrous act of anti-intellectualism. But it happens daily in academia.

The prejudice is by no means only against fantasies; any novel accessible to children is suspect. The principal reason Kipling's *Kim* has very seldom been given its rightful place in the curriculum or the canon of English novels is probably the notion that, since it can give immense delight to a twelve-year-old, it cannot possibly reward an adult reader. That this is a mistaken assumption can be proved by reading *Kim*; but prejudice is easier and safer. Respectability lies in never raising one's eyes from the texts of Flaubert or James, which can at least be guaranteed to bore most children almost as quickly as *The Swiss Family Robinson*.

Lewis Carroll is one of the few writers for children who escapes defenestration – partly, perhaps, because of his mathematical games in the Alice books, which daunt most literary people, and the hoopla about his sexuality, which allows them to speak of him, if not his texts, in adult terms, signaling and sniggering over the children's heads. So much foolishness has been written about Carroll, indeed, that I wonder if I am wise in wanting the critics and professors to talk seriously about children's books. Will they insist on burrowing after sexual perversion in the author as the only way of making the book respectable?

★

I have been asking for thirty years why most critics are afraid of dragons while most children, and many adults, are not. It is a question that really, by now, deserves some answer other than the repetition of mantras; for the restriction of literary fiction to a "mainstream" of realism becomes daily less tenable, more, dare I say, fantastic. It is not only the incursion from South America that must be dealt with, but the frequency of treason and defection in the ranks of contemporary literary fiction in English. What is the critic to do when he sees one of A.S. Byatt's impeccably adult, dourly sophisticated heroines turning slowly and elaborately into a troll? He (the pronoun has been considered and accepted) is being asked to deal with a fantasy: with, as Kroeber puts it, "an artistic experience of confronting as real what one knows cannot be real, the arousal of belief in the unbelievable"[2]

What does it mean, that a woman turns into a troll?

It may mean as much, and have as many meanings, as a girl's turning into Emma Bovary. It may indeed mean more, to more people. Incompleteness and suggestion are very powerful tools for the artist of our time; the impossible, the incredible, the fantastic all suggest the limitations and the falsity of ordinary perception. In the useful words quoted by Kroeber, *Madame Bovary* has "the imposing completeness of a delusion" – but we may prefer, in this age, "the broken fragment of truth."

> The untrained critic, unable to perceive the rules a fantasy works by, may perceive it as meaningless. To excuse or hide failure of comprehension, labels may be stuck onto the story – surrealist, dada, etc. But while surrealism is a subversion of meaning, fantasy is a construction of meaning, perhaps purely linguistic, perhaps more than that. Successful fantasy narrative is notable particularly for its strong inner coherence; its rules are not those of the ordinary world, but it never flouts them. Surrealism subverts in order to destroy, fantasy subverts in order to rebuild.[3]

The untrained mind trying to deal with fantasy is most likely to try to rationalize it – to "explain" it as reflecting an order outside the order of the story, whether a theological order, or psychological, or political, anything so long as it's familiar. But true fantasy is not allegory. Allegory and

---

2 Kroeber, Karl: *Romantic Fantasy and Science Fiction*, Yale, 1988, p. 48.
3 Ibid. p. 48.

fantasy may overlap, as with Spenser, who obeys the rational convention of allegory yet keeps considerable freedom of invention; but Spenser is rather the exception than the model.

Rational inexplicability and avoidance of point-to-point symbolism do not automatically imply moral irresponsibility or social irrelevance. You might think critics would know that from having read the poetry of the last two hundred years; but the lesson seems not to be taken. The tendency to explain fantasy by extracting the fantastic from it and replacing it with the comprehensible reduces the radically unreal to the secondhand commonplace. Thus we have attempts to explain *The Lord of the Rings* as an apologia for Tolkien's Catholicism, or a kind of private mental asylum from his experiences in the First World War, etc. Such rationalizations may be earnestly perceived as a defense of fantasy, but are in fact refusals of it, attempts to explain it away. Only by approaching it on its own terms can a reader begin to apprehend the moral stance and the social relevance of a fantasy.

The purpose of a fantasy may be as inexplicable, in social or political terms, as the purpose (to paraphrase Maxwell) of a baby. To expect to explain or understand a fantasy as disguised ethics or politics is to fall into the reductionist trap. The purposive, utilitarian approach to fantasy and folktale of a Bettelheim or Bly, and in general the "psychological" approach to fantasy, explaining each element of the story in terms of its archetype or unconscious source or educative use, is deeply regressive; it perceives literature as magic, it is a verbomancy. To such interpreters the spell is a spell only if it works immediately to heal or reveal.

Most critics of fiction now eschew such reductive readings; even those who admit that reading a novel may have a profound and lasting effect on the mind and feelings of the reader, possibly including healing and enlightenment, are aware that the effect is not to be prescribed and often may not even be defined. If literary criticism doesn't demand purposive "meaning" of realism, why does it demand it of fantasy?

Probably because critics still equate fantasy with kiddilit. Children's books are particularly defenseless against utilitarian interpretations and judgments. I have been appalled to see my fantasies discussed in journals and columns of children's literature as if they were tracts. That there could be more to a child's book than a brisk story and an explicit ethical lesson – that children need active imagination more than closed moralities, that they respond to beauty in imagery and language, that they read to learn how to ask questions more than to be told answers – this seems to be news to those who judge children's books. But then, how much can you ask of critics and reviewers who are routinely despised and ignored by their peers and inferiors in academia and journalism?

The habit of reducing text to political-economic terms has prevented many Marxian and neo-Marxian critics from reading fantasy at all. If they can't read it as utopian, dystopian, or of clear social relevance, they're likely to dismiss it as frivolous. They see kings, and assume reactionary politics; they see wizards, and assume superstition; they see dragons, and assume nonsense. A literal mind is a great asset to reading fantasy, and so is a liberal mind, but not when either has been programmed too rigidly. Still, I welcome any socially conscious reading of fantasy, so long as it isn't ideologically puristic, for too many modern fantasies are intolerably trivial and complacent in their half-baked feudalism.

The charge that the whole enterprise of fantasy is "escapist" has been discussed by Tolkien and others, and only the ignorant continue to repeat it. It is a fact, however, that much fantasy, especially of the "heroic" kind, seems on the face of it socially and historically regressive: withdrawing from the Industrial Revolution and Modern Times, the fantasy story is often set in a green, underpopulated world of towns and small cities surrounded by wilderness, beyond which the exact and intricate map in the frontispiece does not go. This certainly appears to be a return to the world of the folktale. So it is; and to the world of Homer, Vergil, Shakespeare, Cervantes, Swift, Wordsworth, Dickens – the world of literature and human experience until a hundred and fifty years ago or so. This world is lost now to city folk, but still inhabited by many others, and still accessible to most of us in memories of childhood, hours or days in the woods or the fields, vacations in the mountains or by the shore – the country: the world we call, since it is no longer natural to us, "nature."

Fantasy's green country is one that most of us enter with ease and pleasure, and it seems to be perfectly familiar to most children even if they've never been out of the city streets. It partakes of the Golden Age, whether mythic or personal, though it may also partake of the darkness that ends the golden ages.

Nostalgia is probably essential to it. Nostalgia is a suspect emotion these days, and I will not attempt to defend it, aside from saying that I think it fuels more great poetry, perhaps, than any other emotion. But I will defend fantasy's green country.

Tolkien's Middle Earth is not just pre-industrial. It is also pre-human and non-human. It can be seen as a late and tragic European parallel to the American myth-world where Coyote and Raven and the rest of them are getting things ready for "the people who are coming" – human beings. At the end of *The Lord of the Rings*, we know that the non-human beings of Middle Earth are "dwindling" away or passing into the West, leaving the world to mankind alone. The feeling-tone indeed is less nostalgia than bereavement, the grief of those exiled from dear community, tears by the waters of Babylon.

My Earthsea and the familiar forests and towns of much fantasy are not informed by that great vision: but I think they too imply that modern humanity is in exile, shut out from a community, an intimacy, it once knew. They do not so much lament, perhaps, as remind.

The fields and forests, the villages and byroads, once did belong to us, when we belonged to them. That is the truth of the non-industrial setting of so much fantasy. It reminds us of what we have denied, what we have exiled ourselves from.

Animals were once more to us than meat, pests, or pets: they were fellow-creatures, colleagues, dangerous equals. We might eat them; but then, they might eat us. That is at least part of the truth of my dragons. They remind us that the human is not the universal.

What fantasy often does that the realistic novel generally cannot do is include the nonhuman as essential.

The fantasy element of *Moby Dick* is Moby Dick. To include an animal as a protagonist equal with the human is – in modern terms – to write a fantasy. To include *anything* on equal footing with the human, as equal in importance, is to abandon realism.

Realistic fiction is relentlessly focused on human behavior and psychology. "The proper study of mankind is Man." When fiction disobeys Pope and begins to include the Other, it begins to shade into the ghost story, the horror story, the animal story, or science fiction, or fantasy; it begins the movement outward to the not-entirely-human. Even "regional" fiction, always looked at disparagingly by the modernists, is part of this movement, sliding from human psychology into that which contains it, the landscape.

We need better definitions of terms than the ones we have. Hardy's Egdon Heath is in itself entirely realistic, but its centrality to *The Return of the Native* decentralizes the human characters in a way quite similar to that of fantasy and even science fiction. Melville's white whale isn't a real whale, he's a beast of the imagination, like dragons or unicorns; hence *Moby Dick* is not an animal story, but it is a fantasy. Woolf's *Flush* is an animal story, because Flush is (and actually was) a real spaniel; but of course it is also a novel about the Brownings; it is also definable as a fantasy, since the dog is a central character, and we know what he is thinking; but then we know what the dog is thinking in the hunting scene in *War and Peace*, too, which does not make *War and Peace* a fantasy . . . The clean, sharp definition of what realism is and what fantasy is recedes ever further, along with any justification for despising genre.

I venture a non-defining statement: realistic fiction is drawn towards anthropocentrism, fantasy away from it. Although the green country of fantasy seems to be entirely the invention of human imaginations, it verges on and partakes of actual realms in which humanity is not lord and master, is not central, is not even important. In this, fantasy may come much closer to the immense overview of the exact sciences than does science fiction, which is very largely obsessed by a kind of imperialism of human knowledge and control, a colonial attitude towards the universe.

The only world we know of, now, that isn't shaped and dominated by human beings, is "long ago." "Far away" won't do any more, unless we leap to a literally other world, another planet, or into an imagined future – and these options will be labeled science fiction, even though they may well be fantasies grasping at the specious plausibility, the pseudo-rationalism, provided by popular concepts of "Science" and "the Future."

It is a fact that we as a species have lived for most of our time on earth as animals among animals, as tribes in the wilderness, as farmers, villagers, and citizens in a closely known region of farmlands and forests. Beyond the exact and intricately detailed map of local knowledge, beyond the homelands, in the blank parts of the map, lived the others, the dangerous strangers, those not in the family, those not (yet) known. Even before they learn (if they are taught) about this small world of the long human past, most children seem to feel at home in it; and many keep an affinity for it, are drawn to it. They make maps of bits of it – islands, valleys among the mountains, dream-towns with wonderful names, dream-roads that do not lead to Rome – with blank spaces all around.

The monstrous homogenization of our world has now almost destroyed the map, any map, by making every place on it exactly like every other place, and leaving no blanks. No unknown lands. A hamburger joint and a coffee shop in every block, repeated forever. No Others; nothing unfamiliar. As in the Mandelbrot fractal set, the enormously large and the infinitesimally small are exactly the same, and the same leads always to the same again; there is no other; there is no escape, because there is nowhere else.

In reinventing the world of intense, unreproducible, local knowledge, seemingly by a denial or evasion of current reality, fantasists are perhaps trying to assert and explore a larger reality than we now allow ourselves. They are trying to restore the sense – to regain the knowledge – that there is somewhere else, anywhere else, where other people may live another kind of life.

The literature of imagination, even when tragic, is reassuring, not necessarily in the sense of offering nostalgic comfort, but because it offers a world large enough to contain alternatives and therefore offers hope.

The fractal world of endless repetition is appallingly fragile. There is no illusion, even, of safety in it; a human construct, it can be entirely destroyed at any moment by human agency. It is the world of the neutron bomb, the terrorist, and the next plague. It is Man studying Man alone. It is the reality trap. Is it any wonder that people want to look somewhere else? But there is no somewhere else, except in what is not human – and in our imagination.

If we want to get out of the Mandelbrot set world, that's where the roadmap is. Exact, intricate, inexplicable, and indispensable.

Collectors, Rhymesters, and Drummers

◉

2003

Some thoughts on beauty and on rhythm, written for my own entertainment early in the 1990s, and revised for this book.

COLLECTORS

People collect things. So do some birds and small mammals. The vizcacha, or bizcacha, is a little rodent that digs holes in Patagonia and the pampa and looks like a very round prairie dog with rabbity ears. Charles Darwin says:

> The bizcacha has one very singular habit: namely, dragging every hard object to the mouth of its burrow: around each group of holes many bones of cattle, stones, thistle-stalks, hard lumps of earth, dry dung, etc., are collected into an irregular heap ... I was credibly informed that a gentleman, when riding on a dark night, dropped his watch; he returned in the morning, and by searching the neighborhood of every bizcacha hole in the line of road, as he expected, he soon found it. This habit of picking up whatever may be lying on the ground anywhere near its habitation, must cost much trouble. For what purpose it is done, I am quite unable to form even the most remote conjecture: it cannot be for defence, because the rubbish is chiefly placed above the mouth of the burrow ... No doubt there must exist some good reason; but the inhabitants of the country are quite ignorant of it. The only fact which I know analogous to it is the habit of that extraordinary Australian bird the Calodera maculata, which makes an elegant vaulted passage of twigs for playing in, and which collects near the spot, land and sea-shells, bones, and the feathers of birds, especially bright colored ones. (*The Voyage of the Beagle*, chapter 7)

COLLECTORS, RHYMESTERS, AND DRUMMERS

Anything that left Charles Darwin unable to form even the most remote conjecture has got to be worth thinking about.

Pack rats and some magpies and crows are, I gather, more selective than bizcachas. They too take hard objects, but keep them in their nest, not outside the front door; and the objects are generally notable in being shiny, or shapely, or in some way what we would call pretty – like the gentleman's watch. But, like the bizcacha's clods and bits of dung, they are also notable in being absolutely useless to the collector.

And we have no idea what it is they see in them.

The male bowerbird's collection of playpretties evidently serves to attract the female bowerbird, but has anyone observed crows or magpies using their buttons, spoons, rings, and can-pulls to enhance their allure? It seems rather that they hide them where nobody else can see them. I don't believe anyone has seen a female pack rat being drawn to the male pack rat by the beauty of his collection (hey, honey, wanna come down and see my bottletops?).

My father, an anthropologist with interests that ranged from biology to aesthetics, kept a semipermanent conversation going – like the famous thirty-year-long poker game in Telluride – on the subject of what beauty is. Hapless visiting scholars would find themselves at our dinner table hotly discussing the nature of beauty. An aspect of the question of particular interest to anthropology is whether such concepts as beauty, or gender, are entirely constructed by each society, or whether we can identify an underlying paradigm, a universal agreement, throughout most or all societies, of what is man, what is woman, what is beautiful. Somewhere in the discussion, as it gathered weight, my father would get sneaky, cross species, and bring in the pack rat.

It is curious that evidence for what looks like an aesthetic sense – a desire for objects because they are perceived as desirable in themselves, a willingness to expend real energy acquiring something that has no practical end at all – seems to turn up only among us, some lowly little rodents, and some rowdy birds. One thing we three kinds of creature have in common is that we are nest builders, householders, therefore collectors. People, rats, and crows all spend a good deal of time gathering and arranging building materials, and bedding, and other furniture for our residences.

But there are many nesters in the animal kingdom, far closer to us genetically than birds or rodents. What about the great apes? Gorillas build a nest every night. Zoo orangs drape themselves charmingly with favorite bits of cloth or sacking. If we shared any collecting tastes with our closest relatives, it might indicate a "deep grammar" of beauty – a "deep aesthetic"? – in all us primates, or at least in the big fancy ones.

But alas I know no evidence of wild apes collecting or prizing objects because they seem to find them pretty. They examine objects of interest with interest, but that's not quite the same as stealing something because it's small and shiny and hiding it away as a treasure. Intelligence and the sense of beauty may overlap, but they aren't the same thing.

Chimpanzees have been taught or allowed to paint, but their motivation seems to be interactive rather than aesthetic: they appreciate color and evidently enjoy the act of whacking the paint on the canvas, but they don't initiate anything remotely like painting on their own in the wild; and they don't prize their own paintings. They don't hide them, hoard them. It appears that they're motivated to paint because people they like want them to paint. Their reward is less the painting than the approval of these people. But a crow or a pack rat will risk its life to steal something that offers no reward of any kind except its own shiny self. And it will hoard that stolen object of beauty, treasuring and rearranging it in its collection, as if it were as precious as an egg or an infant.

The interplay of the aesthetic with the erotic is complex. The peacock's tail is beautiful to us, sexy to the peahen. Beauty and sexual attractiveness overlap, coincide. They may be deeply related. I think they should not be confused.

We find the bowerbird's designs exquisite, the perfume of the rose and the dance of the heron wonderful; but what about such sexual attractors as the chimp's swollen anus, the billy goat's stink, the slime trail a slug leaves for another slug to find so that the two slugs can couple, dangling from a slime thread, on a rainy night? All these devices have the beauty of fitness, but to define beauty as fitness would be even more inadequate than most reductionist definitions.

Darwin was never reductionist. It is like him to say that the bowerbird makes its elegant passage "for playing in" – thus leaving the bowerbird room to play, to enjoy his architecture and his treasures and his dance in his own mysterious fashion. We know that the bower is attractive to female bowerbirds, that they are drawn to it, thus becoming sexually available to the male. What attracts the females to the bower is evidently its aesthetic qualities – its architecture, its orderliness, the brightness of the colors – because the stronger these qualities are, the greater the observable attraction. But we do not know why. Least of all, if the sole end and purpose of the bower is to attract female bowerbirds, do we know why *we* perceive it as beautiful. We may be the wrong sex, and are certainly the wrong species.

So: What is beauty?

Beauty is small, shapely, shiny things, like silver buttons, which you can carry home and keep in your nest/box.

That's certainly not a complete answer, but it's an answer I can accept completely — as far as it goes. It's a beginning.

And I think it interesting, puzzling, important that my appreciation of small, hard, shapely, shiny things is something I share with bizcachas, pack rats, crows, and magpies, of both sexes.

RHYMESTERS

Humpback whales sing. The males sing mostly in breeding season, which implies that their songs play a role in courtship. But both sexes sing; and each humpback population or nation has its distinctive song, shared by all citizens. A humpback song, which may last as much as half an hour, has a complex musical organization, structured by phrases (groups of notes that are the same or nearly the same in each repetition) and themes (groups of repeated similar phrases).

While the humpbacks are in northern waters they don't sing very much, and the song remains the same. When they regroup in the south, they all sing more, and the national anthem begins changing. Both the song and the changes in it may well serve to confirm community (like street slang, or any group jargon, or dialect). Every member of the community learns the current version, even when it is changing rapidly. After several years the whole tune has been radically altered. "We will sing to you a new song."

Writing in *Natural History*, in March 1991, Kary B. Payne asks two questions of the whales: How do you remember your song, and why do you change it? She suggests that rhyme may help in remembering. Whale songs with a complex set of themes include "rhymes" – phrases that end similarly – and these rhymes link one theme to the next. As for the second question, why they keep changing and transforming their communal song, she says, "Can we speculate about this, and about whales' use of rhymes, without thinking of human beings and wondering about the ancient roots in nature of even our aesthetic behavior?"

Payne's article reminded me irresistibly of the poet/linguist Dell Hymes's work on oral narratives in his book *In Vain I Tried to Tell You* and other books and articles. One such observation (summarized very crudely) is of the value of the repetitive locutions that mark divisions in Native American oral narratives. Such locutions often begin a sentence, and if translated appear as something like "So, then . . ." or "Now, next it happened . . ." or just "And." Often discarded as meaningless, as noise, by translators intent on getting the story and its "meaning," these locutions serve a purpose analogous to rhyme in English poetry: they signal the *line*, which, when there is no regular meter, is a fundamental rhythmic element; and they may also cue the larger, structural rhythmic units that shape the composition.

Following such cues, what was heard, translated, and presented as a "primitive," purely didactic, moralizing story, given what shape it has merely by the events it relates, now can be appreciated as subtly formal art, in which the form shapes the material, and in which the seemingly utilitarian narrative may actually be the means towards an essentially aesthetic end.

In oral performance, repetition does not serve only to help the performer remember the text. It is a, perhaps the, fundamental structuring element of the piece: whether it takes the form of the repetitive beat of meter, or the regular sound-echo of rhyme, or the use of refrain and other repeated structures, or the long and subtle rhythm of the lines in unmetered poetry and formal oral narrative. (To these latter are related the even longer and more elusive rhythms of written prose.)

All these uses of repetition do seem to be akin to the whales' rhymes.

As for why the whales sing, it is certainly significant that they sing most, or the males sing most, in mating season. But if you can say a song lasting half an hour performed by a hundred individuals in chorus is a mating call, then you can say a Beethoven symphony is a mating call.

Sometimes Freud sounds as if that's what he thought. If (as he said) the artist is motivated to make art by the desire for "fame, money, and the love of beautiful women," then indeed Beethoven wrote the Ninth because it was mating season. Beethoven was marking his territory.

There is plenty of sexuality in Beethoven's music, which as a woman one may sometimes be rather edgily aware of – thump, thump, thump,

BANG! – but testosterone goes only so far. The Ninth Symphony reaches way, way beyond it.

The male song sparrow sings when his little gonads swell as the light grows in the spring. He sings useful information, didactically and purposefully: I am a song sparrow, this is my territory, I rule this roost, my loud sweet voice indicates my youth and health and wonderful capacity to breed, come live with me and be my love, teediddle *wee* too, iddle iddle iddle! And we hear his song as very pretty. But for the crow in the next tree, "caw," said in several different tones, serves exactly the same function. Yet to us, "caw" has negative aesthetic value. "Caw" is ugly. The erotic is not the beautiful, nor vice versa. The beauty of birdsong is incidental to its sexual or informational function.

So why do songbirds go to such elaborate, formalized, repetitive trouble, learning and passing songs down from generation to generation as they do, when they could say "caw" and be done with it?

I propose an anti-utilitarian, nonreductionist, and of course incomplete answer. The bowerbird builds his bower to court his lady, but also, in Darwin's lovely phrase, "for playing in." The song sparrow sings information, but plays with it as he does so. The functional message becomes complicated with a lot of "useless noise" because the pleasure of it – the beauty of it, as we say – is the noise: the trouble taken, the elaboration and repetition, the play. The selfish gene may be using the individual to perpetuate itself, and the sparrow obeys; but, being an individual not a germ cell, he values individual experience, individual pleasure, and to duty adds delight. He plays.

After all, sex, mere sex, may or may not be pleasurable. There's no way to check with slugs or squids, and judging by the hangdog expression on the faces of dogs having sex, and the awful things cats say while having sex, and the experience of the male black widow spider, I should say that if sex is bliss sometimes it doesn't much look like it. But sex is inarguably our duty to our genes or our species. So maybe, to make the duty more enjoyable, you play with it. You fancy it up, you add bells and whistles, tails and bowers, pleasurable complications and formalities. And if these become an end in themselves, as pleasures are likely to do, you end up singing for the joy of singing. Any useful, dutifully sexual purpose of the song has become secondary.

We don't know why the great whales sing. We don't know why pack rats hoard bottlecaps. We do know that young children love to sing and to be sung to, and love to see and possess pretty, shiny things. Their pleasure in such things precedes sexual maturation and seems to be quite unconnected to courtship, sexual stimulation, or mating.

And while song may affirm and confirm community, stealing silver watches certainly does not. We cannot assume that beauty is in the service of either sexuality or solidarity.

I wonder if complication and uselessness are not key words in this meditation. The pack rat seems like a little museum curator, because she has complicated her nest-building instinct with "meaningless noise" – collecting perfectly useless objects for the pleasure of it. The humpback whales can be mentioned along with Beethoven because by adding "meaningless noise" to simple mating calls and statements of community, they elaborated them into symphonies.

My husband's Aunt Pearle employed a useful craft, crochet, with the useful purpose of making a bedspread. By making useless, highly rhythmic variations on plain crochet stitch, she complicated the whole act enormously, because she enjoyed doing so. After months of pleasurable work, she completed a beautiful thing: a "Spiderweb" coverlet, which she gave us. Although it does indeed cover a bed, it isn't, as we women say, for everyday. It is useful, but not simply useful. It is *much more than* useful. It was made to put on the bed when guests are coming, to give them the pleasure of seeing its complex elegance, and the compliment of being given more than is strictly necessary – a surplus, a treat. We take what's useful and play with it – for the beauty of it.

SILENT DRUMMERS

When people are talking about beauty in art they usually take their examples from music, the fine arts, dance, and poetry. They seldom mention prose.

When prose is what's being talked about, the word *beauty* is seldom used, or it's used as mathematicians use it, to mean the satisfying, elegant resolution of a problem: an intellectual beauty, having to do with ideas.

But words, whether in poetry or in prose, are as physical as paint and stone, as much a matter of voice and ear as music, as bodily as dancing.

I think it is a major error in criticism ever to ignore the words. Literally, the words: the sound of the words – the movement and pace of sentences

– the rhythmic structures that the words establish and are controlled by.

A pedagogy that relies on the "Cliff Notes" sort of thing travesties the study of literature. To reduce the aesthetic value of a narrative to the ideas it expresses, to its "meaning," is a drastic impoverishment. The map is not the landscape.

In poetry, the auditory and rhythmic reality of language has stayed alive all through the centuries of the Gutenberg Hegemony. Poetry has always been said or read aloud. Even in the inaudible depths of modernism, T. S. Eliot was persuaded to mumble into a microphone. And ever since Dylan Thomas wowed 'em in New York, poetry has reclaimed its proper nature as an audible art.

But prose narrative has been silent for centuries. Printing made it so.

Book-circuit readings by novelists and memoirists are popular now, and recorded readings of books have gone some way towards restoring aurality to prose; but it is still generally assumed, by writer and by critic, that prose is read in silence.

Reading is performance. The reader – the child under the blanket with a flashlight, the woman at the kitchen table, the man at the library desk – *performs* the work. The performance is silent. The readers hear the sounds of the words and the beat of the sentences only in their inner ear. Silent drummers on noiseless drums. An amazing performance in an amazing theater.

What is the rhythm the silent reader hears? What is the rhythm the prose writer follows?

While she was writing her last novel, *Pointz Hall,* which she refers to below as PH, and which when it was published became *Between the Acts,* Virginia Woolf wrote in her diary:

> It is the rhythm of a book that, by running in the head, winds one into a ball: and so jades one. The rhythm of PH (the last chapter) became so obsessive that I heard it, perhaps used it, in every sentence I spoke. By reading the notes for memoirs I broke this up. The rhythm of the notes is far freer and looser. Two days of writing in that rhythm has completely refreshed me. So I go back to PH tomorrow. This I think is rather profound. (Virginia Woolf, *Diary,* 17 November 1940)

Fourteen years before this diary notation made near the end of her life, Woolf wrote the passage I used to open this book and for its title, where she speaks of prose rhythm and the wave that "breaks and tumbles in the mind." In it she also, lightly, called her remarks on the rhythm of narrative "profound." In both these passing notes on the rhythm of narrative, she knew, I think, that she was onto something big. I only wish she'd gone on with it.

In a letter in 1926, Woolf said that what you start with, in writing a novel, "is a world. Then, when one has imagined this world, suddenly people come in." (Letter 1618) First comes the place, the situation, then the characters arrive with the plot ... But *telling* the story is a matter of getting the beat – of becoming the rhythm, as the dancer becomes the dance.

And reading is the same process, only far easier, not jading: because instead of having to discover the rhythm beat by beat, you can let yourself follow it, be taken over by it, you can let the dance dance you.

What is this rhythm Woolf talks about? Prose scrupulously avoids any clear regular beat or recurrent cadence. Are there, then, deeply syncopated patterns of stress? Or does the rhythm occur in and among the sentences – in the syntax, linkage, paragraphing? Is that why punctuation is so important to prose (whereas it often matters little in poetry, where the line replaces it)? Or is prose narrative rhythm established as well in even longer phrases and larger structures, in the occurrence of events and recurrence of themes in the story, the linkage and counterpoint of plot and chapter?

All these, I think. There are a whole lot of rhythms going in a well-written novel. Together, in their counterpoint and syncopation and union, they make the rhythm of that novel, which is unlike any other, as the rhythms of a human body in their interplay make up a rhythm unique to that body, that person.

Having made this vast, rash statement, I thought I should try to see if it worked. I felt I should be scientific. I should do an experiment.

It is not very rash to say that in a sentence by Jane Austen there is a balanced rhythm characteristic of all good eighteenth-century narrative prose, and also a beat, a timing, characteristic of Jane Austen's prose. Following what Woolf said about the rhythm of *Pointz Hall*, might one also find a delicate nuancing of the beat that is characteristic of *that particular* Jane Austen novel?

I took down my Complete Austen and, as in the *sortes Vergilianae* or a lazy consultation of the *I Ching*, I let the book open where it wanted. First in *Pride and Prejudice*, and copied out the first paragraph my eyes fell on. Then again in *Persuasion*.

From *Pride and Prejudice*:

More than once did Elizabeth in her ramble within the Park, unexpectedly meet Mr Darcy. – She felt all the perverseness of the mischance that should bring him where no one else was brought: and to prevent its ever happening again, took care to inform him at first, that it was a favourite haunt of hers. – How it could occur a second time therefore was very odd! – Yet it did, and even a third.

From *Persuasion*:

To hear them talking so much of Captain Wentworth, repeating his name so often, puzzling over past years, and at last ascertaining that it *might*, that it probably *would*, turn out to be the very same Captain Wentworth whom they recollected meeting, once or twice, after their coming back from Clifton: – a very fine young man: but they could not say whether it was seven or eight years ago, – was a new sort of trial to Anne's nerves. She found, however, that it was one to which she must enure herself.

Probably I'm fooling myself, but I was quite amazed at the result of this tiny test.

Pride and Prejudice is a brilliant comedy of youthful passions, while *Persuasion* is a quiet story about a misunderstanding that ruins a life and is set right only when it's almost too late. One book is April, you might say, and the other November.

Well, the four sentences from *Pride and Prejudice*, separated rather dramatically by a period and a dash in each case, with a colon breaking the longest one in two, are all quite short, with a highly varied, rising rhythm, a kind of dancing gait, like a well-bred young horse longing to break out into a gallop. All are entirely from young Elizabeth's point of view, in her own mental voice, which on this evidence is lively, ironical, and naive.

Though the paragraph from *Persuasion* is longer, it is in only two sentences; the long first one is full of hesitations and repetitions, marked by eight commas, two colons, and two dashes. Its abstract subject ("to hear them") is separated from its verb ("was") by several lines, all having to do with other people's thoughts and notions. The protagonist of the sentence, Anne, is mentioned only in the next-to-last word. The sentence that follows, wholly in her own mental voice, has a brief, strong, quiet cadence.

I do not offer this little analysis and comparison as proof that any paragraph from *Pride and Prejudice* would have a different rhythm from any sentence in *Persuasion*; but as I said, it surprised me – the rhythms were in fact so different, and each was so very characteristic of the mood of the book and the nature of the central character.

But of course I am already persuaded that Woolf was right, that every novel has its characteristic rhythm. And that if the writer hasn't listened for that rhythm and followed it, the sentences will be lame, the characters will be puppets, the story will be false. And that if the writer can hold to that rhythm, the book will have some beauty.

What the writer has to do is listen for that beat, hear it, keep to it, not let anything interfere with it. Then the reader will hear it too, and be carried by it.

A note on rhythms that I was aware of in writing two of my books:

Writing the fantasy novel *Tehanu*, I thought of the work as riding the dragon. In the first place, the story demanded that I be outdoors while writing it – which was lovely in Oregon in July, but inconvenient in November. Cold knees, wet notebook. And the story came not steadily, but in flights – durations of intense perception, sometimes tranquil and lyrical, sometimes frightening – which most often occurred while I was waking, early in the morning. There I would lie and ride the dragon. Then I had to get up, and go sit outdoors, and try to catch that flight in words. If I could hold to the rhythm of the dragon's flight, the very large, long wingbeat, then the story told itself, and the people breathed. When I lost the beat, I fell off, and had to wait around on the ground until the dragon picked me up again.

Waiting, of course, is a very large part of writing.

Writing "Hernes," a novella about ordinary people on the Oregon coast, involved a lot of waiting. Weeks, months. I was listening for voices, the voices of four different women, whose lives overlapped throughout most of the twentieth century. Some of them spoke from a long time ago, before I was born, and I was determined not to patronize the past, not to take the voices of the dead from them by making them generalized, glib, quaint. Each woman had to speak straight from her center, truthfully, even if neither she nor I knew the truth. And each voice must speak in the cadence characteristic of that person, her own voice, and also in a rhythm that included the rhythms of the other voices, since they must relate to one another and form some kind of whole, some true shape, a story.

I had no dragon to carry me. I felt diffident and often foolish, listening, as I walked on the beach or sat in a silent house, for these soft imagined voices, trying to hear them, to catch the beat, the rhythm, that makes the story true and the words beautiful.

I do think novels are beautiful. To me a novel can be as beautiful as any symphony, as beautiful as the sea. As complete, true, real, large, complicated, confusing, deep, troubling, soul-enlarging as the sea with its waves that break and tumble, its tides that rise and ebb.

About Feet

2003

Watching a ballroom dancing competition on television, I was fascinated by the shoes the women wore. They were dancing in strapped stiff shoes with extremely high heels. They danced hard, heel and toe, kicking and prancing, clapping their feet down hard and fast with great precision. The men wore flat-heeled shoes, conformed to the normal posture of the foot. One of them had flashing jewels on the outer side of each shoe. His partner's shoes were entirely covered with the flashing jewels, which must have made the leather quite rigid, and the heels were so high that her own heels were at least three inches above the balls of her feet, on which all her weight was driven powerfully again and again. Imagining my feet in those shoes, I cringed and winced, like the Little Mermaid walking on her knives.

The question has been asked before but I haven't yet got an answer that satisfies me: why do women cripple their feet while men don't?

It's not a very long step to China, where women broke the bones of their daughters' feet and strapped the toes under the ball of the foot to create a little aching useless ball of flesh, stinking of pus and exudations trapped in the bindings and folds of skin: the Lotus Foot, which was, we are told, sexually attractive to men, and so increased the marriageability and social value of the woman.

Such attraction is comprehensible to me as a perversity. A gendered perversity. How many women would be attracted by a man's feet deliberately deformed, dwarfed, and smelling of rot?

So there is the question again. Why? Why do we and why don't they?

Well, I wonder, did some Chinese women find other women's Lotus Feet sexually attractive?

Certainly both men and women may find cruelty and suffering erotic. One person hurts the other so that one or both can feel a sexual thrill that they wouldn't feel if neither was frightened or in pain. As in having a child's foot broken and bound into a rotting lump and then getting an erection from fondling the rotting lump. Sadism and masochism: a sexuality dependent on pain and cruelty.

To let sexual feeling be aroused by pain and cruelty may be better – we are often told it is better – than not having any sexual feeling at all. I'm not sure. For whom is it better?

I'd like to think Chinese women looked with pity, with terror, at one another's Lotus Feet, that they flinched and cringed when they smelled the smell of the bindings, that children burst into tears when they saw their mother's Lotus Feet. Girl children, boy children. But what do I know?

I can understand why a mother would "give" her daughter Lotus Feet, would break the bones and knot the bindings; it's not hard at all to understand, to imagine the circumstances that would lead a mother to make her daughter "marriageable," that is, saleable, acceptable to her society, by torturing and deforming her.

Love and compassion, deformed, act with immense cruelty. How often have Christians and Buddhists thus deformed a teaching of compassion?

And fashion is a great power, a great social force, to which men may be even more enslaved than the women who try to please them by obeying it. I have worn some really stupid shoes myself in the attempt to be desirable, the attempt to be conventional, the attempt to follow fashion.

But that another woman would desire her friend's Lotus Feet, find them erotic, can I imagine that? Yes, I can; but I learn nothing from it. The erotic is not the sum of our being. There is pity, there is terror.

I look at the ballroom dancer's rigid glittering shoes with dagger heels that will leave her lame at fifty, and find them troubling and fascinating. Her partner's flat shiny shoes are boring. His dancing may be thrilling, but his feet aren't. And male ballet dancers' feet certainly aren't attractive, bundled into those soft shoes like big hotdog buns. The uncomfortable fascination comes only when the women get up on their pointes with their whole body weight on the tips of their toes, or prance in their dagger heels, and suffer.

Of course this is a sexual fascination, eroticism explains everything . . . Well, does it?

Bare feet are what I find sexy – the supple, powerful arch, the complex curves and recurves of the dancer's naked foot. Male or female.

I don't find shod feet erotic. Or shoes, either. Not my fetish, thanks. It's the sense of what dancers' shoes are doing to the dancer's feet that

333

fascinates me. The fascination is not erotic, but it is physical. It is bodily, it is social, ethical. It is painful. It troubles me.

And I can't get rid of the trouble, because my society denies that it is troubling. My society says it's all right, nothing is wrong, women's feet are there to be tortured and deformed for the sake of fashion and convention, for the sake of eroticism, for the sake of marriageability, for the sake of money. And we all say yes, certainly, all right, that is all right. Only something in me, some little nerves down in my toes that got bent awry by the stupid shoes I wore when I was young, some muscles in my instep, some tendon in my heel, all those bits of my body say No no no no. It isn't all right. It's all wrong.

And because my own nerves and muscles and tendons respond, I can't look away from the dancer's dagger heels. They pierce me.

Our mind, denying our cruelty, is trapped in it. It is in our body that we know it, and so perhaps may see how there might be an end to it. An end to fascination, an end to obedience, a beginning of freedom. One step towards it. Barefoot?

The Writer and the Character

●

2003

Some ideas written down when I was planning a workshop in fiction, and worked up into a small essay for this book.

Whether they invent the people they write about or borrow them from people they know, fiction writers generally agree that once these people become characters in a story they have a life of their own, sometimes to the extent of escaping from the writer's control and doing and saying things quite unexpected to the author of their being.

My people, in the stories I write, are close to me and mysterious to me, like kinfolk or friends or enemies. They are in and on my mind. I made them up, I invented them, but I have to ponder their motives and try to understand their destinies. They take on their own reality, which is not my reality, and the more they do so, the less I can or wish to control what they do or say. While I'm composing, the characters are alive in my mind, and I owe them the respect due any living soul. They are not to be used, manipulated. They are not plastic toys, they are not megaphones.

But composition is a special condition. While writing, I may yield to my characters, trust them wholly to do and say what is right for the story. In planning the story and in revising it, I do better to keep some emotional distance from the characters, especially the ones I like best or loathe most. I need to look askance at them, inquire rather coldly into their motives, and take everything they say with a grain of salt – till I'm certain that they are really and genuinely speaking for themselves, and not for my damned ego.

If I'm using the people in my story principally to fulfill the needs of my self-image, my self-love or self-hate, my needs, my opinions, they can't be themselves and they can't tell the truth. The story, as a display of needs and opinions, may be effective as such, but the characters will not be characters; they will be puppets.

As a writer I must be conscious that *I am* my characters and that they *are not me*. I am them, and am responsible for them. But they're themselves; they have no responsibility for me, or my politics, or my morals, or my editor, or my income. They're embodiments of my experience and imagination, engaged in an imagined life that is not my life, though it may serve to illuminate it. I may feel passionately with a character who embodies my experience and emotions, but I must be wary of *confusing* myself with that character.

If I fuse or confuse a fictional person with myself, my judgment of the character becomes a self-judgment. Then justice is pretty near impossible, since I've made myself witness, defendant, prosecutor, judge, and jury, using the fiction to justify or condemn what that character does and says.

Self-knowledge takes a clear mind. Clarity can be earned by tough-mindedness and it can be earned by tender-mindedness, but it has to be earned. A writer has to learn to be transparent to the story. The ego is opaque. It fills the space of the story, blocking honesty, obscuring understanding, falsifying the language.

Fiction, like all art, takes place in a space that is the maker's loving difference from the thing made. Without that space there can be no consistent truthfulness and no true respect for the human beings the story is about.

Another way to come at this matter: In so far as the author's point of view exactly coincides with that of a character, the story isn't fiction. It's either a disguised memoir or a fiction-coated sermon.

I don't like the word *distancing*. If I say there should be a distance between author and character it sounds as if I'm after the "objectivity" pretended to by naive scientists and sophisticated minimalists. I'm not. I'm all for subjectivity, the artist's inalienable privilege. But there has to be a distance between the writer and the character.

The naive reader often does not take this distance into account. Inexperienced readers think writers write only from experience. They believe that the writer believes what the characters believe. The idea of the unreliable narrator takes some getting used to.

David Copperfield's experiences and emotions are very close indeed to those of Charles Dickens, but David Copperfield isn't Charles Dickens. However closely Dickens "identified with" his character, as we glibly and freudianly say, there was no confusion in Dickens's mind as to who was who. The distance between them, the difference of point of view, is crucial.

David fictionally lives what Charles factually experienced, and suffers what Charles suffered; but David doesn't know what Charles knows. He can't see his life from a distance, from a vantage point of time, thought, and feeling, as Charles can. Charles learned a great deal about himself, and so let us learn a great deal about ourselves, through *taking* David's point of view, but if he had *confused* his point of view with David's, he and we would have learned nothing. We'd never have got out of the blacking factory.

Another interesting example: *Huckleberry Finn*. What Mark Twain achieves, with great skill and at tremendous risk, all the way through the book, is an invisible but immense ironic distance between his point of view and Huck's. Huck tells the story. Every word of it is in his voice, from his point of view. Mark is silent. Mark's point of view, particularly as regards slavery and the character Jim, is never stated. It is discernible only in the *story itself* and the *characters* – Jim's character, above all. Jim is the only real adult in the book, a kind, warm, strong, patient man, with a delicate and powerful sense of morality. Huck might grow up into that kind of man, given a chance. But Huck at this point is an ignorant, prejudiced kid who doesn't know right from wrong (though once, when it really matters, he guesses right). In the tension between that kid's voice and Mark Twain's silence lies much of the power of the book. We have to understand – as soon as we're old enough to read this way – that what the book really says lies in that silence.

Tom Sawyer, on the other hand, is going to grow up to be at best a smart entrepreneur, at worst a shyster; his imagination has no ethical ballast at all. The last chapters of *Huckleberry Finn* are tedious and hateful whenever that manipulative, unfeeling imagination takes over, controlling Huck and Jim and the story.

Toni Morrison has shown that the jail Tom puts Jim into, the tortures he invents for him, and Huck's uncomfortable but helpless collusion, represent the betrayal of Emancipation during Reconstruction. Freed slaves did find themselves with no freedom at all, and whites accustomed to consider blacks as inferior inevitably colluded in that perpetuation of evil. Seen thus, the long, painful ending makes sense, and the book makes a moral whole. But it was a risk to take, both morally and aesthetically, and it succeeds only partially, perhaps because Mark Twain overidentified with Tom. He loved writing about smart-alecky, go-for-broke manipulators (not only Tom but the King and Duke), and so Huck, and Jim, and we the readers, all have to sit and watch them strut their second-rate stuff. Mark Twain kept his loving distance from Huck perfectly, never breaking the tender irony. But wanting Tom for that final bitter plot twist, he brought him in, indulged him, lost his distance from him – and the book lost its balance.

Though the author may pretend otherwise, the author's point of view is larger than the character's and includes knowledge the character lacks. This means that the character, existing only in the author's knowledge, may be known as we cannot ever know any actual person; and such insight may reveal insights and durable truths relevant to our own lives.

To fuse author and character – to limit the character's behavior to what the author approves of doing, or the character's opinions to the author's opinions, and so forth – is to lose that chance of revelation.

The author's tone may be cold or passionately concerned; it may be detached or judgmental; the difference of the author's point of view from the character's may be obvious or concealed; but the difference must exist. In the space provided by that difference, discovery, change, learning, action, tragedy, fulfillment take place – the story takes place.

Cheek by Jowl:
Animals in Children's Literature

●

2004

This is a reworking and expansion of the Arbuthnot Lecture of 2004, which I had the pleasure of giving at a meeting of the American Library Association. To keep the lecture from going on all night I had to strictly limit my discussion of the books it was about; and the talk as printed in Children & Libraries *could be only slightly longer. In this version, I have time and room to appreciate each book in more detail and dwell on how it may exemplify or define or defy conventions or traditions of the literature under discussion.*

I. Human: Continuum, Dichotomy

I am writing at a desk over which is pinned a painting from the Mexican state of Guerrero. It is in very bright colors of blue and red and orange and pink and green, and shows a village, drawn in the kind of perspective I understand – no vanishing point. There are lots of flowers the size of trees, or trees the size of flowers. This village is busy: a lady is selling pies, men are carrying sacks, a young man is proposing to a young woman, a gentleman is playing the guitar and a lady is snubbing him; people are gardening, grinding corn, cooking, coming out of church, going to school; a cowboy on a horse is herding some cows and a bull; there is a cock-fight going on; a donkey pulls a cart into town; there are rabbits, chickens, and dogs in the house yards, at least I think they're dogs although they're rather hard to tell from the goats – or are they sheep? – next door; horses carrying loads are trotting down a street past the drunk man lying on his back kicking his heels in the air; there are fish in the stream; and up on the bright green hill under the bright golden sun stand two fine stags, one bright white and one bright red.

There are almost as many animals in the painting as people, and all of them are mixed up together, Cheek by Jowl, except for the wild stags, who stand aloof.

If you took the animals out of the picture it wouldn't be a true picture of the village, any more than if you took the people out of it, for the villagers' lives and the animals' lives are totally entwined. Food, drink, transportation, sport: the animals provide all that to the villagers, and therefore the villagers provide for the animals; each is at the service of the other. Interdependent. A community. Cheek by Jowl. And this is the way most of us have lived during the several thousand years of human history, until just the last century or two.

The two stags, the only wild animals in the picture, stand outside the village, not part of it, yet very much part of the picture.

Before history, before agriculture, we lived for hundreds of thousands of years as hunter-gatherers. A hunter-gatherer village typically consisted of people only, with maybe some pets – dogs or baby animals. Such a human community was an element in a predominately nonhuman community: forest, jungle, grassland, or desert, with its stable population of plants and animals, its ecosystem. Each species, including ours, was part of this population, this interdependent system. Each species went about its business on a more or less equal footing – the tribal village, the ant hill, the antelope herd, the wolf pack. As hunter-gatherers, our relationship to the animals was not one of using, caretaking, ownership. We were among, not above. We were a link in the food chain. We hunted deer; lions hunted us. With the animals we didn't eat and that didn't eat us, our relationship was neutral or neighborly: some neighbors are tiresome, some are useful, or liked, or laughable, or admirable.

This neighborliness or fellowship, when positive, was often seen as a spiritual kinship. In that kinship the animals were generally seen as the elders, the forerunners, the ancestors of the humans. They are the people of the Dream Time. We belonged to them, the people of the Deer or the children of the Badger. In the immense, immensely unhuman world of the stone age, the little communities of our naked, soft-skinned species, beset by both realistic and imaginary fears, needed to know and assert their fellowship, their kinship with the powerful, ancient, unchanging animal world all around it. We knew we were different, but we knew also that we belonged.

This was still knowledge to some minds as late as Lucretius, who lived just before the Christian era. In his great poem *On the Nature of Things*,

Lucretius saw no barrier between man and the rest of creation; he saw the non-human world as the matrix in which mankind is formed and nourished, to which we belong as the garnet belongs to the rock in which it crystallized, and to which we will return as the sunlit wave returns into the sea.

But that is not how the tribes of the deserts of Judaea saw it. They saw the earth not as a nourishing matrix but as an antagonist, not a network of interdependence but a kingdom to be ruled. The animal was set entirely apart from both the human and the divine: and mankind was to dominate everything else by divine mandate.

The more we herded and bred animals for food and work, domesticating and dominating them, and the more we lived in cities among other humans only, the easier it was to separate ourselves from other species, to assert difference and dominance, denying kinship and its obligations. In Europe, the idea of community or neighborliness with animals became so rare that St Francis was considered strange and saintly merely for asserting it.

By the eighteenth century in Europe we'd invented "Nature." Nature comprises all the other species and all the places where they live and we don't. Idealized or demonized, Nature is humanity's Other. We stand outside it and above it.

In the forest, the village, or the farm, our interdependence with animals was unmistakable, community was a fact of life; we could despise our domestic animals, bully them, brutalize them, but we couldn't get on without them and we knew it, and so we knew them. But the cities kept growing, and the farms and the wilderness shrinking. After the Industrial Revolution, more and more people lived without any daily contact with other species. In the twentieth century, when the Ford replaced the horse, the last animal to be of essential use in cities, it became possible to live a whole life indifferent to and ignorant of other species. The animals needful to us for food and other requirements are elsewhere, in distant batteries and ranches and slaughterhouses; our dependence on them is so well hidden that we can literally not know it. It takes an informed, active, and uncomfortable imagination even to connect a living pig or hen with the plastic-wrapped slab, the batter-fried lumps. The disconnection is radical, the alienation complete. With the evidence of continuity gone, the sense of community is gone. We have made a world for ourselves alone, in which nothing matters, nothing has meaningful existence, but us. There are no Others.

In this radically impoverished, single-species world, pets have become intensely important links to the nonhuman world. Watching the many animal shows on TV gives us the illusion of being in touch with that world. Bird-watching, fishing, hunting – by now an entirely artificial hi-tech sport, but linked sentimentally to its origins: through all these we seek connection with nonhuman beings, or a reminder, however artificial, that there used to be a connection. That other people used to live here. That we had a family.

Our storytellers offer such a connection.

II. Three Literatures

On my wild and woolly ride through the millennia I pointed out three periods – tribal/prehistoric; farm, village, and city; and hi-tech industrial. Each has its literature of animals, about which I will go on generalizing in the most shameless fashion.

First: The oral literatures of hunter-gatherer peoples are largely myths, in which animals are protagonists, sometimes the only protagonists.

The general purpose of a myth is to tell us who we are – who we are as a people. Mythic narrative affirms our community and our responsibilities. Myths are told as teaching-stories to both children and adults.

For example, many Native American myths concern a First People, called by animal species names such as Coyote, Raven, Rabbit, whose behavior is both human and animal; among them are creators, tricksters, heroes, and villains; what they are doing, usually, is getting the world ready for the "people who are coming," that is, us, us humans, us Yurok or Lakota. Out of context, the meaning of stories from these great mythologies may be obscure, and so they get trivialized into just-so stories – how the woodpecker got his red head, and so on. In the same way, the Jataka tales of India are retold as mere amusements, with no hint of their connection to the ideas of dharma, reincarnation, and the Buddha-nature. But a child who "gets" the story may "get" a sense of those deep connections without even knowing it.

Second: The oral and written literatures of pre-industrial civilizations are, of course, about everything under the sun, but all those I know contain a powerful and permanent element of animal story, largely in the form of folktale, fairytale, and fable, again told both to children and to adults.

342

In these, the humans and animals mingle Cheek by Jowl just as in the Guerrero village.

Third: In postindustrial civilization, where animals are held to be irrelevant to adult concerns, animal story is mostly perceived as being for children. Modern children hear or read stories from the earlier eras, both animal myths and animal fables and tales, retold and illustrated for them, because animal stories are considered suitable for children, and because children want them, seek them, demand them. There is also a modern literature of animal stories, written sometimes for children, sometimes not, but the kids usually get hold of them. Although almost all non-satirical writing about animals is automatically dismissed by literary critics as trivial, authors continue to write animal stories. They are writing in response to a real and permanent demand. Kids want animal stories. Why?

Why do most children respond both to real animals and to stories about them, fascinated by and identifying with creatures that our dominant religions and ethics consider mere objects for human use – raw material for our food, subjects of scientific experiments to benefit us, amusing curiosities of the zoo and the TV nature program, pets to improve our psychological health?

It appears that we give animal stories to children and encourage them to be interested in animals because we see children as inferior, mentally "primitive," not yet fully human: so pets and zoos and animal stories are "natural" steps on the child's way up to adult, exclusive humanity – rungs on the ladder from mindless, helpless babyhood to the full glory of intellectual maturity and mastery. Ontology recapitulating phylogeny in terms of the Great Chain of Being.

But what is it the kid is after – the baby wild with excitement at the sight of a kitten, the six-year-old spelling out *Peter Rabbit*, the twelve-year-old weeping as she reads *Black Beauty*? What is it the child perceives that her whole culture denies?

By raiding my own bookshelves, asking friends, and beseeching the patient and omniscient librarians at Multnomah County Library, I found the books to read for this essay. I hope I included all the real classics. I added some books of less literary merit as exemplary of certain types of animal story. If I knew books were read by children I included them whether or not they were published for children. I had to leave out picture books, or I'd still be reading my way through the Ark. I sadly excluded fabulous or invented animals – dragons, winged cats, etc. – a related but different subject. I had an absolutely wonderful time reading – mostly rereading – all these books, some of them after sixty years. When I tried to organize them it was less fun, and when I tried to wring a thesis or a theory out of them it wasn't much fun at all. All I can offer is a taxonomy.

The organizing principle I settled on is a spectrum, running from jowl to cheek – from purely animal to purely human: from books in which animals independent of human beings are the central characters, through books where the focus is on the relationship of animal and human, to books in which animals exist principally as symbols of human qualities, behaviors, or desires.

As for the thesis, I hoped to find some answers to the question I just asked: why does the child so often, so reliably, turn for stories to the beings who do not speak? I did find some themes, some threads of guidance, but I can say now, I came out of the jungle of Critter Lit with a peacock's feather and a tiger's whisker and a white rabbit's top hat, but with no answers at all.

III. Animals Speaking: Big and Little Languages

A paradox: Nobody has ever heard an animal truly speak in human language, and yet in every literature in the world animals do speak in human language. It is so universal a convention that we hardly notice it.

> "Do you know," asked the Wart, thinking of the thrush, "why birds sing, or how? Is it a language?"
>
> "Of course it's a language [replies Archimedes, Merlyn's owl]. It isn't a big language like human speech, but it's large."
>
> "Gilbert White," said Merlyn, "remarks, or will remark, however you like to put it, that 'the language of birds is very ancient, and, like other ancient modes of speech, little is said, but much is intended . . .'"

> – T. H. White, *The Sword in the Stone*[1]

No other creature talks the way we do. Some birds can imitate our speech;

---

1 White, *The Sword in the Stone*, p. 229.

carefully trained apes can signify wants or interests by signing words in ASL; but evidently no animal except homo sap. has the capacity, activated in infancy, that allows us to learn the full range of human language. Syntax is the key here: not just single words, but combining words, recombining. By arriving with the leash in its mouth and wagging its tail, a dog can certainly signify urgency, willingness, and walking-out-at-opposite-ends-of-leash – accurately represented in language as "It's time to go for a walk!" But I don't know how a dog can say, "She and I might have gone for a walk if it hadn't started raining so hard," and I think probably a dog can't even think it. Not all, but a lot of thought depends on language. To think about what *happened*, to imagine what *didn't* happen – to tell a story or to tell a lie – to say "the thing that is not," as the Houyhnhnms put it – you need grammar, syntax, verb tenses and modes, you need what Archimedes the owl calls "a big language."

But there's a whole lot of stuff you can say or signify without any of that wonderful equipment. Such discourse is different from ours, less than ours, a little language – but why do we refuse to call it language? Merely to ensure that we know we're superior?

As Polynesia the parrot remarks to Dr. Dolittle, "Sometimes people annoy me dreadfully – such airs they put on – talking about 'the dumb animals.' Dumb! Huh!"

Some scientists use language literally as a shibboleth, to draw an uncrossable line between the human species and all other species.[2] Cartesian dualism, Christian exclusivism, and behaviorist theory all have contributed for two centuries to the doctrine that animals are machines, programmed like computers, without minds, thoughts, emotions, communicative ability, even sentience – nothing in common with human beings – despite the curious similarities of our bodies and brains and behavior.

This pseudo-scientific doctrine of absolute difference rises from and reinforces our human clannishness, our prejudice against anybody who doesn't do things the way we do. *Those people don't talk right, they use bad grammar, it's all bar-bar-bar, they're barbarians, they aren't really people. They're*

---

2 For a thoughtful and thoroughly research-supported discussion of animal cognition, see Donald R. Griffin, *Animal Minds*, University of Chicago Press, 1992. Griffin shows how a rational wariness among biologists, zoologists, etc., about interpreting animal behavior in human terms, taken to irrational theoretical extremes, stultified scientific investigation of animal behavior for half the twentieth century. It still lingers on as a mindless dread of anthropomorphizing the animal subject – even when the subject happens to be an anthropoid, patiently signing from its cage, in ASL, "Let me out."

animals. Only we are The People: only we talk real language. There goes the Bandar-Log in full cry!

God in the Bible says, "Let there be light." Only we humans, according to that bible, are in God's image. So only God and We can say "Let there be light."

But I ask you, what is a rooster at four in the morning saying?

Do we really have to believe that there is only one way to talk?

I submit that most children know better. Children have to be persuaded, convinced, that animals don't talk. They have to be informed that there is an impassable gulf between Man and Beast, and taught not to look across it. But so long as they disobey orders and go on looking, they know better. They know that we and creatures physiologically like us are mutually quite comprehensible.

The reason it seems so natural for animals to talk in all folklore and many kinds of literature is that animals do talk, and we do understand them.

We do it by translation, mostly. So do the animals. They don't translate our big language, or not much of it. What the dog probably hears is "Rover, bar-bar-bar walk blah?" but Rover was on his feet before he heard "walk," because he had translated our body language instantly and accurately as "We're going walking now!" And we translate the little languages of the animals – which are mostly "spoken" by body movements and positions and sounds that are meaningful but are not specifically symbolic words – into our big language, with all its symbolism and syntax and subjunctives. So we understand that Rover is saying, very much like T.S. Eliot, "Hurry up, please, it's time!" And the rooster says to the darkness at four a.m., "Let there be light!" And the cat as he walks by waving his tail remarks, "I am the Cat that walks by himself, and all places are alike to me."

As this last example shows, some people are better at translating than others, and we should listen to them if we really want to know what the beasts are saying.

IV. The Animal Biography

The quality of a translation matters both literarily and ethically. A mistranslation can be a mere error, or it can be deliberate, in which case it's misrepresentation – a wrong done to the speaker. Few of the authors I'm talking about deliberately mistranslate animal behavior and communication. But some authors are particularly careful, scientifically careful, about their translations, never ascribing any feeling or intention or thought to the animal except on evidence gained by patient and methodical observation. As in all good science, the purity and austerity of the method is beautiful in itself, and if the tale is well told the result is solidly satisfying.

In the strictest form of the animal biography, the creatures do not talk or think in the "big language." The author presents the animal's perceptions and feelings within its own frame of reference, avoiding interpretation in human terms as much as possible. This "method of least interpretation" sounds cold, but it by no means excludes emotional response, and may even enhance it. It can only come from long, close, real observation of animals, which is likely to lead to identification with them. The animal biographies I selected are all particularly warm and moving books.

My prime example of scrupulous honesty is the book *Red Heifer*, by Frank Dalby Davison. It is not a book many people know of now, but the Australians quite rightly gave it their Gold Medal for Best Australian Novel in 1934. It is a fine animal story, honest and compassionate, with a fiery, fearless, and tragic heroine. It is also – and this theme will turn up again – a lament for a lost wilderness.

The most unusual thing about the heroine is that she isn't a mighty wolf or faithful dog or splendid stallion, but a cow. We don't think of cattle as heroic; only one other book on my list has a bovine protagonist, and he's a born pacifist. The red heifer is heroic: a loner, a rebel, with temperament, and considerable brains, for a cow. Range-bred, she manages to escape the round-up and return to wildness – for a while. But the range is being fenced. And so her story is the story of the growth of human power and the ruin of wilderness.

The "omniscient" narrator tells us what both humans and animals are thinking or feeling, though he does it mostly by showing what they do. What the cows do is totally cow-like; they don't talk, the description of their social interaction is accurate and truthful, and interpretation or translation of their behavior into feeling or thought is done carefully and cautiously. For example: the red cow (never named) finds her calf wandering away instead of staying with the herd. The demands of motherhood bring out her intellect, and at last she concluded that it was time for her to take him with her. This decision had not been quickly arrived at. She had stood over him for an hour or more in vacillating doubt [. . .] She had waited, and watched him get up and wander around [. . .] There had been much subdued lowing and hoof-stamping and tail-switching – indicative of a spirit perturbed – the while she waited for the infallible voice of instinct to speak. It spoke in the affirmative, and so the calf was with her as the herd grazed their way up the ridge.[3]

This is finely observed and delicately told. Understanding, sympathy, and humor should not be taken for anthropomorphization, which I understand rather as an unwarranted co-optation or *colonialization* of the animal by the human.

Davison specifically mentions and dismisses one cherished anthropomorphic myth, reinforced by many horse stories: "She was the leader of the herd, for, in spite of romantic tale-tellers, it is the females among the wild horses and cattle bands who provide the leaders, the males being occupied with duels among themselves and with the propagation of the species."[4] Romance is in short supply here. When the red heifer has won her place in the herd by fighting another heifer, the bull comes "forward to tender the catholic hospitality of the male." The old bull later has to defend his place in the herd against a young bull, and the cows' lack of interest in the long, fierce battle is gently pragmatic: "They know that, whichever wins, there will be one remaining."[5]

The mildness, shyness, peacefulness of the wild herd in the wilderness has an Edenic quality; we are seeing the Golden Age just as it disappears into the mills and slaughterhouses of human greed. How often cattle have been used in paintings of "peace and plenty," rural serenity! But the book is ultimately a lament and a tragedy. At the end the red cow and her calf, last of the wild herd, fenced out from water, go back to their old grazing ground high in the hills, where they will die of thirst and hunger. Those final pages are full of a passionate sense of presence and absence, of yearning, of tragic loss.

Of all the books I read for this essay, perhaps *Bambi* has been most

---

3 Davison, *Red Heifer, a story of men and cattle*, p. 175.
4 Ibid, p. 174.
5 Ibid. p. 166.

misrepresented, sentimentalized, and degraded. If when you read the title *Bambi* you visualize cute skunks with hypertrophied eyes, you are suffering from disnitis. Please, go back and read Felix Salten's book. It is a book that tries to tell what it is to be a wild deer.

The emotions of the deer are fully interpreted in human terms, but their range is plausibly limited. Forest morality consists in doing what one should according to one's kind: each being follows its own being, as leaf, squirrel, or deer, male or female. All the creatures in the novel think in words and talk to one another; interspecies conversations are frequent and charming. But Man is not in the conversation. There is no human viewpoint in the book at all.

Man is seen – by the deer – as a creature of immense, incomprehensible power, about whom they tell stories, "full of blood and suffering," in which "they were unconsciously seeking for some way to propitiate this dark power, or some way to escape it."[6] The fawn Marena has a kind of Christian vision of Man – "They say that sometime He'll come to live with us and be as gentle as we are. He'll play with us then, and the whole forest will be happy, and we'll be friends with Him." But – "Old Nettla burst out laughing. 'Let Him stay where he is and leave us in peace,' she said."[7]

The beauty of the forest is celebrated in tender descriptions of small wild lives, bird songs, leaves – two autumn leaves have a philosophical discussion of life and death – but the brutality of forest life isn't prettified. The book doesn't hide the chanciness of wild lives, the certainty of mortality, death as a fact of life. A charming squirrel's death scene is painful ... but he "replaces himself" next spring. The most fearful episode in the book is a hunt; and the scene where Bambi is taken by the old stag, his mentor, to see a poacher who has been shot, is shocking and haunting.

Deer behavior is realistically presented. The fawns all play together; as they grow up they grow apart. Adult stag Bambi sees doe Faline in season, fights his young stag friends for her, and has his romance; but out of season "she no longer satisfied him completely."[8] Bambi's life is mostly solitary – "He did not much care to stay with the others." Stags are called "princes," elk stags "kings," but this is mere grandeur and majesty of language; nobody rules anybody. There is no hierarchy among the animals, there

---

6 Salten, *Bambi, a Life in the Woods*, p. 125.
7 Ibid. p. 126
8 Ibid. p. 216.

are no leaders of the herd; most of the year there is not even a herd. I am not sure which kind of deer these Austrian animals are, but the behavior Salten shows is perfectly true to the behavior of the European Red Deer as extensively studied and described by Clutton-Brock and others.

If you come to the book with memories of the Disney movie, this strict realism will surprise you. The movie, for all its brilliance and seductive power, betrays the book on every level. Where Salten works from observation of real animals, Disney uses cuteness, stereotype, and cliché. Where Salten portrays violence plainly and sternly, trying to show what the life of a wild animal is and the part human beings play in it, Disney uses fear and violence gloatingly, as dramatic ends in themselves, with no meaning beyond their immediate impact on the nerves and emotions. The awful hunt is replaced with a frightening but morally neutral forest fire. The positive ethic of the movie doesn't go beyond "animals are lovable so we (should) love them." The moral effect of the book, on the other hand, is complex and can't be stated in a few words. Rereading it at the age of seventy-three, I became aware of how its complexity had shaped and penetrated my thinking ever since I was ten or twelve. It is a beautiful book, truthful in its observations and its emotions, disturbing, austere, and subtle.

Many dog stories are animal biographies. Jack London and Albert Payson Terhune are truthful observers of dog behavior and try honestly to interpret it in its own terms, even though both have a very broad romantic streak, verging on the sentimental.

Jack London's *White Fang* is a serious and sympathetic picture of a splendid animal living a hard, chancy life, both in the wild and among men. The vigorous depiction of savage bleakness and brutality gives poignancy to the dog's eventual discovery of trust and love.

Dog behavior is accurately and knowledgeably drawn. We see the world both from human perspectives and from within White Fang's mind. His feelings and thoughts are quite within the range of ideas plausible to a dog. Like Davison and other biographers, London is careful to try to "feel out" how the animal might arrive at his judgments and not attribute improbable abstract notions to him. I am uncomfortable only with London's insistence that to White Fang all human beings are gods. Canines with a hierarchic social system offer their dominant individual pure submission; but is it worship? The spiritual implication seems to me improper, overweening.

Loyal obedience to the alpha of the pack is like a soldier's loyal obedience to command; it does not immediately equate to worship of a deity, though the human alpha male may like to think so.

Salten's deer, too, regard mankind with awe; and a hound in *Bambi*, like White Fang, sees his masters as gods. But to Salten, the wild vision is truer than the tamed one. Taking Bambi to see the dead poacher, the old stag says:

> "He isn't all-powerful as they say. Everything that lives and grows doesn't come from Him. He isn't above us. He's just the same as we are. He has the same fears, the same needs, and suffers in the same way. He can be killed like us, and then He lies helpless on the ground like all the rest of us, as you see Him now."
>
> There was a silence.
>
> "Do you understand me, Bambi?" asked the old stag.
>
> "I think so," Bambi said in a whisper.
>
> "Then speak," the old stag commanded.
>
> Bambi was inspired, and said trembling, "There is Another who is over us all, over us and over Him."
>
> "Now I can go," said the old stag.[9]

London's belief that a dog considers all men to be gods inevitably suggests the equation: as dog to man, so man to god. But, he doesn't follow this logic through. Salten does.

White Fang's "outlook was bleak and materialistic. The world as he saw it was a fierce and brutal world, a world without warmth."[10] Wolf morality is kill or be killed. London relishes these stern brutalities. The dog meets real human immorality in a cruel master, the "mad god," but is rescued by the "love-master," whose patient kindness finally releases his love and melts his fierceness into touching self-surrender.

In a poorly contrived episode late in the book, White Fang kills a vengeful would-be murderer, whom the author in a fit of anthropoid grandiloquence calls "a beast – a human beast, it is true, but nevertheless so terrible a beast that he can best be characterized as carnivorous."[11] This at the end of a story portraying the nobility and dignity of a carnivorous

---

9 Ibid. p. 286.
10 London, *White Fang*, p. 139.
11 Ibid. p. 266.

beast! What was Jack London thinking of? The word "speciesism" is an ugly and awkward one, but it does sum up a vast history of complacency and folly.

Albert Payson Terhune's *Lad: A Dog* is a classic of dog-worship. Like many dog stories, it's a love story. Its sentimentality is innocent, and redeemed from sickliness by lots of adventure. I recall that my brother and I at thirteen and ten snickered at the ever-recurring reference to Lad's "ridiculously tiny white paws," but we devoured this and all Terhune's other books. Lad's loyalty and virtue are rather overwhelming, but then, he is a dream dog, the dog any child would dream of having; and the theme of the animal as companion, rescuer, champion – the Animal Helper – is an old and powerful one. As witness its endless exploitation in the TV series *Lassie*.

In Sheila Burnford's *The Incredible Journey*, the two dogs and a cat who are trying to get back to their people aren't helpers – on the contrary, they need and find human help along their way. Domestic animals born and bred, they move through a wilderness that isn't their world, but which they cope with pretty well – particularly the cat. They don't idolize the human family they're trying to return to, or think of them as gods; they just want to get home. And that theme of home-seeking is another old and powerful one.

Though Burnford allows some large improbabilities (the cat's ability to keep up for hundreds of miles with two fair-sized dogs is a big one), the animals are realistically perceived and described. The dogs' feelings, thoughts, and desires are thoroughly doggy. Mostly we simply see what they do. The cat's mind is largely impenetrable; he just acts – and acts just like a cat – and then washes himself. Their friendship is practical, and so is their morality: while the three are on their own in the wilderness it's kill or be killed, eat or be eaten – no euphemisms about the cat's string of murders. Burnford's realism and sober reticence give her story the credibility it needs, and a strong emotional wallop, too. Straightforward, sympathetic, gently humorous, stoically acceptant, the single-minded story of home-seeking drives straight to its irresistibly moving conclusion.

In the same way, Eric Knight's *Lassie Come-Home* avoids sentimentality and earns its affective power by showing us even more plainly the utter, unreasoning directness of the dog's motives and acts. Neither Knight's book nor Burnford's is a full "animal biography," since they recount only one episode; but in their modesty, their willingness to lay aside human understanding to try to attain an understanding of how it is for the animal, they are true to the lives they tell.

The master of the realistic animal biography is surely Ernest Thompson Seton. Whether it's a bear or a cottontail rabbit or a crow, Seton brilliantly and carefully translates animal behavior to tell us a humanly comprehensible, compassionate, moving life-story.

His intention is frankly didactic. He wants his readers to know what the "lives of the hunted" are really like, and this information has a strong moral purpose. If we know what life is like for somebody else, if we have imaginatively enjoyed and suffered with them, we will be less dismissive, less fearful or scornful of them: we will be more open to love. Our spiritual community will have been enlarged.

I chose *The Biography of a Grizzly* for this essay because it is not an "easy" book. When I was a kid I could only read it when I was feeling brave, because it made me so sad and so angry – like the old, sad, angry bear, driven out of his kingdom, a grizzly Lear.

Wahb the grizzly never speaks, though when he puts a mark on a tree it is translated: "My bath. Keep away! (Signed) WAHB" – in "a language of mud, hair, and smell, that every mountain creature could read."[12] Wahb's thoughts and reactions seem to me excellent translation of animal behavior into human language, without abstraction or self-consciousness: "Revenge is sweet, Wahb felt, though he did not exactly say it, and he went for that red-nosed bear."[13]

This is another tale of the wilderness succumbing to humans, in part – but also resisting human invasion. Men are powerful and have guns, they kill his mother and her other cubs; but Wahb kills three of them when he is adult. He has unchallenged power in his territory, partly by keeping away from human territory, except Yellowstone, where he is safe. Only old age finally defeats him.

We'll be looking at some stories in which there is a tendency to what I call moral regression, where the author uses the animal protagonists as an excuse to regress to a lower ("bestial," "inhuman") moral level – most often, to justify injustice or to wallow in violence. There is some of this regressive gloating in Jack London. There is none in Seton. He does not

12 Seton, *The Biography of a Grizzly*, p. 117.
13 Ibid. p. 106.

use the bear's brutal strength to glorify brutality, but tries to show both the splendor and the terrible sadness of the "way of the wild."

Wahb suffers much in his youth and grows up "big strong and sullen," a solitary, dangerous bear, a rogue male. The book's ethics do not privilege either strength or species: "It was all fair. The man had invaded the Bear's country, had tried to take the Bear's life, and had lost his own." Miners, who are compared to bears themselves, share Wahb's code: "Let him alone and he won't bother you," one says, and indeed the bear doesn't hurt them. He is restrained by "something that in Bear and Man is wiser than his wisdom, and that points the way at every doubtful fork in the dim and winding trail."[14]

Growing old, Wahb loses his self-assurance and lets a younger bear drive him away. He finds his way to a valley of poisonous gases which he has always avoided before. Though this may seem melodramatic or romantic, animals do sometimes choose to die, and Wahb is not shown as clearly understanding what he is doing; he is being guided again by "something wiser than his wisdom." The ending, with the Angel of the Wild Things beckoning Wahb to enter into peace and rest, quietly implies a spirituality of nature not at all dependent on human understanding.

Seton does dramatize his animal biographies; he does anthropomorphize his animal heroes, sometimes to a considerable extent; but I believe his fascination with and knowledge of and respect for the separate, mysterious being of the animal, his marvelous gift of poetic, accurate detail, and his sense of tragedy make him one of the most durably valuable writers a child could be given to read.

With Dhan Mukerji's *Gay-Neck* we move from interpretation of behavior, given in the voice of the boy who owns and trains the pigeon, to autobiographical narration by the bird himself. Early in the book there are passages like this: "Then he cooed, which meant, 'Why do you send me away?' She, the mother, just pecked him the more, meaning, 'Please go. The business on hand is very serious.'"[15] The owner/narrator legitimately translates his close observation into speech expressing emotions assumed to be shared by humans and animals. But later, our human narrator says the bird must tell his own story: "It is not hard for us to understand him

---

14 Ibid. p. 91.
15 Mukerji, *Gay-Neck: the story of a pigeon*, p. 6.

if we use the grammar of fancy and the dictionary of imagination." And Gay-Neck begins, most charmingly – he is, after all, an Oriental pigeon – "O, Master of many tongues, O wizard of all languages human and animal, listen to my tale . . ."[16]

Certainly Gay-Neck is the best one to tell us what it was like to carry messages, on the delicate wings of a bird, over the battlefields of the First World War. The distress, fear, and above all the incomprehension of his narrative are touching and credible: how is a carrier-pigeon to understand mass violence on the human scale? The human species is perceived as owning the power in this world, but not as deserving it. Humans and animals share the world and have responsibilities towards it and towards one another.

At the end of the war, the pigeon and his human companion both come home shell-shocked, traumatized, sick from what they have seen. They find healing in a lamasery. The man learns to pray, "Lead me from the unreal to the real, from darkness into light." The bird, in his own morning worship, flies to salute the rising sun. The book is admirable in its tender but unsentimental vision of man and bird as suffering creatures, equal souls.

The founding classic of the animal autobiography, surely, is Anna Sewell's *Black Beauty*. It is of course a teaching, preaching story, meant to make us walk in horseshoes and feel what horses undergo at our hands. It is also a fine novel with vivid characters and a strong sense of friendship and of delight. It is thoroughly "Victorian" in its acceptance of social and species hierarchy, but never confuses class with virtue: Lady W. and the cab-owner Skinner are as cruel as the cab-driver Jerry and the hostler Joe are kind. Beauty himself is no rebel, but neither is he a snob. Anybody who has ever known a good horse will recognize the quality of his patience and his self-respect.

Beauty tells his story in a strong, clean, direct prose, just what a well-brought-up horse ought to speak; his vocabulary and power of comparison go far beyond anything a horse could think, of course, but his knowledge and observations are singularly convincing. Anna Sewell excels in "speaking for animals" – translating sensation and emotion into words – partly, I think, because the words are direct and yet restrained. It

16 Ibid. p. 69.

is curious how a story so full of pain, fear, injustice, and cruelty can leave one with such a sense of justice and even of nobility; it has a strength and dignity that no other horse story quite matches. I hope it will continue to have many tears wept on its pages. They are the best sort of tears.

Having taken so much exception to the Disney movie of *Bambi*, it is a pleasure to recommend and praise the 1994 film by Caroline Thompson of *Black Beauty*, a touching, light-handed movie, true to the book, and full of lovely, lyrical photography of horses enjoying being horses.

As an example of the continuing tradition of animal autobiography in the cautionary mode, I chose Marion Ashmore's charming dog story, *Lost, Stolen, or Strayed*, now being read by the third generation in my family (*Black Beauty* is in the fourth). Its drama and warning involve dog thieves. The convention in these autobiographies, as in many animal stories, is that the animal can tell his tale to us and understand what human beings say, but does not speak to human beings, only to other animals. Woppets the terrier strains this convention a bit, being improbably afraid of being sent to France because they don't speak English there. But in general he is simply a nice little dog, acting doggy, his psychology interpreted in human terms but with no improbable thoughts or feelings.

As an example of the continuation of the Seton tradition, the animal telling you its life-story so you know what its life is like, I chose Frank Lindermann's *Stumpy*. It is an odd book. Lindermann so faithfully limits Stumpy's voice to the forgetful, happy-go-lucky experience of a small, fast-moving prey animal, that our hero comes off a bit unsympathetic, losing a wife here, a friend there, no big deal ... But then, should a chipmunk have to act out a tragedy? Life in the moment is all there is for Stumpy – curious, interested, distractable, rejecting grief, forgetting fear.

To this small, wild creature, nobody owns the world; who has the power is not really an issue, as it is in so many animal stories. Everybody, including the few humans Stumpy sees, is part of the world; no species has special status. He calls members of other species "pine-squirrel person" or "toad person," even "echo-person," the one who repeats one's call. This is a Native American usage reflecting an acceptance of a nonhierarchical view of animals as persons and persons as animals, everybody on an equal footing in a wild world.

But Stumpy can be a bit dry about us. After he and a friend see an eagle kill a coot they talk about it:

"Everybody has enemies," I told him, feeling a little sorry for the coot.

"Maybe," he said. "But tell me, who is the enemy of the eagle, Stumpy?"

"Man," I said.

"And who is man's enemy?" he asked, as though he had me cornered.

"Man," I said again. And then we both laughed.[17]

A recent, unusual, and delightful example of animal autobiography is Caroline Alexander's *Mrs. Chippy's Last Expedition*, a journal of Shackleton's third voyage to the Antarctic, related by the ship-carpenter's cat. It is a true story, illustrated by photographs. Caroline Alexander knows everything that can be known about those men on that awful trip, and she also writes with aplomb and authenticity in the voice of a tomcat. As the cat sees it, he is in full control of the expedition from beginning to end. It is an extremely funny book, and the hero's serenity in desperate situations is very fine. If I were reading it aloud to a child, though, I might have trouble at the very end. They always say Shackleton never lost a man, but they don't talk about the animals.

V. The Animal Novel

In animal autobiographies, the animals relate their story to us, a pure literary convention. They may understand human speech or they may not, but they don't talk to or with humans, only to other animals. This same separation of human and animal communication holds in my next category of animal-centered books, which I call the animal novel.

We are still on the Jowl side of my spectrum. Animals are the protagonists. Human beings may run the world, but they are secondary characters in the story.

Though animal behavior in these books may be species-characteristic and may have a great deal of observation-based realism, they differ from the biographies in containing a fantasy element: what the animals do is a mixture of behavior proper to their species and human behavior. Black

---

17 Lindermann, *Stumpy*, p. 130.

Beauty and Wahb do only what a horse or a bear would do. Animal novel heroes act from reasoned motives or for ends that (as far as we know) are human motives and aims not shared by any other species. And some of them use tools, wear clothes, drive cars, have wars – owning technologies and acting out patterns of behavior that are strictly human.

There is no explanation, no justification of this blending of animal and human in any of the books that do it. They all simply assume it will be accepted, and it is. Could there be stronger evidence of the felt community of human and animal than such an unapologetic and successful assertion of it? Beatrix Potter was a superb naturalist; her Peter Rabbit is absolutely a rabbit; but he also wears clothes and drinks tea – just as Coyote, in the legends, may carry a bow or make fire.

My first example of this mode is Rudyard Kipling's story "The White Seal." One may forget that less than half the stories in Kipling's *Jungle Books* are about Mowgli; the others are very various, though they all involve animals in one way or another. Every one of them would be well worth discussing; indeed, Kipling, so often dismissed as a blustering imperialist boasting of the White Man's burden, deserves to be recognized as a singularly sympathetic and subtle writer about animals, women, children, and other inferior beings. It was hard to bypass "Rikki-Tikki-Tavi" and several others, but I couldn't talk about all the stories, and so chose "The White Seal."

It begins like a biography, with grand realistic descriptions of a fur seal growing up, and seal colonies, and mating battles; but then it takes off in a new direction, when Kotik realizes – as no seal could in fact realize – that his people are objects of genocide, and that he is called to seek a haven for them where men cannot find and kill them. His odyssey in finding that place makes a great wish-fulfillment story, full of poetry and adventure, that has grown less plausible but even more poignant in the hundred and ten years since it was written.

Two modern classics of the animal novel are E.B. White's *Charlotte's Web* and Robert C. O'Brien's *Mrs. Frisby and the Rats of Nimh*. In both, the animals think and speak like human beings and act out dramas that are a mixture of animal and human problems and solutions.

Charlotte's Web begins with a human point of view, the child Fern, but the point of view shifts quite soon to the animals. They talk, they act; Fern listens. She understands animal language, though she never speaks it. And here we strike a theme that runs deep in animal stories: the child is in touch with animals, but only while she is a child. Only the virgin can touch the unicorn. As Mowgli comes into his manhood, he must leave the jungle. Once Henry Fussy becomes important to Fern, she doesn't listen to the animals any more – she can't hear them.

One reason kids like E.B. White's book, I think, is that it's about justice and injustice. Is it fair for a farmer to kill a runt pig? Has a spider a right to kill flies? These questions are discussed openly and firmly. And it is a mutual aid story, beast helping beast, a fine variation on the folk-tale theme of the Animal Helper. And finally it is a tale of the golden age, the peaceable kingdom, the old rural American dream, the farm children dream of, the farm we wish they could live on . . .

Mrs. Frisby and the Rats of Nimh is totally animal-centered; there are no human characters; but though humans are offstage, they are powerful and dangerous – they control the world. The scientists of NIMH have altered the rats' very nature, enhancing their longevity and intelligence.

The only tame animal in the story, the farm cat, appears as an enemy: it's on the human side, not the animal side. Yet it never speaks, and it acts just like a cat, while the so-called "wild" mice wear clothes, use furniture, have both speech and reason. There are other anomalies of this kind. The rats' intelligence has been artificially enhanced in the laboratory, while the mouse Mrs. Frisby hasn't been "enhanced" like the rats, yet she seems quite as intelligent as they; her "enhanced" husband even taught her to read, though not as well as her children can. There is a certain incoherence here.

Some people are impatient with such quibbles with fantasy – "Well, none of it's real, what does it matter that it's inconsistent?" It matters. The farther a story departs from accepted reality, the more it relies on its own inner consistency. By giving us a "scientific" explanation of why the rats act like humans but no explanation of why the mice also act like humans, O'Brien puts our willing suspension of disbelief into a quandary. That most of us read the book at least the first time without thinking about the inconsistency shows, perhaps, how willing we are to believe and accept our fellow-feeling with these morally troubled creatures.

For *Mrs. Frisby*, too, is about justice. First, the unstated but fundamental question of the right of human beings to imprison and experiment on animals: the rats and mice don't discuss this, but in escaping from the laboratory they clearly state their right to life, liberty, and the pursuit of happiness. Then comes the poignant question, "Where does a group of civilized rats fit in?" They used to live by stealing from humans, but now, as creatures with human intelligence, they see such dependence as ethically wrong, degrading. They must create an independent, new civilization of their own. The unnaturalness of their situation, the risks they run, the fragility of their utopian vision, are vividly described.

The book is again a tale of mutual aid among animals. The sense of the need to collaborate, even to the point of self-sacrifice, is strong. But humans are excluded from the collaboration; they are the enemy, they are what the animals have to help each other against. And though the book has a satisfyingly happy finale, I'm not sure that I have much confidence that the rats' utopia in the hidden valley can endure. There's an awful lot stacked against them. That unstated darkness makes the book all the deeper in the end.

In Brian Jacques' *Redwall* there are no human characters at all. The chief protagonists are mice. A few words, such as "paw" for hand, are used to remind us that the mice have animal bodies, but since they wear clothes, farm with tools, live in a great abbey building, write books, and so on, it is hard to keep their animal bodies in view. These are civilized creatures, leading a human not an animal existence. Readers with literal minds and a craving for consistency may be worried by some aspects of this arrangement. For example, the mice of Redwall Abbey drink goat's milk and make goat's milk cheese, but there seem to be no goats at the Abbey; and even if there were, I for one would like to be told explicitly just how a mouse could milk a goat.

A reader might have a more general question: why are they called mice when they don't do anything mice do, but act just like a lot of bloody-minded feudal humans? The popularity of the Redwall books shows that this question is overly rational. Given the mouse stereotype of small-harmless-cute, simply the fact of calling them mice evidently makes them less daunting to a child reader than bloody-minded feudal humans. And *Redwall* is a fantasy. Brian Jacques makes no pretense of realism. I'm willing to say that my inability to believe his mice are mice is my own problem.

My ethical problem with the book is perhaps more legitimate. In *Redwall*, goodness and badness, admirable and base behavior, are species-specific. Mice are good, rats are bad. A badger, hedgehogs, squirrels, otters, moles, and a hare are on the mouse side – all good; weasels, stoats, and ferrets are on the rats' side – all despicable. A poison adder is, predictably, evil. A few animals are more complex: foxes play both ends against the middle, shrews are independent, an owl threatening but foolish. It's surprising to find a cat helping the hero mouse, but then, he's an aristocratic cat, and the mice are all aristocrats – "gennelbeasts." For the rigid moral hierarchy by species is also a social hierarchy: rats are rabble, moles and such are other common folk who "tug their snouts respectfully" when addressing the noble mice. The good mice and the good badger speak standard English and can read and write; moles and other good but low-class types speak dialect.

The most villainous of the rats organizes an army, and the mice, though natively peaceable, go to war and defeat this threat to their feudal well-being. This is a plot that may well strike a reader of *The Wind in the Willows* as familiar. Indeed, some of the implausibilities concerning size and mechanical ability may seem familiar for the same reason. But *Redwall* was written in 1996, not 1908. Kenneth Grahame lived within the kind of settled hierarchical society, such a favorable environment for the upper classes, so kind and safe for them if for no one else, that Jacques nostalgically evokes. It would be historically unrealistic to ask of Grahame the perspective on the justice of that society that one can fairly ask of any late-twentieth century writer. To offer children a vision of a kind, safe world is a good thing to do; they need such visions. But I'd like the book better if a child reading it found any acknowledgment that status isn't virtue and that being born an upper-class mouse or a low-class rat is undeserved, blind, good or bad luck. I have to admit that all the way through, I was rooting for the rats. But I read the book first as an adult; as a child I'd probably have happily accepted the injustice in order to get the reassurance.

I have a similar but more serious issue with Richard Adams' *Watership Down*. Rabbits are the protagonists of this strong, well-written novel. Power in the rabbits' world belongs above all to humans and their terrible machines and weapons. Weasels, dogs, and foxes are dangers, not superior beings; the rabbits count on escaping and outwitting such enemies; and perhaps even the humans may be outwitted and evaded. This seems perfectly realistic, sound rabbit psychology and sets the scene for a drama of tragedy and hope. The rabbits speak "Lapine" and can communicate with other animals; they have poetry and a kind of religion, but they don't wear clothes, build houses, etc. – they are wild rabbits, living like wild rabbits. Or are they?

The author cites R.M. Lockley's authoritative observational study *The*

Private Life of the Rabbit several times and is insistent upon Lockley as the source of some of the more extraordinary facts of the story (such as reabsorption of fetuses by stressed doe rabbits). He departs radically from Lockley and actual rabbit social behavior, however, in giving the warrens an aggressive hierarchic structure with one Chief Rabbit and a militaristic band of henchmen or soldiers, the Owsla – all male. Doe rabbits, in the book, are mindless breeding slaves. Their only function is to dig holes, provide sex, bear litters, and raise the kittens. The buck rabbits do all the thinking, planning, and acting and are in unquestioned control of the females at all times. The does are so far beneath notice, in fact, that a band of bucks fleeing the home warren to establish a new one doesn't even think to bring any does along; the guys go on for two hundred pages before it dawns on them that it may be hard to establish a new warren without females. So, in good militaristic fashion, they go and rape the Sabines: they carry off females from another warren. That the females might have any voice in the matter is not even considered.

The existence of a "Chief Rabbit" would be authorized by Lockley's term "king" for the dominant male of a group, if Adams did not ignore his equivalent term for the dominant female, the "queen." (The king rabbit wins the most battles and has access to the most females – but not free access: the queen chooses her mate and her dwelling place.) Adams shows wild rabbit society as a militaristic male hierarchy, in the teeth of Lockley's unequivocal statement that "The doe is the centre of the rabbit community, a matriarchy," and his descriptions of a wild rabbit warren as an "expanded population scattered around the queen or matriarch at the heart of the community."

It is quite extraordinary to cite a book as the source of one's information and then systematically misrepresent that information. Adams' excuse might be that Lockley himself, while stating clearly that the female is the center of rabbit society and the founder of both warren and family, prefers to talk about male behavior, which is far more easily observable, and spends much of the book describing individual males. And Lockley makes sweeping generalizations, explicitly including humans, to the effect that all females always want to stay home and tend babies – despite his own statement: "It is always the doe who initiates the new colony."

So some of Adams' sexism is ascribable to Lockley. But the militarism that Adams represents as true to wild rabbit behavior is completely his own invention. When the hero band meets their enemy, the Efrafans, the latter are evidently meant to be a perversion of wild freedom along human lines – but in fact Efrafa is merely an intensification of the oppressive regime of the other warrens. Seeing only active adult males as worthy of interest, the author presents the very limited liberality of Hazel's band as perfect democracy, righteously opposed to the Nazi rigidity of Efrafa. I see both as unrighteous, unrabbitlike, and inhuman.

> The kind of ideas that have become natural to many male human beings in thinking of females – ideas of protection, fidelity, romantic love and so on – are, of course, unknown to rabbits, although rabbits certainly do form exclusive attachments much more frequently than most people realise. However, they are not romantic and it came naturally to Hazel and Holly to consider the two Nuthanger does simply as breeding stock for the warren. This was what they had risked their lives for.[18*]

In this passage the author offers a false alternative: a "romantic" ideal of the male protecting and lovingly faithful to the female, or a "natural" use by males of females as owned objects, breeding stock – thus justifying rape. No other possibility is imagined, such as a relationship of equality, or a relationship that the female initiates or controls some aspects of. Yet to read Lockley is to learn that doe rabbits take the more active and responsible role in *all* situations except male battles for dominance, and that dominant doe rabbits accept or reject male suitors as they please.

I might try to swallow the egregious sexism of the book in order to appreciate its virtues; but I won't, because Adams cheated. He wanted to write a fantasy of male superiority – all right, some people like that sort of thing. But he misrepresented Lockley's actual description of rabbit behaviors. That is cheating. It was clever cheating, too, because in 1972 blatant male supremacism was becoming less acceptable, and Adams got away with it by passing it off as animal behavior. People could say, "Oh well, it's just rabbits, after all." Only it isn't rabbits at all. Rabbits do not behave that way. A book that falsifies animal behavior as a mask for the indulgence of fantasies of morally regressive human behavior is not, to my mind, a book to give any child, or any adult either.

A recent novel, *Fire Bringer*, by David Clement-Davies, has some troubling similarities to *Watership Down*. Like Adams, Clement-Davies had

18 Adams, *Watership Down*, p. 256.

unusually careful scientific observation in highly readable form to rely on: F.F. Darling's and T.H. Clutton-Brock's famous studies of Scottish red deer society. These authoritative studies show that the "harems" controlled by stags are a brief, unstable phenomenon of rutting season; for eleven months of the year stags and hinds don't mingle at all. The only lasting associations between individuals are hinds and their dependent fawns; and the groups, male or female, have no leaders. But Clement-Davies simply flouts their careful descriptions of gender relations; he shows stags leading and dominating females all year long and maintaining a rigid militaristic hierarchy, which degenerates, under a megalomaniac leader, into a cruel, coercive social order along fascist lines, like Adams' Efrafa.

The intrigues and plots and war-making, the deliberate cruelty and torture, the massiveness of the final battle – "The whole plain became a mass of fighting deer" – in all this there is a fundamental disrespect for the very nature, the *deerness* of deer – a willful wrong-headedness. It is a pity, because there are elements in the book of an interesting vision of a religion common to human and animal: Herne, who to the deer is the Lord of the Deer, to the Scottish crofters is Herne the Hunter, the Horned Man – the man-beast figure that goes right back to Old Stone Age cave paintings. But the development of these ideas is confused and strained. A book that brought out a spiritual element in deer existence, while respecting and staying true to the reality of deer gender and society, would be more satisfying. Of course, we have a book that does just that, and I am happy to name it again: it's called *Bambi*.

As I have suggested, Kenneth Grahame may well be the unwitting founder of the lineage of several of the books I've talked about. In *The Wind in the Willows*, as in *Redwall*, virtue is a matter of species: weasels, stoats, ferrets are all bad by nature, villainously vulgar. The book reflects the ruthlessly classed society of England of 1908, along with the widespread human negativity towards certain species. Even given the benefit of historical relativism, this moral genotyping can make the reader a bit queasy. Grahame does assign a fortune and a fine estate to a toad; but Toad is not a noble soul . . . He is, however, a great character. This modest, funny, sunny book for children rises above the limitations of the society it was written in and for, into the universality of literature.

The Wind in the Willows takes huge risks. *Redwall*'s human-acting mice may seem more plausible because there aren't any people in their world. Grahame's animals dress like people, talk like people, go mad over motor-cars like people – and yet there are human beings in the story right along with them. And – here's where the fantasy is wonderfully audacious – the human beings are in the animals' world, not the other way round. When Toad is jailed as a car-thief, the jailer's daughter helps him escape, disguised as her aunt the washerwoman. Shepard's illustration of this is marvelous – is the aunt toad-size or is the toad aunt-size? It does not matter. We are in a world where the human and the animal interact as equals – the world of myth and folktale, miraculously recaptured in this sunlit, nostalgic romance.

It's no accident that the god we meet here is Pan. Like Herne, Pan is very, very old: both man and beast, both forest creature and herdsman, he gives his name to the blind terror of the wild places, yet he cares for the little ones who wander off and are lost. I don't know whether the Pan chapter of *The Wind in the Willows* or the chapter where Mole finds his old home is the more beautiful, but I know that both of them can strike deep chords of feeling, thrilling literary revelations to a child, permanent treasures to an adult.

VI. Jowl Meets Cheek

Now I come to the kind of book that might be seen as the typical animal story – tales of the relationship between human and animal. A boy and a dog. A girl and a horse.

Many of the books I call animal biographies could be put under this heading too: White Fang, Gay-Neck, Lad, Black Beauty, all have strong emotional bonds with their human owners or others. And in almost all the animal biographies and novels, the world animals live in is controlled by or tremendously influenced by human beings. But still, in those books the animal is at the center of the story.

With Will James's *Smoky* we're at a crossover point – *Smoky* is a fine biography of a horse, but it's also a fine portrait of a cowboy, and of the relationship of the cowboy and the horse, and of life on the range. Smoky and his cowboy Clint are at the same time stereotypes and vivid individuals – as the characters in a good Western generally are.

Smoky thinks and "figgers" a good deal, but all in horse terms; the conflation of thought and feeling is strong, easy, and convincing. The book gives a fascinating, knowledgeable picture of the work cowponies and their riders did (and still do), as well as being a morality tale, like *Black Beauty*, about how horses are treated, the good and the bad they meet with at the hands of men. Unfortunately James was less fair-minded toward men than toward horses: the men who mistreat Smoky are mostly Mexicans or "breeds." It's a shame that racial prejudice stains what is otherwise essentially a story about love and trust, and a lovable story.

In these books the central human-animal relationship is positive, involving the growth of trust, dependence, companionship. In some of them it is enabling, liberating, even redemptive – to the animal, the human, or both. But there may be negative connections too, involving the wild animal's only too realistic fear of the human, as in *Bambi* and many Seton stories, or the human abuse of tamed animals, as in episodes in *Black Beauty*, *White Fang*, and *Smoky*.

Straightforward classics of the positive, loving, enabling relationship between child and animal are Walter Farley's *The Black Stallion* and Marguerite Henry's *Misty of Chincoteague* – and all the galloping herd of their descendants by many other authors.

The Black Stallion generally behaves like a horse, but is super-large, super-fast, super-dangerous – a superhorse, embodying a boy's dreams of power, glory, freedom, victory. The heart of the story consists in the growth of trust and loyalty between the boy and the horse. The fascination of the stallion is in his wildness, but that beauty and natural freedom of the animal must be tamed to the purposes of mankind – "conquered."

The stallion is repeatedly described as a killer: "Here was the wildest of all wild animals – he had fought for everything he had ever needed, for food, for leadership, for life itself; it was his nature to kill or be killed."[19] In fact, the only thing wild stallions fight for is ownership of mares, here apparently considered as "leadership." Horses are prey animals. They don't fight one another for their grass or fodder. The competitive streak innate in many horses and bred for in Thoroughbreds is here weirdly exaggerated into a sort of Attila the Hun mentality.

The Black is "conquered with kindness," not with brutality. The growing relationship between boy and horse cast away on a desert island is romantic but not impossible; the scenes of training the horse to the saddle and bridle are accurate. But the race that climaxes the story is just dream

---

19 Farley, *The Black Stallion*, p. 17.

stuff. Farley, who grew up with horses and horsemen, certainly knew how stupid it would be to enter an evil-tempered and headstrong stallion that had never run a race, ridden by a boy who had never ridden a race, against two experienced race horses and their jockeys. Still, one can imagine that if The Black had lost the race, Alec would have loved him almost as much as before. The stallion is in his way the Animal Helper, won by kindness, helping the boy become a manly man.

Wildness is also a theme in *Misty of Chincoteague*, but it's not equated with violent aggression, nor are taming and training glorified as conquest. The children long to capture, ride, and own the semi-feral ponies, but they learn that the only way they can do it is through kindness, patience, steadiness, courage. Their devotion to the ponies brings out the best in them – again, a gift of the beast.

And the final climax of the story glorifies freedom. The Phantom's colt stays to be tamed by the children, but the mare herself belongs to the "isle of the wild things," and the moment of her liberation is a lovely one. *Misty*, like the *Black Stallion*, is a dream story for the horse-loving child, but it's a little closer to the complicated reality a horse-loving child discovers if she actually gets to be around horses.

Enid Bagnold's *National Velvet* was not written for children, but as a delicately satirical comedy of human relationships and ambitions. Horse-loving children got hold of it right away and never let go. And quite right too, for it is a fully sympathetic picture of the particularly intense passion girls may have for horses. The four girls, their mother, and the trainer are the central characters, and the animals are mostly seen through their eyes (the only anthropomorphic moment is a fine comic one, when a terrier answers an inquiry about his love life – "Succulent," he replies succinctly.) The piebald horse is not as romantically glamorous as the Black Stallion, but he is a wonderfully vivid creature; and his training to run in the Grand National and Velvet's training to ride as his jockey are far more plausible and interesting than the race preparations in *The Black Stallion*. The fairytale element is that Velvet does ride the Pie to victory: but it's a victory one can believe – half earned, half luck – and declared invalid by the judges . . . The book has no simple moral message; but the author's loathing of media publicity as shameless, soulless exploitation (a large part of what the story is really about) and her admiration for courage, modesty, steadfastness, and devotion, leave a child, or any reader, on solid ground.

With Walt Morey's *Gentle Ben*, where boy saves bear and bear saves boy, we enter fully the theme of mutual aid, the realm of the Animal Helper. Fred Gypson's *Old Yeller*, where dog rescues boy but boy in the end can't rescue dog, is a fine, sad variation on the theme.

Jean Craighead George's novel *Julie of the Wolves* is a notably successful mixture of several themes and subjects. Her tale of a girl surviving in the wilderness by imitating and to some extent befriending wolves has elements in it of the Animal Helper and the lament for the vanishing wilderness, along with a good deal of both wilderness lore and Native American lore and attitudes.

At the beginning of the story we're in a world where human beings are not all-powerful – anything but. The girl Miyax, lost in the wilderness, is quite literally living a Stone Age existence, where being human does not give her an advantage over everybody else. Among the wolves, she is a weakling, a tolerated beggar and hanger-on, who has to be very careful of her manners just to stay alive. Instead of humans taming an animal, animals "wild" a human. This stunning reversal is the heart of the book's fascination.

Miyax gives the wolves names, but that means nothing to them; their behavior is that of wolves, their social institutions and manners are those of wolves. That they partially include the girl in their tribe or family is attested wolf behavior, and the author's knowledgeable description of it is wonderful. The wolves are Animal Helpers in an unusually literal and realistic sense. They tolerate, semi-adopt, and befriend Miyax. The alpha male leaves her a fresh-killed caribou as a gift. She cannot reciprocate, she just thanks and praises. She makes a song of gratitude for the caribou meat:

> "Amaroq, wolf, my friend,
> You are my adopted father.
> My feet shall run because of you
> My heart shall beat because of you.
> And I shall love because of you."[20]

Her sense of spiritual kinship with the wolves extends deeply to the whole natural world. "Impulsively, she paid tribute to the spirit of the caribou

---

20 George, *Julie of the Wolves*, p. 59.

by lifting her arms to the sun. Then, scoffing at herself for being such an old-fashioned Eskimo, she sharpened her man's knife on a stone and set to work."[21]

In the wilderness, among the wolves, physical superiority is pretty much moral superiority, where might makes right: but, with one mean-natured exception to prove the rule, the wolves are generous and affectionate, and Amaroq, the pack leader, embodies a wild nobility.

In contrast, when Miyax makes her way back to her own kind at last, she finds human morality hideously defective. The father she has longed for and looks up to is the man who shot Amaroq from a plane, laughing, for no reason but to kill. In the larger world she enters at the end of the book, it is the humans who have power, and the wolves and wilderness are doomed. "The hour of the wolf and the Eskimo is over."

The deeply pessimistic ending doesn't entirely fit the story of a thirteen-year-old girl so completely competent in all the ways of survival, so ready to cope with or escape from anything including the feebleminded husband foisted on her, and with such an irrepressibly hopeful and serene spirit. The wilderness is passing and the Inuit are changing, but to say their hour is over comes a little too close to the bad habit of proclaiming that alas! all the Indians are gone! I believe white folks should leave it up to the Inuit and the Indians to decide whether they're gone, and when and where they're going.

The stories of animal-human friendship I've been discussing, all more or less realistic, have a fantasy counterpart for younger children. Some of our animal friends are stuffed. One of them is covered with velveteen. The most famous of them are Pooh and Piglet and that lot. I won't dwell on their part in literature, because I'm only talking about flesh-and-blood animals. But as one who lived for years with stuffed animals, dear friends and active companions, far more autonomous, adventurous, and unpredictable than any doll I ever met, I wanted to mention them, and to suggest that, along the borders of reality and imagination, the human and the animal may truly participate in each other's being. Now I must go back to the unstuffed animals.

Three great works of children's literature and animal literature are *Dr.*

---

21 Ibid. p. 59.

Dolittle, *The Jungle Books*, and *The Sword in the Stone*. They are all about the relationship of human and animal. In each it is different, and each explores it in depth.

Such language may sound a bit fancy, talking of *Dr. Dolittle*, but Hugh Lofting's unpretentious fantasy deserves its classic status. As in *The Wind in the Willows*, animals and people interact without the slightest plausibility and without the slightest hesitation. This is because the animals act like people, mostly. But they act better than most people. None of them does anything cruel or immoral. Gub-Gub is very piggy, to be sure, and the Lion has to be scolded by his wife before he'll help the other animals, but this is the Peaceable Kingdom, where the lion will truly lie down with the lamb. Dr. Dolittle helps animals by sheltering and healing them; they begin to help him in return; and that is the theme and the basis of almost everything in the story. "So long as the birds and the beasts and the fishes are my friends, I do not have to be afraid ..."[22] Every people in the world understood this theme of mutual aid, of the Animal Helper, until we drove the animals out of our streets and skyscrapers. I think every child in the world still understands it. To be friends with the animals is to be a friend and a child of the world, connected to it, nourished by it, belonging to it.

Lofting's morality is entirely sweet and sunny. In Kipling's Mowgli stories, the connections between human and animal are complex and ultimately tragic. Mowgli is a link between his village people and the people of the jungle, and like all go-betweens, all liminal figures, he is torn between the two sides, torn apart. There is no common ground between the village and the jungle; they have turned their back on each other. In every language of the animals Mowgli can say "We be of one blood, ye and I!" – but can he truly say it in Hindi? And yet that is his mother's tongue, his mother's blood. Whom must he betray?

The wolf child, the wild child, both in rare and painful reality and in Kipling's dream-story, can never, in the end, be at home. The ache of exile from Eden is there even in the first story, "Mowgli's Brothers," ever stronger in "Letting in the Jungle" and "The Spring Running." Those are heartbreaking stories. Yet from the *Jungle Books* we may also carry with us all our lives the blessing of those lazy hours and breathless adventures when boy and wolf, bear, black panther, python, speak and think and act in

---

22 Lofting, *Dr. Dolittle*, p. 126.

joyous community: the mystery and beauty of belonging, totally belonging to the wildness of the world.

I want to pay a little further tribute here to Rudyard Kipling, a most uneven genius, one of the most troubling writers of his time, and one of the most badly served by his literary judges. In his book on Kipling, Angus Wilson dismisses the *Jungle Books* in a couple of sentences as silly schoolboy stuff and doesn't deign to mention the *Just So Stories* at all. For the modernist realist, the mere presence of animals as conscious, thinking beings suffices to throw a book out of consideration as literature, while a book for young children is automatically beneath notice. Such critical prejudice, added to Kipling's own self-destructive wrong-headedness and political unpredictability, has been nearly enough to destroy his reputation as a writer. Many people are, I think, ashamed to admit that they like or admire any of his books. Even *Kim*, one of the most beautiful and original novels ever written, is seldom taught in literature courses or mentioned in the canonical lists – tainted, apparently, partly by the fact that it is accessible to children over eleven or twelve. All I can do here is offer a personal tribute: in my life, the *Just So Stories*, along with the Mother Goose rhymes, were the foundation of all poetry and story; and the *Jungle Books* have been for over sixty-five years a perennial, inexhaustible source of joy and discovery.

T.H. White's *The Sword in the Stone* is as full of animals as my Guerrero painting. In the first chapter King Arthur-to-be, currently known as the Wart, takes out a goshawk, loses him, and meets Merlyn's owl Archimedes:

> "Oh, what a lovely owl!" cried the Wart.
>
> But when he went up to it and held out his hand, the owl grew half as tall again, stood up as stiff as a poker, closed its eyes so that there was only the smallest slit to peep through [...] and said in a doubtful voice:
> "There is no owl."
> Then it shut its eyes entirely and looked the other way.
> "It's only a boy," said Merlyn.
> "There is no boy," said the owl hopefully, without turning round.[23]

Merlyn undertakes Arthur's education, which consists mostly of being

---

23 White, *The Sword in the Stone*, p. 33.

turned into animals. Here for the first time we meet the great mythic theme of Transformation, which is a central act of shamanism, though Merlyn doesn't make any fuss about it. The boy becomes a fish, a hawk, a snake, an owl, and a badger. He participates, at thirty years per minute, in the sentience of trees, and then, at two million years per second, in the sentience of stones. All these scenes of participation in animal being are funny, vivid, startling, and wise. (The reason I cite *The Sword in the Stone* rather than *The Once and Future King* is that when incorporating the first book into the trilogy, White revised out some of the finest passages, replacing the snake with a trite political satire about ants, and the cosmic vision with a visit to the wild geese – a nice chapter, but a heavy loss.)

When a witch puts Wart into a cage to fatten him up, the goat in the next cage plays Animal Helper and rescues them all. All animals rightly trust Wart, which is proof of his true kingship. That he goes along on a boar hunt does not vitiate this trust: to White, true hunting is a genuine relationship between hunter and hunted, with implacable moral rules, and a high degree of honor and respect for the prey. The emotions aroused by hunting are powerful, and White draws them all together in the scene of the death of the hound Beaumont, killed by the boar, a passage I have never yet read without crying.

At the climax of the book, Wart can't draw the sword of kingship from the stone anvil by himself. He calls to Merlyn for help, and the animals come.

> There were otters and nightingales and vulgar crows and hares, and serpents and falcons and fishes and goats and dogs and dainty unicorns and newts and solitary wasps and goat-moth caterpillars and corkindrills and volcanoes and mighty trees and patient stones ... all, down to the smallest shrew mouse, had come to help on account of love. Wart felt his power grow.[24]

Each creature calls its special wisdom to the boy who has been one of them, one with them. The pike says, "Put your back into it," a stone says, "Cohere," a snake says, "Fold your powers together with the spirit of your mind" – and: "The Wart walked up to the great sword for the third time.

---

24 Ibid. p. 305.

He put out his right hand softly and drew it out as gently as from a scabbard."[25]

T.H.White was a man to whom animals were very important, perhaps in part because his human relationships were so tormented. But his sense of connection with nonhuman lives goes far beyond mere compensation; it is a passionate vision of a moral universe, a world of terrible pain and cruelty from which trust and love spring like the autumn crocus, vulnerable and unconquerable. *The Sword in the Stone*, which I first read at thirteen or so, influenced my mind and heart in ways that must be quite clear through the course of this essay, convincing me that trust cannot be limited to mankind, that love cannot be specified. It's all or nothing at all. If, called to reign, you distrust and scorn your subjects, your only kingdom will be that of greed and hate. Love and trust and be a king, and your kingdom will be the whole world. And to your coronation, among all the wondrous gifts, an "anonymous hedgehog will send four or five dirty leaves with some fleas on them."[26]

VII. Fables and Psychic Fragments

Now we've come to the purely human end of my spectrum, where the animal exists mixed with or as a reflection of the human.

In the old-fashioned fable, animals represent their species but are scarcely individuals, and their behavior is not observed but stereotyped, archetypal: the wily fox, the timid mouse. In Aesop's fables, the Jataka tales, and my example, the Grimms' *Household Tales*, animals often symbolize and enact human behaviors and qualities.

The Grimms' tales are a verbal equivalent of the painting of the Guerrero village. Of the fifty stories in my Lucy Crane translation, twenty-nine have domestic or wild animals as central or active characters, and in almost every story domestic animals are part of daily life – horses, donkeys, oxen, cattle, dogs, cats, geese. Humanity is the model of behavior and society, but humans and animals are all people on a more or less equal and individual footing. Animals and humans keep house or travel together, fool or cheat one another, Cheek by Jowl. This is the old world, which

---

25 Ibid. p. 306.
26 Ibid. p. 311.

doesn't belong to humans, as our world does. Nobody here is boss.

In general, everybody can talk to everybody else. You can get into an argument with a bean or a sausage. All animal protagonists speak to other animals, and most speak to and are understood by human characters. In most stories where animals play a significant role, they and the humans talk together; animals speaking and behaving rationally are taken for granted. In a few stories animal speech is seen as somewhat miraculous: Falada the horse, whose capacity for speech is specifically mentioned, the talking fish in "The Fisherman and his Wife" and the birds in "The Almond Tree" and "Aschenputtel," all have some element of the supernatural. And in the rather mystical tale of "The White Snake" we meet the widespread theme of the Language of the Animals: a taste of the white snake that the king keeps in a covered dish gives the servant who tastes it the ability to understand what the animals say to one another, from which he gets power and benefit.

Religion as such plays no part in the stories (as selected and translated in this collection). Moral superiority isn't a matter of species, but is individual and unpredictable. As a rule the clever weak defeat the stupid strong, and the compassionate are helped by those they have helped. But justice in folktales is unpredictable and arbitrary; the human hero of "The White Snake" saves the lives of three starving baby ravens by killing his horse so they can eat it. Good for the ravens, hard on the horse.

Two repeated themes are notable: our old friend the Animal Helper, such as the ants who help Aschenputtel sort her lentils so she can go to the ball; and Transformation, where the animal is actually a human being under a spell, as in "The Frog Prince" and the haunting tale of "The Wild Swans." Here the demarcation of human and animal is so weak that one may become, may actually be, the other.

Ever since we lived in caves people have been calling other people greedy as a hog or brave as a lion. What is remarkable about "A Voyage to the Houyhnhnms" is not so much that Jonathan Swift used horses to provide a model of Enlightenment morality, but that he used humans, not animals, to satirize human vice. The honesty and dignity of the Houyhnhnms is not much exaggerated from that of ordinary horses, but they speak, and so are raised above the brute; while the Yahoos have no language, and no virtues, and so are sunk below any brute. Gulliver says, "I never beheld in all my travels so disagreeable an animal." Swift is careful never to compare theYahoos to apes. If theYahoos were mere apes they'd have an excuse for their nastiness. He wants us to see them as men, and we do.

Gulliver's Travels was not written for children, of course, and I don't know how many children these days get a chance to read it, abridged or entire. I think both the story and the satire of the third Voyage completely suitable to older children. Behind Swift's "savage indignation," after all, is the idealism that can conceive of so truthful and gentle a realm as that of the Houyhnhnms. (And any child who wants to know how to pronounce them can read T.H.White's *Mistress Masham's Repose* and find out.)

George Orwell's *Animal Farm* is a less complex satire, more straightforward in its stereotypes, therefore perhaps less disturbing to a young reader; but Orwell is in the end even harsher than Swift, for loyalty and honesty lose out in this modern fable, and whether the story is read as politically topical or as a general warning, its message is merciless.

The last animal satire I'll mention is one I have a little trouble thinking of as satirical, it is so sweet-natured, and perhaps all the stronger for that; I mean *The Story of Ferdinand*. When you come right down to it, Leaf is almost as hard on humans as Swift is, but a good deal more hopeful than Orwell. And is there any other satire in the world that ends, with no irony at all, "He is very happy"?

The last books in this section of Fables are two very different fantasies, a new one and an old one.

Philip Pullman's His Dark Materials trilogy is a long, richly imagined, and deeply incoherent work, in which I'll try only to trace the part animals play. Despite appearances, it is a small part.

The two cats in the story, who have a minor but important role, do what cats have often done in myth and fable: they cross between worlds. Otherwise they're just cats, realistically drawn. Animals are otherwise absent from the books, except for a tribe of polar bears who talk and build forts and use weapons, but who don't have daemons, as humans do.

Daemons are animals in form, and the reason why the trilogy – particularly the first volume – seems to be full of animals is that every human being has one. Until you reach puberty your daemon may take any animal shape at any moment; with your sexual maturity your daemon settles into a permanent form, always of the other gender. Social class is evidently a decisive influence: we are told that servants always have dog daemons, and see that upper-class people's daemons are rare and elegant creatures such as snow leopards. Your daemon accompanies you physically and closely at all times, everywhere; separation is unbearably painful. Though they do not eat or excrete, daemons are tangible, and you can pet and cuddle with your own daemon, though you must not touch anybody else's. Daemons are rational creatures and speak fluently with their owners and with others.

Wish-fulfillment is strong in this concept and gives it great charm: the ever-loyal, ever-present, dear companion, soulmate, comforter, guardian angel, and ultimately perfect pet: as with the beloved stuffed animal, you don't even have to remember to feed it.

But I think Pullman overloads the concept and then confuses it. He implies strongly that the daemon is a kind of visible soul, that to be severed from it is fatal; his plot hinges on the cruelty and horror of this separation. But then he begins changing the rules. We find that witches can live apart from their daemons; in the second volume we are in our world, where nobody has visible or tangible daemons; and, back in her world, the heroine Lyra leaves her daemon on the wharves of hell, and though she misses him, she lives on perfectly competently, and in fact saves the universe, without him. Their reunion seems almost perfunctory.

In a fantasy, to change or break your own rules is to make the story, literally, inconsequential.

If the daemons are meant to show that we are part animal and must not be severed from our animality, they can't do it. They aren't fitted for the job. The essence of animality is the body, the living body with all its brainless needs and embarrassing functions – exactly what the daemons do not have. They are spiritual beings, forms without substance. They are fragments or images of the human psyche given animal shape, wholly contingent, having no independent being and therefore incapable of relationship. Lyra's much-emphasized love for her daemon is self-love. In Pullman's world human beings are dreadfully alone, since his God has gone senile and there aren't any real animals. Except those two cats. Let us place our hope in the cats.

Through the Looking Glass begins with cats. Alice is talking to Dinah and her kittens, who don't talk back, so Alice does it for them, and then she climbs up onto the mantel piece with one of the kittens, and goes through the mirror . . . As noted before, cats cross between worlds.

The looking-glass world and the one down the rabbit hole are dreams, and therefore all the characters in them are aspects of Alice – again, fragments of psyche, but in a very different sense from Pullman's dae-mons. Contingent they may be, but their independence is notable. As soon as Alice gets through the glass into the garden, the flowers not only talk but talk back; they are extremely rude and passionate flowers. As in folktale, all creatures are on an equal footing, mingling and arguing, even turning into each other – the baby becomes a piglet, the White Queen a sheep – Transformation going both ways ... Train passengers include humans, a goat, a beetle, a horse, and a gnat, which begins as a tiny voice in Alice's ear but presently is "about the size of a chicken." It asks if Alice dislikes all insects, and she replies, with admirable aplomb, "I like them when they can talk. None of them ever talk, where I come from."

Alice is a nineteenth-century British middle-class child with a tight, strict moral code of self-respect and respect for others. Her good manners are sorely tried by the behavior of the dream-creatures – whom we can see, if we choose, as acting out Alice's own impulses of rebellion, her passion, her wild willfulness. Violence is not permitted; we know that the Queen's "Off with her head!" is a threat not to be executed. And yet nightmare is never far off. The creatures of Alice's dreams come close to total uncontrol, to madness, and she must wake to know herself.

The Alice books are not animal stories, but there is no way I could leave them out of this essay; they are the purest modern literary instance of the animals of the mind, the dream beasts that every human society has known as ancestors, as spirit-doubles, as omens, as monsters, and as guides. We have spiraled back round to the Dream Time, where human and animal are one.

This is a sacred place. That we got back to it by following a little Victo-rian girl down a rabbit hole is absolutely crazy and appropriate.

VIII. Conclusion

People and animals are supposed to be together. We spent quite a long time evolving together, and we used to be partners.

– Temple Grandin, *Animals in Translation*

We human beings have made a world reduced to ourselves and our artifacts, but we weren't made for it and have to teach our children to live in it. Physically and mentally equipped to be at home in a richly various and unpredictable environment, competing and coexisting with creatures of all kinds, our children must learn poverty and exile, to live on concrete among endless human beings, seeing animals only as a bird high in the air, a beast on a leash or in a cage, a film image. But our innate, acute interest in animals as fellow beings, friend or enemy or food or playmate, can't be instantly eradicated; it resists deprivation. And imagination and literature are there to fill the void and reaffirm the greater community.

The themes I have picked out along the way support this idea. The Animal Helper motif of mutual aid across species, which we see in folktale and as clearly in modern animal stories, tells that kindness and gratitude can't be limited to your own species, that all creatures are kin.

Community is shown as fundamental, a given, by the assimilation of animal to human and the mingling as equals that we see in folktale and in such books as *The Wind in the Willows* and *Dr. Dolittle*.

Transformation of man into beast, which in folktales is usually a curse or unhappy spell, in modern stories is more likely to be enlarging and educational, and even, as in the Wart's last great journey, to offer a glimpse of mystical participation, of an ultimate and eternal communion.

The yearning for a Lost Wilderness that runs through so many animal tales is a lament for the endless landscapes and creatures and species that we have wasted and destroyed. These laments grow urgent, now. We come ever closer to isolating ourselves, a solitary species swarming on a desert world. "Look on my works, ye mighty, and despair."

We go crazy in solitude. We are social primates. Human beings need to belong. To belong to one another, first, of course; but because we can see so far and think so cleverly and imagine so much, we aren't satisfied by membership in a family, a tribe, people just like us. Fearful and suspicious as it is, the human mind yet yearns for a greater belonging, a vaster identification. Wilderness scares us because it is unknown, indifferent, dangerous, yet it is an absolute need to us; it is that animal otherness, that strangeness, older and greater than ourselves, that we must join, or rejoin, if we want to stay sane and stay alive.

The child is our closest link to it. The storytellers know that. Mowgli and young Wart reach out their hands, the right hand to us and the left hand to the jungle, to the wild beast in the wilderness, to the hawk and the owl and the panther and the wolf; they join us together. The six-year-old spelling out *Peter Rabbit*, the twelve-year-old weeping over *Black Beauty* – they have accepted what so much of their culture denies, and they too reach out their hands to rejoin us to the greater creation, keeping us where we belong.

Why Kids Want Fantasy, or,
Be Careful What You Eat

2004

Published under the title "Questward Ho" in Time Out New York Kids, *June–Sept. 2004.*

Fantasy says that dragons exist, magic works, and cats can fly. It denies experience, defies possibility, and ignores gravity. Fantasy is transgressive – which may be the first reason why kids and teenagers love it.

Realism is an upstart kind of fiction that's been around only a couple of centuries and is already showing signs of senility. Fantasy has been here ever since we sat in the lodge and listened to the story of how Raven brought fire to the People. Its roots are in myth, legend, religious parable, the literatures that tell a people who they are. The *Iliad* and the *Odyssey* aren't realistic or historical; they're fantasies. So are the *Aeneid*, the *Mahabharata*, the *Tale of Monkey*. They all defy gravity, though not gravitas.

And as fantasy goes back to humanity's earlier days, so also in an individual life it's likely to be the earliest and most permanent experience of story. Where do we start? "There was an old woman who lived in a shoe ..." *Goodnight Moon* ... Talking locomotives, rabbits who drink tea, Cinderella, *The Story of Ferdinand* ...

Fantasy is the native and natural form of children's story. Not because most kids don't know real from unreal, or need to "escape" from reality, but because their imaginations are working full time to make sense out of reality, and imaginative story is the best tool for doing just that job.

With any luck we're given our first fiction tool-kit early in life: nonsense rhyme and animal fable, folktales and hero tales. Many of us go right on using them throughout life. Some will come to prefer realism. Some will stop reading fiction altogether, because reading is difficult for them, or their culture tells them fiction is unimportant, or contradicts scripture, or whatever. But at nine or ten, lucky kids start reading young adult and adult fantasy, and some will go on doing it the rest of their lives. Fantasy bridges the gap between child and adult as no other form of literature does.

Adolescents struggle fiercely and consciously to understand their world, make sense of it, cope with it, make moral choices. Their struggle is often genuinely desperate. They need help. Story is perhaps the most flexible tool at the disposal of mind. With it we remake reality. We retell events, we imagine alternatives, we figure out how to live according to our desires and according to our needs. The truth of story is not fact. Story tells human truth, serving ethical questioning, human community, and spiritual longing.

When they begin looking for a truth that works for them, a way that they can make for themselves into the dark wood of the world, kids often find it in fantasy – particularly if they're not content to take directions readymade from elders, teachers, and preachers, but seek their own direction. By training the imagination and opening alternatives, fantasy offers self-guidance. Imaginative literature of a high order offers guidance of a high order.

There is, of course, nothing childish about the great works of fantasy. But even now people say with preening self-congratulation "Of course *I* don't read that sort of thing," that sort of thing being Tolkien.

The real, constant, damn-the-critics popularity of *The Lord of the Rings*, and the increase in number and quality of other non-modernist and po-mo nonrealistic fiction, including magical realism, finally showed the irrelevance of modernist dogma to what is – and always was – actually going on. It may be that the greatest fictional legacy of the twentieth century, from Kafka to Borges, from Tolkien to Saramago, will turn out to be – well, call it what you will, but realism it ain't.

However ...

Nothing fails like success.

Fantasy has become a big commercial genre. All you need is a map with weird names. Everybody has a sword and does sorcery, there is no known basis to the economy, and the obligatory War Between Good and Evil is going on. The Good guys and the Evil guys are hard to tell apart since all of them use violence as the response to all situations and the solution to all problems. The Good guys are the ones that win in the third volume of the trilogy.

Fantasy films used to be rare, and mostly animation, because it was difficult to build dragons. Now it's just a flick of the old industrial magic and there's your dragon.

But is he a real one, or a fake? Real dragons can destroy you, and they keep a jewel in their hoard, called wisdom. Fake dragons don't. Fake dragons never get out of the box office.

Meaningless imitation, formula repetition, is always the problem when a genre has mastered its techniques and refined its subject matter. That doesn't matter to the producers of fantasy-by-the-yard; it makes it all the easier for them to produce it. But the stuff they make is shoddy, a fabric that comes to pieces at once.

I recommend caution to both adults and children entering what used to be called Fairyland. Take care. It always was a dangerous place. Wisdom is not easy to come by, and never cheap. Be careful what you eat. Beware of sorcerers who lead you astray by false arts. You'll come out onto the cold hillside and find the money in your pocket has turned to dead leaves and your hair is grey.

But if you seek true guides into the lands of fantasy, if you follow the real wizards, you may not get rich, or stay young, or win any Battle between Good and Evil, but you'll learn something about how to tell the *difference* between good and evil. And that knowledge is the Arkenstone, the jewel of jewels.

National Book Award Medal for Distinguished Contribution to American Letters Acceptance Speech

●

2014

Thank you Neil, and to the givers of this beautiful award, my thanks from the heart. My family, my agent, editors, know that my being here is their doing as well as mine, and that the beautiful reward is theirs as much as mine. And I rejoice at accepting it for, and sharing it with, all the writers who were excluded from literature for so long, my fellow authors of fantasy and science fiction - writers of the imagination, who for the last 50 years watched the beautiful awards go to the so-called realists.

I think hard times are coming when we will be wanting the voices of writers who can see alternatives to how we live now and can see through our fear-stricken society and its obsessive technologies to other ways of being, and even imagine some real grounds for hope. We will need writers who can remember freedom. Poets, visionaries, the realists of a larger reality.

Right now, I think we need writers who know the difference between the production of a market commodity and the practice of an art. Developing written material to suit sales strategies in order to maximize corporate profit and advertising revenue is not quite the same thing as responsible book publishing or authorship. Thank you, brave applauders.

Yet I see sales departments given control over editorial. I see my own publishers in a silly panic of ignorance and greed, charging public libraries for an ebook six or seven times more than they charge customers. We just saw a profiteer try to punish a publisher for disobedience and writers threatened by corporate fatwa, and I see a lot of us – the producers who write the books, and make the books – accepting this. Letting commodity profiteers sell us like deodorant, and tell us what to publish and what to write. Well, I love you too, darling.

Books, you know, they're not just commodities. The profit motive often is in conflict with the aims of art. We live in capitalism. Its power seems inescapable. So did the divine right of kings. Any human power can be resisted and changed by human beings. Resistance and change often begin in art, and very often in our art – the art of words.

I have had a long career and a good one. In good company. Now here, at the end of it, I really don't want to watch American literature get sold down the river. We who live by writing and publishing want – and should demand – our fair share of the proceeds. But the name of our beautiful reward is not profit.

Its name is freedom.

Thank you.

Acknowledgements And Credits

387

Ursula K. Le Guin (1929–2018)

Ursula K. Le Guin is one of the finest writers of our time. Her books have attracted millions of devoted readers and won many awards, including the National Book Award, the Hugo and Nebula Awards and a Newbery Honor. Among her novels, *The Left Hand of Darkness*, *The Dispossessed* and the six books of Earthsea have attained undisputed classic status; and her Annals of the Western Shore series won her the PEN Center USA Children's literature award and the Nebula Award for best novel. In 2014 Ursula Le Guin was awarded the National Book Foundation Medal for Distinguished Contribution to American Letters. She lived in Portland, Oregon before she passed away in 2018.